Olivia Leady

# THE HEALING POWER OF DREAMS

Patricia Garfield, Ph.D.

SIMON & SCHUSTER
New York ◇ London ◇ Toronto ◇ Sydney ◇ Tokyo ◇ Singapore

Simon & Schuster
Simon & Schuster Building
Rockefeller Center
1230 Avenue of the Americas
New York, New York 10020

SIMON & SCHUSTER and colophon are registered trademarks
of Simon & Schuster, Inc.

Designed by D'Amario/Levavi & Levavi
Manufactured in the United States of America

1   3   5   7   9   10   8   6   4   2

Library of Congress Cataloging in Publication Data
Garfield, Patricia
The healing power of dreams/Patricia Garfield.
p.     cm.
Includes bibliographical references and index.
1. Dreams—Therapeutic use.   I. Title.
RC489.D74G37   1991                          91-9098
616.89'14–dc20
CIP
ISBN 0-671-68622-4

# Disclaimer

Please be aware that this book is not intended to replace appropriate medical care. Also, don't be alarmed if you find yourself dreaming about various illnesses and injuries as you read the book; it's a natural reaction to the content. Many people have dreamed they were dying of fatal diseases and are alive and thriving dozens of years later. Look at your dreams from a psychological as well as from a physical point of view. Later life events will often reveal the meaning of dreams that were unclear at the time. Accept your dreams as they come—as gifts from another part of yourself. Be open to their messages, but realize they vary in degree of accuracy. Watch for recurrent patterns—this is where you are apt to find the greatest teachings.

# Contents

# List of Illustrations

# Acknowledgments

This book owes its existence to the many professionals, friends, and family who contributed to my healing from a severe wrist fracture.

In particular, I wish to thank hand surgeon Leonard Gordon and his staff at the University of California, San Francisco, who surgically corrected a grievous error in diagnosis and ordered treatments that set me on the road to recovery.

My special appreciation also goes to the devoted physical therapists at the Hand Clinic of the University of California, San Francisco, then under the direction of Pamela Silverman (now of Hand Therapy of San Francisco), with the able assistance of Marilyn Armbruster. Their ministrations were psychological, in addition to physical, as they persuaded frozen digits to loosen, weak joints to strengthen, and taught new ways to function.

Patients, who remain anonymous from these two busy clinics, freely offered the stories of their traumatic injuries and their accompanying dreams.

People who keep regular dream diaries, professional and

laypersons alike, kindly extracted portions of their journals for my use. Jill Bond Caire and Rita Dwyer, especially, let me have access to large sections of their dream records. Others, friends or colleagues, collected dream records especially for this book— Jordan Beyer, Kris Getz, Alice Kales, Arlyn Zones, to mention only a few. The late Irene Roseman, among several, gave liberally of her experience in the midst of discomfort. Still other people shared artwork along with their accounts of injuries or illnesses, notably Alex Pellegrini and Phyllis Clark Harvey. The late Charisse Kranes showed me drawings of exceptional value that her husband Winston Pickett later made available for further examination.

A workman who got injured, a girlfriend who developed an ovarian cyst, a daughter who came down with pneumonia, a sister-in-law who underwent surgery—all told me their stories as they happened. I began to realize that almost *everyone* eventually endures injury or illness to a greater or lesser degree. Although it's not possible to name them all, I'm thankful to those who shared as they struggled to overcome their afflictions.

Experts in various fields contributed explicit knowledge. Alice Kalman of the Monterey Institute of International Studies, in particular, among others, made relevant translations from the Russian text by Vasilii Kasatkin. Physician and friend Stanley Nudelman kindly examined several chapters of this book for medical errors, but of course any that remain are my responsibility. He also put me in touch with patients who were willing to discuss their dreams prior to their surgery. I appreciate the time and generosity of art psychotherapist Evelyn Simon, of Phoenix, who reviewed this book's illustrations with me and made pertinent suggestions for using art to help the healing process, as well as commenting on my techniques. Ann Wiseman, an expressive arts therapist from Boston, whose workshop on Body Image I attended, outlined another approach to using art to accelerate healing. Dreamworker Aad van Ouwerkerk, of the Netherlands, suggested an additional way to use art with dream imagery. The lucid dream techniques of Stephen LaBerge, of Stanford University, evoked yet another dimension to healing.

Patricia Maybruck, Monique Lortie–Lussier, Jayne Gackenbach–Snyder, Deirdre Barrett, Fariba Bogzaran, Robert van de Castle, Stanley Krippner, Pierre Étévenon, and Roger Broughton—friends and fellow members of the Association for the Study of Dreams were inspiring, challenging, and altogether stimulating. Our organization has evolved into a thriving international dream community since Strephon Kaplan–Williams first founded it in 1982, with myself as one of the original six co-founders.

The Greek Tourist Board deserves credit for sponsoring my trip in 1984 to visit the Greek dream temples; viewing these sites stirred my fascination with ancient Greek healing techniques and led to fruitful adventures.

Thanks to my agent, John Brockman, whose confidence in the concept of this book helped bring it from idea to the written page. Thanks, too, to my editor, Barbara Gess of Simon & Schuster, who patiently coaxed more of the manuscript through an earthquake and threat of war.

Friends Linda Dancer, Carol Schoneberg, Thomasine Kushner, Alison Rivin, Ping Li, and Hsiu-Ming Lee were especially supportive during my original crisis. My mother Evelyn, my godmother Kathryn Lee, my daughter Cheryl, my stepdaughters Wendy and Linda (who just graduated from medical school), my stepson Steven, my brother Fred, and their families, each contributed to my well-being and my understanding of dream imagery.

My husband Zal was continuously present—a bit distraught while I was in danger, but ever loving and giving.

Family, friends, colleagues, professionals, and patients—my gratitude to all of them. May the gifts of these generous people flow through my writing to nourish all who read this work.

—Patricia Garfield
San Francisco
New Year's Day, January, 1991

Remembering my father, Fred Cameron Goff,
whose skilled hands created paintings and puppets,
toy airplanes, kites, and houses for my brother and me,
and whose loving heart remains a
heritage to all who knew him,
especially his daughter.

# YOUR BODY IN DREAMS

Your dreams can help keep you healthy, warn you when you are at risk, diagnose incipient physical problems, support you during physical crises, forecast your recuperation, suggest treatment, heal your body, and signal your return to wellness. All this becomes available to you each night as you learn to use the healing power of your dreams.

I am not suggesting that you substitute your dreams for the advice of qualified physicians and appropriate medical treatment. I *am* saying that you can use your full dream resources to improve the quality of your life, especially when you become ill or have an accident. You can add inner awareness to external advice. You'll be able to consult with your physician more effectively. Your dreams are packed with information about the functioning of your body. They speak to you each night; all you have to do is listen and learn. This book will show you how.

I discovered many of the principles described here the hard way—from suffering and personal pain. When I broke my left wrist, I was suddenly propelled into a world of anguish, hospitals, surgery, and physical therapy and equipment. My dreams underwent a radical transformation. Each phase in the slow and difficult process of recuperation was dramatized in my dreams; each step in recovery from the injury was characterized by specific dream content. My injury eventually led to an understanding of universal concepts about dreams and healing. Since then, I have discovered how much the ancients already knew about dreams and health.

My own experience was later supplemented by the dreams of dozens of injured or ill women and men whom I interviewed as they struggled back to health. I searched the literature for scattered gems about the correspondence between dreams and health. I interviewed physicians as well as patients; I talked with surgeons, anesthetists, nurses, and physical and art therapists. All contributed their thoughts about the relationship between dreams and health. Then I synthesized the material. This book charts a path through unexplored areas. The map is far from complete—there is unknown territory and confusing signposts— but enough is clear that, with this diagram in hand, your journey toward health may be made safer and surer.

Although you may not recognize them, your dreams broadcast nightly bulletins about your health—news flashes that are critical for your well-being. I had recorded my dreams for over forty years, and had written four books[1] on the topic of dreams prior to this one. Still, I was not fully aware of how closely linked our dream images are to the condition of our bodies until I severely injured my left wrist. In a sense, this book chose me. Before writing it, I had selected other areas of dreams that I wanted to explore. Now I had no choice.

## ◇ THE RELUCTANT HERO

Like it or not, will it or not, I was hurt; and my dreams taught me how to move from injury to wellness. In mythological terms, one could say I had received the "call to adventure," one in which I had no wish to participate. If I could have avoided this particular experience—what Joseph Campbell calls "the hero journey"[2]—I gladly would have done so. Since I could not, I was determined to make the best of a dreadful situation, and reluctant or not, I undertook the journey. You may find yourself in a similar situation.

In myths or fairy tales, the hero or heroine sometimes

leaves home because he or she is bored, or longs for something more in life. Other times the journey begins because the hero is struck by destiny. Whichever form the call to adventure takes, the departure begins from home base. If you face a serious illness or unexpectedly experience a traumatic injury, you, too, are thrust into a hero journey as surely as if you deliberately set out in quest of the Holy Grail. You cross a threshold.

The strange new space you encounter is often portrayed in myths and stories as a trip into the wilderness or a descent into a cave or hell. For many people, being admitted to a hospital is like being transported to an unknown land where one must undergo tests and trials. There in the unfamiliar territory is where the "initiation" takes place. People who are seriously ill or injured have metaphorical dragons to battle; they may be mutilated, dismembered, near death, and profoundly discouraged. The nadir of the hero journey is sometimes depicted in legends as a dangerous sea crossing at night or as being trapped in a labyrinth or in the belly of a whale. For those of us who are ill or injured, a particular treatment or operation may seem worse than the actual health problem. Descending into the unconsciousness of anesthesia or struggling with painful treatments, we find that survival requires courage. Not surprisingly, we sometimes despair before we discover the way to cope with a disease or an accident.

If we are lucky, we encounter people—or even animals in dreams—who help us to recover and find our way, as well as tempters who confuse and misdirect us. We become initiated into new knowledge about life and about ourselves. We discover a treasure. Holding fast to our prize, we pass through remaining dangers. Sometimes those people who die first manage to communicate what they have learned, thus enriching the lives of those who remain. The departed may leave behind a blessing.

To return to the everyday world whole—but transformed —is like a rebirth. We have changed in some important way, not only physically, but also psychologically. We know what the descent was like and how to ascend. We learned to endure in both worlds. We share what we have discovered with one another.

The eminent Swiss psychiatrist Carl Jung believed that we have an opportunity to become more complete people, what he called "individuated," when we are forced to cope with catastrophic illness or severe injury.[3] Becoming sick or suffering pain forces us to constructively re-evaluate what is truly important. We can reframe our pain and loss into a growth experience, whether or not we are restored to physical health. We have the option of dealing with unfinished elements and forming a new, positive relationship to life.

Part of my own healing was the realization that I had something important to tell other people who become injured or ill. As a dream expert and a clinical psychologist who had been physically traumatized, I noticed that there were crucial pieces of information about the condition of the body in dreams that were not generally recognized. By organizing what I discovered in my own experience—and in those of others who were also struggling to recover—I helped myself heal. I hope this book will guide you and those you care about to better health.

We may not be able to choose when we fall ill or get injured, but we *can* choose how we respond to it. The right choice is to face the unknown and learn from it. Once we have been called to an adventure, embracing it may lead us to discoveries that illuminate our lives.

Before turning to the little-known area of dreams and healing, let's briefly review some fundamental concepts about dreamwork. (If you are already familiar with them, you may want to skip ahead to page 29, "The Body in Dreams.")

## ◇ BASIC PRINCIPLES OF DREAMWORK

### ◇ Recalling Your Dreams

Your dreams are part of an innate biological rhythm; in a cycle, they ebb and flow throughout your sleep like waves upon the shore. Every ninety minutes or so while you sleep, in progressively longer periods, your central nervous system undergoes activation.

When you first fall asleep, your brain waves begin to slow down, your breathing becomes more regular, your heart rate lowers and steadies, your body temperature falls, and your large muscles relax. These changes continue through four stages of progressively deeper sleep.[4] After a phase of profoundly restful sleep, you gradually reascend through increasingly lighter stages until, about ninety minutes after falling asleep, your brain waves suddenly accelerate, your breathing gets irregular, your heart rate quickens, and your temperature rises slightly. Despite a slight twitching around the lips and in the fingers, your large muscles lose their tone. Yet the sexual organs, responding to the ongoing activation of your central nervous system, become aroused. Males develop an erection; in females, the vulva and clitoris engorge with blood and the vagina becomes moist. This is when rapid eye movement (REM) begins—the swift back-and-forth darting that occurs in the eyes.

In your brain stem is a group of nerve cells—called gigantocellular tegmental field (GTF) neurons—that periodically fire.[5] These cells are a kind of switch that turns on REM. Usually these cells are inhibited by another group of neurons in the brain stem—called locus coeruleus—that act as an off switch. As the GTF cells become excited, they stimulate the lower brain, where emotions originate, and the visual and sensory cortex. When the GTF cells peak in excitation, there is a burst of REM, and you begin to dream.

Throughout the night this pattern continues, bringing "high tides" of dreaming. By the time you awaken, you will have spent about 25 percent of your sleep time in REM, totaling about ninety minutes to two hours each night, if you sleep eight hours. This REM time is divided into four or five distinct periods—the earliest is about ten minutes long, with the later phases progressively increasing until the final REM period, which lasts about thirty to forty-five minutes. This is the dream period that most people remember when they report a dream.

Originally scientists thought that all dreaming occurred during REM sleep; now we know that many dreams occur during the remaining time as well.[6] There are two types of sleep, REM and non-REM, and each contains distinctive types of dreams. When people are asked to describe dreams during or after a REM period, they report dramatic events resembling horror films or spy stories; for a non-REM period, they tend to report events that are more calm and thoughtlike, as if in a documentary film. Apparently our minds are constantly busy during sleep, with low tides of dreaming interspersed between the high tides.

Some scientists think that the periodic activation we undergo during sleep is a kind of "self-test" to make sure that all circuits are operative. Others speculate that this alternation of activity and rest is a switching of brain hemispheres, as if to keep both sides in working order. Researchers also suspect that we have a similar schedule of heightened fantasy that fluctuates during the daytime.[7] Thus, we are possibly undergoing a rhythmic cycle of dreamlike thoughts during the day as well as at night.

Your best opportunity to catch a dream is right at the end of the longest dream period, after several hours of sleep, or following a dream in an afternoon nap. Here are some suggestions for heightening your dream recall:

1. Accept and value each dream, regardless of how foolish or fragmentary it may appear at the time. It may fit into a larger pattern that will only become apparent later.
2. Before going to sleep, plan to recall whatever dreams appear. Place a notepad and pen—or a voice-activated tape recorder, if you prefer—within easy reach of your bed.
3. Suggest to yourself as you drift into a drowsy state, "Tonight I'll remember a dream." Picture yourself waking from a dream and describing it.
4. Select an unpressured period of days, such as a weekend or vacation, to focus on improving your dream recall. Allow yourself to awaken spontaneously from a dream, rather than by alarm clock or some other disruption to your natural cycle.
5. Lie still and let the dream images flow through your mind. The last scene of a dream often lingers; use it as a hook to reel in previous scenes. If no images occur, think about the important people in your life; visualizing them may trigger associations to a recent dream.
6. Record any dream imagery in your mind on the notepad or onto the tape, keeping your eyes shut if possible. You can prevent overlapping lines by bracing your little finger upright as you write. Use your other fingers to judge the edge of the pad.
7. Record the dream in the order recalled, except when there are unique verbal expressions fresh in mind. Poems, unusual names, and phrases should be described first, as they are most easily lost. Don't try to understand the dream at this point; just remember it and write it down.
8. When you have finished recalling dreams in the body position in which you awoke, move gently into other

usual sleeping positions to promote additional dream recall, which seems easier in the body position used during the dream.

9. Keep your eyes closed for as long as possible while recording your dream on the notepad or onto the tape; opening them often disrupts recall. If you must get up, open your eyes briefly, then return to bed and close them. Later on, when your dream recall habit is secure, you won't need these precautions. You'll be able to sit up, move around, turn on the light, and record your dream without losing it.

10. The most vivid dream recall occurs right after the REM period finishes. By following these suggestions, many people find they can awaken themselves after each dream to make notes. You may not wish to emphasize dreams this much. Simply accept those dreams that surface and work with them. If you suddenly recall a dream during the course of the day, record it as soon as you have a chance.

11. If you still have difficulty remembering dreams after following these suggestions, you may wish to try another method to increase your recall, such as having a friend stay up to observe your rapid eye movements, and after giving you time to get into the dream, gently awaken you. Some people prefer to set an alarm clock at ninety-minute to two-hour intervals to catch an ongoing dream.

12. Sharing a dream with a friend sometimes helps set the memory of it and leads to insights as you describe it. Joining or creating a dream-discussion group almost guarantees dream recall. Be sure to write down the dream, however, so you have a record for comparing past and future dreams. Remembering your dreams gives you the raw material for self-understanding and personal growth.

## ◇ Recording Your Dreams

After you have gathered notes about your dreams during the night or in the morning, put them into a more permanent format sometime during the next day, or as soon as possible. This dream document will help you recognize and express emotions that you weren't fully aware of, understand your own dream language, discover meaning in your past experiences, give you guidance for present and future behavior, evaluate your current condition, and discover joy in living. Here are some suggestions for maintaining useful dream records:

1. Decide how you'll keep your dream record. Some people write in a bound notebook; others like an artist's sketchbook; still others prefer loose-leaf pages with a three-ring binder; still others use their computers, or even index cards, to store and sort dreams. Whatever works for you is fine, as long as you create a written document in a consistent way.

2. Before you go to sleep, enter the date in your permanent record and jot down what you have done and felt during the day. This paragraph of "facts" needn't be long but should include the salient events and emotions you experienced. This may hardly seem necessary but two months or two years from now you will find it invaluable. Be sure to include the pleasurable flavors of your day, however small, as well as the dregs.

3. If you travel often, as I do, you may wish to indicate where you slept, along with the date, at the top of the page. This sometimes makes it easier to locate a particular dream record later.

4. The day after you've made rough notes on a dream, rewrite them into a legible record, using the present tense to help you get back into the feeling mode of the dream.

5. Give each dream a title based on some unique feature it contains. This "naming ceremony"[8] is useful for later dreamwork.

6. You may wish to leave a wide column for sketches or diagrams of dream elements that are unusual or hard to describe. You can also add drawings by pasting or taping them into your dream journal.

7. Explore the most intriguing images that arise in your dreams. Some people feel overwhelmed with dreams after they develop their recall skill. Not to worry—simply pick the dream images that fascinate you and work with them. Discovering things about yourself and finding insights in your dreams increases your recall and makes

recording dreams worthwhile. (Perhaps you'll want to add your responses to the activities given in later sections to your permanent dream record.)

8. Be patient. The full meaning of a particular dream sometimes takes a long time to unfold.

### ◇ Understanding Your Dreams—Six Steps

Dreams are problem-solving devices, available to you every night. As you grow in understanding your dreams, you are better able to use these inner tools for guidance in dealing with problems and for creating novel solutions.

Today's dreamers have many methods available to explore their dreams. Most methods, however, have certain core steps in common. Below I briefly describe my technique for processing dreams; it shares elements with others, but has its unique slant.[9] Notice that the initial letter of each step combine to spell the word "dreams." This acronym makes the method easy to remember and apply.

### 1. DESCRIBE THE DREAM IN THE PRESENT TENSE.

By writing or telling the dream as though it were ongoing, you are able to recall the emotions in it more clearly and begin to discharge any anxiety associated with the imagery. If you have followed the instructions for recalling and recording dreams, you have already completed this step.

### 2. REFLECT YOUR FEELINGS DURING THE DREAM.

What was your overall feeling about the events in the dream? Did your emotions change during the course of the dream? When were they strongest? What was the worst part of the dream? What was the best?

### 3. EXPRESS WAKING EMOTIONS AND EVENTS RELATED TO THE DREAM.

What has happened recently in your life? What were your responses to these events or thoughts in the last few days? It's important to know that dream images exaggerate and overdramatize reality. The waking emotions that dreams represent are likely to be similar but less powerful; they are resemblances, not replicas. Can you see any connection between your dream feelings and current waking life feelings? Do your dream feelings *correspond* to waking life feelings or do they represent a sharp *contrast?* When you relived the feelings in the dream as you wrote them down, did they remind you of anything in your waking life? Connect the dream world and the waking world. (Sometimes this step is easier to do after you have completed step four, so keep it in mind as you consider the next guideline.)

### 4. ASSOCIATE TO THE KEY IMAGES IN THE DREAM.

First, consider the main action. What was the dream about? Then determine the oddest thing about the dream. What was this? If it was a person, ask yourself, who is this person? What's special about him or her? Was it about an animal? What is this kind of animal like? How does it differ from other similar animals? Describe the person or animal as if to a child who does not know either of them. Do it simply and concretely.[10] Tell what is characteristic about them; list their general qualities. Observe the qualities you emphasize. How are these qualities important to the dream? Is there a composite dream character, such as a bird-cat or two people blended into one? If so, define each part separately, then tell what it would mean if these two things were combined. Now imagine yourself inside one of these dream images. What does it feel like to be that image? If that image could speak, what would it say?

What does the setting of the dream suggest to you? What does it feel like to be in that locale? Are there unusual objects or colors or other elements in the dream? What do they remind you of? Describe the image fully, but also tell what it makes you think about.

Repeat this associative, amplification process for all the main images in the dream, especially for anything that seems important or evokes strong emotion in you. Remember that dreams are multileveled; they reveal information about your physical and psychological condition and sometimes even your spiritual or creative aspects. Stay aware of these three beautiful strands woven into one rich braid.

### 5. MEDITATE ON THE MEANING OF THE DREAM BY SUBSTITUTING YOUR PERSONAL ASSOCIATIONS FOR THE ACTION IN THE DREAM.

By associating to the key dream images and then substituting these associations for the images and actions in the dream, you will find that a clear message begins to emerge, almost as if you were making a translation from a foreign language. Step four, associating to key images, is like looking up separate definitions of each word. In step five, you make a smooth translation. Be sure to use the dreamer's exact words.

For example, suppose your dream was, "John F. Kennedy is dead." In step four, you will have made associations to John F. Kennedy that are unique to you. You may have said, "JFK was an idealistic politician," or "JFK was a womanizer," or some other association. Each dreamer will have unique associations. The second key image in this dream is "dead." Death in dreams is usually a metaphor for "nonfunctional, inactive, as if dead."

Whatever your associations were to the key images in the dream, you now substitute them for the action in the dream. Step five in this case might yield the translation, "the idealistic politician part of myself is no longer functional," or "the womanizer part of myself is now inactive." Some people like to write their original dream text on one page and put the "translation" on the opposite page. This step takes practice to get the most benefits.

### 6. SUMMARIZE WHAT YOU PLAN TO DO ABOUT THIS SITUATION IN YOUR WAKING LIFE.

You may decide to "wait and see," or you may opt to act as a result of your dream exploration. In the sample dream about John F. Kennedy being dead, you might decide to "resuscitate" the politically idealistic aspect of yourself, and become reinvolved in politics, supporting a candidate whom you admire. Images that die in dreams can be brought back to life when you're awake. Instead, you might be content to have this part of your life over, as in the case of the womanizer aspect being inactive. Whatever it is, put your decision into words. Some people like to phrase the summary into a dream "proverb" or concise saying, such as, "I will follow my ideals." You can gradually build a set of personal proverbs that apply to your life.[11]

This method of understanding your dreams provides the basic groundwork for more advanced dreamwork. Each future chapter, as already mentioned, provides activities to further your dream skills. However, there's one more tool you should have at the outset.

◇ The Secret Language of Dreams—Metaphors

A growling dog with teeth bared, a gardenia plant in full bloom, tree branches covered with ice, a woman drowning—the images in our dreams are special kinds of pictures: they are metaphors. The word *metaphor* comes from the Greek words *meta*, meaning "over," and *pherein*, meaning "to carry." Thus, a metaphor carries something over from one thing to another. A metaphor is usually thought of as a figure of speech in which one thing is likened to another, different thing; it is an implied comparison, as in the expression "screaming headlines." Newspaper headlines cannot literally shout, but in size and visual impact they can imply a loud voice. A metaphor differs from a simile, in which the comparison is explicit, containing the words *like* or *as*. For example, "Her tears flowed like wine."

People often have the notion that metaphors are limited to poetry, drama, and art. In fact, we use metaphors constantly in everyday talking, thinking, and acting.[12] One man, for instance, says, "I'm running out of gas," when he is bored with a project. Awake or asleep, we think in metaphorical terms.

The Greek philosopher Aristotle, over two thousand years ago, stated, "The most skillful interpreter of dreams is he who has the faculty of observing resemblances."[13] You will see in the next section the importance of recognizing resemblances between dream images and body forms and functions. In general, however, dream images are metaphors for our emotions. They are a kind of picture language for how we feel.

When we dream of falling, for example, it is often a symbol for feeling disappointed or failing in a project. Our dreaming minds equate "lack of emotional support" with "falling." In waking speech, we might say "so and so let me down," or "I lost ground." Metaphors help us understand our emotional reactions to our experiences by comparing a more abstract concept —such as disappointment over lack of emotional support—to a more concrete one—such as plunging downward through space. Metaphors put handles on more abstract concepts by likening them to more familiar ones.

If we dream of animals with sharp teeth, the images are often metaphors for our own feelings of anger. Here the implied comparison is "biting anger." When we are furious without expressing it, or when we fear someone is angry with us, we may dream about a biting, snarling animal, as if harsh words could inflict physical wounds. If we dream of drowning, it is often a symbol for feeling overwhelmed by some situation. A woman who was getting divorced dreamed of helplessly floating on the sea, about to drown. The dream image likened the emotional excess of her situation to literal inundation with water. Getting divorced made her feel as if she were drowning.

In one of his interviews with television commentator Bill Moyers, mythologist Joseph Campbell pointed out that primitive people do not think of themselves as "running like a deer;" they *become* the deer. Similarly, we become the metaphors in our dreams: we are the burning house; we are the hurt puppy; we are the broken machine.[14] Certain dream images are typical metaphors for the body.

## ◇ THE BODY IN DREAMS

In daily speech, we often refer to parts of bodies as if they were other objects or animals. A pregnant woman is sometimes said to have "a bun in the oven," when referring to the fetus in her womb. A sexually aroused woman may be said to have "a fire in her furnace," or to be "a hot pussy," speaking of a condition of sexual heat in her genitals. These sayings are based on a more general metaphor—the body is a container. In dreams, two of the most common metaphors for bodies are houses and vehicles.

### ◇ The Body as a House

A house has an inside and outside. It is divided into parts: it has a foundation, framework, basement, and ground and upper floors. The house contains pipes, ducts, and wires that transport heating, cooling, and energy from one area to another. It has windows and doors. All these structures are analogous to parts of the human body in shape or function, although the images used to represent them vary from dreamer to dreamer. Here are some common correspondences between a house and a body that appear in dreams:

| *HOUSE PART* | *BODY PART* |
|---|---|
| staircase | spine |
| framework | skeleton or bones |
| windows | eyes ("the window of the soul") |
| front door | mouth or vagina |
| back door | anus |
| furnace | stomach or womb |
| pipes | blood vessels or ducts |
| electrical wiring | nerves |
| room | inner space (e.g., vagina) |
| balcony | breasts |
| chimney, tower, or turret | penis |

When a house, skyscraper, cottage, or castle, or parts of them, appear in dreams, the dreamer is often—but not always—symbolizing his or her own body. An entire dream house may represent a part of the body, as when a high-rise or a silo stands for an erect penis; a barn containing animals may symbolize a woman's womb with unborn children. In these cases, the metaphor is based on similar structural shapes. Psychologically, a house in a dream symbolizes the dreamer's current life-style or attitude.

If you dream about a house as a metaphor for your body, the emphasis is on the structure and condition of your body. Therefore, it's important to pay attention to the condition of your dream house:

Is the house too small or is it spacious?
It is shabby or well cared for?
Are parts of it in disrepair?
Is something broken or disconnected?
Is the house harmonious or unattractively decorated?
Is the foundation strong or shaky?
Are there rooms that you never knew were there?

Noticing these elements in the dream house often reveals something about the current condition of your body; these qualities usually contain psychological information as well. If a house in a dream often tells something about the structure and condition of the dreamer's body, different metaphors emphasize the dreamer's body in action.

### ◇ The Body as a Vehicle

Cars, trucks, airplanes, ships, bicycles—these and other vehicles often symbolize the dreamer's body in action. "The body is a vehicle" is another variant of "bodies are containers." Cars are the most common vehicular metaphor for the body. In preautomobile times, the dream image chosen to represent the dreamer's body was frequently a horse or a horse and carriage.

The word *automobile* derives from the Greek word *autos*, meaning "self," plus the Latin word *mobilis*, meaning "movable." Like organic bodies, an auto requires an energy input of fuel and has a residual waste output of exhaust. These processes parallel our functions of eating food and excreting wastes. An auto, like a body, requires maintenance to function well; it may break down or have an accident; it can go too fast, too slow, or just right.

When you dream about a car as a representation of your body, you are emphasizing the degree of control of your body and its movement through space. You still may learn about your body's condition and structure, as you did in dreams about a house, but in dreams about vehicles, the focus is on your body's functioning. Here are some common correspondences between a car and a body that appear in dreams:

| AUTOMOBILE PART | BODY PART |
| --- | --- |
| body (outer shell) | body surface |
| steering wheel | mind-set, control of direction |
| brakes | ability to control level of activity |
| headlights | eyes |
| horn | voice |
| fuel | energy level |
| engine, other concealed parts | inner organs |
| tires or wheels | legs |

If you dream about an automobile as a metaphor for your body, you should consider:

Which brand is it?

Which model is it (sedan, convertible, sports, racing)?

What condition is it in?

How well does it function?

Are you at the steering wheel? If not, who is in control?

Is the car going too fast or too slow?

Do the brakes work?

Is the car moving properly on the road or has it swerved off?

Is it stuck in a rut?

Is there danger of a crash?

Is there a flat tire?

Are the inner parts malfunctioning?

Is the exterior rusty or polished?

Is there enough gas?

The same concepts apply to other vehicles, but the questions vary somewhat. Answers to these questions will reveal how your body is functioning at the moment.

There are numerous other metaphors operating in dreams, such as, the body is a "machine," an "animal," a "plant," a "garment," and so forth. Because no one metaphor gives complete expression to the body's condition, functioning, or our emotions about it, we use many metaphors in our dreams. Each expresses what is important at the moment, while downplaying or hiding other aspects. Each highlights exactly those aspects of the experience that are relevant at the time. Together, as we will see in the following chapters, several metaphors combine to give a comprehensive picture.

◇ Normal Bodily Processes in Dreams

Have you ever dreamed of eating a scrumptious meal and awakened to find yourself feeling ravenously hungry? You might think that the dream banquet created your hunger, but it's more likely that your stomach was experiencing hunger pangs as you slept and your mind, registering these sensations, conjured up images of food. Each organ in the body has a voice in our dreams.

Most men have awakened at times from a passionate dream with an erection or, especially in teenaged boys, even an ejaculation. Did an erotic dream provoke the erection and ejaculation? Or did an accumulation of seminal fluid in the testes create swelling pressure that stimulated the dream? The answer is yes to both questions. Researchers report that sexual arousal in males and females is a natural part of the activation of the entire central nervous system that occurs during dreaming in rapid eye movement (REM) periods.[15] Investigators also find that penile erections are firmer and stronger during sensuous dreams; increases in vaginal blood flow are often associated with overtly sexual dreams.[16] When the dreamer is sexually deprived or excessively stimulated, the usual sexual arousal during dreaming is intensified and often results in dreams involving lust or passion.

Throughout their menstrual years, women experience constant rhythmic contractions of the uterus. During deep sleep, these contractions of the reproductive organ occur the least (an average of 118 times an hour, one investigator found). During the waking state, they occur more often (about 127 times an hour); during the dream state, uterine contractions are the most frequent (about 137 times an hour). Thus, a nonpregnant woman of menstrual years has uterine contractions one to three times every minute. This continuous activity of the uterus is thought to be exercise preparing the organ for the demands of menstruation, reproduction, and labor, because the frequency of contractions decreases after menopause.

When a woman is pregnant, her uterine contractions grow stronger, intensifying toward the end of her term.[17] These periodic tightenings of the uterus, called Braxton-Hicks contractions, are believed to fortify uterine muscles in preparation for the hard labor of childbirth. Thus, a woman's most powerful uterine contractions occur during her dreams when she is pregnant. Small wonder that a pregnant woman begins to have very realistic dreams of labor during the last few months of her term. Her mind, as well as her body, is practicing for the forthcoming labor while she dreams.

Almost everyone has had dreams of wanting to urinate and waking with an insistent need to void the bladder. Images of looking for a bathroom or sitting on a toilet are likely to occur toward the end of a dream story. It's no mystery that the internal pressure created by a full bladder after several hours of sleep amplifies until it instigates dream scenes involving bathrooms or toilets. The pressure on the internal organ eventually escalates enough to awaken the dreamer.

A full bladder or colon, a stomach cramping with hunger

pangs, a contracting uterus, and congested testes—each of these normal, recurring conditions lead to dream images associated with satisfying the momentary need. Since normal bodily processes create sensations that are converted into dream pictures, we should not be surprised that abnormal body processes—ones that occur in illness or injury—also take shape in dreams. In fact, when our bodies become disturbed, our dreams are often the first to know.

### ◇ Abnormal Bodily Processes in Dreams

As normal bodily functions go awry, the disturbances take on dream form. While we sleep, our sensory organs continue to register impressions that impinge upon us from the environment; we also register sensations inside our bodies that are produced by our internal organs. If these sensations become intense enough to pass a threshold, we will awaken. The threshold is determined in part by our motivations. The sleeping mother who "listens" with part of her mind for any sound her baby makes will awaken to its cries without an alarm clock, while other sleepers continue to sleep without responding to the baby's cries. The sleeper whose expanding bladder becomes overfull will awaken in order to empty it. So, too, the injured or ill person will be awakened by sensations of pain or discomfort that penetrate into dreams. *However, if these external and internal sensations remain mild, disturbing but not enough to arouse the sleeper, they are twined into ongoing dream stories.* Here is where we can learn from our dreams. Peering through the windows of our dreams, we can watch our bodies at work.

Suppose, for example, you fall asleep feeling fine, but as you sleep you develop a headache. You most likely would be getting a common tension headache from fatigue or be coming down with an infection and a fever. (Of course, some headaches have more serious causes, such as hormonal changes, vascular abnormalities, hemorrhage, encephalitis, tumors, or obstructions.) Inside your head, certain changes are occurring that cause pain. In the two most common types of headaches—tension and migraine—these changes are partly vascular constrictions and dilations. The exact mechanism of many headaches is still controversial, but all involve changes in the normal functioning of the head.

While you dream, these changes in your head will be depicted. The exact shape of the dream image depends upon a number of factors, but the form almost always shows something on a head, something happening to a head, or a reference to a head. I have examined over forty dream reports from people who awoke with headaches they did not have before they went to sleep—some from my collection of people's dreams, others from research studies.[18] Here is a summary of various dream images typical of headaches in dreamers:

### 1. INTENTIONAL OR ACCIDENTAL BLOW TO THE HEAD:
- dreamer is hit on the head with an ax by an assailant
- dreamer is hit on the head with books by a student
- dreamer is hit on the head with a rifle butt by an enemy
- dreamer is struck on the head with a baseball bat
- dreamer is struck on the head by falling material as a building collapses
- dreamer strikes head on a bridge railing after losing control of a vehicle

### 2. INJURED OR DISTORTED HEADS:
- dreamer is attacked by wolves who gnaw his head
- dreamer is shot in the head by a man
- dreamer sees animals with big heads and horns
- dreamer sees monsters with deformed heads

### 3. WEARING OBSTRUCTIVE HEADGEAR:
- dreamer wears a large fur hat that obstructs vision
- dreamer wears a big helmet that obstructs vision
- dreamer wears an uncomfortable, tight hat

### 4. HOT OR COLD SENSATIONS ON THE HEAD:
- dreamer washes hair in hot, then cold dirty water
- dreamer's hair is on fire

### 5. WEIGHT ON HEAD:
- dreamer carries food and raw meat on head

### 6. REFERENCES TO THE HEAD:
- dreamer is disoriented by a headache, then hunts for aspirin
- dreamer is to have an operation on head

You can see that dreamers who awoke with headaches were picturing the following in their dreams:

- painful sensations in the head (blows)
- feelings of injury or distortion in the head (attacks or odd shapes)
- unpleasant sensations around the eyes (obstructive head-gear)
- changes in cranial blood circulation (hot or cold)
- sensations of pressure on the head (weight)
- concerns about pain in the head (fear of an operation)

Yet most of these internal sensations were greatly exaggerated and overdramatized. The dreamer was not actually being attacked by wolves, but felt pain in the head area where the dream animals appeared to be chewing. Every change in the body's normal processes—from a simple headache or stubbed toe to a broken bone or diseased organ—is portrayed in dream content directly or symbolically.

Our dreams about disturbances in our normal body functioning often show us:

1. the exact location of the disturbance
2. the symptoms of the disturbance
3. the malfunctioning involved in the disturbance

This information is extremely useful because it allows us to assess changes. When we are injured or ill, our dreams demonstrate what is happening in the body *at the moment*, and enable us to compare this moment to past and future conditions seen in dreams; thus, they permit us to evaluate our stage of healing.

You will see how dreams announce when we are in danger, alert us to damage occurring in our bodies, and change content as we worsen or improve. By using certain dream images in visualizations and in art activities, we can move more rapidly toward psychological, and possibly physical, wellness.

## ◇ DREAM ACTIVITIES: GETTING STARTED

### ◇ 1. Begin your dream journal tonight.

Those of you who have kept dream journals in the past know how much they can teach you about yourself, guiding you toward a fuller life, as you work with their images. If you are injured or ill, keeping a diary of your dreams provides special benefits for your recovery of well-being. You might want to make this project exclusively a recovery/discovery journal. It can help you:

- contact unrecognized emotions about what's happening to your body
- understand your reactions to treatment
- express troublesome emotions and rid yourself of their negative impact, relieving tensions
- transform your emotions
- discover your personal symbols for ill health, vibrant health, and changes in health
- assess progress in stages of healing
- learn from past injuries and illnesses
- obtain creative solutions to difficulties
- warn you about present or future health dangers
- contact curative powers within your mind
- find a lighthouse midst the chaos of physical pain
- recognize your personal components of joyful living

◇ 2.  Review the suggestions on recalling your dreams,
if needed.

If you are in the hospital, you are likely to be awakened often; use these times to scan your mind for recent dreams.

◇ 3.  Read over the suggestions on recording your
dreams and gather any necessary supplies.

Maintaining a dream journal when you are in pain may require imaginative methods. For example, if you are right-handed and have broken your right arm, there's no way you'll be able to easily record your dreams. This may be the time to exercise your uninjured hand. Some people find that it's easier to express emotions and get in touch with subliminal thoughts with their non-dominant hand.

Perhaps you'll be able to use a voice-activated tape recorder and describe your dreams aloud for a friend to transcribe later. Or maybe a friend will write down your dreams directly as you describe them. Family and friends often feel better in a crisis when they are given a specific task to do for a loved one; it reduces their sense of helplessness. Computer-wise dreamers may be able to get a portable machine to use while in the hospital or confined to a bed. Simply describing your dream aloud is better than holding it inside. In whichever way is possible for you, even if it is retrospective notes, make a record of your dreams, along with your reactions to any accident or disease and the methods of care. This journal may become an important document in your recovery. At the very least, it will provide a means for self-expression and insight.

◇ 4. Enter the facts of the day in your dream journal, along with a brief description of your feelings.

If you are injured or ill, you may find it useful to include comments on your physical health during the day. What was the worst time? What seemed to help? What equipment did you use? What exercises did you do? What medication did you take? What were your emotions? What was the highlight of the day? Any small pleasure counts.

◇ 5. After you sleep and dream, describe it in your journal.

The written record of your dream is called the "dream text." Be sure to include the characters that appeared in the dream: people, animals, and superhuman creatures; the setting and atmosphere of the dream; the objects that were central to the content; any outstanding colors; the action that took place; and how you felt during the dream.

◇ 6. Now explore the dream text using the six-step method D-R-E-A-M-S described above on page 25 (or any other technique you find useful).

If you are injured or ill, pay particular attention to the body parts mentioned in the dream. The activities in the following chapters will help you understand these images.

Once you have your dream diary underway, you'll be able to get the most benefit from the activities that appear at the end of each chapter. Since this book is laid out according to a plan, each chapter builds upon what you learned in the preceding one. You might wish to read the book straight through, experimenting with the techniques as you go. Later you can return to those strategies that were most beneficial. You're on your way to dreaming well.

# 2

## DREAMER, HEAL THYSELF

Tuesday, March 1, 1988 was a brisk, sunny day in San Francisco. The winds from the sea were fresh after weeks of wintry rain. I had been immersed for the past two months completing the revised manuscript for my book *Women's Bodies, Women's Dreams.* Now the remainder of the book had been mailed. This was my first free day.

My girlfriend Linda and I planned a special outing to celebrate. The day was so beautiful, we thought a walk before lunch would be invigorating. I love the view of the ocean from the cliffs near my house. We set out at a stride. As we turned off Lake Street onto El Camino del Mar, I realized that Linda was going at too fast a pace for me. I hesitated to say so, deciding instead it might be good for me to quicken the rate.

We'd been talking and walking for about twenty minutes—then it happened. I don't know what exactly, since there was a short blank space. My extremely vivid memory was of the sidewalk rapidly rising toward my face—not that I had fallen so much as *it* was rising. I could see the fine grainy texture of the concrete as it rushed toward me with tremendous speed, and I knew the impact would be hard.

Instinctively I threw out my left arm to protect my head. I felt the thunk of my body, padded by the tweed jacket I wore. Even with leather gloves on, I could feel my hand scraping the rough sidewalk as it took the impact, and I knew my left knee was lacerated. The left side of my forehead struck the concrete with force, protected somewhat by my sunglasses, which hit first and clattered off. I lay there stunned, noticing a large rusty nail inches from my brow.

Linda, who was much alarmed, helped me to sit up. I knew at once from the sharp pang in my left wrist that I'd sustained serious damage, probably broken it. I would certainly have to go to a hospital for X-rays.

Another friend of mine who was driving by stopped her car and drove us home, where I called my orthopedist friend, who agreed to meet me at the hospital in a few minutes. I grabbed a bag of frozen peas from the freezer to ice my wrist, then Linda drove me to the hospital. My arm was swelling rapidly and severe pain was setting in. Despite an inner jitteriness, I felt efficient and practical about what must be done. It was a pity, a dreadful inconvenience, but simply needed to be taken care of promptly.

In the emergency room, I was glad to see the familiar face of my orthopedist, who said he'd return as soon as I was checked in and had X-rays taken. While I went through the seemingly endless registration procedure, I began to feel weak and faint.

A compassionate nurse sat me down in a wheelchair and gave me some water, then whisked me into the X-ray room while Linda called my husband, Zal. The pulling and turning necessary to take the X-rays was extremely painful, and I almost passed out. I began to feel nauseous, so I was helped onto a gurney and wheeled to the casting room, where I lay in a stupor for a few minutes until the orthopedist reappeared. He announced, "Well, despite the way you look and feel, it's only a sprain. There's no dislocation or break." I couldn't believe it. My wrist was acutely painful and already enormous in size. "There's evidence of past trauma in that wrist—a fracture at one time." He added blithely, "Nothing recent."

"But," I protested feebly, "I've never broken this arm before. Is it possible I could have broken it without knowing it?"

"Maybe—this is only a sprain. You'll feel better when I immobilize it."

A strange euphoria was creeping over me. I wasn't badly hurt after all. The authority had said so. I would soon be fine. All I wanted to do was go to sleep on the gurney. Endorphins, I thought as I drifted in and out of awareness. Drowsy, almost tipsy, I thought vaguely how dangerous this state could be if one were hurt in an isolated setting . . . all that mattered was sleep.

Zal appeared at the door, ashen-faced. He was reassured by the orthopedist that there was nothing seriously wrong. We spoke for a few minutes before he kissed my brow, then went back to the psychotherapy patient whom he had left waiting in his nearby office. Meanwhile, the orthopedist put a light plastic splint on my arm, instructed me to rest, and ice my wrist. Then he told me to take pills for pain and to come into his office in two days. Linda helped me with the awkward job of dressing and drove me home, fortified with supplies of hydrocodeine to kill any pain.

Having taken an analgesic before I left the hospital, I began to feel lighthearted. What a relief! It was nothing serious after all—a few days of discomfort, no more. But by the time we reached home, the first painkiller was wearing off and my arm started to hurt again.

Linda arranged a snack, and helped me disrobe. I crawled into bed, propped with pillows under every appendage. Sleep would soon mend me, I thought. Linda left, knowing that Philippe, our live-in French student, would be home shortly to help if I needed it. I took another analgesic and drifted into a brief oblivion.

When I woke up, I still felt dreadful, but Philippe was busy preparing dinner, so when Zal arrived with a magnificent bouquet, I went downstairs to eat. The evening passed tolerably.

That night, however, was agonizing. I woke repeatedly. I discovered I could no longer move without excruciating pain in "the" arm—it was no longer mine. Involuntarily, I screamed when I tried to get up or down in bed because the attempt to do so brought on unbearable muscle spasms in my forearm. I woke Zal in the middle of the night with a shriek. I dreamed about a death warning: an acquaintance who had committed suicide was back in town. Obviously, I felt I had badly injured myself.

When daylight finally came, I could not sit up or lie down without assistance, because the pain was so acute. The painkillers barely touched it. My hand and forearm were swollen beyond recognition. Zal arranged for a cousin and her baby to keep me company. Although I still had torturous cramps, I minimized them by keeping my whole body as immobile as possible.

That night I again woke every three hours, but Zal and I had devised a better prop using a large wedge-shaped pillow as a base so that I slept sitting halfway up and could move a little without setting off spasms. My dream was an incomprehensible fragment.

On Thursday morning Zal drove me to the orthopedist's office, in my pajamas with a jacket over my shoulders. He told me, "You're much too swollen for the nature of your injury." He said the excessive swelling was because I wasn't moving my arm enough. I countered that moving it brought on unbearable spasms of pain. "You must move it!" he insisted. "You're holding tension in your hand and have to break it up." He instructed me to make a fist. The fat-sausage fingers could barely budge. I struggled to follow his instructions with tears streaming down my face.

Sure enough, if I forced myself to endure the pain, I could bend the fingers and the swelling did begin to recede as I clenched and unclenched my fist. I was told that I must keep my hand active, to elevate it above my heart when lying down, and to wear the splint as little as possible. He asked me to demonstrate the lying-down and sitting-up movements that brought on the cramps, but I refused—not for anyone would I deliberately evoke those. He re-emphasized that I must wear the splint for as short a time as possible and use my arm as much as I could.

The rest of Thursday I had the help of another friend, who sponge bathed me and fixed meals. That night I dreamed of falling into the sea and climbing out over rough concrete. Friday was somewhat better. I even managed to work a little, sitting up in bed, making notes and phone calls. But by late afternoon, the pain returned and I felt weak and shaky. However, I slept and dreamed more and needed less painkiller.

The next few days passed in a mix of moderate undulating pain, with periods of respite. I always felt better when I wore the splint, but I dutifully removed it for several hours, clenched my fingers and moved the arm. My sleep, though chaotic, was better. I seemed to be ravenous for nourishing food. I went back to work on my manuscript, which had been returned for further revisions, hoping the whole unpleasant injury would pass away.

One week later, the battered arm was less swollen, but looked and felt extremely fragile and vulnerable. I could barely move it. It was still hot with inflammation over the wrist and it looked deformed to me. I had been a hand model in my college days, posing for magazine photographs and television commercials in which I turned appliance knobs or dialed telephones— even appearing handcuffed on the cover of a detective story magazine. The shape of my hands is still important to me. The orthopedist, however, whom I saw every few days, said the deformed appearance of my wrist was because of the residual swelling. "Just keep moving it," he advised.

Any movement of the arm still brought on pain. I started carrying a stiff pillow with me to support it. I was only to use the splint when pain was excessive. I worked hard to increase flexibility.

About ten days after I was injured, I dreamed that my arm was broken. Perhaps this dream was the impetus I needed to confront the orthopedist on my next appointment, which was about two weeks after the accident. I still had considerable pain in my arm, which seemed inappropriate for a sprain; the area over the wrist continued to feel hot. My black eye was almost gone, my contusions had vanished, but my swollen, bruised, and tender arm still looked misshapen and I was determined to find out why.

"Look at this!" I said in his office. "Something is wrong! I want more X-rays."

"I agree," he replied, examining it. After the X-rays were taken, I sat in the cold room waiting for the results, shivering with anxious near-certainty over what the outcome would be. I dreaded hearing my fears confirmed.

When the radiologist clipped the X-rays onto the light box, he commented, "That's quite a complex fracture you've got!"

"It's supposed to be a sprain," I said weakly.

"Oh, no—look. Here are two breaks in the radius, and see how the wrist bones are jammed into a dropped position."

"How do these compare to the first X-rays?" I asked grimly.

He sent for them. Half an hour later the sets hung side by side. The progressive worsening was apparent even to my untrained eye. My injury was far more extensive than the day it happened.

"We've got a problem," said the orthopedist with a blanched face. To his credit, he added, "I made a mistake. I'm really sorry." He launched into a lengthy explanation of how my arm required immediate surgery to repair the damage, and it would have to be rebroken since it had begun to heal in a deformed fashion. It would be a two- or three-month procedure. He could perform the surgery along with an associate. I determined on the spot that he would never touch me again. I was maddened, terrified, and shocked. I had thought my arm was broken all along and he had never listened to me! He wanted to explain the situation to my husband, so he said I should return to the office with him as soon as possible. Now I was forbidden to move my arm the slightest bit and to keep the splint on at all times.

I walked over to Zal's office in a daze and, after his patient left, I gave him a tearful account of the situation. We returned to the orthopedist's office. I could feel Zal's hand shaking with anger as he held mine, listening to the explanation of the problem. I said I wanted a second opinion. The orthopedist gave us some suggestions, urging haste.

We spent the evening telephoning every physician we knew, and friends on university staffs, for recommendations for a hand surgeon. A small list was formed, with the oft-repeated name of Leonard Gordon, a microsurgeon at the University of California, San Francisco. The chagrined orthopedist arranged for us to see the specialist the following day, a Thursday. I scarcely slept and remembered no dreams.

Dr. Gordon was unable to see me until Friday. That Thursday night I slept poorly again and had a nightmare about a great catastrophe. Friday morning we conferred with Dr. Gordon and his staff for nearly three hours in order to decide which of three alternatives to pursue: (1) I could have my arm cast as it was, which would leave me with a deformed wrist and the inability to turn my arm over; (2) without opening the arm, a surgical attempt could be made to pull the bones into place with the pins of an "external fixator," which would be inserted through the skin and muscle layers into the bones with the hope they would heal strongly enough to hold; (3) I could have the wrist capsule surgically opened, the bones rearranged, and a metal plate pinned to the radius to hold it in place. Each procedure had its risks and benefits. We chose the third option, which offered the only chance for near-complete recovery; it also involved the greatest risk and required months of physical therapy to restore functioning to my hand. At least we felt fully informed of the possible dangers and outcomes.

Time was of the essence because the bones were healing incorrectly; we had to schedule the surgery promptly. A sturdy cast was applied to my broken arm, then Dr. Gordon sent me to have pre-operative tests done while his staff tried to obtain an operating room for that evening.

I was sent directly to have my blood taken, my urine sampled, my chest X-rayed, and my heart checked on an electrocardiogram, with the probability of being admitted as a patient in a few hours. My anxiety level sky-rocketed. I felt as though my well-being were out of my control. By the time I reached the electrocardiogram station, I was extremely agitated. The young technician urged me to calm down, but I could not. The recording pen was zigzagging off the paper. Finally I asked the frustrated young technician to get my husband, and she complied.

Zal's skills as a psychotherapist and loving mate were never so appreciated. He began talking to me in a soothing voice, telling me to close my eyes. He stroked my forehead rhythmically. "Think about the spring," he suggested, "and we're traveling in the south of France. Can you see it? What does it look like?"

"Lavender fields," I mumbled.

"Now we're walking through the lavender fields," he continued. "See how lovely they are . . . the color . . . inhale the fragrance."

I began to breathe deeply and evenly and to drift with the sound of his voice, accompanied by the sensation of his hand moving across my brow. I was vaguely aware that the electrocardiogram was being taken.

There was no operating room available that evening, so I was sent home with the possibility of returning in the morning for surgery. I slept fitfully and dreamed of a fire-damaged house that was being restored. In another dream, I was talking in the back seat of a car when it suddenly took off. I screamed, "I can't go!" Clearly, I hoped my body would be repaired, symbolized by the restored house, but I did not want to face what was required—major surgery.

Saturday morning we learned that all the operating rooms were committed until Monday, so my surgery was squeezed into the Monday schedule at noon. Saturday night I dreamed that my husband and I were both to have operations. We had to separate, and I entered a strict hospital where I felt pushed around, frightened, and criticized. Somehow I missed the appointed time for the operation and was mistreated by a nasty nurse. The pre-operative tests had already given me a sense of the dehumanization that many patients report.

Sunday passed in a blurred mixture of pain and pleasure. Zal was treating me royally to help pass the time, but underneath it all ran a current of extreme anxiety. I had been in pain for three weeks and would have to endure more. The thought was appalling. Sunday night I had an amazing dream about falling into a bog, climbing out, and seeing a rare mythological creature—a blue dog wearing a red life jacket (described in Chapter 5, *Crisis Dreams*).

Monday morning came at last and we drove to the hospital. Being admitted to the hospital became a journey into the unknown. Perhaps that was why I felt so frightened about it. Like most of us, I had heard of people who were hospitalized to have a routine operation and never returned. Would I be one of those? Even if the operation was successful, would I be able to recover full use of my hand? Would I have a permanently deformed hand? Would my bones be too weak to endure the repair procedure? Would I be forced to endure further gruesome pain? Not even my surgeon was sure this attempt would work. The last three weeks had been so difficult that my resilience was worn down. I had hardly slept for the three nights since I learned that I must have my arm rebroken. I felt resentful over the misdiagnosis, exhausted and wounded. I didn't want any more pain. I wanted the whole thing to be over and to be myself again. A wave of compassion flooded through me for those people with more widespread injuries or disease.

In the crowded hospital-admissions room we had to wait for an hour. It was an exercise in anxiety. People entered looking pale and terrified; others were weeping or showing signs of acute distress. An agonized-looking old man with a cane was reclining awkwardly on a couch. A red-faced woman in a wheelchair was given a stuffed bear dressed in blue aviator gear and goggles; she clutched it to her bosom, sobbing over and over, "I love it!" There was a general air of doom. I felt invaded by other people's ordeals as well as my own.

Eventually the intake clerk called my name and my husband and I went to her cubicle to complete the essential forms. Then we were sent to the family lounge, where our medical-student daughter joined us for a while. Even my close family members, who were busy chatting, seemed to be at a great distance from me. Although my hand was being held and they were showing me much affection, I felt alone. No doubt they were trying to distract me with general talk, but it seemed as though no one knew what I was about to face. I felt frustrated and finally said, "I need your full attention right now!"

That was the moment before we were called to make the trip to the surgical-preparation room. Zal and I held chilly hands as the elevator ascended to the surgery floor. In a small area curtained off with yellow translucent fabric, I was helped to disrobe and put on a hospital gown. The eerie yellow light made me think of Virginia Woolf's childhood memory of her bedroom at a beach house, where she felt like she was inside a grape.

It seemed as though at least a dozen masked and gowned attendants popped their heads into the curtained area to ask my name and confirm which operation I was having on which arm. This precaution apparently prevents the appalling mistake of performing the incorrect operation on the wrong side of the body.

When the anesthesiologist came to give me the required warnings about the dire possible results of general anesthesia, Zal insisted that he stop. As a psychotherapist who sometimes uses hypnosis, Zal knew how open to suggestion I am, and that I would be better off not hearing a list of the potential dangers. The cheerful anesthesiologist chatted some more, then informed me that I was ready for surgery. I had noticed him occasionally glancing above my head, but did not realize until then that he was checking my readings on the monitor. He explained that a recent study had shown that fifteen minutes of pre-operative talk with a patient prior to surgery proved more relaxing than pre-medication, and resulted in fewer complications. My blood pressure had lowered to an appropriate level.

My gurney was set in motion and I was wheeled down the long corridor, finally letting go of Zal's hand and now truly on my own. I still felt afraid, but somehow it was better since the event was imminent. I remembered my dream about the blue dog in the red life jacket—the mythological creature who turned out to be real. Surely that augered well for what was to come.

We reached the operating room, swerved to the right, and came to a halt under a bank of blazing lights with shiny metal and pale green glass everywhere. I glanced at the large black-

and-white wall clock; it read 1:30. The smiling brown eyes of a nurse appeared above a mask; it comforted me that she resembled a favorite cousin. Someone was attaching the intravenous equipment to my right hand. A few greetings were exchanged, then all went black. It was not a fading or a gradual going under, as I have experienced before, but more like a switch being thrown, and the world around me shut off.

The first few hours following the surgery were miserable. I came partially awake in a gray gloom, with no sense of time having passed. I later learned the operation had taken two-and-a-half hours. Through the murkiness, I heard people urging, "Open your eyes. It's all over. Look at me. It went beautifully." I vomited and felt ghastly. There was an area of undifferentiated pain surrounding my left arm, which was propped high above my heart on a stack of pillows. I could only force my eyes open for short intervals. Vague notions of people suctioning vomitus from my mouth, noise surrounding me, lights. I could hear myself moaning and feel myself moving my legs about restlessly, with no way to get comfortable.

Somewhere in this murky half-world, I had a sense of labored breathing, like lifting a weight up and down. I thought to myself that it was only the effect of the anesthetic. But people around me seemed to become agitated. Concerned voices started asking me, "Is it hard for you to breathe? Is it like when you had teenage asthma? Did anyone in your family have heart trouble?" Obviously something was wrong.

Someone put something under my tongue. "Is it any better? Does it burn? Do you feel any change?" I felt nothing from the first pill or the second. Gradually the weight lifted. Someone was taking a blood sample—what a quantity had been extracted in the last few days.

Slowly the nausea passed. I emerged from the gray gloom and was able to hold my eyes open for longer than a millisecond. The surgeon and the anesthesiologist appeared, commenting about how perfectly I did, how much stronger my bones looked than they anticipated, and how well the surgery went.

I soon began to feel better—in comparison—and sat up to eat some dinner, and much later, even breakfast. I was mystified as to why I was still in the recovery room. People all around me were moaning and vomiting. I was kept in the recovery room from about four o'clock the day of the surgery for the next twenty-four hours. The lights were bright and I didn't sleep at all. I was extremely weary and extremely worried.

During this time, a new and unexpected situation emerged. I was informed there had been a minute change on the electrocardiogram. The doctors said, "If we hadn't happened to have been looking, we would have missed it. We're just being conservative—just to wear a belt and suspenders." A cardiologist was called in to consult and pored over my record with a frown. Blood tests were ordered to check if there had been any damage to the heart. Each of these tests, which took several hours to evaluate, kept coming back equivocal. Above a certain level, I would have definitely been diagnosed with heart damage, but I was right on the borderline.

Many hours later, after much consultation among the specialists, and the administration of four units of potassium, it was determined I was to be sent to the cardiac ward "just to be safe." The cardiologist explained that he thought I had a mild underlying heart disease; we couldn't take the chance of putting me in the orthopedic ward and missing something. The crisis had escalated from arm pain to one of life and death. And so, a full day following the operation, I was trundled off with a cardiac monitor slung upon my chest and my arm propped heavenward for the next stage of this trial by hospitalization.

In the cardiac ward, I was greeted by a girlfriend with some of my favorite cookies, fresh lemon for my water, and a story read aloud to me. Since it was now late afternoon, Zal was back in his office seeing patients. As the attendant wheeled me into the semi-private space, I protested that I was scheduled for a private room. There were none available in the cardiac ward. My friend persuaded someone to create a waiting list for the first available private room, with my name at the head, then she returned and entertained me until another friend arrived.

After my friends departed, the nadir of the whole hospital experience took place. I pressed the button for a nurse and requested a bedpan. A disgruntled attendant appeared; it took her half an hour to return with a bedpan. She stuck it under me roughly, jerking my injured arm in the process, left the pan there, and disappeared. It was impossible for me to remove the pan myself. My left arm was in a heavy cast and my right hand had an intravenous needle in it. Soon, with the bedpan filled to the brim, the urine overflowed onto the sheets. When the obnoxious attendant finally returned and I asked her to place something dry under me, she vanished again. I was left lying in the puddle of urine for two hours. Ringing the bell was futile. My roommate was busy with her visitors and paid no heed.

By the time Zal arrived, I was hysterical. A relatively healthy woman, in full possession of her senses, intelligent and with substantial resource, I was still unable to help myself. I was furious. And immobilized, with my operated arm elevated, my other arm linked to the intravenous line, and the cardiac monitor weighing on my chest. Not only was I frightened and in pain, but I was forced to lie in my own urine for hours. If I could be reduced to this, what of the aged and frail? Every patient needs an advocate.

I complained bitterly to Zal, who went and brought the attendant back himself, insisting that she put dry sheets under me right away. When the assistant surgeon appeared, I expressed my disgust to him as well. He explained that he was unable to do anything because this ward was out of his jurisdiction. It was a catch-22—the orthopedist wanted to help, but the cardiologist had precedence and he wasn't available. Zal assured me that he would get a private nurse in the morning if I still wanted one; he would not leave me alone, but I just had to stick it out for the night. I agreed, and he went home to bed.

I hadn't counted on the roommate. This grim-faced woman was watching television, changing the channel every few seconds with her remote control. At the same time, she tore open the bag of potato chips her guests had brought and was crunching them one at a time. Click—crunch—click—crunch. There I was in a stuporous morphine daze, staring at the flickering lights of the TV screen reflected on the ceiling, without strength to raise my voice over the blare of the TV to ask her to lower the volume or turn it off.

It must have been shortly after midnight that a friendly face peered over the bed railing to ask if I felt able to be moved to a private room. "Yes, please!" She, the new charge nurse, had seen the written request. A room had opened up, but if I waited until morning, it would be gone.

The attendants unlocked my bed and rolled it past the dragon near the door, her TV still blaring, her chips scattered about. She announced, "Well, I drove another one away! That's three!" Her triumphant note faded as we rounded the corner to a blessedly dark, quiet space. The tide turned. Heavily sedated, I slept at last and began to recover.

The following two days and nights were a blur. Drugged, I saw visitors come and go, gazed at the flower painting on the wall for hours, or watched clouds change shape over the wind-blown pines that were visible from my window. I made the first staggering trip to the toilet with my heavy cast dangling above my head. Washing my face and brushing my teeth for the first time in two days felt divine. Late afternoons and evenings were difficult times. The pain always escalated then, in addition to the constant fear I felt with the heart monitor heavy on my chest.

On the third day after the operation, I was to practice walking in the hallway so that my heart could be monitored under stress. Zal supported me on one side to balance the weighty cast draped across my head to keep it above my heart. The cardiac functioning continued to look good. In fact, there had been zero change since the brief split second that indicated a potential problem.

However, I felt shaky and weak. Even though I felt much more comfortable, I found myself crying several times a day. The morphine injections had been shifted to codeine pills to kill the pain; it didn't occur to me that my labile emotions were attributable in part to the medication. Whether it was fear, the medication, or sleep deprivation, I certainly felt peculiar. I hadn't had a good night's sleep in six days—the three at home since I knew I must have the operation and the three nights of disrupted sleep in the hospital, where I had no dream recall—a rarity for me.

During the daytime hours, I practiced two exercises faithfully. Because people who have had a general anesthetic need to expand their lungs fully to expectorate the mucous that has accumulated during the operation, I had been given a "spirometer," a plastic instrument consisting of a calibrated cylinder containing a ball. Attached to the cylinder was a tube into which I was to exhale forcefully in an effort to raise the ball in the cylinder. A few hours after the operation, it was almost impossible for me to exhale powerfully enough to raise the ball; I coughed violently with each attempt. But, with persistence, I tried to raise the ball higher three or four times at the beginning of each hour when I was awake. By the fourth morning, there was a remarkable improvement in my lung capacity.

The other exercise involved mobilizing the fingers that extended beyond the cast of my injured arm. Since muscles that are immobilized atrophy rapidly, I had been urged to practice curling my fingers toward the edge of the cast. I could barely budge my fingers because my arm was exceedingly swollen, a muscle and a ligament had been surgically cut, and a metal plate with screws had been inserted into the radius bone. Yet, with considerable effort, I managed to curl the fingers by trying to do so ten times at the beginning of each waking hour. I'm sure that practicing deep breathing and attempting to curl my fingers helped speed my recovery, giving me something to do to actively help myself.

On the fourth day, I was to be discharged if the cardiologist agreed. It was a busy morning. I had awakened at 5:00 A.M. in anticipation. Zal arrived at about 8:00 A.M., to be present when the cardiologist came. The specialist continued to express his belief that I had a mild underlying heart disease; the chances were 70–30, he told us, that something was wrong. Of the four enzyme tests that were taken, two were equivocal and two were normal. The only test that would convince him that the very brief heart malfunctioning was not something serious would be a negative treadmill test. I had to make an appointment to take this test before he would permit my discharge. This accomplished, he said I could go home with supplies of nitroglycerin to use in case of heart pain.

My surgeon stopped by later to check on my progress and agreed on the discharge. When I told him what the cardiologist said regarding my heart, he replied, "That's nonsense! It was just a reaction to the anesthetic." Such was the consensus of medical opinion. I felt the surgeon was right. I'd never had heart trouble, but the authority of the cardiologist impressed and alarmed me.

There turned out to be no problem with my heart. I took the treadmill test several weeks later with trepidation, and it came out totally negative. With his own instruments providing proof, the cardiologist conceded that I had no heart problem, that it must have been a reaction to the anesthetic, and that I could do whatever I wished. However, I spent that month in fear that I had heart disease. If this had been the case, the "cure" could have scared me to death.

After the dismissal interviews the morning I was released, the assistant surgeon removed my heavy cast, dressed the surgical wound, and reapplied a lighter cast. A girlfriend arrived to help me pack. A male discharge nurse gave me clear instructions about what to look for in my hand that might indicate trouble. Any change in color, especially blueness; a change in sensation, such as numbness; a change in temperature, colder or hotter; or a change in degree of swelling should be immediately reported. He helped me to dress, gather my belongings, get into a wheelchair, and go to my friend's waiting car. What a sense of relief —I felt like a prisoner being freed from jail!

Once home, another loyal girlfriend soon arrived and the two of them helped me to undress and get settled in bed, with necessities within my good arm's reach. One friend set up a simple two-way intercom so that I could speak to whomever was downstairs in the kitchen. She also brought a huge supply of cassette tapes of fiction to pass the time. The other prepared a delicious lunch. We ate together, with me propped on a bedrest, one of them sitting on the bed, and the other in the armchair. We laughed ourselves silly over the various misadventures in getting home—it felt like a group therapy session.

Then, as I grew weary, one of them read aloud to me. Both of them left in the late afternoon. Another devoted friend moved in for a week to cook for me and help me wash and dress. Zal took the night shift, making tea or reading to me until a painkiller took effect.

After a reviving dinner that first night home, I fell asleep at 9:30 P.M. I was awakened by a violent nightmare at 1:00 A.M. I felt as though I might die momentarily—it was true panic.

What was happening? Why did I feel such terror? How did this dreadful dream relate to what was going on? There I was, one of the world's leading dream experts, having a nightmare. Help!

## ◇ DREAM ACTIVITIES: EXPLORING YOUR STORY

This chapter describes my story—what happened to me, how I felt about it while awake and asleep, and how these thoughts and emotions influenced what followed. It's important to be able to tell other people about any traumatic event we experience. By telling what happened and how we felt and continue to feel about it, we start the process of recuperation. Holding pain inside prolongs recovery. In contrast, expressing our physical pain and our emotional reactions to it can "desensitize" us to our discomfort and allow us to begin to heal. My story continues later. Right now it's time for you to tell your story.[1]

◇ 1. Tell your story.

If you have recently had a physical trauma, it will be fairly easy to contact your emotional responses to it. Think about what led up to this difficult time. If you have not recently had an accident, operation, or illness, let your mind drift back to an earlier time, even one in your childhood when you were not well. Remember a time when your body was hurt.

On a new page in your dream journal, write down your story, or have someone record it for you if you cannot. Tell what happened, who was present, when this occurred, where you were, and how and why you think this event took place. Be sure to include how you felt physically and your emotional reactions to your injury or illness. Researchers find that the mere act of putting pain into words can reduce anxiety and set you on the road to recovery.

◇ 2. Find your image for loss.

What was the most disturbing part of this experience for you? Was it the loss of control? The recognition of your vulnerability? The loss of a body part? Loss of your sexuality? Being blemished? What produced the greatest sense of loss for you? This loss is almost always emotional as well as physical. Putting your loss into words may be difficult. Yet the very act of naming it depletes its power to inflict harm.

As you consider the traumatic event you went through, let an image form in your mind that epitomizes your loss. Perhaps this image will be part of the traumatic event, perhaps a symbol of it, or perhaps it will be an image from a relevant dream. Make a note of your image of loss and/or sketch it in your journal.

◇ 3. Find a meaning in loss.

If your injury or illness were to have a meaning, what would it be? For example, I broke my arm at a time when my dreams were urging me to "slow down," that I was "going too fast," that I was "out of balance." My accident forced me to stop and reassess how I was functioning.

Was there anything positive about your accident or sickness? What could it be? Transform any answers to these questions that pop into your head into a proverb. My proverb was, "She who goes too fast, fast falls down."

*1a. Post-Traumatic stress response: Earthquake*

Drawing by Patricia Garfield

*Illustrating a traumatic experience helps reduce a person's anxiety reaction to the event. The picture should include not only what objectively happened, but also the person's feelings about it. This drawing shows the date and time of an earthquake I experienced, the walls and my feet shaking, books tumbling, and objects breaking, as well as my tremulous emotional response.*

*When you make a drawing of a traumatic event, you begin the process of defusing residual fear.*

*1b. Healing visualization for post-traumatic stress: The centered self*
Drawing by Patricia Garfield

*After you have expressed your emotional reactions to a traumatic event, the next phase is to re-center yourself. Remember how you felt prior to the traumatic event. Is there a deep inner core that remains untouched? See if you can contact that portion of your inner self and depict it in a drawing. If your center feels completely lost, re-invent it.*

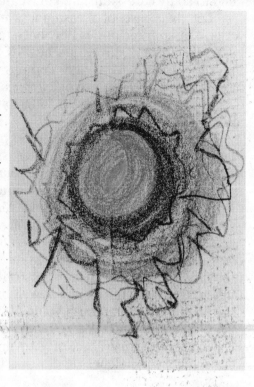

*The picture shows my outer layers agitated by the recent earthquake. Within lies a glowing, golden center that comforts me to recall. What does your image reveal about your thoughts and feelings? Such drawings of the inner center help you re-collect yourself and continue the process of healing.*

Seeing a meaning in a physical trauma does not mean that we *caused* the trauma or wished it to happen. It's merely a way to notice that something can be learned from any painful event.

## ◇ 4. Find an image for wholeness.

Now settle yourself as comfortably as possible. (You may wish to have someone read these directions to you or listen to them on a cassette tape.) Take a few deep breaths and let your muscles relax easily. Close your eyes or just let them glaze over. Rest gently at ease. Let your breathing grow slow and regular.

Now begin to scan your body with your mind's eye. Let it roam the landscape of your body, outside and inside. Find the place or spot in your body that feels most comfortable, no matter how minute. Which area feels most pleasant? Focus there.

Move your mind's eye closer. Regard the shape of this good feeling, its color, and its texture. Allow the fingertips of your mind to softly caress this area of well-being.

Let the sense of pleasantness expand. See it spreading wider. Let your memories flow back to a time when your entire body felt glowing, alive, and healthy. Just enjoy the vibrancy, the pure wholeness of health. Perhaps you are a child, or even a baby, or perhaps you are older, engaging in a vigorous sport, dancing or swimming, or making love. You feel marvelously alive.

Soon you may see or sense a symbol, a shape or pattern that expresses this sense of wholeness. Let yourself watch the symbol appear that encapsulates your sense of complete wellness. It may be a part of your past or an image from one of your dreams. Let it grow clear and vivid. Memorize it.

This sense of vibrant well-being can be part of your life again. It will be evoked, perhaps, in a different way, but it can come again as part of your present life. For the moment, just let it be in your mind. Cherish it. Absorb it into yourself. And continue to relax into the feeling of well-being. Let the memories of this time restore and refresh you. . . .

Gradually, when you're ready, open and clear your eyes. Feel the invigorating effect of your memories. Make a note of your symbol of wholeness and, if possible, sketch it.

◇ 5. Fortify yourself with pleasure.

You may not presently be able to do any of the things that have brought you joy in the past. But there is bound to be *something* you can do at this moment that will give you pleasure. It may be a small, simple thing. Perhaps you'll inhale the fragrance of flowers nearby, remembering fond associations. Perhaps you'll reread some special poem. Perhaps you'll listen to a favorite piece of music. For the next ten minutes, do something you love.[2] Delight yourself.

Every day, from this day forward, set aside at least ten minutes—then fifteen, then twenty—to do something that gives you joy. No matter how much you may be suffering, or how busy you may be, there is something within your capacity to do. Take a daily pleasure pause. You'll be doing your body and spirit a great favor.

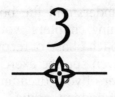

# THE SEVEN STAGES OF
# RECOVERY FROM PHYSICAL
# TRAUMA

Each phase of sickness and returning wellness is traced in our dream imagery. Our dreams resound with alarm bells when we sense trouble ahead; they darken with disaster when we are in crisis. Often suppressed by medication during an operation or chemotherapy, our dreams rebound with a vengeance after medication is lessened or withdrawn. When we have a fever, our dreams grow agitated; and they glimmer gently in response as healing begins. Dreams mirror convalescence, and finally, our dreams glow with new images as health is restored. Thus our dream metaphors about our bodies constantly change throughout the course of recovery.

Regardless of the type of injury or illness, the body and its dreaming mind travel the same mountainous route: we are hurt, we reach a crisis, we react to it, we worsen and die or improve and live. Even if we do not survive, we can grow in self-understanding as long as we are alive.

I have observed seven stages in the recuperation from accidents and diseases. This chapter presents an overview of these seven stages of recovery. At the end of the chapter, you'll see how to explore and understand the body metaphors in your dreams. In the remaining chapters, you'll learn which dream pictures are typical of each phase of recovery and how to assess each step. You'll be given specific exercises to assist your own imagination—the power of your dreaming mind—to accelerate your healing and/or self-understanding.

## ◇ DREAM METAPHORS CHANGE WITH EACH PHASE OF RECOVERY

### ◇ Stage 1: Forewarning Dreams

Accidents happen by chance. The word *accident* derives from the Latin word *accidens*, meaning "falling." Many times we have no control whatsoever over getting into an accident. The ski lift breaks while certain people happen to be on it; the drunk driver on the wrong side of the road plows into someone's car; the earthquake shatters the foundation of a building that crashes down on those inside; the crane at the building site collapses onto the people below. The victims have little warning or chance to escape injury or death.

Likewise, we rarely choose to become sick. People happen to stay in a hotel where the air-conditioning system is circulating an infectious mold; someone drinks a glass of typhoid-infected water; a person cuddles a child who develops measles the following day; someone with a virus sneezes into another person's face. These unforeseen events and mishaps are no one's fault.

### VULNERABILITY TO ACCIDENT AND DISEASE

Yet there are times when all of us are especially susceptible to accidents or illnesses, and we are alerted to this by our dreams. Many people experience a "post-project droop." The business person who has pushed relentlessly to obtain a special contract; the playwright who has completed a work, seen it through dress rehearsal and the opening—both people may collapse after the crisis. When you are eating poorly, exercising irregularly, sleeping inadequately, distracted by worry, pressed by overwork, or have just completed a big job—these are the times when you are more likely to get hurt or fall ill. Your dreams often ring the first warning bell. Dreams sometimes give you a chance to act to avoid harm.

Be on special guard whenever you are excessively busy, preoccupied, or worried. The director of a leading hand clinic in San Francisco, Pamela Silverman, said that many of the wounded men she has treated with physical therapy had wives or girlfriends who were pregnant with their first child. The preoccupation these men felt about their situation distracted them at work, leaving them vulnerable to serious injury. One of the women I spoke with had injured her hand badly, severing a nerve, on the day she brought her husband home from the hospital after he had a heart attack. She was fixing him a sandwich with an extremely sharp knife and was so distraught that she accidentally cut herself. Conditions of overwork, anxiety, or bodily neglect show up clearly in our dream content; such dreams can help us protect ourselves.

The season, climate, and external conditions, such as air pollution and sanitation, influence our health, too. Researchers report that traumatic life events—such as the death of a spouse, getting a divorce, and so on—are also experiences that render us susceptible to disease.[1] However, not everyone who undergoes these events has the same response of weakening. It is our *reaction* to traumatic events that makes us more or less resilient. Our psychological state affects our ability to cope. By monitoring our dreams, we may be able to observe whether the effect of an external event is damaging and see what we can do to help ourselves.

Here are a few typical forewarning dreams that preceded the dreamer's actual illness or injury:

- dreamer is driving a car very fast, with no brakes
- workers at hard labor on construction begin to collapse
- dreamer is warned by a wise figure to slow down
- dreamer who is clinging to a window ledge faints
- dreamer's house is broken into and damaged
- dreamer sees dead relatives
- a terrible storm is coming with black clouds and wind

In general, these forewarning dreams indicate *going too fast* (the car without brakes); *nearing the point of exhaustion* (collapsing laborers, fainting person); *danger ahead* (the storm on the horizon); and *damage underway* (the broken-into house).

The ancient Greeks paid close attention to certain dreams that seemed to predict illness; they called them "prodromal," from the Greek words *pro*, meaning "before," and *dromos*, meaning "running," thus, a forerunner. In medical terms, a prodrome is a symptom that signals the onset of a disease. Over two thousand years ago, Hippocrates, the Greek physician called the father of medicine, thought that specific dream images prognosticated future ailments. Such dreams are probably responses of the brain to minute bodily sensations that are magnified and dramatized during sleep. Symptoms of illness, we shall see, often appear in dreams long before they are observable while awake. As you learn the common dream signs of both poor and vibrant health, and discover your personal images for illness and improvement, you have the opportunity to pick up forewarnings each night. When the images are dire, you can take action to protect yourself. For instance, if you dream that you are driving a car that's going too fast and its brakes have failed, you should find a way to slow down your waking lifestyle before you crash.

### ◇ Stage 2: Diagnostic Dreams

Dreams can sometimes provide a diagnosis that is highly accurate, as in my dream about my arm being broken when I was told it was only sprained. My case is not unique. Our dreams are able, at times, to sift puzzling symptoms and synthesize the clues into a diagnosis.

If dreamers are trained to scan their dreams for danger signs, they will be able to seek treatment earlier rather than later, to help themselves swiftly restore health. Physicians who are sensitive to diagnostic dreams could create a preventive medicine of dreaming based on this concept. Physicians and their staff could be trained to screen for any dreams that have dangerous implications.

One women dreamed about a disease demon who forced her to sit on a hot pipe.[2] In the dream, she felt a burning pain between her legs that awakened her. The same dream recurred on a subsequent night. A psychoanalyst might well interpret this dream as a sexual one, likening the hot pipe to a phallus, and observing that her attitude toward sex was negative, or diseased. However, the woman consulted her physician instead, who found an acute cystitis, or inflammation of her bladder.

Notice how this diagnostic dream informed the dreamer of the exact location of her afflicted body part. It portrayed her pain as caused by something hot, which represented the inflammation present. The dream even implied the functioning of the body part by the image of a pipe, which has the shape of the urinary canal through which the bladder empties. Recurrent dream images of pain, such as this one, are crucial to observe.

Here's an example of a diagnostic dream experienced by a man. In the dream, he fell from a wharf into the water between the wharf piles. A yacht was moored alongside. The yacht squeezed him onto the pier structures.[3]

In this case, the man had complained about a "fluttering feeling" in his stomach just after returning from vacation; he mentioned his dream to his physician. On the basis of this dream, his doctor administered an electrocardiogram and found evidence of a myocardial infarction that was later confirmed by hospital tests. The two significant health clues in this scene were the dreamer's immersion in water and the sensation of being squeezed. You will see later how excessive amounts of water in dreams suggest fluid retention in the body, a condition that is characteristic of heart patients. The squeezing pain associated with heart attacks is clearly present in this dream.

Be sure to monitor your dreams for clues to body disturbances, such as:

- extreme heat
- extreme cold
- excess water
- dryness
- itchiness
- pain

Pay particular attention to any dream about a body part that portrays severe wounding or squeezing pain, or strenuous physical effort combined with breathlessness or drowning. If such dreams are especially intense and/or recur, it's a good idea to check with your physician.

Also be alert to dream images of:

- people, animals, or plants that are injured or die
- buildings or objects that are damaged or destroyed
- people or things that are impaired
- normal flow of liquid that is blocked
- machines or equipment that malfunction or break

Overall, these dreams show *damage taking place* (destroyed objects, injured or dying people and animals); and *impaired functioning* (malfunctioning machines and equipment, blocked flow). Although each of these dream images has psychological implications as well, these very images are often clues to some disorder in your body. Each of us can learn to monitor our dreams, recognize signs of disturbance, and get proper assistance.

### ◇ Stage 3: Crisis Dreams

Whenever the integrity of our bodies is threatened, the dreaming mind interprets the situation as a crisis. If we have sustained a severe injury, developed a disease, or we are facing an operation, the mind turns on a nightly show of its catastrophic dream images. The dreaming mind likens any bodily injury to a physical attack. No matter that an operation is meant to cure a problem, the dreamer will frequently depict surgery as an invasion by knife or bullet or phallus, by wild animal or warrior.

When I had to confront having my arm rebroken in order to set it properly, I dreamed that there was a disaster in a city in which ten million people died; happily I was among the few survivors in my dream. In part of our minds, an operation is compared to a brutal attack upon our bodies.

Here are some other samples of dreams from people who were expecting surgery in the next few days:

- beef is being cut into pieces
- people are cutting a board
- black clouds are covering the sun
- a huge fire is decimating a city
- people wanting to cut the dreamer's throat
- bloody death in a car accident

These dream images indicate, in general, a *fear of being surgically cut* (cut beef, board, and throat); *fear of destruction* (decimating fire, car accident); and *depression* (black clouds blocking sun).

Other dream images during a physical crisis continue to depict the location of the disturbed body part, any sensations of heat, cold, moisture, dryness, or itching experienced in it, and any current malfunction. Replays of accidents are common.

Breaks in bones and skin, rips in muscles, and amputations are dramatically portrayed, frequently in broken buildings, objects, or clothing. In one dream at this stage, I saw myself wearing rags filled with holes; I considered having the outfit mended, but decided to throw it away. My dreaming mind seemed to be comparing the breaks in my body to holes in clothing. I wanted to start over with a "new outfit."

Many hospitalized dreamers feel a loss of identity. Thus, their dreams often contain images of losing identification papers, passports, purses, or wallets. Having been stripped of their personal possessions and been tagged, like a prisoner or an inmate, they don't know what's coming next. They are no longer themselves but a diseased or malfunctioning body.

If you are facing an operation or have an acute illness, remember that catastrophic dreams are only one stage of a larger process. Disaster dreams are normal when you are seriously ill. Later on, you will see that dreams return to happier subjects and, if you allow them, they can soothe and encourage you in your healing.

Among the dreadful images that are typical at this phase, there are scattered a few hopeful ones. Attempts to repair or reconstruct damaged dream objects usually represent hopes for improvement following surgery. Some dream images are purely inspirational, such as the blue dog in the red life jacket (which I will discuss later). Learning to recognize and attend to those positive images is an important part of sustaining ourselves during the crisis and in accelerating the recovery process.

◇ Stage 4: Post-Crisis Dreams

Because of anxiety, many people facing a physical crisis sleep poorly. If you are about to undergo surgery, you are not likely to dream much at all during the night or two before and after the operation. The operation itself turns day into night and disrupts the body's normal cycles. Afterward, most patients find themselves in a stupor from the repercussions of a general anesthetic or from post-operative pain and medication to suppress it. Following complex surgery, it often takes two weeks or so to restore normal sleep and dream patterns. Likewise, the physical aftereffects of chemical treatments dampen dreaming. Most people couldn't care less about dreams at this stage; they are too busy surviving.

Many medications suppress dreaming. When we take pain-killers, we often drowse intermittently; all barbiturates change sleep patterns and affect the ability to dream. In addition to disrupted sleep patterns because of medications, hospitalized patients frequently sleep poorly due to pain and to being awakened by noises from roommates and attendants. Thus, the hospitalized patient usually suffers from sleep deprivation. This condition makes a person agitated; emotions become labile, with angry outbursts or weeping. It sets the stage for violent nightmares.

As pain medication is reduced, the brain experiences what is called "REM rebound." This phenomenon is a state of intense, vivid, often terrifying dreams. It is the natural outcome of having had dreams suppressed for several days. The brain needs to compensate for its dream inhibition. When you are deprived of sleep, and have a chance to make up for it, your body will first undergo a few hours of deep, restful sleep; then wild, chaotic dreams will follow. If you are forewarned that dreams during this phase may be horrific, it should help you accept them with less distress. They will soon pass. You may even be able to change the nightmares when they occur, using some of the strategies for coping with nightmares, or else by becoming lucid within the dream (techniques described in chapters 6 and 8). REM rebound is a sign that your brain is trying to restore its normal functioning.

Here are a few samples of immediate post-crisis dreams:

| DREAM IMAGE | RECENT CRISIS |
| --- | --- |
| dreamer is raped by two strangers | hysterectomy |
| bulldozers break garage door and steal car | abortion |
| dreamer sees deceased person or dead animals | various types of surgery with general anesthetic |
| grief over something lost | surgical removal of a body part |
| replay of traumatic injury | war wound, car crash, calamity, or disaster |

In general, post-surgical dreams depict the *destruction or damage inflicted on the body by the operation* (the images of rape and the destroyed garage door/cervix). People who have had some parts of their body removed depict this fact in their dreams by *lost or stolen objects* (the stolen car/fetus and the lost object/organ). Post-surgical dreams also dramatically portray the *fear of death* (the images of deceased people and dead animals). Patients often compare the unconsciousness resulting from a general anesthetic to a kind of death. Don't be unduly distressed if you dream about deceased people or other characters, including yourself, who die after having had an operation. Death and replays of traumas are common dream themes at this stage.

In addition to dreams of the deceased or corpses, people who are enduring a physical crisis also frequently dream of dead or injured animals. Eileen, a woman of late middle years who had just had a hysterectomy with a complication, was in an intensive-care unit for three days when she had a dreadful dream of this sort. "I was looking out onto a field that sloped uphill," she told me. "I walked out and saw dead animals lying around. Some of them were wild animals; others were little ones like rabbits. I was so shook up, I retreated into the building." Again, the unconscious state associated with the bodily injury sustained during surgery was being likened to death. Animals often represent the basic life force in dreams. Almost two weeks after surgery, Eileen still found this imagery difficult to discuss. Such dreams are quite frightening to the patient who doesn't realize how typical they are.

People who have just experienced a physical crisis also express feelings of grief. Nan, an elderly widow who had broken her hip and arm in a fall while crossing a street, was confused and distraught. "Each time I close my eyes," she told me, "I see weeping willows—lots of green and gold—all over the place. Maybe they were sad, too, that I fell, sad because of me." Previously, she added, her husband had been at her side when she was in trouble; now she had to confront her difficulty alone. Although the weeping willow was a waking image, it was a metaphor for Nan's own feeling of sadness about her situation, in the same way that dream images are. Because this image troubled her, she tried to avoid closing her eyes, thus depriving herself of sleep, which is the natural restorative remedy. Don't be surprised if some of your dream images show that you feel sorry for yourself. This, too, is a common response.

Post-traumatic stress dreams following a catastrophe are universally terrifying. The degree of bodily damage undergone and the extremity of the situation under which it was inflicted determine how intense and how long such nightmares will continue. Methods for coping with such dreams (discussed in Chapter 6, *Post-Crisis Dreams*) involve learning how to change the dream content by taking action within the dream. Hippocrates said, "Prayer indeed is good, but while calling on the gods a man should himself lend a hand."[4] We will see how taking action within dreams is the key to changing nightmares.

We continue to dream about the afflicted body part, displaying its sensations of pressure, pain, heat, cold, itchiness, and functioning. Dreams at this stage often involve treatment apparatus or hospital personnel. Eileen, whose surgical wound was closed by staples, told me, "I feel like Frankenstein's monster." Arm and leg casts, splints, stitches, wires, pins, and tubes that are attached to or inserted into our bodies are especially portrayed in dreams, along with the way they make us feel.

The finding that dreams monitor the body's condition is important. Patients are frequently assailed by nightmares like those samples described above during the first few days after surgery. These dreams are exceedingly stressful and may even exacerbate the patients' condition. Such dreams are the patients' attempts to master their difficult situations and work through conflicts they have about treatment. Resolving their conflicts in dreams may partly explain why patients tend to feel less anxiety during the second half of their hospitalization. Researchers have found that patients who are hospitalized are extremely anxious during the first half of their hospitalization—more so than during the second half.[5]

Ideally, the hospital or specialized psychological staff should be familiarized with the pattern of post-surgical dreaming, be trained to inform patients about normal responses, routinely question them about the presence of disturbing dreams, and be prepared to render basic "first-aid" for nightmares. This early period of anxiety is when attention to the patients' dreams is essential. Cognitive psychologist Robert Haskell, at the University of New England, suggests that patients' ". . . dreams should be considered just as much a part of their treatment as nutrition."[6] If this were so, it would become possible to mitigate the worsening effects of nightmares that are typical at this stage.

Until that time, dreamers must rely on themselves to be

prepared about what to expect and how to cope with night-mares. They can also share their experiences with other people who are bombarded by bad dreams after a crisis.

#### ◇ Stage 5: Healing Dreams

As we return to health, several signposts appear in our dreams. We may even experience significant healing *within* the dream. Slowly, interspersed among the nightmares or unpleasant dreams, the injured or ill person will notice new elements aris-ing. Although negative dream content may continue for some time, depending upon the nature of the trauma and the prog-nosis for full recovery, positive images signal the beginning of a return to health. The two patterns frequently are intermixed for a time.

Dream images indicative of returning health are often of "new" things. Hippocrates put it succinctly: "New objects indi-cate a change."[7] Here are a few samples of dreams that arose as the dreamer's physical healing and improvement began:

- dreamer sees a beautiful view from a window
- dreamer holds hands with a group of people in danger
- dreamer prevents a car from crashing
- dreamer maneuvers a car well on a hazardous road
- dreamer sees green grass and lush fields
- dreamer sees blossoming trees
- dreamer picks flowers
- dreamer plants a garden
- dreamer notices a house being restored or a new building constructed
- dreamer finds a lost watch
- dreamer sees a newborn puppy
- dreamer watches animals play happily
- dreamer tries on attractive new clothes
- dreamer removes debris from an injured leg
- dreamer accepts advice from a helpful figure

Some of these dream signs of returning health are meta-phors for the *new body image* that is evolving as the dreamer heals (new or restored house; restored watch; new clothing or plant growth; animal birth). Others depict the dreamer's *return-ing sense of control over life* (preventing a car crash; maneuvering down a hazardous road; removing debris from an injured body part). Two images show *feeling supported or loved* (holding hands with a group; helpful figure giving advice). One portrays the *restoration of energy* (playing animals).

Throughout the entire process of injury or illness and recuperation, the afflicted body part enters into our dreams. Our perceptions of how it feels at the moment and how it functions are vividly portrayed. Pay particular attention to dreams in which you are using your injured body part in a normal fashion. These often herald the return of functioning to the repaired part. While I was still in a cast, I dreamed of seeing my arm out of the cast, looking thin but well formed and moving gracefully. A few days later, with the cast off, I observed that my arm had the shape depicted in my dream, although I could not yet move it much. Later I dreamed of scratching the middle of my back with my repaired arm—a movement I was incapable of doing at the time. Not long afterward I was able to perform this action. Perhaps in dreams the brain recalls memories of former, well body movements, helping us to actualize the dream behavior.

Researchers have reported cases in which people have dreamed that a body part was damaged, only to discover upon awakening that this unfortunate dream experience had truly materialized. For example, several cases have been recorded of people who dreamed that their legs were paralyzed, and who awoke to find this was actually the case, though their legs had appeared normal prior to the dream. The dreamer was perceiving a disturbance of the body during the dream that persisted into the waking state. Rarely do we hear of a dream healing carrying over into the waking state.

Yet people have related amazing experiences of dream healing. The most dramatic case is one in which a full recovery occurred during the dream. A woman whose arm had been paralyzed for some time dreamed that her pet dog had been attacked; she began to beat the attacking animal in her dream with her paralyzed arm.[8] When she awoke, she was astonished to discover that her paralysis had vanished, and she was able to move her arm once more.

In another case, a young woman who was suffering from arthritis found that her condition improved in a dream.[9] Previously, her dreams had contained such images as having her arms in a strait jacket; her dreaming mind had compared her limited mobility to the forced restriction of the jacket. However, when she dreamed that she slipped on ice, but was able to get up easily, she awoke to find her arthritic condition greatly improved.

Research into dreams and health too often emphasizes the negative. For example, hypertensives are said to have dreams containing conflict and hostility.[10] Asthmatics are reported to have dreams with themselves as victims who are dependent on mother figures.[11] Migraine and arthritic patients have described dreams in which they show oral aggression such as biting.[12] Perhaps we are overlooking the powerful healing resource in our dreams. Instead of staying stuck in negative descriptions, we need to look carefully at the instances where people have been able to recover by performing specific actions in the dream state. We can teach hypertensives to express their anger in their dreams, rather than label them as "angry" and dismiss the matter. We can also teach asthmatics to abandon the victim role in dreams, to confront and conquer their dream dangers.

If moving a paralyzed arm in a dream precedes the restoration of its waking function, let us teach paralyzed patients to use their limbs in their dreams! The possibilities of deliberate and lucid dreaming for improved healthy functioning are monumental. *If the premise that dream behavior precedes waking function is true, it is imperative that we begin to "practice" healthy functioning in our dreams.*

◇ Stage 6: Convalescence Dreams

There is no clear demarcation between dreams of healing and dreams of convalescence; rather, there is a gradual shift in emphasis. Convalescence is the latter stage of healing. When this phase occurs depends upon the severity of the disorder. Although energy and mobility may still be limited, the injured or ill person begins to dream more normally.

Certain dream themes decrease. People who have been injured or ill may still dream replays of their accidents or operations, but these become less frequent. Nightmares are rare. When they occur, they often relate to conflicts about returning to normal life functions or fears about the inability to do so.

Other dream themes increase. Improvement in the afflicted body part and the reduction of symptoms continue to be reflected in dream content. Dream images that are typical of the healing phase appear more frequently: new clothing and buildings, flourishing plant life, frisky animal life, and new births inhabit the dreamscape.

If there is no damage in the genital area, pleasant sexual dreams begin to reappear as a person recuperates and vitality returns. One woman who had undergone knee surgery felt eager and ready to engage in sex, though the pain still present in her knees inhibited her mobility and prevented full participation. Her dreams announced her body's readiness, aside from her knees, in passionate encounters while she was asleep. She said she had "incredible sexual dreams about making love with someone I didn't know." A woman who was recovering from pneumonia found herself inundated with scenes of delicious sex. When we have been ill or injured, delightful sexual dreams indicate a resurgence of normal energy levels.

Dreams of restored appetite for food also suggest returning strength. Eileen, the middle-aged woman who had a hysterectomy, was obliged to have a tube inserted through her nose and into her stomach to remove its contents. She had been on liquid food for three days prior to her operation and was fed intravenously for some time afterward. Although her first dream after surgery was a horrific one about dead animals, her second one was more encouraging. Several days after her operation, during her nine-day stay in the hospital, Eileen dreamed of being in a fancy restaurant with three other people, sitting at a square table with a white tablecloth and pink flowers, waiting for some delicious food to be served. "I could almost smell it," she told me. In part, of course, this dream symbolized Eileen's wish for solid food again, but it also contained images that suggested hopefulness—the pink flowers, white tablecloth, and forthcoming good food.

Dreams that dramatize optimistic thoughts about a restored body—such as new clothing, building construction, plant growth, or newborn animals—need to be noticed and reinforced. We will see how drawing these images and using them in visualizations help encourage the healing they represent.

Convalescence is particularly characterized by dream images that integrate the formerly injured or ill body part into a new body image. Here are some examples of convalescence dreams:

- dreamer decides to have a baby
- dreamer makes love with pleasure

- dreamer's clothing incorporates surgical scar
- dreamer's clothing accommodates removed body parts
- dreamer participates in an inspirational ceremony
- dreamer functions well at work

In general, dream themes during convalescence indicate *restored energy* (making love); *hope for restored functioning* (doing well at work); *new body image* (clothing incorporating a scar, or accommodating removed body parts); *optimism about the future* (deciding to have a baby or attending an inspirational ceremony). Convalescence dreams are directed more toward the tasks and interests ahead instead of the pain and fright in the past.

◇ Stage 7: Wellness Dreams

When we have regained our well-being, our dreams return to mainly pre-trauma topics—we struggle with our mates, our parents, our children, and our colleagues. We strive to succeed at work, to solve our daily problems, to be creative, to develop our talents, and to increase our enjoyment of life. We dream of our fears and hopes for the future.

By this stage, we have integrated our new body condition into our dreams. During earlier phases, we replayed our injuries or illnesses, sometimes making our condition worse. Then, as we improved, we were able to struggle to change images in our dreams. Finally, our new behaviors and conditions become the standard. We accept our newly integrated body and dream about other things.

What does the vigorously healthy person dream about? Hippocrates answered this question over two millennia ago. He said that the following dream images indicate health:

> To see the sun, moon, heavens and stars clear and bright, each in the proper order, is good, as it indicates physical health in all its signs. . . .[13]

> To see and hear clearly the things on the earth, to walk surely, to run surely, quickly and without fear, to see the earth level and well tilled, trees that are luxuriant, covered with fruit and cultivated, rivers flowing naturally, with water that is pure, and neither higher nor lower than it should be, and springs and wells that are similar.[14]

In other words, *when dreamers are well, their dream images show the dreamer functioning normally and with assurance; the elements of nature likewise appear to flourish, without suffering from excess or deficit.* The person's dream clothing and footwear appear attractive and in the right size, neither too large nor too small.[15] Dream objects appear clear, bright, and pure in the healthy dreamer, rather than dark, dull, and dirty.[16]

Mark all your positive images in your journal of recovery. Notice them, nourish them, draw them, and visualize them while you're awake. See yourself functioning in this well-ordered world. Activity sections in each chapter will guide you.

People who have been ill or injured often celebrate their return to wellness by external symbolic behavior. Some of these actions are straightforward "freshening up," such as getting a haircut or having a manicure. Others are "finishing up" behaviors, such as writing to or meeting with a physician against whom you have harbored a grudge, to confront him or her and express what has been left unsaid.

Still other "wrap-up" actions symbolize your transformation to health. I was fascinated with people who performed these wellness rituals, such as a man who melted down his arm splints to make a sculpture, a woman who turned her treatment equipment into Christmas ornaments, and a woman who cooked a festive dish from the beans she had used as a weight for her wrist exercises. By transforming equipment associated with suffering into objects of art or nourishment, men and women triumph over their pain and concretely honor their revival—new bodies for old—their reborn self.

### ◇ The Delicate Body Balance

The ideal dreamscape described by Hippocrates appears only occasionally in the sleep of modern dreamers. In sickness and in health, life demands continuous readjustment. We rise and fly, we slip and fall, we rise again. Awake and asleep, we strive to maintain the balance where life is good.

After you have been injured or ill, your dream repertoire has gained fresh symbols. If you bear permanent scars or disabilities, they become assimilated into your current dream body image. Don't be alarmed if an occasional twinge, a sore scar, or a rainy day that triggers an ache brings back dreams of injury.

Whenever you feel afraid, vulnerable, helpless, or out of control, you may once again find yourself in your dreams in an accident or hospitalized or in surgery.

Now, too, there is a new strength—the knowledge that you were able to survive. You know the difficulty of the journey and the joy of return. You have discovered the precious quality of life every moment. You can sustain others when they stumble, and, above the rough road, hold high a light.

### ◇ Garfield's Dream Aphorisms

Suppose we could have a few short, pithy sentences that would summarize our knowledge about the correspondences between dream imagery and conditions in the dreamer's body. This thought intrigued me for days after reading about ancient medical aphorisms. I had learned that the Greek sages composed sayings that concisely conveyed kernels of medical knowledge. On the inner walls of the Greek dream temples built at the town of Cnidos (pronounced *NAI*dus), in what is now western Turkey, some of the key aphorisms were inscribed.[17]

Carved in stone, these sayings were available for ready reference by the physicians and priests of the temple. The aphorisms were famous in the ancient world as the "Cnidian sentences." The original maxims are lost, but some, it is thought, were preserved in the writings of Hippocrates. His most famous aphorism is: "Life is short, Art long . . ."[18] Of course, the original is in Greek, and the best-known translation is the Latin one: *"Ars longa, vita brevis . . ."*[19]

I decided to try my hand at condensing the information I was uncovering about dream metaphors for the body and put them into aphorisms. The results serve as a forecast of the many body metaphors that you'll be encountering in this book. You may wish to use the couplets as a tool to alert yourself to possible similar body metaphors that occur in the dreams you are recording in your dream journal. Remember, however, that every dreamer has his or her own idiosyncratic version. (The concluding section of this chapter offers guidance in discovering your own dream metaphors.)

#### AFFLICTED BODY PART:
*When body parts come to dream harm,*
*The sleeping mind signals alarm.*

### EXCESS PRESSURE ON BODY PART:
*Heavy earth or weight on chest,*
*Probably the lungs congest.*

### SHARP PAIN IN BODY PART:
*Bullet wounds or stabs with knife,*
*Intense pain may threaten life.*

### SQUEEZING PAIN IN BODY PART:
*Squeezing pain or short of air,*
*Caution dreamer to beware.*

### EXCESS HEAT IN BODY PART:
*Sunburn and destructive fire,*
*Inflammation, fever higher.*

### INSUFFICIENT HEAT IN BODY PART:
*Freezing rain, frost, ice, or snow,*
*Body circulation slow.*

### EXCESS MOISTURE IN BODY PART:
*Drowning deep or throat all clogged,*
*Body tissues waterlogged.*

### INSUFFICIENT MOISTURE IN BODY PART:
*Arid earth, plants wilt and die,*
*Body tissues overdry.*

### OBSTRUCTED FLOW IN BODY PART:
*Flowing waters drip or drop,*
*Body fluids slow or stop.*

### BREAKAGE OR MALFUNCTION IN BODY PART:
*Crooked pipes or tubes with rocks,*
*Broken bones or vessel blocks.*

### IMPROVEMENT IN BODY PART:
*Babies, blossoms, clothes all new,*
*Morning brings good change for you.*

The following activities will help you discover principles
about your own dream images.

## ◇ DREAM ACTIVITIES: IDENTIFYING YOUR BODY METAPHORS

#### ◇ 1. Select a dream to explore.

Look over your dream journal and choose a dream to work with that you think relates to what is going on in your body. If you are currently injured or ill, look for any action that relates to the afflicted body part. If none of the entries seem to fit, pick any dream that intrigues you.

#### ◇ 2. Highlight direct references to body parts.

Examine the text of the dream you have chosen and circle or underline or highlight any body part that is mentioned in your journal. Also, mark any reference to body parts of other dream characters.

*Example:* Let's say you have chosen "my hand" in the dream text.

#### ◇ 3. Ask yourself questions about the body part:

A. How am I using the body part? (Or how is someone else using his or her body part?)
B. What is happening to the body part?
C. Is this normal behavior?

If your answer to question C is yes, you probably do not need to pursue this image for information about your body, though it may yield information about your psychological state. If your answer is no, then you can benefit from studying the dream image.

Hippocrates believed that the repetition of natural daytime actions and thoughts in dreams signified health. "But when dreams are contrary to the acts of the day, and there occurs about them some struggle or triumph, a disturbance in the body is indicated, a violent struggle meaning a violent mischief, a feeble struggle a less serious mischief." [20] If the way the body part in your dream is being used, or what is happening to it, is odd, or a sharp contrast to normal usage, ask yourself this further question:

D. How would you describe this body part simply, as if to a child?

If you were explaining to a child what this body part is, what would you say? How does this particular body part differ from other similar ones? (Describing the key dream image is part of step four in the D-R-E-A-M-S technique discussed on pages 25–27.)

### EXAMPLE DESCRIPTION OF BODY PART

My hands are what I use to do things in the world. I make things with them. I take care of myself with them. I use them to touch people I love. I write books and paint pictures with my right hand. People have always said my hands are beautiful because the fingers are long and slender. When I was in college, I was a hand model.

In a similar fashion, ask yourself questions about other key images in the dream. How would you describe a particular object, animal, or person to a child who does not know them? What are its important characteristics? How does it differ from other, similar objects or animals? This technique, originally suggested by the Swiss psychologist Carl G. Jung,[21] helps dreamers discover the meanings of their images. The definitions do not need to be literally true, simply true for the dreamer.

The images in your dreams are comments upon your state of mind or state of body—sometimes both. Answering questions A through D will help you comprehend whether the dream imagery is:

- a psychological commentary about your current life
- a direct portrayal of a physical disturbance
- a symbolic portrayal of a physical disturbance

We will explore these possibilities and how to understand your own imagery in the forthcoming chapters. As a preview, the following are three brief dream examples—each involving a hand or arm, each with a different meaning.

### EXAMPLE DREAM: THE GRANDFATHER CLOCK

"My right hand is placed underneath a grandfather clock." In the dream, I experienced no pain or discomfort; I simply noticed its position. I do not normally, nor have I ever, put my hand underneath a grandfather clock. Thus, the dream image was contrary to my natural behavior. My right hand differs from the left one in that I use it for writing and painting. A grandfather clock differs from other clocks in that it is exceedingly heavy—to put my hand under it would crush, if not destroy it.

The image made me laugh because, at the time I dreamed it, I was under "heavy" time pressure to finish a piece of writing. The abstract concept "time" had become a large, heavy clock in my dream. The scene was a reminder of the "weight" of time "pressure" and the necessity to speed up my writing. It was a metaphor for my current situation, a psychological commentary, not information about my body.

## EXAMPLE DREAM: THE DIAGRAM

"I see a man making a diagram of a break. I recognize that it is my broken arm." (This body image was part of a long dream described fully in Chapter 4, *Forewarning and Diagnostic Dreams*.) To me, a diagram explains the structure of something and how it functions. The dream diagram of something broken was a metaphor for my broken left arm; *during the dream*, I recognized that it represented my broken arm. This dream image was a contrast to what I had been told in the waking state, that my arm was sprained, not broken. My dreaming mind knew something my physician did not.

## EXAMPLE DREAM: THE ICY TREES

"I see trees with branches and twigs covered with ice." This image was part of a dream described fully in Chapter 5, *Crisis Dreams*. From much experience working with dreams, I know that dreamers often liken their arms and fingers to tree branches and twigs. I realized that the icy "limbs" of my dream trees were a metaphor for my fingers, which were cold because of reduced circulation from a nerve injury. The dream image compared my cold fingers to ice-covered twigs. This metaphor symbolically pictured a literal physical sensation; it warned me to do something to prevent further damage to my hand.

Symbolic dream images about body parts—like twigs representing fingers—are harder to recognize, but as you work with your own dreams, you will discover more and more about your inner picture language. You will be able to make the connection between a dream metaphor about your body and your waking condition—psychological and somatic. This information is extremely valuable for safeguarding your health.

### ◇ 4. Record any metaphors you discover in the dream.

Do these metaphors seem to involve direct or symbolic references to your body, a psychological commentary about your life, or a combination of your body and your emotional state?

There is no way to be absolutely certain whether a metaphor is physical or psychological or both. Unless you are suffering with an existing condition that clearly corresponds to the dream image, you should stay open to both possibilities. Look at your dream from both points of view: (1) your dream may be a comment about your current psychological state; or (2) it may be a warning of incipient physical problems. If the dream is a psychological comment, you will probably get an impression of accuracy about it. You will sense the perfect fit to your present situation; you'll recognize its rightness. If the dream is a warning about an embryonic physical disorder, only the future development can prove whether the dream was correct or not. It may be better to heed the warning than to wait and see if you fall ill or get hurt.

### ◇ 5. Pinpoint the location of any afflicted body part in the dream.

In Chapter 1, I mentioned that dreams about parts of our bodies are capable of revealing three things:

1. the exact location of an afflicted body part
2. the sensations within that part
3. the functioning of that part

In this activity, we'll work with locating the afflicted body part. Later on, you'll be invited to explore the sensations and functioning of the afflicted body part, and see how to use these images to improve your well-being.

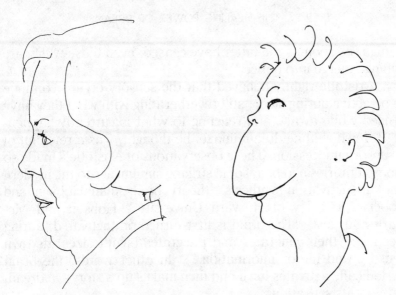

*2a. Objective appearance: Post-Oral surgery*

*2b. Subjective sensations: Post-Oral surgery*

Line drawings by Patricia Garfield

*The objective appearance of a person following injury or during illness may be quite different from the person's subjective sensations. The day after I had oral surgery, the swelling in my cheeks, upper lip, and eye area were actually moderate, as shown in the first drawing, 2a. The subjective sensations were much more dramatic, as shown in the second drawing, 2b. My upper lip felt huge, with underlying pain in my gum; my eye felt swollen almost shut; I felt frazzled and miserable, as shown by the disheveled hair.*

*These exaggerated sensations are the elements that need to be expressed in drawings of illness or injury. You may find it easier to draw the actual situation first, then dramatize or caricature these sensations. As with metaphors in dreams, exaggerated images depict emotional feelings and physical sensations. Expressing these feelings and sensations in dreams and drawings helps relieve their pressure.*

When we have a disturbance somewhere in our body, we perceive it as an image in our dreams. Probably because we are not distracted by external events and stimuli while we are asleep, we become sensitively attuned to inner sensations. Aristotle astutely observed that even minute sensory impressions seem considerable during sleep. He said that by day, sensory impressions derived from within the body often are ". . . extruded from consciousness or obscured, just as a smaller is beside a larger fire, or as small beside great pains or pleasures, though, as soon as the latter have ceased, even those which are trifling emerge into notice."[22]

Aristotle rightly believed that the sensory organs continue to be active during sleep, still reverberating with what they have sensed while awake and reacting to what is currently happening.[23] Each shifting dream image, he thought, was a remnant of a sensory impression. These observations of Aristotle's made so many centuries ago bear some striking similarities to the modern "dream activation-synthesis" theory of J. Allan Hobson and Robert McCarley of Harvard University.[24] Hobson and McCarley suggest, "The brain is first turned on (activated) during sleep and then generates and integrates (synthesizes) its own sensory and motor information."[25] In other words, the brain periodically activates itself and then makes up a story—a dream —about its sensations.

Regardless of what the explanation of the mechanism of dreaming turns out to be, most researchers agree that some internal body processes find their way into dream imagery. This is especially so when body conditions deviate from the norm. Here are some verbatim examples of how minor and more severe dysfunctions in body parts appear in dreams:

| DREAM IMAGE | PHYSICAL STATE |
|---|---|
| • a stairwell painted pink, covered with scratches | sore throat |
| • dreamer is impaled on a sharp pole in the anus | hemorrhoids |
| • dreamer is eating pickled cucumbers or coleslaw | heartburn |
| • dreamer's house is on fire | peptic ulcer |
| • dreamer is eating pizza when stomach breaks open | perforated ulcer |
| • dreamer is wounded in the stomach in a war | appendicitis |
| • dreamer is drowning in yellowish, dirty water | bronchitis |
| • man holding world stands on dreamer's chest | pneumonia |
| • man shoots dreamer on left side of the head | migraine |

| | |
|---|---|
| • pet wolves eating someone's body | arthritis |
| • four villains shooting bullets through heart, causing it to bleed | heart attack |
| • dreamer visiting a spouse's grave, hands squeezing throat and heart | heart attack |

These actual dream examples include images that *directly depict the afflicted body part* (anus, stomach, chest, head, throat, and heart); others *portray the body part symbolically* (the stairwell is the dreamer's throat; the burning house is the dreamer's stomach; the person being eaten by wolves is the dreamer). Most of the dream images, in addition to pinpointing the location of the disturbance, *dramatize sensations being experienced in the body part*.

Notice how the same dream image can serve different purposes. In Chapter 1, I mentioned that a staircase sometimes represents the spine in dreams; the emphasis is on the shape of the spine and its steplike vertebrae. In other dreams, climbing a staircase is symbolic of sexual intercourse; the shape of the staircase suggests the slender vagina and the movement upon the steps resembles the thrusts of sexual intercourse. In the previous example, the long shape of the stairwell corresponded to the dreamer's throat. *There is no invariable meaning to a dream image.* All three instances share the similar elongated shape of a staircase—the spine, the vagina, the throat—but each has a different meaning, according to the associations of the dreamer, and what he or she is emphasizing.

Likewise, in Chapter 1, I discussed how a house in a dream often represents the dreamer's body. However, sometimes a house in a dream stands for a part of the dreamer's body; in the previous example, it symbolizes the dreamer's stomach and the fire depicts his sense of burning pain that is causing destruction to the organ. At other times, a house in a dream may represent the dreamer's general life-style.

There are no hard and fast rules about the meaning of a dream image. You need to make your own personal associations to the images in your dream, and notice which qualities and functions you are emphasizing. Dream images are *your* personal language.

◇ 6. List any sensations in the body parts in
the dream.

Observe how each dream image symbolizes perceptions of pain
in the area of the body. The "scratches" on the stairwell correspond to the dreamer's scratchy throat; the sharp pole in the
anus depicts the pain in that spot.

The sensation of weight upon the chest is characteristic of
lung disorders, such as influenza, bronchitis, pneumonia, and
severe colds. The eight-year-old boy who dreamed of a man
holding the whole world while he stood on his chest was suffering from pneumonia. He was feverish; this dream recurred three
times before he recovered and had "the weight of the world" off
his chest. From a psychological point of view, he felt "op-
pressed" by his illness; it was "too much for him to bear."

The sensation of the burning pain in heartburn or in a perforated ulcer is indicated in dream images of eating food that
can create a burning sensation—the pickled cucumber, coleslaw, and pizza.[26] A young man dreamed of eating pizza when
his stomach broke open the very night before his ulcer perforated. Another patient with stomach trouble dreamed of drinking vinegar. Burning pain is also depicted by dream images of
fire, as in the burning-house dream of the ulcer patient.[27] The
dreamer shouted for help, but no one came to rescue him and
he woke up feeling terrified.

Notice how the sensation of intense pain is portrayed by
dream images of wounds in the body. A healthy Russian officer
dreamed of fighting in a war and being wounded in his stomach,
clearly seeing the wound in his lower right stomach. When he
awoke in the morning, he was unwell and went to his doctor; he
was diagnosed with appendicitis.[28] A teenaged girl who dreamed
that a man broke in through her bedroom window tried to escape to the bathroom when the man shot her on the left side of
her head; she awoke with a severe migraine in that area.[29]

The sensation of squeezing pain is particularly important
to note. From the previous list of examples, the man who
dreamed of being shot in the heart by four attackers saw blood
pouring from his wounds and, in the dream, he died; the dream
culminated in a scene where a giant began to strangle him.[30] He
awoke with pain in his heart and throat. His cardiologist then
found that an arterial infarct had affected the apex and anterior

wall of the man's heart. The woman who dreamed of visiting her husband's grave when arms reached up, and bony hands squeezed her throat and heart, also had a heart attack.[31] Dream images of the chest and throat being squeezed are characteristic of heart trouble.

Obviously, it's wise to pay special attention to any dream images that involve sensations of pressure or pain that is wounding, burning, or squeezing any body part. In addition to perceiving pressure or pain in an area of our body in a dream, we also need to observe whether any other unusual qualities are present. Sensations of heat, cold, and itching should be noted as well. (You'll be given guidance for exploring these sensations in the activities in the next chapter.)

When pressure in dreams is a purely psychological metaphor, it refers to situations that are "too heavy to bear," burdensome, or intolerable. When images of dream pain are psychological, they suggest emotional wounds or injuries, as in the expressions, "he cut me to the quick," or "she broke my heart," or "he's a pain in the ass."

◇ 7. Read over metaphors you wrote in your dream
journal.

Describe how they apply from a physical and psychological point of view, keeping in mind the cautions described in activity four.

◇ 8. Transform these metaphors into dream
aphorisms.

As you discover principles about your own dream images, you may want to put them into couplets for easy recall like the ones on pages 75–76. Try describing the dream image in the first line and follow this with the implication it has for you in the second line. It's a good way to heighten awareness about the meaning of your dream imagery.

You have begun the process of understanding your secret language of dreams. In the next chapter, you'll see how you can apply these skills to the warnings and diagnoses your dreams offer when you are in danger. You'll continue to refine your ability to recognize dream metaphors about the body that can guide you toward better health.

# 4

$\diamond$

# FOREWARNING AND
# DIAGNOSTIC DREAMS

The night before I fell and broke my arm, I had a profound warning dream. Monday had been hectic. I was wrapping
up the final details on my current book. Having worked through
the weekend, I felt frazzled. Indeed, for the past few months, I
had been working under unusual pressure, not only on the book,
but also on tax information that was due, and a special celebra-
tion that I was hosting for my husband's birthday, complete with
out-of-town guests and a grand party. The tax project had been
finished and the party was a splendid success. Then on Monday
I made corrections on the bibliography to my book, typed labels,
had the material reproduced, and finally went to the post office
to mail the manuscript. In addition, I ran numerous household
errands: to market, to the shoemaker, to the cleaner, to the
hardware store, to the stationer's, to the drugstore, and to the
bookstore. I was deliberately doing more than customary because I planned to take the whole next day off, enjoying it with
a girlfriend. Although I relaxed in the evening watching television with my husband after dinner, I found it hard to get to sleep;
I was too keyed up. I had felt zippy and well during the day,

but my dreams pointed out dangers. At the climax of the first dream:

> A family friend—a very maternal-type older woman—is gently but firmly scolding me. She tells me that I've been behaving improperly lately. The gist of it is that I've been running around too much, being too frenetic and not attending to my crucial inner feelings. I accept all this because I respect her opinion.

The warning continued in the second dream of the night:

> At one point, I get into a car and find a key in the radio. When I pull out the key, I hear something on the radio about how I was protected by a spirit in a foreign place where I once lived, but not necessarily here. I pull out a faded flower that is stuck in the radio, as the key was. I toss it to the earth to regenerate. I wonder how I can ensure the spirit's protection in this new place.

These dreams should have made me more cautious the next day. The main themes—too much frenzied activity and a lack of protection—are potent warnings. Unfortunately, I didn't pay attention to them and got carried away with the momentum of the day. I left the house early to join my friend, and ended up in the hospital. Having felt pressured for weeks finishing my book, I did not heed the clear forewarnings in my dreams to slow down. I went head over heels crashing onto the sidewalk. I hope this chapter helps you learn to recognize and respond to your own warning dreams.

## ◇ FOREWARNING DREAMS

### ◇ Rita Dwyer's Fate

Rita Dwyer owes her life to a recurrent nightmare her colleague had.[1] Some thirty years ago, Rita was a research chemist. Her job involved synthesizing and testing high-energy propellants that were hazardously unstable. She and her co-worker Ed Butler had been employed together, fresh from college. They were pleased to become pioneer researchers in the new field of aerospace systems. Rita and Ed were close friends without any romantic links. Researchers in the area of paranormal dreams have often observed that telepathic communication is facilitated by two minds having common associations between them.[2] Rita and Ed had a lot of common associations. Their laboratories were adjacent at their workplace.

When Ed began having recurrent nightmares about Rita being hurt in an explosion and his saving her, he was troubled. He decided not to tell her about these bad dreams, because he didn't want to alarm her. Unfortunately, one day Ed's nightmare came true. He was in his laboratory when he heard the muffled sound of a nearby explosion. He heard Rita screaming. Rushing to the doorway of Rita's laboratory, he peered through the smoke and fumes. He saw a foot sticking out of the flames.

Ed dashed over to Rita. He grabbed her foot and pulled her to the doorway where the safety shower was located. Then he jerked the emergency chain that released gallons of water onto the woman's burning body. After the flames were quenched, he dragged her to a nearby laboratory and ran to the emergency telephone. When he returned, Rita was being cradled in the arms of a lab technician.

Rita remembered the flaming liquid and shattered apparatus blasting into her face and upper body. She had not been able to see because of the damage to her safety glasses. Her hands and arms were on fire, preventing her from using her lab coat to smother the flames. She deliberately screamed for help. She was sure she was dying and uttered a prayer. Then her pain seemed to disappear. She heard a strange sound that swept her into a black whirlpool.

When Rita regained consciousness, she was being held by the technician. She had no idea how she had been removed from the flames. Rita was rushed to a hospital, where she was in critical condition for a long time and remained in a serious condition for many months. Her survival was considered miraculous. Round-the-clock nurses tended her under the supervision of a plastic surgeon who was a burn specialist. Only a few family members and one close friend were permitted to visit. Rita later learned that it was Ed who saved her from the fire, and she heard about his previous nightmares.

Rita, like others who have had a severe trauma, relived the explosion in nightmares for years afterward. How this trauma changed Rita's life and how her dreams led her to her eventual psychological healing are described in later chapters.

◇ Precognitive Dream Alert

Precognitive dreams as vivid as Ed's are rare, but they do exist. Ed thought his ability to act quickly had been a reflex conditioned by these dreams, and that their horrifying images had prepared him to save Rita's life.

If you should have a dramatic dream about yourself or someone close to you, what should you do? You can begin by asking yourself these questions:

1. Was your dream exceptionally vivid?
2. Did the emotional atmosphere in this dream differ from your usual dreams?
3. Did your dream take place in a known location with realistic details?
4. Has your dream recurred?
5. Were there images of communication present in the dream, such as telephones or wires?[3]
6. Did you have a special "feeling" that your dream was prophetic?

If your answers to a number of these questions are yes, then extra caution is advisable. You may want to change plans or take precautions. There's no point risking that your dreaming mind had a valid intuition. and then ignoring that warning. Such dreams may help us protect a loved one or avert disaster. Forewarning dreams can, as Ed's did for Rita, save lives.

If you experience a dream that is precognitive, be sure to mark it as such in your dream journal. Some dreamers who consistently have such dreams—ones they later find confirmed in newspapers—clip out the "proof" and put this into their journal. Noticing which dreams turn out to be predictive can help alert you to any such dreams in the future. Most of us, however, just receive simple dream messages to "slow down" or "speed up" or "start it" or "stop it" that relate to our daily behavior. Brenda's case is characteristic.

BRENDA'S BLACK LUNG

This attractive woman in her thirties was a heavy smoker when she dreamed one night:

My sister and I are looking at X-rays taken of our lungs, which are black. I woke up feeling dreadful.

Not long after this dream, Brenda quit smoking for good. Her dream, I believe, helped her avoid serious complications. When we listen to our dream forewarnings, as Brenda did, we never know whether we would have developed a disease or not, or whether any minute symptoms would have gone away instead of being followed by disease. That's all right. Better to take action and be well, than ignore a dream warning and fall ill.

### NELLIE'S SMOKE RINGS

Nellie, too, had alarming nightmares about her smoking. For years, she had this recurrent dream:

> I am walking through a very formal cemetery (I hate these—they are like death). I see a cube of opaque, smoky glass, as in a car. If I stand close to the cube, I can see a slab (like a hospital gurney) with a woman on it. Then I see that I am the dead woman, with long hair. There is a chest X-ray over her/my head.

Nellie speculated that the "smoky cube" represented her own chest. By standing close to it, she saw a projection into the future. This dream still recurs because Nellie has not yet listened to its warning. I hope she hears it in time.

Dreams like Brenda's and Nellie's are typical forewarning dreams. Whether we pay attention to such dreams or not is up to us. And when we are already in pain or feel sick, our dreams sometimes tell us why.

Smoking, by the way, seems to have an adverse effect on dreaming. Researchers have studied seven heavy smokers who were measured in a sleep laboratory after days of smoking and after days of withdrawal.[4] They found a significant difference in the amount of REM sleep and in the content of dreams under the two conditions. After days when dreamers had refrained from smoking, there was a marked increase in the amount of REM sleep at night, and their dreams were more intense and unpleasant. This suggested that smoking suppressed the normal amount of REM sleep and that withdrawal from smoking provided the chance to compensate—a REM rebound effect. Perhaps not smoking is better for our dreams as well as our lungs.

## ◊ DIAGNOSTIC DREAMS

I had the following dream ten days after I was injured. Recorded in my journal at the time, it later provided evidence of a truly diagnostic dream. It came at the end of a series of remarkable dreams about an elaborate ritual in which I participated in an initiation dance, doing intricate, rhythmic steps, gliding in a line of dancers going from balcony to balcony, pausing to form marvelous patterns. This was all part of a cycle of ceremonies that admitted me to a realm of special knowledge.

In my last dream of the night, I understand some profound secret to the meaning of life: we are all one. This is true; I know it. I am part of an exceedingly complex story. At some point, all the parts fit together and I am able to comprehend the whole picture.

I seem to be with a group of people outside a large hotel where a man—one of the two other people who also understand the secret—is explaining about a problem that a man has—a break in something.

As I watch him make a diagram on a clipboard, I have a revelation: "Don't you realize?! *That's my broken arm!*" I say. (Supposedly, it's really a sprain, but it surely feels broken.) "We are all one! Everything's connected. All the things that have been happening are all related to the others." The man has long suspected this but has been unwilling to face it.

Then the man is loading a van full of women for a night drive up the mountain. The women are all inside, leaving just enough space for him to lie down at the driver's seat. He's putting on a Sherlock Holmes-type double cape. (Is this a clue?) I'm afraid they're going to crash on the way and all be killed because of something that has happened before.

The other person who also knows the secret, a woman, arrives with some people. I say to her, "I know. It's all connected. You know, too." She is weeping and thrashing around; she knows more than I do and wishes to disbelieve it. I understand how everything is important; everything one does affects something else. The van begins to climb the hill and I see some things slide out. I say, "Now it looks like a hearse. Are you willing to take that chance?" I wake in discomfort.

When I awoke from this dream, I was deeply concerned. I have learned that "initiation" scenes in my dreams are often associated with predictive or clairvoyant information for me. This dream made me almost certain that I was indeed walking around with a broken arm.

It was Friday, however, and I was not sure enough to insist on seeing my physician over the weekend when I had an appointment on the following Wednesday. He had been so positive that I had a sprain, and that I was creating my own discomfort by not using the arm enough. I was in considerable pain, but less than originally, so I opted to wait. I felt reluctant to announce that I knew my arm must be broken on the basis of a dream.

How did I know my arm was broken in the dream and almost know when I awoke? The evidence was abundant: in the dream, I "learned a secret"; the two other dream figures who also knew it were "reluctant to face it" or "knew more than I" about it. The diagram in the dream actually showed the location of the break. A Sherlock Holmes-type cape or cap is always connected to a clue in my dreaming mind. I was afraid for the group of women because they seemed to be heading into a dangerous (the mountain road at night) and perhaps deadly situation (the hearse). The images in this dream were almost screaming aloud that there was something I was not facing, an important clue, a danger to physical life that was connected to a break in my arm. Furthermore, the dream said, everything was part of a pattern; this had to mean, among other things, that the dream pictures were connected to my waking experience. In retrospect, I was foolish to have waited even a few more days. My wrist looked deformed and was hot and swollen; when I took the splint off, as I had been urged to do as much as possible, I had agonizing pain. I had to take painkillers to get through the next few days.

The dreams during these next few nights involved:

- an oven that needed cleaning
- an approaching storm
- a marquee advertising "The Rocky Horror Show" that broke off from a theater and almost crushed me and my husband
- a building that was broken into
- a mother who was almost hit by a truck fell; a glassful of blood flowed out of her head

Certainly these were dream images that underscored the notion of danger to my body beyond a mere sprain. I had, in fact, struck my head in the fall and must have been bleeding internally because my face was black and blue.

People who are injured often do not realize how important it is to have their physicians listen to them. We often do not trust our own impressions enough to require our views to be thoroughly investigated. All too easily we yield to the authority figure who labels the situation without taking a stand based on our own perceptions. We tend to disbelieve our dreams that proclaim the situation as we sense it. When we have been so badly injured that we cannot participate in our care, we are even more helpless. Then we need the advocacy of our friends and loved ones to make certain that our rights to full and adequate care are received.

If I am ever again in a situation where an injury is not responding to treatment, I will demand additional X-rays within a week. Then I will make certain that all available X-rays are compared in my presence. If I ever again have that much disabling pain, I will insist on further scrutinization and other medical opinions.

What would have happened if I had shared my dream about the broken arm with my doctor? Nothing except the dismissal of it as foolish anxiety, I expect. Yet the day may come when physicians not only listen to the dreams of their patients but actively solicit them. Our dreams, I have come to believe, contain some of the most valuable diagnoses available.

Would a doctor who was familiar with the connection between dreams and injury or disease have been able to make a swifter and more accurate diagnosis? Can physicians really learn to diagnose physical illness by assessing the patient's dreams in addition to examining the body? You will see, as you become familiar with your own dream symbols for wellness and illness, that it is often possible to recognize when your body needs medical attention. The idea that dreams are valuable diagnostic tools has deep and ancient roots in history from which we can still draw knowledge.

◇ Chinese Roots of Dream Diagnosis

As part of any complete examination, a physician in ancient China asked his patient to describe his dreams. Dreams were considered vital clues to physical problems. In fact, in what is believed to be the oldest medical book in existence, *The Yellow*

*Emperor's Classic of Internal Medicine,*[5] there is a section devoted to the relationship between certain dreams and illness.

These ideas are extremely old. The perhaps legendary Yellow Emperor is said to have lived from 2696–2598 B.C. The text purports to be a dialogue between this sage and his minister, discussing ideas about dreams, health, and treatment that have been traditional in China for centuries. Historians speculate that the book was written around 1,000 B.C., but it was most certainly in existence by 200 B.C., when it was referred to in other documents.

In the ancient Chinese system, health is regarded as a harmony or balance between two forces: "yin" and "yang"; disharmony brings disease and possibly death. Many Westerners are now acquainted with the idea that yang is the more active force —fiery, hot, and dry; yin is the more passive force—watery, wet, and cool. To be healthy, according to this tradition, one must have these two powers in balance.

Applying this idea to dreams, for example, the ancient Chinese said that dreams of "wading through great waters which cause bad fears" indicate that "yin is flourishing."[6] This means that dreams of excessive water indicate too much fluid is present in the body (too much yin), and there is a lack of sufficient vital energy (too little yang). Dreaming of "great fires which burn and cauterize" was thought to reveal that "yang is flourishing." This means that dreams of fire indicate the body processes are hot, dry, and overactive (too much yang). When yin and yang are both flourishing, there are dreams in which both forces destroy and kill or wound each other. "Fullness of the lungs" was believed to cause dreams of "sorrow and weeping." Dreams of flying were associated with a "flourishing upper pulse," while dreams of falling indicated a "flourishing lower pulse."

Although such ideas seem alien and improbable to modern Westerners, when they are recast in familiar terms, they become more comprehensible. I have already mentioned that current researchers, for instance, have observed dreams of drowning (in great waters) among heart patients whose water retention is excessive (or when "yin is flourishing"). We may find hidden in such ancient texts valuable information for modern medicine.

### ◇ Greek and Roman Roots of Dream Diagnosis

People in most ancient cultures believed that dreams revealed or predicted the dreamers' health, and sometimes offered cures.

#### ASKLEPIOS' DREAM CONTRIBUTIONS

The cult of the healing god Asklepios flourished for nearly a thousand years, from the end of the sixth century B.C. until the end of the fifth century A.D.[7]

Greek legend says that Asklepios was the child of the sun god Apollo and a human woman whose name, Coronis, means "dark, crowlike." Therefore, this god was thought to combine the radiance of the heavens inherited from his father with the darkness of the earth from his mother. He thus controlled the celestial powers as well as the chthonic (deep dangerous powers of the earth). There are many versions of the myth. One says that Asklepios' mother Coronis was unfaithful to Apollo by marrying a human. As punishment, the pregnant woman was slain by Apollo's sister and placed upon a funeral pyre. As the flames leapt up, Coronis gave birth and died. Apollo snatched the newborn Asklepios from his mother's corpse. He gave the infant to the centaur Chiron, who was said to have raised the boy in the mountains and taught him the secrets of medicine. Asklepios became so skilled in healing that he could even resurrect the dead. This behavior, reserved for the gods, eventually invoked the anger of Zeus, who struck Asklepios dead with a thunderbolt. Then he elevated Asklepios to the divine rank of a healing god and set him into the heavens as the constellation Orion. In fact, Asklepios was probably once a human physician who was so revered he was raised to the rank of a god.

The priests and followers of Asklepios established dream temples where people sought healing or advice from the god in dreams. Some four hundred of these dream temples were built throughout the Greek islands and along the coast of Asia Minor (now western Turkey). In 1984, I visited the ruins of some of these dream temples in Epidauros, Corinth, and Ephesus and was much impressed by the beauty of their sites.

During the height of the Greek and Roman civilization, "incubants" made pilgrimages to these magnificent dream temples where—after purifying themselves in sacred springs, offering sacrifices and prayers, chanting and singing hymns, watching musical performances and theater, and participating in other rituals—the pilgrims underwent "temple sleep" in the sanctuary in hopes of receiving a curing dream.

Although these practices may seem strange today, when we investigate their process, they have much of value to offer people who are injured or ill. These practices suggest ways to solicit our dreams for answers, to incubate dream solutions, as we will see.

"Asklepios" is my preferred spelling for the healing god, rather than "Asculapius," because the former contains the English word *ask*. Asking for information or advice or health and other problems was the purpose of consulting Asklepios. We can, by remembering Asklepios, recall the importance of consulting our dreams for information about our lives.

## HIPPOCRATES' DREAM CONTRIBUTIONS
In Chapter 3, I mentioned some of the beliefs Hippocrates (who is thought to have lived from 460–377 B.C.) had about the connection between dreams and health. This celebrated physician was carrying on the tradition that the followers of Asklepios had espoused for centuries, as well as adding his own observations and stressing the value of careful examination of the patient.[8]

Hippocrates reminds us to notice when our dreams deviate from their normal course and to pay attention to ones that contain excessive or deficient heat and moisture. In this respect, his ideas were similar to the Chinese concept of yin and yang. (We will see how to apply some of his ideas to our own dreams in the next chapter.)

## ARISTOTLE'S DREAM CONTRIBUTIONS
We also saw in Chapter 3 that one of the greatest intellects of the Western world, the Greek philosopher Aristotle (384–322 B.C.), in his short treatise on dreams, expressed his belief that sensory organs continue to be stimulated while we sleep.[9] He thought that each person was more finely tuned to the minute, inner sensations during sleep than when awake. Aristotle, too, is relevant for today's dreamers.

Take, for example, Ashley, who had been seriously ill for a month, with a respiratory infection. She thought she was completely recovered when she had a dream containing the following images:

• She eats chocolate chip cookies (which are not good for her)

- Her cellar ceiling cracks and collapses
- A woman rolls off something and gets hurt
- She thinks the woman might have had a heart attack
- She dials the emergency number for help
- Cold air blows through a window, indicating a storm
- She lets two little cold ducks into the house
- Her husband looks ill and clasps his chest
- She arranges things in a medicine chest

Ashley's dream was filled with images of impending danger; it was exaggerated and highly dramatic. There were two recurrent images: "chest" and "cold." A chest was mentioned or implied three times in the dream: the woman's possible heart attack; her husband clasping his chest; and the medicine "chest." This repetition of negative images implied that Ashley had sensory impressions of some kind in her own chest, which had to do with poor health.

The image of "cold" was repeated twice: two little cold ducks and the cold air blowing through the window. The approaching storm, along with the collapsing cellar ceiling, further underscored the idea of weak foundations (in her body as well as in the dream cellar) and trouble ahead.

Whenever images recur within a single dream or over several dreams, they provide clues to the meaning of the dream. *Recurring images suggest not only recurrent thoughts and emotions, but also recurring sensations in the body.* Ashley's single dream contained a large number of images indicating poor health.

Indeed, within a week, Ashley had a full-fledged relapse of her chest infection and had to return to bed confinement for another two weeks. Was her dream simply a warning or did it express the presence of continued infection? There's no way to be absolutely certain. Perhaps by taking preventive care, Ashley, on the basis of her dream, might have averted her relapse.

Aristotle thought that diseases about to occur in our bodies are more evident when we're asleep and dreaming than when we're awake. If this is true, as I believe it is, our dreams contain nightly reports on the state of our health. We need to listen carefully to these health forecasts.

## GALEN'S DREAM CONTRIBUTIONS

Galen, who lived from 129–199 A.D., was one of the most illustrious physicians of antiquity. He was born in Pergamon, a

Greek city on the western coast of Asia Minor (now Bergama, Turkey). This city was famous for its great shrine to the healing god Asklepios. Its presence influenced Galen's whole life.[10]

The son of a famous architect named Nikon, Galen took up the study of philosophy at sixteen. One night his father dreamed that the god Asklepios appeared and commanded him to raise his son as a physician. Nikon complied, sparing no expense to have his son trained by the most competent physicians of the time, financing travels to Rome and other medical centers. Galen embraced his studies with a passion.

During the next years, Galen made several important medical discoveries. At the time, dissection of the human body was forbidden. Galen was able to study anatomy using the animals at his father's farm at slaughtering time. Later he treated the wounds of gladiators and was able to learn much about the functioning of the human body. He established that the arteries carried blood, not air, which had been the belief for the previous four hundred years. He showed how the heart set the blood in motion. He made more discoveries in anatomy and physiology than anyone ever had. His writings were voluminous. The Latin translation of his works (the ones that have not been lost) fills twenty-two volumes. His ideas were found in every area of medicine for centuries to follow, and influenced later medical researchers, such as William Harvey, the British physician who discovered the circulation of blood.

During his lifetime, Galen was continuously guided by his dreams. When he was twenty-seven, he fell gravely ill with a subdiaphragmatic abscess (a collection of infected fluid located within the abdominal cavity, under the diaphragm and over the liver).[11] He went to the incubation shrine of Asklepios where he had two dreams that showed him how his ailment could be cured. He dreamed that he should open an artery in his hand between his thumb and forefinger, letting it bleed spontaneously until it stopped. He performed this operation on himself—faith, indeed, in dreams—and was cured.

Although dreamers who are not physicians should observe any such dreams with extreme caution, Galen's dreaming mind was probably synthesizing much of his medical knowledge. Opening an artery to drain the infection was actually the correct treatment for his physical problem, though today such surgery is usually done directly at the site of infection.[12]

Galen mentioned two other dreams that were crucial to

him. When he was thirty-eight, he was the personal physician of Marcus Aurelius, then emperor of Rome.[13] Galen dreamed that Asklepios forbade him to follow his employer into the war zone. He obeyed this dream, too, whether from the god's commandment or from his own wish. Later, when Galen was forty-eight, he had gathered material he felt revealed the secrets of vision. He was reluctant to publish all of his treatise on the anatomy and function of the eyes until he dreamed he was being censured for failing to do so; he published the entire work. Galen's patients were often given remedies and treatments based on his dreams, a policy unlikely to be applauded today.

Like Hippocrates before him, Galen believed in using dreams as a diagnostic tool for medical conditions. He followed the prevalent theory of the time stating that the body contained "four humours": yellow bile, black bile, white phlegm, and red blood. Imbalance in one of these "humours" was thought to cause disease. Dreams of fire, Galen believed, indicated an imbalance caused by too much yellow bile. Dreams of smoke, mist, fog, or profound darkness suggested an overabundance of black bile. Dreams of snow, ice, and hail indicated too much cold (white) phlegm. Dreams of blood suggested an overabundance of blood and a need for the dreamer to be bled. Dreams of feces suggested putrefaction in the bowels. Galen noted how patients who were experiencing critical sweats often dreamed of diving into warm water or being immersed in it.

Galen thought that dreams of drinking were related to thirst; dreams of eating, to hunger; and that a man's sexual dreams were due to his genital organs being full of semen. He stated, "It seems that during sleep the soul enters into the depth of the body, becomes separated from external sensation, and senses only what happens inside the body, and the sleeper has the impression as if everything that he desires is already present."[14] This was the concept of wish fulfillment in dreams long before the work of Freud. (Again, we will see how some of these ancient ideas have validity in modern terminology.)

## ARTEMIDORUS' DREAM CONTRIBUTIONS

The grandfather of all dream interpreters was a Greek philosopher named Artemidorus Daldianus who was born in the second century A.D. in Ephesus, an ancient city on the west coast of Asia Minor (now Turkey).[15] He was a contemporary of Galen's, living just a few hundred miles south of Galen's home in Pergamon. He traveled throughout the civilized world, collecting and categorizing dreams from native people and professional dream interpreters. His purpose was to form a uniform set of laws about what dreams revealed or predicted; he produced five books that are called the *Oneirocritica*, from the Greek word *oneiros* (pronounced oh-*NYE*-rus), meaning "predictive dreams." Most modern dream dictionaries are based upon his works, but usually without understanding the concepts behind them.

Artemidorus did not simply say that to dream of a certain thing was good or bad, as modern writers of dream dictionaries often do. Instead, he put great importance on taking into account the dreamer's age, sex, occupation, personal habits, finances, health, and other identifying characteristics, as well as the customs of the land in which the person was raised. A dream interpreter, he believed, could not accurately apply the same rule to the same image in different dreamers; rather, he must consider the individual's condition and beliefs—advice that is valid today.

### ◇ Russian Dream Diagnosis

At least one contemporary researcher in the Soviet Union is developing some of these ancient ideas about a dreamer's awareness of bodily processes into a system of diagnosis. At the Leningrad Neurosurgical Institute, the psychiatrist Vasilii Kasatkin and his associates are reported to have saved many lives by using dreams to diagnose physical illnesses long before they could be picked up by conventional tests.[16] I was fascinated to work with some translators on key portions of his work.

Kasatkin has amassed a large collection of 1,642 dreams from 247 patients suffering from a wide range of disorders, ranging from minor tooth and skin problems to brain tumors. He noted that 90 percent of these dreams were extremely unpleasant; only 54 percent of them, however, contained actual physical sensations of pain. The amount of dreaming and its unpleasant character did not always depend upon the seriousness of a patient's condition. For instance, patients with brain tumors experienced fewer dreams than those people with less serious physical problems.

Kasatkin observed changes in dream content shortly before an illness appeared, often preceding other clinical symptoms of the disorder. These changes lasted throughout the illness and did not disappear until the patient recovered. The quality of these changes in dream content differed from one disorder to the next, depending upon the degree and duration of the illness, the area affected, and the specific process that took place when a certain organ or system was affected.

In general, dreams announcing the onset of a disease were frightening, even nightmarish. They included visual scenes of war, fire, fighting, and being wounded or experiencing damage to the part of the body affected by the disorder. Blood, raw meat, corpses, graves, dirt, muddy water, spoiled food, mountainous terrain, falling, and hospital-related images were typical. Gloomy thoughts and feelings of alarm, loneliness, or terror were often present. The dreams were found to parallel the course of the disease. As the symptoms worsened, so did the dream content; as the symptoms abated, the dream images grew less unpleasant.

With small, localized disorders, such as a boil, the dream content was milder, depicting changes in form, color, temperature, or itchiness of the area. With more serious afflictions, the dream content was dramatic and violent. In almost every case, the patient's dream images involved the appearance of the affected organ or body part, showing its location, its sensations, and its malfunction.

Kasatkin has come to believe that recurrent dreams of bodily wounds are the most grave; he thinks they often indicate an impending serious illness. For instance, repeated dreams of a chest wound are said to indicate a possible heart attack; recurrent dreams of a stomach wound suggest liver or kidney disease.

Furthermore, Kasatkin says that different illnesses follow clearly defined dream patterns. He hopes to develop a system of early warning about health hazards from dreams, and recommends that people with recurrent dreams about some body parts see their physicians for investigation. Your dreams may be night sentries standing guard duty over your health.

◇ American Dream Prognosis

The concept of the diagnostic potential in dreams is just beginning to be recognized in the United States. One person investigating this notion is physician Robert Smith, who is an associate professor of medicine and psychiatry at Michigan State University. Using carefully structured interview techniques, Smith asked forty-nine patients who were hospitalized for serious disease about their dreams. These included patients with heart disease, malignancy, lung disease, infection, or other severe illnesses.[17] The descriptions the patients gave were recorded and rated. These dreams were compared with the outcome of the patient's disease. Smith used a clear-cut measure of recovery—survival—versus the patient being readmitted to the hospital or dying.

Smith and his fellow researchers found that certain images in the patients' dreams predicted their prognosis. Men whose dreams contained references to death and dying were, in fact, those most likely to die of their illness or to have a relapse. Women whose dreams contained references to separation and leave-taking were the ones who were most likely to die or relapse.[18] The worst prognosis was for those patients who had little or no recent dream recall, a finding reported by other researchers. In contrast, an absence of dream references to death or separation was associated with a stable condition or improvement.

Another investigator of dreams and illness, Abraham Kardiner, has described dreams of death presaging the actual deterioration of patients with coronary artery disease.[19] In patients who worsened, dreams of death and destruction continued and eventually dreaming itself often disappeared. In those patients who improved, there was a gradual shift in the dreams away from themes of death and destruction.

Were the patients aware of the future outcome of their illnesses at the dreaming level of their minds? Or were their dream images of death and dying a response to the seriousness of their disease without necessarily being a prediction? Like Kardiner, I found that patients recovering from surgery often dreamed of deceased people or of dying, yet most of them recovered and thrived. If a dream therapist had worked with those patients with negative dream imagery to help them counteract it, would it have increased their survival rate? I believe it might. We have much to explore in this unfamiliar territory as we help ourselves move toward full and vital health.

## ◇ Did Freud Overlook a Prognostic/Diagnostic Dream?

Sigmund Freud, the father of psychoanalysis, recorded a dream that seems to be predictive of the throat cancer that eventually killed him.[20] Early on July 24, 1895, Freud, then thirty-nine, awoke from a dream he had while on a summer holiday.[21] This dream was immortalized as the "specimen dream" that Freud used to demonstrate that dreams are repressed wishes in his classic book, *The Interpretation of Dreams.* (A full description of this dream may be found in the reference notes.[22]) The central image is one in which Freud is examining the mouth of his patient "Irma":

> She then opened her mouth properly and on the right I found a big white patch; at another place I saw extensive whitish grey scabs upon some remarkable curly structures which were evidently modelled on the turbinal bones of the nose.—I at once called in Dr. M., and he repeated the examination and confirmed it.

Some twenty-eight years after having this dream, Freud consulted an oral surgeon who recorded the following observations about Freud's throat: ". . . papillary proliferating leukoplakia [a white patch] at the right anterior palatinal arch [the right palate, near the nose] . . . (Histolog. carcinoma)." This correspondence between the dream symptoms of Irma and Freud's own symptoms many years afterward was pointed out by a psychologist from San Francisco, Jill Caire, in an important paper, "A Holographic Model of a Psychosomatic Pattern: Freud's Specimen Dream Re-Interpreted."[23]

One may well object that Freud's dream could not be predictive of a fatal illness so far in advance. One may assert that it is merely an odd coincidence that his dream character is described with a condition he himself exhibited some twenty-eight years later.

Yet, consider these facts. At the time of his dream, Freud was being treated by a colleague and friend, Wilhelm Fleiss, who was an ear, nose, and throat specialist. Freud suffered at that time from an annoying drainage of his sinuses. Fleiss had advised the local application of powdered cocaine to Freud's nasal passages—a procedure that Freud carried out. In fact, Freud had been the first to notice the painkilling properties of cocaine, but was not yet fully aware of its addictive character.

Furthermore, Freud had permitted Fleiss to perform several minor operations on his nasal passages. At the same time, Freud was addicted to cigar smoking. Although the connection between smoking and cancer was not then clearly established, Fleiss had urged Freud not to smoke. Freud was well aware that smoke irritated the mucous membranes of his nose and mouth. However, he believed himself incapable of stopping smoking because he thought he needed nicotine to be creative. He also thought that smoking was a substitute for masturbation. He refused to cease smoking.

Although Freud did not notice a painful swelling on his palate until some twenty-two years (in late 1917) after his famous dream, and he was not certainly diagnosed with a cancerous growth of the mouth until twenty-eight years (on April 4, 1923) after the dream, Freud's nasal and mouth passages were afflicted and had been operated on by the time of his dream of Irma. It is not unreasonable to speculate that, as a physician, Freud's dreaming mind was able to diagnose his current symptoms and project them to a future possibility. This conjecture is strengthened by the fact that Freud dreamed Irma was complaining of symptoms that later paralleled his own:

> "If you only knew what pains I've got now in my throat and stomach and abdomen—it's choking me"—I was alarmed and looked at her. She looked pale and puffy. I thought to myself that after all I must be missing some organic trouble.

These dream symptoms of Irma's were not part of her actual complaints. Freud commented, "Pains in the throat and abdomen and constriction of the throat played scarcely any part in her illness."[24] These symptoms were, however, the very ones from which he later suffered. Freud eventually underwent three major operations to remove cancerous portions of his palate and more than thirty minor excisions of portions of it. In his later years, he had to wear a prosthesis that made eating and speaking painful.

Freud had several valuable psychological insights about himself from his dream of Irma. He was even reminded of some concerns about his own physical health by the condition of Irma's mouth in the dream, particularly his concern about the long-term effect of using cocaine to reduce nasal swelling. However, if Freud recognized the warning of serious disease for himself that this dream contained, he did not share it with others or, so far as we know, change his behavior to avert the danger that the dream predicted.

In the next case, a contemporary dreamer took his dream about his throat seriously.

◇ A Journalist is Tortured in the Throat

We have said that dreams magnify small physical sensations during our sleep, and that these may be signs of impending illness. Bernie Siegel, a surgeon at Yale University who has worked successfully with what he calls "exceptional cancer patients"—those who survive instead of dying as predicted—relates the case of Marc Barasch's diagnostic dreams. Barasch, a journalist and editor who developed cancer of the thyroid gland, recalled two terrifying dreams before signs of his disease appeared in the waking state. In one of these, torturers were placing hot coals beneath his chin:

> I distinctly felt the heat start to sear my throat and I screamed, the sound becoming hoarser, a raw, animal desperation, as the coals gnawed my larynx. [25]

Lying in bed after this dream in a shaken state, Barasch received a call from his girlfriend in Colorado, who had just had a horrendous dream of being with him in a bed filling with blood. What could it mean? Barasch was sure: "It means I have cancer. I have cancer growing in my throat." Barasch's close relationship with his girlfriend probably stimulated her apparent telepathic awareness of his distress.

This dream diagnosis was confirmed months later when Barasch finally consulted a physician because he felt symptoms while awake, as well. By now he had had another dream in which medicine men formed a circle around him and stuck hypodermic needles into what in the dream he called the "neck brain." In both of these dreams, he had wounds in his throat. As Kasatkin in Russia found out, such dream images are a key diagnostic sign.

Barasch's physician, however, was skeptical about the implication from these dreams that Barasch had a disease in his throat. He thought the man was a hypochondriac—until the results of the checkup several weeks later confirmed the serious

condition. Fortunately, Barasch's dreams alerted him to the possibility of physical damage so that he was able to seek help
rapidly when symptoms emerged. Our best bet of coping with
serious illness is to catch it early, and that's where our dreams
are our first line of defense.

### ◇ A Nurse Recognizes a Worm

Another person who took her dream diagnosis seriously, also
described by Bernie Siegel, was a nurse who had been sick for
weeks without anyone being able to figure out what was wrong
with her. She dreamed the following:

> A shellfish opened, a worm stood up inside it, and an old woman
> pointed at the worm and said, "That's what's wrong with you." [26]

When the woman woke up, she was certain that she had hepa-
titis—an infection of the liver caused by a virus in contaminated
food. As a nurse, she knew that hepatitis-A was caused by con-
suming shellfish from contaminated waters. Her dreaming mind
equated the virus to the worm inside the shellfish in her dream.
Subsequent tests confirmed the woman's dream-inspired diagnosis. When we are able to recognize the "culprit" in our
dreams, we may be able to hunt it down while awake.

### ◇ Jung Makes a Diagnosis from a Dream

Dream diagnosis can sometimes be so highly sophisticated that
it seems unbelievable. On one occasion, in 1933, Carl Jung was
asked by a fellow physician to interpret the dream of a patient,
without any information about him other than the following
dream:

> Someone beside me kept asking me something about oiling some
> machinery. Milk was suggested as the best lubricant. Apparently
> I thought that oozy slime was preferable. Then, a pond was
> drained and amid the slime there were two extinct animals. One
> was a minute mastodon. I forgot what the other one was. [27]

Jung correctly diagnosed this patient as having an organic problem—a blockage of the cerebro-spinal fluid, probably due to a

tumor. It seems nearly incredible that someone who has medical knowledge, in addition to understanding dream symbolism, could make such an accurate diagnosis based on complex reasoning. However, although few of us would recognize the source of the dreamer's physical problem, everyone is capable of observing the dream image of a malfunctioning machine in need of lubrication. This dream image alone suggests an impairment in some part of the body. If physicians could become fluent in dream symbolism, it might be possible to expand our knowledge of a patient's medical problems. Meanwhile, we can learn to sharpen our own dream skills.

## ◇ DREAM ACTIVITIES: WATCH FOR HEALTH WARNINGS

### ◇ 1. Review the dreams recorded in your journal for evidence of precognition.

It may be helpful to reread the questions on page 89, to remind yourself about the characteristics of precognitive dreams. If you have observed events in your immediate environment or the world at large that seem to confirm a precognitive dream, add a note in your dream journal to this effect. If evidence has appeared in print, make a copy of it or clip it out to insert in your journal. Try to analyze what is unique about your precognitive dreams compared to your everyday ones. Don't be concerned if you have no precognitive dreams; they are comparatively rare.

### ◇ 2. Observe whether your recorded dreams contain any forewarnings about your health.

Think of a recent time when you have not felt well or had an accident. Glance through the dreams you recorded immediately prior to this incident. Were there any alarm signals you might have noticed? If so, mark these in some special way, perhaps underlining them with red pencil. You might wish to make a special list of "Forewarning Images" on a separate page in your journal. Review these images periodically so you will recognize one when it arises in your dreams. Update the list over the next few months. You'll be creating a useful tool for years to come.

◇ 3. Observe any dream images that you have
recorded when you were feeling exceptionally well.

Think of a recent time when you felt comparatively vigorous.
Examine the dreams you recorded around this time—before and
during the peak of well-being. What characterizes these images?
Again, you may wish to create a list on a separate page of
"Wellness Images." These, too, will prove useful in your dream
activities. Whenever one of these images of good health appears
in your dreams, welcome it.

◇ 4. Watch for changes in metabolism: too slow.

One important clue to your health in dreams is contained in the
rate of activity in your dream images. The pictures in dreams
sometimes show the rate of your body's basic processes. I believe that when your metabolism changes from normal to too
fast or too slow, your dream figures grow correspondingly overactive or inactive.

What is the current rate of activity in your dream characters? Skim through the dreams you have recorded in your journal. Do the people in them seem to be as active as they usually
are? Notice any instance of unusual slowness or rigidity if it
appears in the people in your dreams.

Although it is uncommon, people sometimes dream of inactive or rigid dream characters as a metabolic disorder begins.

### EXAMPLE OF SLOWED METABOLISM:
### RIGID WAX BODIES

Prior to her falling into a coma, Elizabeth, a woman in her
sixties, had had many dream warnings that her metabolism was
dangerously low.[28] For several months before she became
acutely ill, Elizabeth had dreams that involved ominously still
characters. In one, she walked into a kitchen where the seated
people seemed to be waxlike figures. In another, she saw people
sitting rigidly immobile on a lawn. In yet another dream, Elizabeth saw corpses sitting upright in an undertaker's parlor.

When Elizabeth first discussed these dreams with me, we
looked at them only from a psychological point of view, and
concluded that she didn't feel involved enough in life. In retrospect, the physical warning in them is easily recognized.

One day, Elizabeth was discovered in a deep coma. She

was rushed to the hospital where she underwent diagnostic tests. Although she had emerged from the coma, she was confused and disoriented, making repetitive hand motions. After several days of testing, it was determined that Elizabeth's calcium level was perilously low. She had been suffering from myxedema coma, a potentially fatal condition that results from fluid retention as a consequence of an underactive thyroid gland. Intravenous calcium and thyroid replacement restored her mental health in a few days. Her dreams of the oddly inactive characters had been a measurement of her failing metabolism.

Now in her early eighties, Elizabeth is more energetic than when she was years younger. Her dreams reflect her restored vitality with mobile characters. Had the significance of the deadly still figures in her dreams been understood early enough, she might have been spared much agony.

## EXAMPLE OF SLOWED METABOLISM: WOMAN INTO STONE

Another woman was not so lucky. Neurologist Oliver Sacks, in his fascinating book, *Awakenings*,[29] gives an account of the dreams of a woman who became a victim of sleeping sickness (encephalitis lethargica). In 1926, "Rose R." was a healthy, high-spirited young woman of twenty-one when she was suddenly struck with a form of sleeping sickness.

The acute phase of Rose's illness was heralded by a series of terrifying dreams that she had the preceding night. There was a single central theme to these nightmares: the dreamer was immobilized. In one dream, Rose was imprisoned in an inaccessible castle that had the form and shape of her own body. In another, she dreamed of being enchanted, bewitched, and entranced; in yet another, she dreamed she had become a living, sentient statue of stone. She also dreamed the world had come to a stop, and that she had fallen into a sleep so deep she could not be awakened. Finally she dreamed of a death which was somehow different from death.

The next morning after Rose had these dreams, her family had difficulty waking her. They pleaded with her to get up, asking, "What's the matter?" Rose lay still. She could not reply. Her dreams had become reality.

The local physician who was called in diagnosed her condition as catatonia, and declared that she would be fine after a week of rest and nourishing food. Instead, she never recovered.

She did regain the ability to speak in short sentences and could make a few sudden movements before she "froze" again. She was able to describe the dreams she had the night before her illness struck. Rose's family lovingly cared for her at home for nearly ten years. As her siblings left the house and her parents aged, Rose developed signs of Parkinson's disease and full-time nursing was required. Eventually she had to be admitted to a New York hospital where Oliver Sacks met her some forty years later; she was treated with L-dopa but never fully recovered.[30]

Although the dreams of Elizabeth and Rose shared a common dreadful "stillness," there were some important differences in them. Elizabeth saw dream characters that were waxlike; Rose saw herself as made of stone. Rose was identifying herself with the rigidity of stone in her dream castle and statue; Elizabeth still had the distance of seeing this rigidity in others. Furthermore, Elizabeth's dreams took place over a period of months; Rose's nightmares were concentrated into one night.

The examples of Elizabeth and Rose represent extreme changes in the functioning of the body. It's unlikely that you would experience similar ones, but should such dreams arise, consider them seriously. We do not have records of Rose's dreams prior to her night of crisis. Would they have displayed signs of increasing rigidity? If so, which I think is probable, could recognizing the danger sign of immobile figures have allowed prevention of the full-fledged onset of her illness? There is much we need to learn about the implication of immobile figures in our dreams. But this much is certain: if a dreamer's living characters become strangely still and rigid, we need to consider the possibility of a metabolic slowdown. A thorough physical checkup may be advisable, especially if dreams of immobility continue over time or increase in severity. Most often, however, this type of dream represents a sense of feeling entrapped emotionally rather than physically.

### ◇ Psychological Meaning of Dreams of Entrapment

Dreams of becoming entrapped or paralyzed sometimes occur in physically healthy dreamers for psychological reasons. One man I spoke with, for instance, had recurrent dreams of being buried alive. When he was able to extricate himself from his unhappy marriage, these dreams ceased. Being buried alive had been a dream metaphor for the feeling of entrapment in the marriage. A middle-aged woman whom I interviewed, also in an unhappy marriage, dreamed of being locked in a jail cell. In another dream, she was being stuffed into a kitchen oven by her husband who then turned on the gas. Such horrific imagery relates to the dreamer's sense of emotional entrapment, rather than an impending physical affliction. As always with dream images, examine both issues—the physical and psychological.

We have considered how the body's perception of a disastrously slowed metabolism can appear in dreams. What if the dreamer's system becomes too rapid? How is this portrayed in dreams?

◇ 5. Watch for changes in metabolism: too fast.

When a person is overmedicated, he or she sometimes exhibits this fact with overactive dream characters—especially, of course, if the medication is a stimulant of some kind.

### EXAMPLE OF ACCELERATED METABOLISM: MAN INTO BEAST

Oliver Sacks, again in his book *Awakenings*, describes the case of "Leonard L.," a highly intelligent man who had suffered encephalitis and was almost totally "petrified"; he was one of the first people Sacks treated with L-dopa.[31] After two weeks on medication, Leonard felt reborn; he could walk and speak fluently. After two months, he began to feel "charged up," with a surplus, a pressure, of sexual and aggressive feelings during his waking hours.

In his dreams, Leonard ". . . was a burly caveman equipped with an invincible club and an invincible phallus; a Dionysiac god packed with virility and power; a wild, wonderful, ravening man-beast who combined kingly, artistic, and genital omnipotence." These feelings became overwhelming and unabating, whether he was awake or asleep. Awake, Leonard was not only excited but frenzied and manic; asleep, he had erotic dreams and nightmares each night. He finally had to be restrained. He was withdrawn from the medication and he once more fell into his motionless and speechless premedication condition poignantly portrayed by Robert DeNiro in a recent film.

Treatment with any drug is exceedingly complex. Since our dream images are so responsive to changes in the body condition, including medication, we can use them as a gauge to assess whether the dosage is too high or too low. The physician who is aware of the almost momentary effect of medication on dream activity might find dream reports useful for monitoring the correct dosage levels for those who must undergo treatment. By watching our own dream imagery, we become scouts in the service of our own health.

### ◇ Psychological Meaning of Dreams of Overactivity

Whenever I am overdoing things, my mind registers this condition with dreams of frantic activity, such as laborers rushing to complete some construction. If I am able to respond to the warning in time, it's possible to avoid trouble. Such dreams of overactivity more often suggest the dreamer has been too frenzied in the waking state, rather than implying an overactive metabolism or a condition of overmedication.

### ◇ 6. Give yourself a daily dream checkup.

As you review your dreams from the previous night, give particular attention to whether:

- any dream characters are rigid or immobile
- any dream characters are overactive or frenzied
- any dream characters, including yourself, have a physical illness or infirmity

Remember, when you dream about a physical infirmity or illness in yourself or another dream character, there are three possibilities:

1. *The dream image of ill health is a metaphor of your psychological condition.* For instance, you might dream of a blind person to indicate to yourself that something important is "not seen" or has been overlooked.
2. *The dream image of ill health is a portrayal of minute, current physical sensations.* In this case, you might dream of a blind person when you are experiencing a literal dimming of vision, perhaps temporary eyestrain. Remember, dreams exaggerate. Such a dream cautions the dreamer to take preventive care of the eyes.

3. *The dream image is a combination of metaphor and physical sensation.* You might dream of a blind person when you are experiencing poor vision and also have not given adequate attention to this fact.

### EXAMPLE OF COMBINED METAPHOR AND PHYSICAL SENSATION: BROKEN FINGERNAILS

Molly, a widow in her late middle years, had broken a fingernail during the day. It was mildly annoying, but certainly not a serious problem. That night she dreamed:

> All of my fingernails are breaking, one after the other. I am very upset.

Puzzled by this dream, Molly asked me what it could mean. I asked her to tell me what a fingernail is, very simply, as if explaining it to a child. She replied, "A fingernail is something that covers the end of your finger. It protects the fingertip. Sometimes you can use your fingernails as a tool."

"So, then," I said, "in your dream language, something that usually protects you (fingernails) and is useful to you, is not active at the moment. Is there some recent change in your life that makes you feel more vulnerable than usual?"

Molly's face lit up with the expression of someone who has just made a connection between a dream symbol and waking life. "My brother's out of town," she said in astonishment. "I live alone. When he's around, I feel safe. I can call on him anytime if I need him. Now he's far away for several weeks."

Molly's dream had been a combination of the actual physical sensation in her newly broken fingernail, exaggerated and dramatized to become all of her fingernails, and the discomfort she felt by the absence of her protective brother. Having lost her husband, Molly relied heavily on the next closest male in her environment. Her dream probably further expressed the concern that her brother's temporary absence might become permanent, leaving her quite bereft of protection.

From serious metabolic disturbances to trivial broken fingernails, our dream images display our important emotions, which are often unrecognized.

The appearance of an illness or infirmity, of overactivity or underactivity, in one of your dream characters or in yourself, should lead you to ask, "Have I been having an actual problem with that recently?" If your answer is yes, and the problem could be significant, a physical checkup or a change of behavior may be in order. If you have such a dream, watch your condition carefully over the next few days to see whether any symptoms resembling those in the dream develop. If your answer is no, that you have had no physical difficulty with the body part as depicted in the dream, contemplate what metaphorical meaning the image might have for you. What does the dream suggest about your psychological condition? Take action to correct any deficit or excess in your waking life. Continue to monitor your dreams, staying alert for any recurrent body images.

Next we examine how dreams change when we confront a major physical crisis.

# CRISIS DREAMS

A great catastrophe. I see myself and my husband in a city
where a huge fire is burning. Hundreds of people are running up
an incline to look. An airplane has landed to evacuate the
population. The door is open, but I refuse to enter because I can
see we would soon be trapped by the fire. Later we have taken
refuge in an underground cave when we hear a huge explosion
on the surface. I know that ten million people have died; we
survive in safety under the earth.

Author's dream diary
Two nights before operation

When the body is threatened by injury or surgery or
illness, the dreaming mind interprets the situation as a crisis.
Knowing that nightmares are a natural response to a physical
crisis may help allay our anxiety.

My own dreaming mind portrayed my fright in grand-opera
style. The night I found out about the error in diagnosis and the
probable necessity of rebreaking my arm, I was in such shock
that I had zero dream recall, or indeed, little sleep. My head
was in a whirl. The following night, my dreams portrayed the
disaster just described. I woke up sobbing at 5:00 A.M.

Dreams of a natural or man-made cataclysm, like mine, I
discovered, are frequently found at this stage of an acute illness
or injury. The dreaming mind interprets threat to body integrity
as a threat to life itself. Oliver Sacks, a neurologist who injured
his leg while hiking, said he thought the hospital admissions
clerk told him, "Execution tomorrow." He knew the clerk must
have said, "Operation tomorrow," but he heard it through fe-

verish fears.[1] Emotionally, an operation seems like an attack upon the body.

In my dream, I portrayed this threat to my body first as a great fire that was burning down a whole city, then as an explosion that destroyed millions. In fact, there was considerable heat being generated from the inflammation in my fractured arm. No doubt this sensation produced the image of fire in my dream. My waking concern was expressed by the "hundreds of people" running to look. There seemed to be a way out offered, by means of the airplane, but I knew this was not safe. Instead, I withdrew deeper into myself, "into a cave." From this sanctuary, I could hear in the distance the destruction of millions of people with a horrendous detonation that I inferred was somehow caused by the airplane or the fire. The news that I must undergo major surgery was thus being compared in my dream to a massive explosion. Underground, with my family and a few friends, I survived. The dream imagery suggested that I felt able to live through the disaster I faced. As always, dreams exaggerate, overdramatizing our life situations.

When we are injured or ill, our dreams are full of fears about the unknown we must face, our hopes for eradicating the pain, and our emotional reactions to the injury or illness. Also within our dreams are pictures that can help us to heal.

## ◇ INJURED BODY PARTS SYMBOLIZED BY DREAM IMAGES

After we have an accident or get sick, our injured body part is depicted directly or symbolically in our dreams. I described in Chapter 1 how buildings, vehicles, machines, clothing, and other objects frequently represent the dreamer's healthy body. Therefore, when we fracture a bone, tear a ligament, tendon, muscle, or have an amputation in waking life, it is often portrayed in dreams as a defective or broken part of a building, automobile, machine, or clothing.

### ◇ Broken Building Parts

DREAM OF A COLLAPSING BANISTER = BROKEN RIBS
Sue, in her early sixties, had broken two ribs, but appeared to be healing well. A few weeks after the accident, however, she

overdid lifting things in her home. Her fracture split open again. That night, she dreamed:

> There is an earthquake. I go outside and see a brown split opened up in the earth. The bricks on the patio are falling. I try to hold onto the railing on the back steps. The right banister gives way. I fall into a pit. I wake up with my ribs hurting.

Here Sue's dreaming mind likened her body first to the earth cracking apart. Then, as she tried to support herself by grasping the banister, it collapsed. In fact, it was her right ribs that gave way, just as it was the right hand banister—the symbol for her ribs—that crumbled in her dream. The pit into which Sue fell probably represented the dark situation in which she felt temporarily trapped.

At times, dreamers represent their afflicted body part by destruction to part of a building, as Sue did. At other times, they portray damage to a whole building. In my case, it was an entire city being destroyed.

## ◇ Defective Objects

Broken furniture and tools, shabby material and equipment— these images often appear in the dreams of an injured person, representing the damage done to the body. One man who was to undergo surgery in a few days, to have part of a damaged blood vessel removed to clear a vascular blockage in his leg, dreamed about defective objects in eleven out of his fourteen pre-operation dreams.[2] These images included a stove that was torn down for repair, a broken hospital bed, a switch with rusty pipes, and a plugged-up septic tank. Many dreamers equate their blood vessels to pipes in dreams. One woman who was to have her gall bladder removed dreamed about a house with its front wall removed, torn museum drapes, and worn-out record jackets—defective objects that seemed to represent her stomach wall.[3]

## ◇ Defective Cars

Dreamers frequently picture the disorder in their bodies as mechanical problems in their cars. The man who was to have a vascular operation on his leg dreamed of a car or truck with a clutch that wasn't going up and down properly.[4] The malfunctioning clutch stood for his damaged leg. A man due for an operation on his ulcerated stomach dreamed about a car being chained to a bed; he was trying to free it.[5] This image probably represented the dreamer's sense of entrapment by his illness rather than the body part itself. Still another man who was to have a hip replaced dreamed of being in a speeding car that went off the end of a pier. We will see how dreams about speeding cars often symbolize the dreamer's sense of loss of control, as well as mechanical problems in the body.

When the dreamer attempts to repair defective objects, or to reconstruct damaged or destroyed equipment and buildings, it suggests the presence of an active attempt to cope with the waking physical crisis. The dreamer's attitude is more hopeful than when he or she simply succumbs to a collapsing structure or does nothing about damaged equipment in a dream.

### ◇ Psychological Meaning of Broken Structures and Defective Objects in Dreams

When a healthy person dreams about buildings, automobiles, machines, or objects that are breaking apart or defective, the dream may be a warning about a possible breakdown in the dreamer's health. Often, however, such dream images in a healthy dreamer refer to an emotional relationship that is not "working" properly. When one woman's marriage was breaking up, she dreamed about a bookcase that was coming apart; it could only be held together temporarily with clamps. Dreams about buildings being toppled by earthquakes are not unusual when a relationship between lovers grows "shaky."

Since structures of buildings, machines, and vehicles often symbolize our bodies in dreams, being alert to these images helps us comprehend how we feel about what is happening to us. Give special attention to any such images whenever you have a physical problem. Even if you are feeling well, these images can spotlight an emotional situation that needs attention.

## ◇ PHYSICAL SYMPTOMS REPRESENTED BY DREAM IMAGES

We have seen how, after an injury or onset of an illness, the body part appears in dreams, sometimes with its exact location pinpointed. I have already mentioned that dreams during injury or illness also reflect the sensations present in the afflicted body part and show how this part is functioning. Now we will look more closely at this concept.

### ◇ Dreams of Fire or Heat = Body Part Too Hot

Excessive heat in a dream may indicate the presence of inflammation or fever in the dreamer's body. In my dream at the opening of this chapter, I pointed out the image of a huge fire destroying a city. In another dream that occurred during this time, I saw a house that had been badly burned being reconstructed. These dream images of fire no doubt were stimulated by the inflammation around the breaks in my arm. As I worked with other people who had been injured or were ill, I found that inflammation and fever are often portrayed in their dreams as destructive fire. I summarized this observation in my dream aphorism:

*Sunburn and destructive fire,*
*Inflammation, fever higher.*

#### DREAMS OF FIERY HAIR = HEADACHE
Ashley, for example, when she had a severe headache, dreamed that her hair was on fire, streaming out in flames. The blood vessel flow in her head and neck had altered, generating an intense sensation of heat. Likewise, people who suffer from migraine headaches often draw flames in the head area to represent their sensations of burning pain.[6]

#### DREAMS OF FIERY FOODS = BURNING PAIN IN STOMACH
Patients suffering from heartburn dreamed of eating foods that cause a burning sensation, such as sauerkraut, herring, pickles, and pizza.[7] A patient with stomach trouble dreamed of drinking vinegar. The burning taste of the food in such dreams is triggered

by the actual burning sensation the people are experiencing as they sleep.

## DREAMS OF HOUSES ON FIRE = FEVER OR BURNING SENSATION

A patient with a peptic ulcer dreamed his house was burning down. The burning sensation in the dreamer's ulcer was being experienced during sleep and stimulated a dream of fire destroying his home. Several physical ailments, including ulcers, are activated during REM periods.[8]

Artemidorus, in the second century A.D., reported a man's dream that his father died in the flames of a house on fire. Not long after this dream, the dreamer himself died of a high fever, perhaps caused by pneumonia.[9] Jung cited a somewhat similar case.[10] Hippocrates thought that to dream of seeing ". . . the earth black, or scorched" is not good because ". . . there is danger of catching a violent, or even a fatal disease, for it indicates excess of dryness in the flesh."[11] These cases were severe illnesses leading to dreams of fire; most often fire appears in dreams as a result of a temporary, passing fever or inflammation.

## DREAMS OF HOT OBJECTS = SENSATION OF BODY HEAT

In addition to dream images of burning houses, hair, and food, other hot objects may depict the dreamer's sensation of intense heat in the body. A woman with an inflamed sore about to erupt on the back of her right hand dreamed a neighbor touched her in that spot with a lit cigarette.[12] A woman with a bladder infection dreamed of being forced to sit on a hot pipe—an image stimulated by the developing inflammation in her urinary canal. Once when I had a sore throat, I dreamed that a devil stuck a hot pitchfork into my neck, striking exactly where it was most painful inside my throat.

Victims of burns often draw pictures containing a scorching sun or a summer beach scene showing hot sand.[13] These drawings seem to be related to the burning sensations in the patients' skin in the same way that fire in dreams is related to sensations of extreme internal body heat.

## DREAM ANTIDOTES TO SYMPTOMS

Lila, a woman in her late thirties, began to feel itchy and ill. Thinking perhaps she had hives, she went to her physician for tests. That night she had the following dream:

> I have poison oak. There is a brown pus-filled spot on my forehead shaped like a fire hydrant.

The next day, Lila's physician called to say that the tests showed she had adult chicken pox. Soon a pus-filled spot appeared on her forehead in the exact spot where the fire hydrant was in her dream, along with numerous other eruptions all over her body. It seemed as though Lila's dreaming mind sensed the forming spots as they were about to erupt and compared them to poison oak, which she had before.

Throughout the course of her chicken pox, Lila had a low-grade fever, and twice she dreamed about: "Streets on fire and buildings crashing; there may be a flood." The crashing buildings—a typical symbol during illness—probably represented her general sense of collapse. The fiery streets were her fever. Yet, the image of the fire hydrant is most unusual. Perhaps Lila was providing herself with the means to extinguish the fire she felt being unleashed in her system. Such idiosyncratic imagery is important.

Whenever your dream includes an image that can counteract a present physical symptom or that reduces your general anxiety, note it carefully. In Lila's dream, the fire hydrant and the possible flood were images that could counteract her other dream image of fire in the streets. I call such dream pictures *refocusing images*. They serve as antidotes to the affliction. (You will see how to use them at the end of this chapter.)

## EMOTIONAL IMPLICATIONS OF FIRE AND HEAT IN DREAMS

While dreams about fire in the ill or injured dreamer are related to fever or inflammation, dreams about fire in the healthy dreamer may suggest that the dreamer is sexually aroused, or "aflame" with erotic passion, or that the dreamer is passionately angry, or "burned up" about some situation. Such images may also portray feeling "burned out." Passionate feelings tend to produce dream images of extreme heat.

◇ Dreams of Ice or Cold = Body Part Too Cool

Although some areas of the body may feel burning hot, other areas may feel abnormally cool because of deficient body heat. If there has been nerve damage and, consequently, reduced circulation to the body part, excessive cold is almost sure to appear in dreams, as summarized in my dream aphorism:

> *Freezing rain, frost, ice, or snow,*
> *Body circulation slow.*

### DREAMS OF ICY BRANCHES = ICY FINGERS

Despite feeling feverish over the undiagnosed broken wrist that compressed my ulnar nerve, my ring and little fingers felt cool and numb. This symptom, too, appeared in my dreams. About a week after my injury, toward the end of a dream that included driving through a landscape with palm trees and poor immigrants who had temporary wooden shelters, the scenery changed:

> Then my husband and I are driving through an area of icy trees. It's incredible. The bare branches are covered with ice. As the wind blows through the thousands of trees, it makes an eerie, wailing sound. He is driving carefully, but there is a sudden lurch and our car jams. Will we be stuck in this cold, awful place of icy trees?

Here, my fingers were being compared in my dream to branches on a tree. The ice on the branches, of course, was the coldness I sensed in my fingers. This contrasted sharply to the hot area of palm trees, representing inflammation. The wailing sound was probably my own fear crying out at being "stuck" in this deplorable condition. Like the poor immigrants of my dream, my "shelter" was inadequate.

### DREAMS OF COLD OBJECTS = INADEQUATE
### BLOOD CIRCULATION

The image of ice in dreams seems to be a typical symbol for reduced circulation. The man who had vascular blockages in his legs that caused nighttime cramping, coldness in his feet, and limited mobility, dreamed he was driving a car with great difficulty, trying to get up an icy incline.[14] His dream contained several references to snow, ice, and cold, and as he discussed the dream afterward, he referred to the ice as being "two feet thick," unconsciously alluding to his own two cold feet. He perhaps also had "cold feet" about the upcoming operation.

Women who were unfortunate enough to have a fetus die in the womb have reported dreams involving cold and the unborn child, prior to waking knowledge of the fetus death. Psychologist Robert Van de Castle described the dream of a pregnant woman who saw her infant baby on the examining table with her obstetrician when he discontinued the examination because the baby was too cold[15]—her child had died in the womb. In another case described by Van de Castle, a pregnant woman dreamed that her mother was baby-sitting for her child; she discovered that her mother had put the baby into a refrigerator, where she found it icy cold. Later, in fact, this woman's child was born dead.[16] It seems as though the dreaming minds of these women were sensing the abnormal coldness of the fetuses they were carrying. Obviously, not every dream involving cold and a baby is going to have this meaning for a pregnant woman, but such a dream theme may be a warning signal. These are extreme cases; more often the cause is less drastic.

## EMOTIONAL IMPLICATIONS OF ICE AND COLD IN DREAMS

Snow, frost, and other cold weather conditions in dreams often underscore an emotional "coldness" in the dreamer's environment, or "chilly," fearful feelings in the dreamer. In psychological terms, dream images of ice, snow, or cold suggest fear of a "dangerous" or "slippery" situation.[17]

Frost, ice, snow, freezing rain, and similar cold images in dreams may signify a condition of overall body chill or inadequate blood circulation. Sometimes such dreams are simply caused by a cold room or a dislodged bedcover.

If you should dream of ice or snow after an injury, however, it may well relate to a body area with inadequate circulation. Notice where such imagery appears in your dream and whether it might correspond to an area of your body. If so, it's a good idea to discuss this finding with your physician. You may want to practice specific visualizations (such as those discussed at the end of this chapter) relating to the affected area.

◇ Dreams of Excess Water = Too Much Body Fluid

Overabundant fluid in the body tissues is often pictured by too much water in dreams, as in my dream aphorism:

> *Drowning deep or throat all clogged,*
> *Body tissues waterlogged.*

Perceptions of excess fluid and excess heat in the body may be combined into one image, as they were for the feverish woman who saw a pool filled with hot water in her dream.

### DREAMS OF EXCESSIVE WATER = BODY EDEMA OR MUCOUS PRODUCTION

Two conditions seem to stimulate dreams of excessive water: when a person has edema (water retention); and when a person has a lung condition that creates large amounts of phlegm or mucous. Such conditions may lead to dreams of drowning or of difficulty breathing. Patients who have suffered a heart attack need to be particularly alert for dreams of drowning, which may suggest a dangerous degree of water retention.

Dreams of drowning are often associated with excessive body fluids. These ailments include chronic lung disease, bronchitis, and pneumonia, as well as less serious chest infections. A patient who had a bad case of bronchitis dreamed of walking with friends along a dirty mountain road and having difficulty keeping up with them, when he fell into a river and began drowning in the deep, dirty, yellowish water. He thought he was dying and woke up in fear with a headache.[18] The dirty, yellowish water symbolized the thick, discolored expectorant of the dreamer.

Robert Bosnak, a Jungian analyst at Cambridge, described the poignant case of one of his patients, Christopher, who developed AIDS.[19] As the young man's health deteriorated, he contracted pneumocystis (a severe pneumonia that AIDS victims are susceptible to) but managed to fight it off. At the start of one psychotherapy session, he reported, "I seem to be dreaming about water a lot . . . I've had two dreams in a row with polluted water." In one of these dreams, the water in a lake was "mucky" with a "vile green slick," reminding him of not being able to breathe when he was in the hospital. In the other dream, he was separated from a beautiful woman by "icky" water. Although there are many levels of meaning to this patient's dreams, it seems to me that on a physical level, the man was portraying the infection regathering in his lungs. Indeed, not long after these dreams, Christopher came down with a second bout of pneumocystis; the third attack eventually killed him.

Although their condition is rarely fatal, asthmatics have similar excess water dreams because the histamine reaction of the asthmatic's body causes too much fluid to be secreted. One young woman with bronchial asthma dreamed a man was trying to kill other women by suffocation, holding them under water for three minutes. She woke up wheezing.[20] The water in the dream was a metaphor for the excess fluid in her own bronchial tubes.

People with various types of lung infections dream of drowning because, in my opinion, they perceive the excess fluid in their lungs while asleep and their dreaming minds liken this sensation to drowning.

I was astonished to discover, as I researched ancient writings on dreams and health, that Hippocrates had described this same significance of excess water in dreams many centuries ago. He called such conditions "moist phlegm" and said they were sometimes associated with dreams of heavy rains, storms, tempests, or hail. "If the dreamer thinks that he is diving in a lake, in the sea, or in a river, it is not a good sign, for it indicates excess of moisture."[21] Heavy sweating associated with fever, Hippocrates noted, sometimes stimulates dreams of being immersed in water or drowning. I observed this in a young woman's dream. When Jo was hospitalized for breast cancer, she was feverish and sweating profusely. She dreamed of drowning in a lake that bore her own last name.

Hippocrates also pointed out, "To see the earth flooded by water or sea signifies a disease, as there is much moisture in the body."[22] (We shall see later how negative dream imagery like this can be used to custom-design visualizations to counteract excesses.)

## EMOTIONAL IMPLICATIONS OF EXCESS WATER IN DREAMS

Images of excessive water may also suggest the dreamer is feeling overwhelmed by some situation in the environment or by some inner emotion. One woman dreamed of being inundated with high waves when she was struggling with a romantic relationship that she felt was too much for her.

If you are going through an illness that produces feverish sweating, or you are retaining water, or you are suffering from a respiratory infection, don't be surprised if you dream of drowning or being immersed in water. Such dreams will abate when the excess fluid in your body is reduced. (Meanwhile, you may find some of the visualizations described at the end of this chapter helpful.)

### ◇ Dreams of Dryness = Too Little Body Fluid

When body tissues do not have enough fluids present, dreams of scorched land, or burnt or dried-up objects may occur, as in my dream aphorism:

> Arid earth, plants wilt and die,
> Body tissues overdry.

I have already mentioned that people who have suffered severe burns often depict scenes of hot summer sun and hot sand in their drawings, which are metaphors for the burning heat and overly dry conditions they are experiencing. A patient whose cerebro-spinal fluid was blocked dreamed of a malfunctioning machine that needed lubrication.[23]

Two nights before he was to have an operation, the man who had a vascular blockage in his leg dreamed of trying to climb over rocks sticking out of a partially dried-up riverbed.[24] The half-dried river appeared to symbolize the reduced circulation in his leg. He mentioned stumbling and staggering over boulders "the size of feet," thus underscoring the connection between the rocks in his dream and his own impaired leg.

Images of feeling too dry or thirsty sometimes arise when the dreamer is feeling parched or has eaten very salty or spicy food. Freud described a dream that he could produce at will after going to bed thirsty from eating olives or anchovies; in it, he would drink large amounts of water, wishing to quench his thirst.[25]

EMOTIONAL IMPLICATIONS OF DRYNESS IN DREAMS

Dreams of people or things that are too dry are relatively rare. If you find yourself having such a dream when you are well, consider whether any area of your life has "lost its juice" or feels "all dried up and withered."

Dream images of scorched or burned objects and landscapes may occur in conjunction with excessive body heat. On the other hand, the dreamer may only be sleeping in an overheated dry room, or directly in front of a heater.

If, when you are injured or ill, you have any dreams that portray scorched or parched objects or people, consider whether this could correspond with insufficient lubrication or excessive dryness in some part of your body.

## ◇ FUNCTIONING OF AFFLICTED BODY PARTS

### ◇ Malfunctioning Flow Level

Pipes, tubes, wires, hoses, channels—these are the structures often associated with the movement of fluid and energy in the dreamer's body through blood vessels or nerves. Channels sometimes correspond to the dreamer's blood vessels, but may symbolize other passages in the body. Hoses frequently stand for the canal in which the semen moves. Wires are often associated with the dreamer's nerves. Moving bodies of water, such as rivers and streams, may become metaphors for the dreamer's circulating blood.

As in other cases, Hippocrates had long ago observed dream occurrences of uneven blood flow. He said, "When rivers are abnormal, they indicate a circulation of the blood; high water excess of blood, low water defect of blood." [26] He also said, "Impure streams indicate disturbance of the bowels," and, "Springs and cisterns indicate some trouble of the bladder." [27] He believed, "A troubled sea indicates disease of the belly." [28] If we dream of a disturbed flow of water or fluids in dreams, especially if the fluid is too much or too little or is polluted, we should consider the possibility of a fluid level disturbance in the body.

I have often noted dreams of abnormal water flow relating to menstruation. When I was having an exceedingly heavy menstrual period, I dreamed of a sink overflowing with water that I could not turn off. The sink was a metaphor for my uterus and the overflowing water represented the heavy blood flow.

Men sometimes depict the flow of their seminal fluid through the urethra by dreams of gasoline being pumped through a hose. Too much or too little gasoline in a dream may be significant information about the flow in this body part. Women, too, may dream about a hose pumping gas into a tank as a metaphor for sexual intercourse. Likewise, dreamers sometimes depict seminal fluid in dreams as a fluid being transported through pipes and faucets.

Obviously, modern dreamers do not limit themselves to natural bodies of water such as rivers and springs; they also incorporate the taps and sinks, hoses, tanks, pipes, and faucets of plumbing to indicate how the fluids in their bodies are moving.

### EMOTIONAL IMPLICATIONS OF FLUID OVERFLOW AND UNDERFLOW IN DREAMS

Psychologically, dreams of fluid overflow or underflow suggest an overabundance or deficiency of energy in the life current— the state of feeling at "flood tide" or a "low ebb." When we are healthy, dream images of overflowing fluids may suggest an excessive emotional situation. Dream images of inadequate fluids may suggest a situation that seems insufficient to nourish us.

### ◇ Blockages

When there is a blockage in the natural flow of a body fluid, this often appears as an obstacle in dreams, such as rocks sticking out of a half-dried riverbed. A man with chronic peptic ulcers who was to have surgery dreamed of standing on a ladder, trying to remove a ball that was stuck in telephone wires. This corresponded to the removal of his stomach obstruction (the ball in the dream) by fixing a nerve (the wire in the dream) that was involved in causing the obstruction.[29] His dreams also contained several images of narrow or constricted passageways; these were thought to symbolize the actual restriction of food passing through his gastrointestinal tract.[30] Yet another man who had just undergone surgery to remove an advanced tumor from his colon dreamed about a spring box with pipes that had been plugged.[31] The researchers who worked with this patient thought the plugged pipes in his dream referred to his bowels, which had been "shut off" by a colostomy.

If, when we are unwell, we have dreams in which some natural flow is blocked or the functioning of an apparatus is prevented, we should consider whether there might be any obstruction present in our body.

## EMOTIONAL IMPLICATIONS OF BLOCKAGE IN DREAMS

Psychologically, the presence of an obstacle in dreams indicates a frustration to our purpose or to our ability to act. People often represent difficulties in emotional relationships with trouble operating a machine in a dream. Healthy people who dream of trying to make a telephone call, but are unable to get through or get the wrong number or the connection breaks off, are usually symbolizing their difficulties in communication with an important person in their life. Answering machines have recently made dream appearances, as in the case of a man who dreamed there was a garbled message on his machine from his father. These motifs in healthy dreamers suggest problems in an emotional relationship, rather than a physical blockage. The images are metaphors for a difficulty "connecting" to another person.

### ◇ Dreams of Malfunctioning Vehicles = Malfunctioning Body

### DREAMS OF LOW FUEL TANKS = LOW ENERGY RESERVE

Cars, trucks, airplanes, and other vehicles often represent the healthy dreamer's body (as described in Chapter 1). We saw how, when your body is malfunctioning or in need of repair, such vehicles are likely to appear in your dreams in a damaged condition or a risky situation. The fuel level is an important metaphor for body energy.

When my husband, Zal, for example, who rarely remembers his dreams, was due for a hernia operation, he dreamed of adventurously flying a small, old-fashioned airplane, going to or from combat, when he noticed that the gas gauge was less than half full. Although he probably had enough fuel for the trip, he was concerned.

As a man in his middle sixties, Zal's body, like the airplane in his dream, was more "old-fashioned," but he was still enjoying the challenge of the journey of life. He thought of this type of airplane as "highly responsive, exciting, and romantic," and he associated "fuel" with "energy resource." A "gas gauge," he said, "measures how much energy is left." Zal realized that his dream imagery reläted to his upcoming hernia operation and his concern about how much physical resource he had left. In his dream language, Zal was expressing anxiety about whether he had enough energy to continue his journey onward. The dream said that the resource was more than half gone, yet it was probably sufficient for the trip. Indeed that operation—more than four years ago—went smoothly, and Zal bounced back as vigorous as ever.

Each dreamer has characteristic dream imagery and individual metaphors. For many dreamers, it is an automobile that represents their movement through life and/or the condition of their physical body.

## DREAMS OF EMPTY FUEL TANKS = ENERGY DEPLETED

Robert Bosnak's patient, Christopher, who was dying of AIDS, reported a dream in which the convertible he was driving was about to run out of gas.[32] He saw the fuel gauge practically on zero. Then the car ran out of gas and stopped, implying depleted waking energy. More common is the motif of losing one's brakes.

## DREAMS OF CARS GOING TOO FAST = LOSS OF CONTROL

Brad, a man in his early seventies, was scheduled for a hip joint replacement, since walking had become exceedingly painful for him. During the two weeks prior to his surgery, Brad recorded four dreams that he shared with me. He had the following a week before his operation:

> I'm in the front seat of an auto. Joe [a former friend who is a too-clever businessman and no longer close to me] is driving. We're going out a long pier, faster and faster, and go off the end. It's a long time before we hit the water. The two of us come up. My God, we've got to swim all the way back—a half mile! People are shaking their fists at us. The dream dissolves.

In his dream, Brad depicted his body—represented by the automobile—as out of control. Someone else—an unreliable person—was steering and speeding. The image of going off the end of the pier and into deep water suggested the danger of total collapse. But Brad surfaced to confront the long swim to safety. In describing this, Brad commented, "I was once a competitive swimmer. Now I'm a shell of my former self." The anger he felt at his predicament was portrayed in the dream by people shaking their fists. The dream suggested that Brad was trying to cope with his feelings of anger and his anxiety about the upcoming operation. It said that he'd have a long struggle to get back on firm ground. Six months after the surgery, Brad was walking smoothly without a cane. He'd made the long swim back.

## DREAMS OF CARS WITHOUT BRAKES = OUT OF CONTROL

Dreamers use car imagery to represent their bodies and their life situation regardless of age. Rosie, who was only six, had the following terrifying nightmare about an uncontrollable car after she returned home from a week in the hospital with pneumonia:

> I was in Mommy's car and I wasn't supposed to be there. The brakes went out and the car ran away. Suddenly there was a big witch in a shiny red car. I was afraid I would never be able to get back to Mommy. [This dream frightened the child so much, she went into her mother's bedroom for comfort.]

Here the little dreamer indicated not only that she felt her body and her life situation were out of control, in the same way that the dream car lost its brakes, but also she seemed to blame herself for what happened, as if it were her fault the brakes "went out." Rosie's mother, who slept overnight in a cot by her daughter's bed during her hospitalization, had become extremely upset over the treatment of her child in the hospital, describing herself as becoming "hysterical" with the staff. Perhaps the witch in Rosie's dream also represented the "uncontrolled" mother. If so, it's small wonder she wanted to get back to her familiar Mom as well as to her normal state of health. Notice how Zal, Brad, and even Rosie depicted the distance to recovery as a physical space.

If you must have an operation, observe how your dreams portray the situation. You are almost certain to depict your body in some form, either directly or symbolically. It may be in the form of a vehicle or as a machine or as a building. What does your dream convey about the condition of this body image, its malfunctioning, the general situation, the difficulties of the journey, and the possibilities for successful completion? (You'll find more suggestions for understanding such dreams at the end of this chapter.)

*3a. Illness: In the hospital with pneumonia*       Drawing by Rosie Schoneberg

*In this drawing of an illness, 3a, six-year-old Rosie shows how she felt when she was in the hospital for a week with pneumonia. Her mother (the smaller figure seated to the left) is holding the child's hand and wearing a smiling, consoling expression. The child's size, larger than her mother, depicts herself as the center of her own life. Rosie's face looks sad but she and her mother are connected.*

### ◇ Dreams of Insects and Foul Matter = Invasion by Toxins

Diseases sometimes take the form of insects in dreams. A man with an ulcerated stomach dreamed of having "wood moths" or "wood eaters" on the roof of his house that might damage or destroy the trees.[33] The wood moths were a metaphor for the acidic ulcers "eating" his stomach lining.

The Russian psychiatrist Vasilii Kasatkin quoted the case of a "Patient N." with chronic gastritis, who, during the time of his attacks, had a series of disgusting dreams. In one, he was in a sauna filled with feces and felt nauseous; in another, he was eating raw fish with a vile dressing; during his worst attack, he dreamed of pulling mucous out of his throat that had roots covered with moving spiders and worms; and also of walking alongside a dirty river with rotting fish on the coast.[34] After each of these dreams, the patient awoke feeling ill. These repugnant images represented the dreamer's sensations of discomfort in his stomach while he slept. Dreams about insects are almost uniformly unpleasant.

### EMOTIONAL IMPLICATIONS OF INSECTS
### AND FECES IN DREAMS

Psychologically, dreams of insects or feces may indicate dreamers' feelings about people and situations that "bug" them or that they find "shitty." Sometimes such dream images indicate a more severe mental disturbance.

We have seen how disorders in the body may be pictured in dreams. We now turn to the dream responses people have when they become hospitalized.

## ◇ DREAMS ABOUT HOSPITALIZATION

People generally respond to hospitalization with a feeling of loss in three areas: control, identity, and dignity. Patients are usually fearful about upcoming surgery or other medical procedures. They hope they will soon be restored to normal. Each of these concerns becomes a topic of dream images for the hospitalized person.

Pre-operative procedures can be agitating in themselves, particularly when an emergency necessitates surgery. Because of an accident or the discovery of a critical condition, the body's systems first go into a shock reaction followed by a high level of arousal. Planned operations remain a threat to the body's integrity, but one has time to pack a bag, reschedule one's activities, alert a support system of friends and relatives and, in general, exert some degree of control over the situation.

### ◇ Loss of Control

The shock of an accident is the most intense threat to the body. We saw how dreams of vehicles out of control are common at this stage. Again and again, victims of traumatic accidents say, "It happened so fast. It was over so quickly."[35] The suddenness of injury may cause confusion about exactly what has happened and also leads the victim to feel disoriented and sometimes even dissociated.[36]

*3b. Nightmare post-hospitalization: Car out of control*

Drawing by Rosie Schoneberg

*This drawing, 3b, depicts another level of Rosie's feelings, a nightmare (described on page 131), soon after she came home from the hospital. Rosie's breathing was painful and difficult, and hospital procedures had been frightening. Rosie drew herself in the "runaway" car that had lost its brakes—a typical dream symbol for physical illness and for feeling out of control about one's life.*

*Notice how Rosie's dream car is heading away from her mother (the slashed figure on the far left). The woman in the pointed hat is the witch who suddenly appeared in Rosie's nightmare. During Rosie's hospitalization, her mother was very angry at the staff over perceived inadequate treatment of her child, describing herself as "becoming hysterical." The witch probably represents the "bad side" of her uncontrolled mother that every child fears. Here it is the witch and the mother who are in contact, and the witch stands between Rosie and her "normal" mother. The anger that Rosie witnessed made her momentarily fearful that she "would never be able to get back to Mommy." Rosie's nightmare combined fear about being ill, being in the hospital, and her mother's behavior. When she awoke from the nightmare, Rosie's mother was comforting, helping restore the child's confidence.*

*By drawing their nightmares, dreamers defuse the anxiety their imagery expressed and start the process of regaining lost control.*

## BEYOND THE CURTAIN

Nan, a woman in her eighties, had a serious fall while crossing a busy street; it resulted in a fractured hip and arm, as well as contusions. She was hospitalized promptly and her surgeon planned to operate the next day. Although generally alert and capable, she became severely confused the night of her injury, perhaps in part from the sleeping medication she was given. Nan told me of waking up in the middle of the night and seeing the flowers and dividing curtain. She said, "Suddenly I felt quite sure that on the other side of the curtain was my home. I pulled everything away from my legs. I took this rubber thing off. I began to shout, 'Where am I?! It's not my house!' "

This nightmarelike experience probably arose in the drowsy state just prior to sleep; dreamlike imagery is common during this hypnagogic period. I mentioned earlier how Nan attempted to stay awake to avoid seeing the images of the weeping willow —a metaphor for her sadness. Despite her efforts, she finally began to drift to sleep and became disoriented. Nighttime is often the worst time for patients, or any anxious person, especially if they feel confused and alone.

Even young people who are suddenly hurt can become disoriented, especially if they are feverish or given medication. Don't be alarmed if this should happen to you as a patient. Don't allow yourself to become increasingly upset. Relax as best you can and you'll soon be oriented again. Using active visualizations and positive imagery is one of the ways you can help yourself restore a sense of control.

### ◇ Imagery Produces Physiological Responses

When I first realized I might have an operation within a few hours, my agitation was soothed by imagining lavender fields that had a profoundly relaxing effect. If you ever find yourself facing a crisis, try bringing to mind the most restful and beautiful scene you can conjure. Use all your senses to depict it—see it, hear it, touch it, smell it, even taste it.

What you imagine and what you dream about influence your very heartbeat, in addition to your internal secretions and the functioning of all your systems. By visualizing peaceful pictures in your mind, you can, to a large extent, counteract the onslaught of perceived or actual threats to your physical integrity. You will see how using certain images from your dreams can help carry you safely through stormy emotional seas.

## ROSSI'S MIND/BODY CONNECTION

Ernest Rossi is a clinician and hypnotist in Los Angeles who has worked extensively with the connection between the mind and body. He believes that researchers have identified a three-stage process whereby the mind influences the cells: (1) When we think, or imagine a picture, or feel an emotion, the frontal part of the cerebral cortex generates nervous impulses; (2) These impulses are filtered through the emotional areas of the limbic-hypothalamic system; (3) Then the nervous impulses are converted into chemical impulses called neurotransmitters, or messenger molecules.[37]

Thus, information carried from the cortex enters the hypothalamus in the form of nerve signals and exits in the form of biochemicals. These neurotransmitters travel through the bloodstream, seeking receptors on the outside of cells in the tissues and organs throughout the body, where they fit like a key into a lock and turn on a response at the local site. In this way, the mind influences the biochemical functions of all the major organ systems and tissues of the body by way of the autonomic nervous system. In other words, what we think, imagine, or feel has a specific effect on the functioning of our body, which becomes exceedingly important in our recuperation from illness or injury.

Positive emotions, thoughts, and images have specific biochemical correlates that influence how our body works. By refocusing our attention on, and directing our imagination and emotions to, different areas of the body, we actually alter the direction of blood flow, dilating or constricting our blood vessels. Several suggestions are given in the activities section at the end of this chapter, and in the following chapters, on how to use your inner powers to ameliorate your condition.

### ◇ Restoring Control

Maintaining some degree of control is a key to reducing stress. Several studies have demonstrated that the greater the degree of control people feel they have over their lives, the less emotional stress they are likely to experience.[38] Being able to make one's own decisions increases one's sense of control. A person who is hospitalized suddenly loses control over most areas of his or her life. When we engage our minds and our power to imagine in our own service, we help to restore some of our lost control.

◇ Loss of Identity

Another common reaction to being injured is the sense of depersonalization that often accompanies becoming a patient. Loss of dignity usually comes later. Many hospitalized people—stripped of personal possessions and tagged like a prisoner or inmate—feel a loss of identity.

### THE BLUE DOG IN THE RED LIFE JACKET

During the final night before my operation, my dreams portrayed many images of damage and danger, including the loss of my identity cards. The following is the middle of a long, complex dream I had: [39]

> As I return to the castle grounds, I'm stunned to see a creature that people have often described but no one believed existed—a mythological creature. It's a large blue dog wearing a red life jacket. There may be three or four of them. I'm so startled by seeing the unbelievable creature with my own eyes that I drop my belongings into a bog by the road. I, too, either fall or stumble into it. I manage to climb out, but when I turn to grab my purse, airline tickets, and other things, they have sunk beyond retrieval.

The dream concluded on a more positive note (described on page 140). Notice how the imagery in my pre-operation dream was a distorted replay of my accident. Injured people frequently depict the original accident in dreams; these may be exact replays or distortions of the original. I had fallen onto a sidewalk, not into a bog. By substituting a bog for the sidewalk, my dreaming mind created a metaphor that emphasized my feeling of being "stuck" in a messy and difficult situation. In the dream, this event caused me to lose my valuables. Airline tickets, to me, refer to the ability to move about freely. My purse contained all of my identification papers, money, makeup, and credit cards.

*4. Focusing image: The blue dog in the red life jacket*

Drawing by Patricia Garfield

*Making a drawing of a positive image from one of your dreams gives you a concrete place to focus healing energy. The blue dog in the red life jacket was a hopeful image for me, derived from a dream I had a few nights before (surgery described on page 137). Watching for positive dream images, depicting them, and concentrating upon them helps dreamers alleviate fears and sustain hope in much the same way that icons do for religious followers. These images may be used as the basis for meditation or for visualization exercises. Because such images are created from the dreamer's own emotional depths, they have extraordinary healing power for the dreamer.*

Whenever dreamers lose identification materials, as I did, they are depicting the loss of identity that is so common among patients. I was no longer a psychologist who was an expert on dreams, an author, a consultant, a loved and loving wife, a mother; I was a patient facing the unknown—pain and perhaps even death. It's a feeling that many patients experience.

If you are facing an operation or have an acute illness, remember that catastrophic dreams are only one stage of a larger process. Disaster dreams are normal when we are seriously ill. Later on, you will see that dreams return to happier subjects and, if you allow them, can soothe and encourage you in your healing.

Don't be surprised if you dream about going on a journey, especially if you are actually packing a bag for a stay in the hospital. You are going on a trip into the unknown. The following pages provide a map with the route marked all the way home.

### ◇ Restoring Identity

Remember who you are. You are not just a disordered body part. You are yourself—a whole human being—regardless of whether any parts are damaged or missing. Do not allow yourself to be treated unkindly or unfairly. Working with your personal dream imagery is a fundamental way to stay in touch with your inner self and remember your unique identity. (See the guide at the end of this chapter for specific suggestions for dreamwork, drawings, and visualizations.)

## ◇ FEARS AND HOPES SYMBOLIZED BY DREAM IMAGES

### ◇ Fears about Being Cut

Facing surgery is a highly stressful experience. People about to have an operation confront a double threat: bodily injury and possible death. Men and women generally react to this crisis with fear, anxiety, dependency, and/or anger; some of them react by denying the seriousness of the situation. There is a period of inner agitation in which the patient attempts to mobilize defenses against the anxiety he or she feels. Many people in one study of patients facing surgery were preoccupied with fantasies of punishment, mutilation, or death. In dreams, the patient attempts to master his or her fears about the stress.

In a carefully controlled study, researchers Louis Breger, Ian Hunter, and Ron Lane collected dreams from five patients for four nights before surgery was scheduled.[40] These patients slept in the laboratory and were awakened following REM periods. They produced forty-nine dream reports prior to their operations which were then compared to the forty-five dreams they reported in the three nights following their operations. These reports were compared to those of two control subjects who were not undergoing surgery.

### DREAMS OF KNIVES AND SAWS = FEAR OF SURGICAL KNIVES

As mentioned earlier, patients confronting surgery often picture cutting instruments in their dreams. This imagery is thought to represent a fear of the surgeon's knife, because it is far more common prior to surgery than afterward. Cutting, combined with defective or damaged objects, appeared in an average of 80 percent of the pre-operative dreams collected by Breger and his associates, but in only 53 percent of the post-operative dreams.

Patients dreamed about elements related to surgery—doctors, patients, hospitals, medical examinations equipment, or operations—in more pre-operative dreams than in post-operative dreams (an average of 42 percent compared to 13 percent).[41] People who were not facing surgery had scarcely any images of cutting, defective objects, and hospital-related people or objects in their dreams.[42]

### ◇ Hopes for Recovery

Dreamers about to undergo surgery depict their wishes for the outcome, as well as represent their damaged body parts and their fears of being cut. Thus, not all pre-operative dreams are unpleasant. The following is the conclusion of my dream about the blue dog:

> I'm not too concerned about losing my belongings and continue into the castle grounds, passing many people carrying strange animals—one creature has green fur; another is a rabbit with long hair that he combs and parts. Now it seems to be an outdoor fair or festival with models of tigers with bulbous clown noses. I squeeze through a tight place, encouraged by a woman.
>
> Later, I'm inside the castle with Zal, being interviewed by reporters and liking the attention. I tell them I've lost my purse with airline tickets and other valuables. Somehow I know these lost things are likely to be replaced when the story is printed. A hairdresser gives me beautiful postcards of the castle and grounds with exquisite views I've not yet seen.

This final dream scene provided a resolution. I sensed that my missing valuables would be restored. Animals in dreams frequently refer to the animal life of the dreamer, his or her instincts, or the basic vitality of life—mine appeared to be lively.

I believe that even in the worst of situations and in the worst of nightmares, there are elements upon which to base hope. In order to dream well, we must search for and find these elements in the dream. These pictures, fragile as they seem, are powerful images that can connect us to inner resources and give us sustenance. For me, the image of the blue dog in the red life jacket held such hope.

I associate the color blue with the elements: sea and sky, water and air, as well as spiritual things; it's an unreal color for a dog. I think of red as the color of blood, fire and fiery emotions, sex and anger, as well as the Red Cross and help. Together, blue and red convey to me a sense of survival of physical and spiritual life. Remembering this image as I was wheeled into the operating room helped me stay calm and confident. Just as I had survived in my catastrophic dream about the death of millions, so in my last pre-operative dream, there were elements of hope.

## DREAMS OF CURLY HAIR = HOPEFUL THOUGHTS

Fiona, a woman in her late forties, had been experiencing pain in her jaw. She'd recently had root-canal work done; now she perceived some discomfort underneath the root canal and there was an ulcer on the gum that would not go away. Her dentist decided that the underlying bone was decaying from an infection in the jaw and the area must be cleaned out immediately.

Fiona is especially skittish about dental procedures, so she was exceedingly anxious the night before the dental surgery, which was to be done under a general anesthetic. She dreamed:

> All night long I was in the dental chair and I could feel the drill. But when he was finished, I woke up (in the dream) and looked in the mirror. I had a new face. There was not a crease in sight. I looked sixteen years old. Not only did my teeth look wonderful, my hair was all curled and puffed up, bouncy—all I'd ever wanted in life. I looked sparkly. All the pain and fear was worth it. The result was wonderful!

This encouraging dream may have helped Fiona approach the operation more positively. Certainly it expressed her wish that something good come out of the operation beyond fixing her tooth—a fresh new face, skin, and hair. After several more difficult procedures, Fiona was finished with that ordeal. Very possibly, the dream helped her through the trying time.

## DREAMS OF NEW CARS AND CLOTHES = HOPE FOR A NEW, IMPROVED BODY

Hopes for a "new, improved self" are fairly common when facing surgery. These wishes often take the form of new clothing, remodeling of buildings, repaired machines, new cars, and other replacements and reconstructions. The man who was to have surgery for his peptic ulcer dreamed he was shopping for a new car.[43] Women more often represent their wishes for an improved body after surgery by dreams about new clothes. A young woman in the Breger study was scheduled for exploratory surgery with possible removal of her gallbladder. She was overweight, a condition frequently associated with gallbladder problems,[44] and hoped that the operation would help her reduce. In one of her pre-surgery dreams, a woman was cutting material to sew a new dress; in another, the dreamer was wearing "different clothes."[45]

I've mentioned my pre-surgery dream of being dressed in rags as a symbol for my "tattered" body. Shopping for new clothing, buying clothes, making them, being given them—all such images relate to the injured dreamer's hopes for a better body, and maybe even a better life, after surgery is complete. Cutting out material, mending it, or sewing it relate to the act of surgery itself, reconstructing the material of the body. Such reconstruction of the body may also take the form in dreams of remodeling houses or other structures. Be alert for such images in your dreams.

## ◇ DREAM ACTIVITIES: DISCOVERIES IN YOUR DREAM IMAGERY

◇ 1. Scan the dreams recorded in your journal for images that indicate:

- excessive heat or fire
- excessive cold, ice, snow, hail, or sleet

- excessive water or fluids
- excessive dryness
- inadequate or overabundant fluid flow
- blockages
- insects or foul material
- broken or damaged structures or machines
- wounded, sick, dying, or dead people and animals
- hopeful images
- refocusing images

◇ 2. Think about and feel these images from the
physical and psychological perspectives.

You may find it helpful to review the sections in this chapter on
"Injured Body Parts Symbolized by Dream Images," "Physical
Symptoms," and "Functioning of Afflicted Body Parts." Jot down
your findings in your dream journal.

◇ 3. Select one of your dreams about a vehicle
in trouble.

Answer the questions in the following section about your particular dream vehicle.

## DREAM CARS IN TROUBLE

If you dream about being in another vehicle, such as a truck,
bus, airplane, or ship, adapt the questions to fit the particular
vehicle. Ask yourself how this vehicle differs from others similar
to it. Be sure to notice:

### THE CONTROLLER
1. Who is at the steering wheel?
2. If not yourself, what is this person like (spoiled, reckless,
   crazy)?
3. Where are you sitting (driver's seat, passenger's seat,
   back seat, floor)?
4. Who are the other passengers, if any?

### IMPLICATIONS OF CONTROLLER
Whoever is at the steering wheel indicates the aspect of yourself
that is currently in control. Your location in the vehicle indicates

how you assess your position. Consider whether any other passengers are people whom you associate with helpful support, threat, stress or other attributes.

## CONDITION AND FUNCTIONING OF VEHICLE

5. What is the condition of the vehicle? What is its make, color, size, state of repair? What are your associations to it? Is it big and difficult to handle or big and luxurious? Is it small and cramped or small and flexible?
6. How is it functioning? Are the brakes working? Is it going too fast or slow? Can you steer? Do internal parts break down? Do you have enough fuel?

## IMPLICATIONS OF VEHICLE CONDITION AND FUNCTIONING

Answers to these questions often relate to feelings you have about your physical body or the way you are currently moving through life. Going too fast or being unable to use the brakes suggests you are pushing yourself too hard. Going too slow and low fuel indicate inadequate energy. Steering ability relates to degree of control. Breaking down suggests body impairment or difficulty in some relationship.

## ROAD CONDITIONS

7. What is the condition of the road? Is it muddy, icy, slippery, full of ruts, uphill, downhill? Is it a freeway, a superhighway, or country lane?
8. What are other conditions of the environment? Are you on the ground, in the air, in the water? Is it snowing or raining? Are there obstacles blocking your path?

## IMPLICATIONS OF ROAD CONDITIONS

Answers to these questions suggest feelings you have about conditions and obstacles. Ice and snow often indicate feelings of treacherous, slippery, or tricky situations. Mud usually relates to messy conditions. Ruts, obstacles, and uphill driving indicate strenuous conditions. A "freeway" means easy going to some dreamers and dangerous conditions to others. If the road is inappropriate for the vehicle, such as a huge trailer truck on a country lane, something is out of place for the dreamer.

## GOAL ORIENTATION

9. Is there a direction, purpose, or goal to your trip? Are you on track? Stuck in a rut? Missed a turn?
10. How do you feel about the journey?

## IMPLICATIONS OF GOALS

Answers to these questions relate to your present purpose. Getting off track or being stuck in a rut suggests difficulties in achieving the current purpose. Missing a turn indicates a missed opportunity. Even if the road is difficult, you may still arrive at your destination. If you feel pleased to be making the journey, your goal is worthwhile; if the journey is burdensome, you may be depicting a distasteful duty.

## "REDREAM" YOUR RIDE

Assume that your dream car (or other vehicle) represents your physical body moving through life at the moment. What do your answers tell you about the current condition of your body or your mode of traversing life? If there are any conditions you do not like, visualize a way to make the situation better. What is missing? What do you need to improve the situation? Spend two minutes picturing your vehicle and the road you travel in a better way. Use all your imagination, seeing it, hearing it, sensing it.

### ◊ 4. Draw your crisis.

It may seem peculiar, but one of the best ways to overcome the emotional effects of a traumatic incident is to draw it. Most people react by saying, "I don't want to draw it. I don't even want to think about it!" Art therapists sometimes coax a patient into making a drawing of an accident or an illness by telling the person that the drawing can be torn up afterward. Getting the incident on paper, "externalizing" it, helps get it out of your system. Make a concrete record of your crisis.

As a psychologist, I know that talking about a painful or difficult incident in a safe place to a trusted person can begin the process of desensitizing the sufferer to the discomfort. It defuses anger and anxiety. Drawing a pain in the shoulder (or anywhere else) can reduce the actual experienced pain. Making the red, orange, and black zigzag lines for pain can leave the artist feeling less pain. Once the trauma has been drawn, it can be discarded, if the artist still desires to do so. Some people find the act of making the drawing so anxiety- or pain-reducing that they decide to keep the drawing. A collection of drawings throughout a course of healing is a fascinating record of an emotional as well as physical journey.[46]

To try this process for yourself, get some plain paper and a box of colored pencils or crayons. Depict the traumatic scene as you remember it and as you reacted emotionally. Show everything you want to show. Pretend it is a dramatic scene in a play or film, but make it your story. Be sure to date the paper and jot down any thoughts that occur to you as you work on the drawing. Tear it up or keep it, as you wish. Remember, you don't need to be able to draw well to benefit from these exercises; the important thing is to express your feelings and sensations. Follow your heart.

*5. Accident: Broken wrist*                    Line drawing by Patricia Garfield

*People who have been traumatically injured or suddenly become ill can help themselves get an overview of their situation by drawing their*

◊ 5. Draw your afflicted body part.

If you have time, it is also useful to draw the way your injured or ill body part *feels* at the moment. It need not be an accurate drawing. My original drawing of my broken wrist was of a wooden block attached to the wooden arm bones by a rigid hinge; the fingers dangled like useless strings. If possible, use a range of colors to depict hot and cold areas, and painful and numb spots.

Such drawings may tell the artist a great deal about what needs to be accomplished to recover, as well as expressing any current discomfort. They also serve as an excellent gauge of progress as you go through the stages of healing. If you keep this initial drawing, be sure to date it. Interesting comparisons can be made to later drawings.

## TRACE YOUR LIFE LINE

Another approach to using art to accelerate healing is very simple—all you need is a piece of paper and a pencil. Set the pencil on the paper and let it move as you recall what has happened to you. Just let the pencil travel, indicating your movement through life when the accident or illness occurred. Show by the quality of the line what it was like; let your marks reflect your sense of what happened. Now go on. Let the line continue. Show what you feel like now and the obstacles ahead. Find a way forward

---

*experience as a concrete line, as described in the Trace Your Life Line activity above.*

*This picture shows my life line as I experienced it about three weeks after I broke my arm. It reads from the bottom upward. I was going along in my normal way—the curving line lowest on the drawing—when suddenly my life was disrupted by the fall that broke my arm. This accident is shown by the large jagged lines. The intense pain and gloomy fear I felt is pictured by the black patch, followed by sporadic pain shown in smaller jagged lines. When I drew this picture, I knew it was necessary to have surgery to rebreak my arm. The gap in the line depicts the gap in consciousness I expected. I anticipated that it would be difficult to get going again, as seen in the wiggly line, but then I thought life would return to normal, depicted by the rhythmic line that commences toward the top of the page. The drawing helped me keep my perspective on the upcoming surgery as part of a larger process.*

in your drawing. Show yourself going through the operation, if there is to be one, and beyond. What will the rehabilitation be like? What will happen to you then? My drawing showed a rhythmic line with a sudden explosion (the break), followed by jagged lines (the pain), reaching a blank space (the operation and the unknown); the line picked up with a jerk that gradually smoothed and began to flow rhythmically again. Show your story in a line.[47] Date the drawing and put it away. Later you will see how it compares to the future.

### ◇ 6. Describe your injury or illness in writing.

Of course, not all of us are able to draw following an injury or illness. Writing about your problem is also therapeutic. Describing it into a tape recorder or dictating it to a friend accomplishes a similar purpose. Researchers have found that the mere act of putting down a traumatic event in writing decreases anxiety. So, if you can't draw after an injury, write or, at least, tell about it on tape or describe it to a friend whom you'll ask to record it. You'll be setting out on the road to recovery.

### ◇ 7. Draw your nightmare.

If you have been troubled by a nightmare prior to surgery, while you are in the hospital, or while being treated for an illness, draw a picture of it. Making drawings of our nightmares helps defuse them of their power to alarm us. Be sure to include the main characters and the setting. Depict the action. For some dreamers, this will be an exact or a distorted replay of what actually happened. For others, it will be entirely symbolic. In any case, show the worst moment in the dream. It's the best way to start transforming your problem. Date this drawing, too, and save it.

### ◇ 8. Find and use your refocusing image.

The images of our dreams are potent because they have been created from the depths of our emotions. Formed by feelings, they evoke feelings. When we encounter a picture in one of our dreams that intrigues us, that has a fascination, or that tugs on our heartstrings, we have a treasure. Jung referred to dream images that hold power for the dreamer as "numinous." These are often idiosyncratic, odd images that don't make logical sense; they make perfect symbolic sense. They almost seem like a magic icon, a picture that is said to encapsulate some of the energy or spirit of the figure depicted. For the dreamer, they work like magic because they are a direct link to the dreamer's emotions.

I use powerful dream pictures as "refocusing images." The red dog in the blue life jacket was such an image for me. I held it in mind as I was wheeled down the hall on a gurney to the operating room; it gave me a sense of calm and confidence. If you are facing surgery, watch your dreams carefully for the image that can calm and reassure you.

If you are ill, you can use a refocusing image to help counteract your symptoms. The fire hydrant in Lila's dream was the direct opposite of the low-grade fever she was experiencing, accompanied by dreams of streets on fire. By picturing the fire hydrant open, gushing water, washing down the flaming streets and cooling them, she would be helping to cool and lower her temperature. Such images are not just fantasies. They are effective because they are formed in our body, which is receptive to them. Our imagination literally affects our body processes. By visualizing vividly on a regular basis, we can help ourselves move toward health.

Scan your dreams for any image, no matter how insignificant, that gives you contentment and select it for your refocusing image. If you have the time or the inclination, make a sketch of your chosen image. It doesn't need to be "good," it just needs to capture the feeling it gave you, to remind you of itself. The act of drawing alone helps you to concentrate on your refocusing image and comprehend its meaning. If you prefer, find a photograph or drawing that evokes the feeling of your dream. Keeping your refocusing image near your bedside will help you visualize it when you want to do so. Find your image, give it waking shape, and hold it in your mind's eye.

Now picture this image inside your body, nurturing it, easing its discomfort. Place it into any nightmares you may have had. Cherish it—for this image from your deepest self has much to teach. Above all, through it all, do the things that help you understand and believe in your own self, your own power.

# POST-CRISIS DREAMS

I am totally alone and extremely frightened. Then I see a man in a shack and I go to speak with him. I feel afraid of people or things that I've seen. One of these is a place with a broken pipe or large pipe connection that causes too much pounding in the pavement. I realize I am afraid of having a heart attack and dying.

At one point, I see my father (who died of a heart attack at the age of sixty-two). It doesn't look at all like him, but I know it is he; in the dream he has dark hair with a white tuft in the front. When I see him, I rise into the air, moving over a kind of railroad track on the ground below. As I rise, I seem to become invisible, a wraith. I awake with the conviction that this imagery of floating up into the air after having seen my dead father means that I am about to die.

Author's dream diary<br>Four nights after operation

That was the dream I had on my first night home from the hospital. It was the fourth night since I had had surgery on my left arm under a general anesthetic, and the first time I had a period of unbroken sleep from 9:30 P.M. until I woke up in terror from this nightmare at 1:00 A.M. I was so traumatized that it didn't even occur to me that I was experiencing typical REM rebound.

In retrospect, it's obvious that my brain, having gotten a respite of deep sleep, was compensating for the missed nights of dreaming. In my distraction, I had forgotten that this was to be expected. Following periods of sleep and dream deprivation, rapid eye movements become exceedingly intense, and when eye movements are intense dream content is almost always unpleasant.

In addition, I had a new and seemingly realistic fear: possible heart trouble. Besides, I felt quite peculiar, so maybe something *was* wrong with me. I didn't realize that the odd sensation of shakiness I had was due to the painkilling medication, along with the aftereffects of the general anesthetic and the postoperative morphine. Drug withdrawal alone can produce REM rebound. It was not until months later that I began to realize how typical my nightmare after surgery was.

## ◇ TYPICAL DREAM THEMES AFTER SURGERY OR TREATMENT

Dream reactions to the stress of surgery or medical treatment for an injury or illness fall into several general categories:

- fear of death
- sense of having been attacked
- replay of the original trauma
- fear of relapse or further harm
- symptoms or malfunctions of an injured body part
- change in body image

If you find yourself having these dreams, you can be confident that you are having a typical response.

### ◇ Dreams Indicating a Fear of Death

My nightmare on my first night home was an expression of my fear of death—an anxiety that many patients share after surgery. In my dream, the shack represented my battered body. The "broken pipe," or "large pipe connection that caused too much pounding in the pavement," referred both to the repaired break in my arm and to the "pounding" in my heart—from fear and from medication. The sight of my deceased father led me to rise into the air, resembling a spirit myself. It was this imagery that petrified me, not flying with pleasure, as I usually do, but leaving the earth as though already dead. The railroad track made me think of an inevitable destination, with little hope of escape. The dream really alarmed me.

During the remainder of that night, the dreams continued in abundance. However, each became less terrorizing. In one of these dreams, there was an injured, dying dog that turned on its owner and bit her arm. Before the dog died, however, it gave birth to a new puppy that the woman cared for tenderly. In another scene, a woman who had fallen and sprained her back was being nursed to health. The next morning I felt considerably encouraged that my end was not imminent. Although apprehension hung over me for several weeks until the dreaded treadmill test was done, the refreshing, restoring quality of deep sleep and full dreaming had begun to heal me.

Later, as I convalesced and talked with many other patients who had experienced traumatic accidents and illnesses, surgery, or other stressful medical procedures, I came to realize that my nightmare was not unique. In fact, although its details were specific to my case, its emotional tone was typical. I was not alone. But each dreamer had felt as isolated as I had felt. Fear of dying is a common reaction to being seriously injured or ill.

### ◇ Dreams About Being Attacked by Men or Beasts

I have already mentioned that dreamers often symbolize surgery as a brutal or fatal attack, which can take the form of a physical assault with weapons, a sexual assault, or an attack by animals.

#### DREAMS OF REPEATED RAPE = PAIN IN GENITALS

Mimi, a woman in her forties, had a hysterectomy. When she first woke up after having surgery with a general anesthetic, she sensed, ". . . a big, red amorphous thing extending from my breasts down and out of my body. It looked as though I were four months pregnant." This sensation may have partly contributed to the nightmares Mimi told me she had while still in the hospital. In the first, she dreamed:

> I am with a college boyfriend who is forcing me to have sex in fifty different ways. I am totally helpless.

In another dream during her hospitalization:

> Two young strangers are raping me. One awful episode follows another. I can hardly move.

Obviously, Mimi felt her body had been brutally invaded. She had never been raped in waking life, nor had she previously dreamed of being raped. She was comparing the pain of the operation to an imagined pain of sexual assault. The waking sensation she had of an unpleasant pregnancy was "explained" by her dreaming mind as being caused by rape.

### DREAMS OF A PAINFUL DELIVERY = PAIN IN GENITALS

Bejay, who's the same age as Mimi, also had a hysterectomy because of fibroids, but she depicted her post-surgical pain in a different dream metaphor:

> I am lying down delivering something, as in childbirth. I keep pushing this thing down and down, and when it finally starts to come out of my vagina, I can see that it's half of a car fender! The hard metal edge is all jagged and sharp. It's so big—how can I ever get this out of me?!

Bejay's dreaming mind attributed the painful sensations of abdominal and genital discomfort, along with severe gas pains, to a difficult delivery of an unnaturally large, hard-edged, cutting object.

When the integrity of the body image has been broken, as it is by damage resulting from an accident or by surgical procedures, people must change their body image. Before being able to rally and return to full health, injured women and men must begin to positively incorporate the changes in their bodies into their new self-images. (We will see in later chapters how this took place for Mimi.)

### THE MAD DOG SURGEON = METAPHOR FOR PAIN FROM SURGERY

Sometimes surgical wounds are likened by the dreaming mind to gashes caused by a savage beast. Nina, a woman in her fifties, is a nurse who suffers from rheumatoid arthritis. She had surgery to have nodules removed from one of her hands, with plans to have them removed from the other hand later. When she showed me the results of her surgery three weeks after it was completed,[1] she commented, "It looks like I've been attacked by a pit bull, but it was really Dr. X."

In light of her comparing surgery to an attack by a vicious dog, I was fascinated to learn that Nina owned a pet dog (a schnauzer, not a pit bull) and that one of her dreams involved looking for her pet, because it was missing. She described a schnauzer as "a very sensitive type—one that responds to the owner's emotions." Her dog "puts her head on my lap if I cry or I'm sad." To dream of this pet as missing suggested that Nina felt out of touch with her own feelings. She was feeling mauled and sore from the surgery that her conscious mind compared to an attack by a ferocious dog; her dreaming mind said she felt deprived of a sensitive part of herself.

When dreamers picture their surgery as a brutal assault, they usually realize the procedure is necessary for their health and well-being. Dreaming of an operation as an attack on the body is an *emotional* reaction to having one's body invaded by surgical instruments. As such, it feels cruel, even though we know its purpose is to help us.

## DREAMS ABOUT WILD BEASTS = FEAR OF NATURAL DISASTER

Wild beasts and brutal assassins are probably selected by the dreaming mind to represent the traumatizing agent because their force is savage, unpredictable, and uncontrollable.[2] This is true whether the pain the dreamer suffers was caused by an accident, by surgical incisions, or by a violent upheaval of nature. Many kinds of trauma, in addition to surgery, may be represented by wild animals in dreams.

A man from South Carolina, who was traumatized by Hurricane Hugo in 1989, dreamed that he was being chased, first on land and then in the air, by a flying alligator.[3] In most dreams of flying, only the dreamer is capable of the superhuman act of flight, but the alligator's ability to fly expressed the dreamer's extreme sense of helplessness and loss of control during the disaster that traumatized him.

Many people were also disturbed by nightmares following the 1989 San Francisco earthquake.[4] My first dream relating to the earthquake was one of surveying the general destruction; it was a straightforward replay of the first few days. The imagery in my second dream about the earthquake showed signs of change:

> I seem to be standing on a plot of grassy ground. Suddenly the whole thing begins to shift and move beneath my feet, and I realize that what I thought was solid ground is really an animal with grasslike hair. I'm in danger of being toppled over.

In this dream, there was a transformation from ordinary earth, which probably represented everyday life, to the trembling, unstable ground of an earthquake, and then into a dangerous, hairy beast who could be a direct threat. Yet this very change, making the event more of a fantasy than a replay of reality, meant that my mind was beginning to move on, to accept the disaster, and go forward with life. The fear was still present, but it was less real.

Why do traumatized people seem to torment themselves with nightmares replaying their original or even worse misfortunes? Why do they transform their trauma into symbolic form in dreams?

## ◇ POST-TRAUMATIC STRESS DISORDER

When people experience an event that is outside the range of usual daily life, one that would be distressing to almost anyone, they may develop a reaction that needs professional attention. This "post-traumatic stress disorder" may take place if you or someone you love has been threatened with death or bodily harm. It can occur whether you were traumatized directly—such as in an attempted murder or a rape—or indirectly. Being a witness to a disaster is also traumatizing: if you see your home or community suddenly destroyed, as in a fire, in a bombing raid, or in a natural disaster, such as the San Francisco earthquake; or if you see another person seriously injured or killed as the result of an accident or physical violence, such as when a group of schoolchildren in California witnessed their classmates being shot by a man with an automatic rifle, it is traumatizing.

When such a trauma occurs, the person to whom it happened or who witnessed it may re-experience the event in recurrent and intrusive recollections. The person may have distressing dreams about it, sudden flashbacks of it during the day, or have intense disturbances when exposed to events that resemble the original situation. For days after my fall, I "saw" the sidewalk looming up toward my face, and vividly relived the situation without wishing to do so. It took many weeks, even after my arm was repaired, before I could walk in the area where I had been hurt without feeling a stab of anguish. Those people who have been more severely damaged may develop a lifelong phobia.

Traumatized people may try to avoid thinking or feeling about the tragedy, and they may try to avoid activities that resemble the original event. They may be unable to recall parts of the trauma. Sometimes they become disinterested in activities that formerly were appealing or lose skills that they formerly had. They may try to protect themselves from further emotional suffering by detaching their emotions from other people, by feeling unable to love, or by developing a sense that they do not have a long future.

People suffering with post-traumatic stress may also have difficulty falling or staying asleep, become irritable, or have difficulty concentrating. Mood swings, stomach disorders, headaches, fatigue, and coldlike symptoms are common. At first, traumatized people often feel dazed and confused; then they sometimes become hypervigilant to any danger in the environment, overreacting to minor things with a startle response, and they often have physiological reactions to events that resemble the trauma.

Survivors of the 1989 San Francisco earthquake reacted violently to mild aftershocks, or even trucks rumbling by—any vibration reminded them of the major quake. Veterans of wars, victims of torture, and survivors of concentration camps and other catastrophes frequently have a severe post-traumatic stress reaction. Such persons may become and remain angry or anxious. Those of us who experience less extreme events still may be traumatized enough to have a strong response that endures.

It's quite natural to have some of these feelings and reactions during the first few days and weeks after a trauma. If, however, the symptoms persist beyond one to two months, or recur several months later, it's probably advisable to seek consultation with a psychotherapist.

Several of the people I interviewed who had been injured in a traumatic way relived their accidents in their dreams. It seems as if their minds were stuck in a groove, from shock, playing over and over the same unhappy event like a stuck record player needle. Therapists think these replays of the trauma may be an attempt to absorb the incident, to accept the unacceptable, before being able to move on with life.

## ◇ Dreams Replaying an Injury

### THE ARTERY/HOSE OUT OF CONTROL

Peter, a carpenter who severed the nerves and artery of his left hand when a circular saw "kicked back," had violent nightmares replaying his injury in exact detail and he suffered flashbacks of it during the day.[5] While he was awake, Peter told me he said to himself, "Bad thought!" He added, "I put it in a compartment with other bad thoughts, like ex-wives." During the night, however, he was not able to dismiss the dreams. He had been assaulted by the nightmare a number of times with increasing frequency. "That's what bothers me—I'm going to have to deal with it," he confided.

### THE MONSTER/LAWN MOWER

A person can suffer from post-traumatic stress whatever his age. Nine-year-old Billy had had several of his toes and the top of his foot cut off by a power lawn mower. His physical recovery from the surgery to repair the damage was good, but he began to awaken screaming. He described repetitive nightmares that the lawn mower was in a closet in the house and would soon come out to get him.

### THE EVIL MACHINES

As I spoke with many people who had been traumatically injured by mechanical equipment, I found that men and women alike frequently transformed the machine by which they had been injured into a monsterlike creature who deliberately wanted to harm them in their dreams.

Dee, whose left hand was severely injured when her glove was caught in the rollers of an industrial machine and pulled her hand into them, had three violent nightmares about all the machines at work closing in on her, as though to devour her.[6] The third time, Dee recognized it was a nightmare and woke herself up. She explained to me that, in fact, each machine is bolted to the floor and cannot move. Yet the dream seemed so real she could not bring herself to return to the factory where the accident happened. (Dee was helped to reduce her fears by some of the visualization activities described at the end of the chapter.)

This dreamer exaggerated the already traumatic experience. The machines that were closing in on her in the nightmare, as though in a concerted attack, were ones that could have inflicted greater damage. They seemed malevolent and intent on mutilation.

## THE OUT-OF-CONTROL MACHINE

This pattern of dramatizing an already horrendous situation, making it far worse, is a common characteristic of trauma in dreams.

George, like Dee, found himself subjected to nightmares about the machine that caused his injury. He had almost lost his left hand when he was operating a machine at work; it went out of control, chipping two of his wrist bones, severing nine finger tendons, and slashing his median nerve. George had a long and painful recovery with little hope of full restoration.

The first dream that George recalled after surgery was one in which he was using his hand normally in a fist. This man in his prime of life felt understandably angry about his situation. The next several dreams were replays of the accident that exaggerated what actually happened. In one of these nightmares, the same machine completely severed his left hand, leaving it dangling by a piece of skin. In another, the machine:

> . . . kicked-jumped off the table and became tangled in my sleeve, digging a deep channel up my arm. While I was fighting it off with the other arm, I got two fingers of the right hand cut off.

When I asked George what it would mean to injure his right hand as well, he replied, "My life would be over." Since his right hand was dominant, as long as he had the use of it, he felt he could function. The machine that had damaged his left hand became animated in his dreams, actively seeking to harm him like a villain. In other dreams of the same time, George would hear the machine in his basement spinning out of control across the floor.

An important turning point in George's healing process occurred when he acquired some protection from the machine in his dreams, as we'll see in "Strategies for Coping with Nightmares" on page 165.

## TRAUMATIC REPLAY NIGHTMARES

A team of hand therapists and physicians reported finding that injured people who had exact flashbacks, including nightmares, of their original traumas were more likely to return to work sooner than those who had exaggerated flashbacks about their injuries.[7]

About half of the sixty-one patients in this study experienced flashbacks such as Dee had in her nightmares, depicting the original injury with danger of additional impairment; about a third had exact replay flashbacks such as Peter's nightmares; and only a little over 10 percent of the subjects had flashbacks such as George's nightmares of the original impairment being more severe, damaging the other hand as well.[8]

The researchers reasoned that each category of flashback served a different psychological purpose.[9] Replay flashbacks, they thought, had a more positive purpose. The patient appeared to be actively searching for ways to have altered the outcome, thus preventing the injury. These patients seemed to develop a greater sense of control and feel more able to guard against such accidents in the future. The patients who imagined suffering worse injuries than they actually sustained had increased anxiety and tended to avoid situations that were associated with the trauma. They had less sense of control and remained afraid of being hurt further.

The more sense of control we have over what has happened to us in a past accident or illness, the more control we have over preventing injuries in the present and the future, the better able we will be to adapt to our problem and get on with our lives. The more we feel that what we do makes a difference, the quicker our rehabilitation will be.

Regardless of the type of nightmare you might have after an injury or onset of an illness, replaying it exactly or making the affliction worse than it was, you start the process of gaining control when you are able to change the dream content for the better. What can you do to increase your sense of control? First of all, you need to express whatever it is you feel about being injured.

### EXPRESSING THE EMOTIONS

Getting your feelings out is essential. Don had lost several fingers of his hand when a co-worker turned on a machine without realizing that Don's hand was in the way of the blades. After he had surgery to graft skin onto the areas where it had been torn off, Don was tormented by nightmares replaying the accident for six out of the nine nights that he was hospitalized. During the daytime, Don tried to talk with nurses to explain what he was experiencing, but they never seemed to have time enough to hear his whole story.

It was only when Don's girlfriend arrived from out of town and he was finally able to describe the accident in detail, fully expressing his emotional reactions, that he got relief from his nightmares. As he held his girlfriend's hand in his uninjured one, relating the part of the incident where he heard his bones breaking, he felt his girlfriend's hand "wince." He told me, "I knew she was really listening then, and that made all the difference."

Injured people need to talk about their accidents and any nightmares; they need to vent their feelings and fears to a compassionate listener. Otherwise, the pain stays inside them, gets covered up, and festers in nightmares for years to come.

When Bobby, a boy who had been crippled, awakened weeping from a nightmare, he was told by the night nurse to go back to sleep and stop disturbing the other children. Perhaps this nurse was too busy or uninterested; she may have had no notion of what to say to the child to ease his bad dreams. Fortunately, when the day nurse arrived and heard that Bobby had been sobbing hysterically from a nightmare the previous night, she managed to find time to hear the boy's dream that his father had been killed in the war. Just telling a nightmare can be the first step in overcoming it. After I had the nightmare described at the beginning of this chapter, I awoke my husband to tell him about it. Psychological healing is as important as physical recovery. Like myself, Don and Bobby found relief from a compassionate listener.

Coping with your feelings about what has happened to you is an essential step in your recovery process. Another major step in healing completely is to resolve your sense of increased vulnerability. Many men and women who have sustained serious injury or illness feel as though the world has become a more dangerous place.

### ◇ Dreams Revealing Increased Vulnerability

At first, this fear is often realistic. A person who has broken a limb needs to exercise caution that the bone is not further stressed or bumped. A raw wound from surgery has to be protected from irritation or pressure. Among the recovering people I spoke with, several cited a fear of crowds. Being in a situation with hundreds of people, as at a movie theater or sporting event, increased their anxiety about being hurt again. Even going into a crowded store or market could make some recovering people break out in a sweat. During this stage, it is helpful to wear a protective apparatus, such as a splint, that signals to others a need for physical space. Having another person accompany you is also a good idea. If a person who has been injured continues to feel excessively cautious, beyond the point when physical healing has taken place, a psychological problem can develop.[10] These fears of being re-injured often become topics of dreams.

During the first two months or so following surgery for a severe injury or illness, people do need a protected environment. Under the umbrella of caring relatives and friends, as well as professional contacts, they can regain skills, learn new ones, and gradually move toward restored self-sufficiency. But it is their own actions—their efforts to pleasurably participate in life —that are most potent.

### ◇ Dreams Indicating a Fear of Relapse

One of the fears that hangs over the person who has been seriously ill or injured is the danger of relapse.

### EDITH RESTERILIZES THE BOTTLES

Edith, a woman who had to have an emergency angioplasty to clear a blocked artery, had the following dream shortly after her return from the hospital. In view of what happened later, I can't help wondering whether this dream was predictive, as well as expressing her resentment over having been ill:

> It is my duty to collect mother's milk for impoverished babies who need it. My grand-daughter, or a baby her age, is playing with the mother's milk with grimy little hands. I get so angry I try to spank her and pinch her. I'm really mad that I have to resterilize the bottles.

In this dream, Edith vented her anger at herself, her "naughty child" who made it necessary to go through a whole process of cleaning bottles again. Her "bad little girl" was causing trouble. "If I had exercised more, if I had eaten more healthfully . . ." Wounded or sick dreamers often wish they had behaved better in the past. Edith had even commented to me, "I'm going to be a good girl," before mentioning this dream. When I asked Edith to tell me how mother's milk was different from regular milk, she replied that it was "life-giving nourishment, like oxygen." Obviously the milk in her dream was a metaphor for the precious oxygen she needed to function well; it was being contaminated by the thoughtless child part of herself, infuriating the dreamer. Dreamers frequently blame themselves for becoming ill or having an accident.

Edith had done well on a treadmill test a little over two weeks after the original procedure. However, about six weeks following the first crisis, she began experiencing some of the same symptoms again. Tests revealed that the same artery had started to reclose. Perhaps the "resterilization" of the bottles in Edith's dream was a forecast of the need that arose to repeat the angioplasty.

A larger balloon was used for the second angioplasty, with apparently good results, and a second treadmill test went well. Understandably, Edith feels "a little shaky about the whole thing." She hopes to avoid having to undergo bypass surgery. So far, all looks promising and Edith has returned to work.

Anger, as well as fear of relapse, may be a part of postoperative dreams. Don't be surprised if you find yourself having to cope with either of these powerful emotions.

## GILDA RADNER COMBATS THE HAMMER-MAN

Gilda Radner, the late delightful comedienne, had been diagnosed with ovarian cancer only two years after her marriage to actor Gene Wilder. In her book, *It's Always Something*,[11] Radner gave a courageous account of her battle with this disease, which has low odds of survival. Although she ultimately died at the age of forty-two, about two-and-a-half years after she was first diagnosed, Radner made a number of discoveries about the value of healthy living and loving that are a worthy memorial.

Radner described how frightened she felt when she returned from three weeks in the hospital after having had a total hysterectomy.[12] Over a year later, Radner appeared to be doing well. She had completed chemotherapy treatments and radiation therapy, as well as various other procedures. Her health seemed to be returning, her career was thriving, and her spirits were high. Then one of Radner's friends from her therapy group died from cancer. The sadness over the loss of her friend probably reawakened her fears for herself, because at that time she dreamed:

. . . that a very thin and hollow-eyed man in a hospital gown stood on our bed with a hammer ready to bludgeon Gene [her husband] and Sparkle [their dog] to death. I ran in and jumped on the bed to stop him. He turned and viciously threw the hammer at me. With great dexterity and finesse, I caught the hammer in my hand. Then I woke up.[13]

Radner did not comment on the images of her dream, but it is obvious that the thin and hollow-eyed man is the specter of illness and death; she described herself in much the same terms after her first hospitalization for cancer. Here Radner's most precious relationships were being threatened—images that probably stood for her innermost self. She was defending them with "great dexterity and finesse." Indeed, her response was a valiant attempt to fight off the recurrence that eventually killed her. At the time of this dream, she seemed to be successful, and blood tests taken a few days afterward were reported to be fine, but a little over three weeks later tests showed ominous changes. Then the blood tests that had been reported as normal actually turned out to be a computer error; the signs of change for the worse had been present at the time of her dream. Fear of relapse is a realistic one that people who have been seriously ill constantly battle. But, in catching the dream hammer, Radner was still actively engaged in combat. We all need such courage.

We have seen that fear of a further injury or illness, feeling increased vulnerability, and having nightmares that replay or worsen the incident are typical responses to a trauma. If you have been traumatized by a natural disaster, or by an accident leading to an injury, or by surgery for an illness, there are some crucial steps you can take that will help you avert a severe post-traumatic stress reaction or assist you to vanquish an already present negative response.

### ◇ Self-Help After a Trauma

Here are some of the vital steps you can follow to help yourself overcome a trauma:

#### 1. TALK ABOUT THE TRAUMA.
Your friends will understand a need to talk about what has happened to you and how you feel about it. Sharing your emotions with them eases the psychological impact.

## 2. WRITE ABOUT THE TRAUMA.

If you don't have a friendly ear available, and it is possible to write, describe the accident or illness in words. Studies have shown that the mere recording of unpleasant events can have a psychotherapeutic effect. If your injury prevents writing, or no people are available, talk into a tape recorder. Record your emotions onto paper or tape.

## 3. RESUME YOUR USUAL ROUTINE AS SOON AS POSSIBLE.

Resuming daily activities restores a sense of control over the situation. Work itself may be therapeutic, when practical. Sometimes alternative forms of conducting business can be arranged, such as giving dictation rather than writing. Surround yourself with friendly, familiar routine—people and environment—as much as possible.

## 4. KEEP LIFE IN BALANCE.

Eat nutritious foods, drink fluids, and get adequate rest and exercise. Increasing physical activity helps relieve stress.

## 5. ASSIST OTHERS WHO ARE IN DISTRESS.

The activity of helping others can reduce your own suffering. Give verbal and physical comfort. But remember that concentrating on others may delay dealing with your own emotions. Be sure you give yourself the emotional expression you need. This will enable you to better help others as well as to heal yourself.

## 6. JOIN A SUPPORT GROUP TO DISCUSS REACTIONS.

Sharing traumatic experiences with other people in a group reduces their painful intensity. If you have suffered a severe physical trauma or personal loss, seek individual therapy or counseling. Don't deny feeling agitated or out of control; denial can increase unpleasant emotions. Stay aware of your feelings and work with them as they emerge.

## 7. ENGAGE IN SELF-NURTURING ACTIVITIES.

Give yourself careful, loving attention. Undertake only such new projects as you can comfortably and pleasurably do; consider postponing major, stressful projects. Practice relaxation or meditation techniques or prayer.

## 8. CONFRONT THE CIRCUMSTANCES OF THE TRAUMATIC EVENT.

When you feel able to do so, and if it's applicable and practical, return to the scene of the trauma, with supportive friends and/ or equipment that make you feel safe. Being able to confront the same or a similar situation may prevent the development of a phobic reaction to it.

Most traumatic experiences leave people feeling helpless and out of control. Whatever you can do to re-establish a sense of control is helpful. If you have survived an earthquake, or another natural disaster, such activities as storing supplies, learning evacuation routes, and making preparations for any future recurrences are helpful. If you have fallen ill and suspect your diet or life-style habits have contributed, changing to more nutritious eating and healthful exercise will give you a sense of being able to avert further trouble.

Another tactic for coping with post-traumatic stress is becoming active in any nightmares you may have about the trauma, as suggested in the next section.

## ◇ STRATEGIES FOR COPING WITH NIGHTMARES

### ◇ Characteristics of Nightmares

Whether a person has just had a physical or an emotional crisis, the nightmares that typically follow are of two types:

#### 1. CHASE OR ATTACK.

The dreamer is chased or attacked. He or she attempts to escape from harm by running away or hiding.

#### 2. OTHER HORRIFIC HAPPENING.

The dreamer has a horrendous experience, which may be a replay or worsening of a trauma, or it may be a depiction of current pain.

In both of these dilemmas, the dreamer usually:

- feels afraid
- feels helpless
- has little or no control
- gets hurt, dies or is killed

### RUNNING AND HIDING

If you are the victim in a chase or attack nightmare, the probability is that you respond in the dream in the typical way—by running away or hiding, as we saw in the preceding examples. You may find yourself in a dream trying to escape some animal or object that represents your physical trauma, like George's machine. It's a very common nightmare after a crisis. Fortunately, you can use the following techniques to cope with such dreams.

### HOPELESS AND HELPLESS

Sometimes there is no specific villain in a nightmare; bad things just happen. We saw how Bejay dreamed of giving painful birth to a jagged car fender; she was a victim without an attacker. When I was terrified in the dream by a pounding on the pavement, the sight of my deceased father, and rising into the air like a wraith, I was suffering without a specific person or animal or thing causing it. Nonetheless, these images represented current pain and fear.

As we saw, people who have been through extreme traumas such as violent accidents dream replays of it, duplicating the exact incident or exaggerating it.

All nightmares are characterized by feelings of fear that range from moderate discomfort or frustration to outright terror. There is usually a sensation of helplessness and hopelessness in the dreamer. It seems as though nothing can be done to circumvent the harmful or fatal outcome. Sometimes this feeling is underscored by images of being paralyzed or trapped. Helplessness is often associated with the dreamer's sense of having no control. Nightmares involving cars with failing brakes or going off cliffs emphasize the dreamer's inability to change the ongoing scenario. The climax of a nightmare often comes the second before the dreamer is about to be fatally wounded. Sometimes the dreamer, or some other dream character, is badly injured, suffers, dies, or is killed, and the dream proceeds to further awful events.

#### ◇ Tactics for Coping with Nightmares

We can break the cycle of a worsening nightmare, or a series of recurrent bad dreams, by *changing our behavior within the dream.* This may seem impossible if you have never tried it, but it can be done, and has been accomplished by numerous dreamers. Changing your behavior in the dream not only transforms the nightmare, it changes the way you feel in the waking state. Learning to become an active participant in your dream, rather than a passive victim, develops your self-confidence. It dissolves the feeling of helplessness and begins to restore a sense of control in your life.

If you find yourself troubled by a nightmare, examine the following methods and try applying them to the next bad dream. Even if you haven't had a nightmare, the techniques are useful tools for coping with any that might arise in the future.

## 1. FACING YOUR DREAM ENEMIES

When you first find yourself pursued or attacked by a villain in a dream, turn around and face it/him/her. You can actually remember during the dream, "I don't have to run and hide. I can turn around and face my dream enemy." You can order the pursuer to stop: "You're only a dream image!" Sometimes merely confronting the villains in your dreams is enough to deprive them of their power. Take action. Tigers sometimes shrink into pussycats.

## 2. FIGHTING YOUR DREAM ENEMIES

If you are being attacked in a dream, you can fight back. Psychologically, it is better to fight back than to run and hide from dream villains; it's a more adaptive response, with a better chance of success. I call this principle: "Confront and conquer danger in your dreams." Get help if you feel overwhelmed by the dream enemy. Remember, it's your dream. You can bring anyone or anything into it to help you cope. Any figure you think of as strong or protective can be called to appear in your dream. Draw upon your inner resources. Create allies and dream friends to assist you.

Fighting back is easier to remember and carry out in a dream than befriending a dream enemy. Once you have discovered that it's possible to change an ongoing dream, and that you have more power than you realized in dreams, you may decide you would rather question your dream attackers, asking what they want and how you can help them, rather than demolishing them.

### 3. RECONCILING WITH YOUR DREAM ENEMIES

Some people are troubled by the idea of combating a part of themselves in imagery or in dreams. They prefer to approach negative dream figures in a spirit of reconciliation, questioning these images. Dreamers can bargain with threatening dream figures, offering desirable behavior changes in exchange for something. Engage in constructive dialogue. Anthropologist Barbara Tedlock, who studied dream interpretation with a Mayan shaman in Guatemala, said that in this system, dreamers are advised to "complete" the dream.[14] Interacting with your dream figures, talking with them, and asking them for advice are some ways of completing a dream. Your threatening dream figures can be transformed into friendly ones who can provide help. You can even ask your dream figures for advice or gifts to remember them by.

### 4. LOVING YOUR DREAM ENEMIES

Still other people like the idea of embracing the threatening figures in their dreams. Stephen LaBerge, a pioneer in the field of lucid dreaming, reported a milestone dream in which he was able to tell a horrific giant that he loved it, incorporating the dream image into himself during the dream.[15] Other dreamers have surrounded their dream villains with golden light, transforming them into benign or even beneficent images.

### 5. REDREAMING

Help yourself realize the options you have during a dream. Close your eyes and think about your nightmare. Pretend you can see it again, exactly the way it happened. Now, in your imagination, think of something else that could happen. Make the dream better. Turn it into a good dream. Change it. Maybe a superhero or religious figure helps you. Maybe you are rescued by people using special equipment. Perhaps you discover a magic weapon. Maybe you make friends with the thing that frightened you. Make the dream different in any way you want. Picture the dream the way you want it to be. See the details, the colors, the shapes, and the sounds. You may even want to draw a picture of this new dream.

Jung called the practice of working with dream images in waking fantasy "active imagination."[16] Redreaming an improved dream helps you diffuse anxiety about the original dream, shows you that there are other possibilities than what happened, and gives you the chance to practice using them.

## 6. LUCID DREAMING

Another approach to coping with frightening dreams is becoming conscious during them. This consciousness within a dream, called "lucid dreaming," is a technique that can be learned and then utilized as a tool in many areas of your life. (Suggestions on developing lucid dreaming are given at the end of the next chapter.) If you become aware of the fact that you're dreaming during a dream, realize that you no longer need to be afraid. You are dreaming and can do anything you want. You may want to act out your redream in the dream.

### ◇ Dissociating from the Afflicted Body Part

I have previously explained how one of the protective reactions people adopt when they have been hurt is to dissociate themselves from the injured body part. They speak of "the hand" instead of "my hand," etc. Because the body part is not functioning in a normal fashion, it feels foreign and is psychologically rejected. The body part is viewed as a thing rather than a living extension of the person. One of the chief goals of physical therapy is to assist the patient in reintegrating the injured body part. Dreamers register their dissociation from their ill or injured bodies by images of dead or inorganic appendages, especially if numbness is present.

### OLIVER SACKS'S INORGANIC LEG

Sacks's account of his nightmares following surgery to repair his quadriceps tendon is a valuable example of this reaction.[17] He demonstrated the amazing variety with which the injured body part can appear in dreams. Having lost all sensation in his leg, Sacks said he was tormented by hundreds of nightmares in which his leg was made of plastic, marble, cement, or sand. The damaged limb almost always seemed to be formed of some inorganic material in his nightmares. These dreams portrayed the feeling of being dissociated from his injured part and the perception of having a cast upon his leg; they also depicted his loss of sensation in the limb. In other nightmares, his cast was empty, made of mist, or his leg was a chalky envelope. In still other bad dreams, Sacks saw his leg filled with a verminous mass of bones, bugs, and pus. The worst nightmare of all was one in which his leg was composed of darkness or shadow—it seemed as though life could never return to such a leg.

Eventually, through a series of treatments and activities, Sacks was once again able to perceive his leg as a normal part of himself, and he became able to use it naturally.

### ◇ "Reowning" Your Afflicted Body Part

If you have been impaired, try to maintain a psychological connection to the injured area. Deliberately speak of "my" finger, "my" foot, "my" breast, or any other hurt area of your body. It was yours, it is yours, and even if only a portion of it remains, it is still a part of you.

At times you may notice yourself emotionally disconnecting from a wounded or diseased area, speaking of "it" as though this part were independent of your whole self. Readopt this damaged body part, even if it is disfigured, mutilated, or deformed. Love it, cherish it, cradle it. Know that this part of yourself has served you well in the past and is capable of learning to do so again, even if its service will be different.

If you have totally lost a part of your body, through accident or surgical removal, you will undoubtedly grieve over this loss. This is, of course, a normal response. You may continue to perceive sensation in a missing limb or digit, as amputees sometimes do with the so-called "phantom limb." Such people may experience pleasant sensations as well as painful ones in the "ghost" of the missing part. I have heard reports of people getting pleasure from imagining the missing part being massaged or stroked soothingly. You might wish to try soothing the missing part. In any case, cherish what a lost body part has done for you in the past. Ask your body to take over the tasks of the missing part.

In a psychological sense, disowning an injured area of your body can slow your recovery, preventing the wounded area from being reintegrated into normal body movements and processes. Accepting, and better yet, actively loving the site of destruction, whether whole or in remnants, cannot hurt you and may allow healing to occur more rapidly. When you reintegrate an injured area of your body in your thinking, you speed reintegration on every level.

*6a. Recovery from the flu: Sickness*     Drawings by Patricia Garfield

*This pair of pictures had been drawn on the front and back of the same sheet of paper. The drawings are mirror images of sickness and wellness. The image originally on the front of the paper, Sickness, 6a, depicts my subjective experience: stuffy head, draining sinus, hot, aching eyes, and irritated throat. A mist of sickly green and purple gloom surrounds me. The image originally on the back of the page, Wellness, 6b, depicts my hoped-for recovery. I visualized brilliant golden light emanating from a jewel located in the middle of my forehead, its radiance clearing and healing my sinus, nasal, and throat passages. A soft golden light streams outward from my face and body. I used cooling colors for my drawing on the reverse side of the paper, to*

*(continued)*

*6b. Recovery from the flu: Wellness*          Drawings by Patricia Garfield

counteract the hot, feverish feeling I was experiencing in my head and throat.

By drawing wellness on the reverse side of an illustration of your illness, depicting the opposite conditions, you help yourself focus on contrasting, healthier feelings. By concentrating on these better conditions, you may even improve blood flow that can speed your recovery.

## ◇ DREAM ACTIVITIES: USING ART AND IMAGERY TO HELP YOU RECOVER

### ◇ 1. Monitor your dreams for any changes in the affected body part, its symptoms and its functioning.

We have seen how the damaged body part appears consistently in the dreams of people who have developed an illness or sustained an injury. The afflicted body part debuts when the disturbance first appears and it does not bow out until normalcy has been restored. By now you realize how houses and vehicles often represent the dreamer's body, and that parts of houses or vehicles often symbolize the afflicted area of the body. You have been alert to any dream that suggests damage or malfunctioning in a dream house or vehicle, noticing the forces that impinge upon it and how you, as yourself in the dream, act to deal with the situation.

After a crisis, it's important to continue monitoring your dreams to watch for any changes in your afflicted body part. Watching what is happening to your body part in dreams allows you to assess how your healing is progressing.

### EXAMPLE: FREUD GOES HORSEBACK RIDING

Freud reported that he had only one dream that could be attributed to a somatic source. He had been suffering from boils—in particular, a painful one the "size of an apple" that arose at the base of his scrotum and gave him the most unbearable pain with each step. He managed to carry on with his busy schedule but was exceedingly uncomfortable. One night he was only able to sleep with the aid of a poultice applied to his perineum, the area between the genitals and anus. These facts were dramatically rendered in his dream:

> I was riding on a grey horse, timidly and awkwardly to begin with, as though I were only reclining upon it. I met one of my colleagues, P., who was sitting high on a horse, dressed in a tweed suit, and who drew my attention to something (probably to my bad seat). I now begin to find myself sitting more and more firmly and comfortably on my highly intelligent horse, and noticed that I was feeling quite at home up there. My saddle was a kind of bolster, which completely filled the space between its neck and

crupper. In this way I rode straight in between two vans. After riding some distance up the street, I turned round and tried to dismount, first in front of a small open chapel that stood in the street frontage. Then I actually did dismount in front of another chapel that stood near it. My hotel was in the same street; I might have let the horse go to it on its own, but I preferred to lead it there. It was as though I should have felt ashamed to arrive at it on horseback. A hotel "boots" was standing in front of the hotel; he showed me a note of mine that had been found, and laughed at me over it. In the note was written, doubly underlined: "No food" and then another remark (indistinct) such as "No work," together with a vague idea that I was in a strange town in which I was doing no work.[18]

Freud explained that he had never ridden a horse, that he had never dreamed of riding before, and that he was certainly not fit to do so. He saw his dream as a denial of his illness, and a wish not to be afflicted with the boil on the perineum. Freud noticed that the gray color of the horse was the precise shade of the salt-and-pepper-colored jacket of his colleague in the dream; he associated this color with his own taste for highly spiced food, which may have caused the boils. He commented that this particular colleague liked to "ride his high horse." He described another friend who had commented that Freud seemed "firmly in the saddle" in a particular situation. The dream obviously combined psychological elements with images stimulated by his physical condition. There was also a pun on the phrase "my bad seat," referring not only to his horsemanship but also his physical problem. Freud seemed to be prescribing for himself in the dream as well, suggesting he would do well to stop work and eliminate highly spiced food for the time being.

From the physical point of view, notice that the pressure created by the swollen boil probably suggested to Freud's dreaming mind the notion that similar pressure would be produced in this same area of the body when horseback riding. The poultice applied to the painful area that enabled Freud to get to sleep was transformed in his dream into the image of a bolster-saddle on which the dreamer rode. (We saw how it is important to be alert for any images in your dreams that seem to be exerting pressure on a specific area of your body.) Freud's dream indicated that he was not ready to resume normal activity and seemed to be warning him about the dangers of highly spiced food for his body.

What do your current dreams reveal about the stage of your physical recovery?

◇ 2. Select a metaphor for your injury or illness.

In general, the strategy for using art to help you heal involves three steps:

1. Select a metaphor.
   Ask yourself, "What does my injury/disease feel like?" Your answer will be your metaphor. If you wish, select a metaphor for your illness or injury from one of your dreams.
2. Draw a picture of how your afflicted body part feels.
3. Visualize a positive change in the afflicted area.

Each of these steps has several components. You might wish to read the following section and then try applying the concepts to yourself. If you do not have an injury or illness at the moment, select an area of your body that sometimes troubles you. Discover what you can learn about yourself by going through the following procedure. If you have already drawn a picture of your afflicted body part, you may wish to make another drawing now that shows how you feel currently and compare it to the previous drawing.

◇ 3. Draw your injured or ill body part.

Drawing your pain can reduce its intensity. There is something about expressing a physical discomfort on paper that drains its power. Here's how to do it:

A. GATHER ART SUPPLIES.
Ideally, set up an area to work with standard-sized paper and a box of crayons, markers, or pencils with a wide assortment of colors, including warm and cool colors, strong and weak, dark and light, colors you like and those you don't. If these supplies are not convenient, black pencil on white paper is better than not drawing. The important thing is to make marks that represent the sensations in your injured body part. If your dominant hand is damaged, use your other one.

## B. STUDY SENSATIONS IN THE AFFLICTED BODY PART.

Close your eyes for a moment and tune into the way your body feels at this moment. Concentrate your thoughts on the injured area and allow yourself to fully perceive it, regardless of the degree of discomfort. Ask yourself, "How does my injury feel right now?" Open your eyes and pick up a drawing instrument.

*Examples:* "My leg feels like a skinny stick from being in the cast so long. My foot feels totally flat; I can't feel any arch. My toes are swollen puffy and fluffy. There's no feeling at all in my great toe"; "My stomach feels like everything is going to fall out, as though there were an open space, or a blown-up balloon in my stomach"; Virginia Woolf, the British novelist and critic, described her migraine headaches as "enraged rats gnawing at the base of my brain"; Dennis Potter, the contemporary British television writer and novelist, described the arthritic psoriasis in his feet as "feeling as though rats were chewing off my toes."

*In this example of objective appearance versus subjective sensation, the emotional reaction a woman had to her eye infection becomes progressively clearer. The first drawing, 7a, the objective appearance, shows the irritation, burning sensation, and itchiness she was experiencing. The second and third drawings, 7b and 7c, the subjective sensations, more dramatically depict the pain and sadness that were associated with her discomfort and her current condition.*

*Be sure to include your emotional responses in any drawings of an illness, an injury or a dream.*

Drawings by Phyllis Clark Harvey

*7a. Objective appearance: Eye infection*

*7b, c. Subjective sensations: Eye infection*

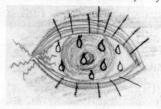

## C. DRAW THE INJURED OR ILL BODY PART.

Show the whole afflicted body part, with or without the rest of your body attached. Either way you do it is fine. Examine the drawings in this book for examples of illnesses and a variety of injuries. How is your injury or illness different and how is it similar?

## D. DEPICT SPECIFIC SENSATIONS IN THE AFFLICTED BODY PART.

Answer the following questions with your marker:

> Where is the pain greatest?
> What area does the pain cover?
> What shape is the pain?
> What color is the pain?
> Are any areas too hot?
> Are any areas too cold?
> Are any areas swollen?
> Are any areas itchy?
> Are any areas wounded?
> Are any areas broken?
> Are there any other sensations present?

*Examples:* Look at the sample drawings that show the location of the pain, often drawn in jagged lines. Areas that are too hot are often in warm colors; areas too cold are often in cool colors, but not always. A victim of an explosion that burned him depicted hope in yellow.

## E. DEPICT THE FUNCTIONING OF THE AFFLICTED BODY PART.

When you try to move or use the body part, what does it feel like? Put your answer into the picture.

*Examples:* "It's as though there is a stiff hinge in my wrist attached to blocks of wood"; "It's as though my neck were the base of a lightbulb that's screwed in wrong"; "There are knots in my shoulders"; "My hand feels like a mitten with three fingers"; "I feel like I'm all toes"; "There's a burning red spot in my lower back"; "My back is like a tight band twisted all in one direction"; "My chest is like raw beef"; "Electrical flashes run up my leg."

### F. DEPICT EMOTIONS.

How do you feel about the condition of your injured or ill body? Represent these emotions in the drawing, too. You may use lines, masses of color, symbols, or objects—whatever feels appropriate.

*Example:* A child who had been badly burned and permanently scarred in a fire drew her face covered with small scars that turned into tears.

### G. IDENTIFY THE DRAWING AND COMMENT ON IT.

In the corner or on the back of the drawing, put your name and date. Add any brief remarks you wish to make as you regard your work. Save the drawing for future comparisons. Drawings collected over the first few months following a trauma usually show dramatic differences.

*Example:* People suffering from burns often have initial drawings full of hot colors, red and orange, or black, including fire, burning suns, erupting volcanos; as their fevers recede and they begin to heal, cool greens and blues and the sea emerge in their drawings.

Congratulations! You've made a giant step on the road to accepting and coping with your condition. You've allowed yourself to look your pain squarely in the face. You'll be able to assess changes, temporary setbacks, or leaps forward as they occur. You've located some of the anchors on which to hook healing imagery.

◇ 4. Let your image speak.

Now that you've found an image for your injury or illness, and drawn it, give your image a voice. Pretend you can talk with the image of your injured or ill body part. What would it say? What does it want to do? Ask your afflicted body part:

1. How does it feel to be as you are?
2. What is good about it?
3. What don't you like about it?
4. What do you need to feel better?

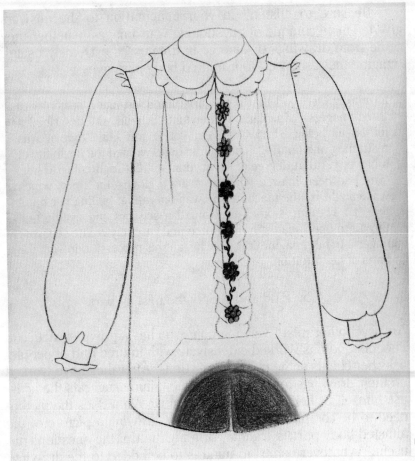

*8. Healing Dream Image: The "Caretaker Smock" speaks*

Drawing by Patricia Garfield

The Caretaker Smock was an image in one of my dreams the night after I had oral surgery to remove an infection at the root of one of my teeth (an apicoectomy). Early dreams of that night expressed unpleasant feelings evoked by the operation. The most positive part of the series of dreams that night was the idiosyncratic image of the caretaker smock in the third dream, so I chose this one to draw and to endow with a voice. Its message was that now I could begin to take care of myself—this helped facilitate my healing:

"I am fresh, clean, and white. I slip on easily over any clothing because I'm roomy. I have large patch pockets for carrying all sorts of useful tools wherever I go.

"I am decorated with cheerful colors. The rising sun at my base reminds the troubled person that a new day begins each morning. The flowers on my buttonholes depict bright new growth. I make people

(continued)

Be sure to "listen" in your imagination to the answers given. This technique of questioning your images, whether they come from drawings or emerge in dreams, is extremely useful. Imagine the responses your injured body part gives.

*Example:* Dee said that her injured hand felt like a mitten with three "fingers." Speaking for her injured hand, she described a mitten as being warm and safe, yet at the same time it was restricting and limiting. The injured hand wanted the flexibility of a glove, yet that degree of separation still felt frightening to her. (She had been injured while wearing a glove—the tip of which was caught by the machine she was operating, pulling her hand into it.) The hurt body part wanted a scissors and needle and thread to open seams in the mitten and carefully create separate fingers. In her imagination, Dee began this process, following the hints of her intuition.

### ◇ 5. Find and supply the missing part.

Art psychotherapist Evelyn Simon, who has a private practice in Phoenix and has worked extensively with injured and ill people, asks her clients some pointed questions. After they have worked on their drawings for a period of time, Simon suggests the artist ask himself or herself, "What is missing? What does the picture need to be complete?" Whether one is drawing a picture of the afflicted body part, a trauma, or a nightmare, the questions are useful. Whatever comes to mind is to be added to the drawing. Simon believes, "The artistic resolution of the artwork parallels the solution to the problem"[19]

*Example:* When I asked myself this question about the first drawing I had made of my injured left hand, the answer was obvious. The wooden blocks and stiff hinge desperately needed flexibility. What is missing from your drawing?

---

*happy to look at. I'm beautiful and practical. Smocks are worn by artists—I am the art of caring.*

*"I have been worn by many people during this difficult time. I was worn by the dental assistant who stroked your cheek during the operation. I was worn by your surgeon when he greeted you kindly. I was worn by your daughter when she petted your leg and when she held your arm. I was worn by your husband when he read to you although his voice was tired. Anyone can wear me. Even you."*

◇ 6. "Satisfy your image."

Once you have imagined what might help your injured or ill body part, the next step is to provide it in the drawing and in visualizations.

Ann Sayre Wiseman, an expressive-arts therapist in Boston, has evolved fascinating techniques for coping with negative images, whether they arise in nightmares or from traumas people have experienced during the day. In her book, *Nightmare Help*, Wiseman summarizes one of her approaches: "Draw the dream. Cage the monster. Add your helpers. . . . Let the picture speak. Direct the rescue action. Create a good solution. Just draw help into your picture. Invent a safe place."[20] It's good advice.

Wiseman says that once we have an image for our hurt, emotional or physical, we need to "satisfy the image." We can supply what the afflicted area of our body needs in further drawings or simply by closing our eyes and letting our imagination roll out the inner pictures.

◇ 7. Transform your injury or illness image
by visualization.

### A. OPPOSITION IMAGERY

Some dreamers find that visualizing the opposite of what the injured or ill part feels like is comforting. Observe the force and direction of discomfort in your afflicted body part. Picture this force flowing, turning or moving in the opposite way. Take the parts that feel stiff or rigid and imagine them being flexible and free. Take the parts that feel too loose or unstable and provide, in your mind's eye, strengthening props. Give your afflicted body part what it needs.

*Example:* Maureen, the woman who felt her back was "like a tight band twisted all in one direction," imagined that she was able to reverse the twist. She pictured little men turning a crank to twist her back in the opposite direction until she could see her spine straight again.

### B. DILUTION IMAGERY

"Diluting" the intensity of the pain is another useful tactic. Picture the painful area of your injury or illness dissolving, becoming calm and soothed. You might find that images of water—warm or cool, depending on what seems to feel good—can help disperse the pain. Some people feel that the imagery of light pouring onto a disturbed area is especially beneficial.

*Example:* Peg, the woman whose pain in her back felt like a "focused red spot," visualized the hot spot dissolving, dispersing, and turning a pale pink.

## C. DIRECTIONAL IMAGERY

Picture a source of what your injured or ill body part needs and imagine it flowing into you. See sunlight, firelight, or another comforting heat radiating onto areas of your body that are too cold; see the heat penetrating and warming the chilled spots. For areas of your body that are too hot, picture a cool running stream, an icy waterfall, or fresh crisp snow; see it flowing or falling onto the overheated areas of your body; see them being soothed.

*Example:* People who suffer from migraines usually have constricted blood vessels of the neck while those of the head are dilated. They are often helped by picturing their *hands* becoming warmer; for example, by imagining they are warming their hands near a fire or holding a cup of hot chocolate or coffee in both hands. Imagery of this sort can actually ease physical discomfort by altering blood flow; the blood vessels in the hands dilate when visualizing heat, bringing the excess blood down from the head.

## D. COLOR IMAGERY

Some people find that their afflicted body parts are eased by visualization of colored light shining on them. Picture a favorite color as beams of bright light pouring onto your injured or ill body part. Choose a warm color such as rose, or a cool color, such as turquoise, depending upon whether you want the area to feel warmer or cooler. Perhaps you will prefer a brilliant white or golden light. Let the rays of the shining light bring healing energy.

*Examples:* Dawn, recovering from an operation on her face, was comforted by visualizing healing green light gleaming on her aching face. Barrie pictured shining white light coming from heaven and pure blue light coming from earth, meeting in the area of her body disturbance and healing it.

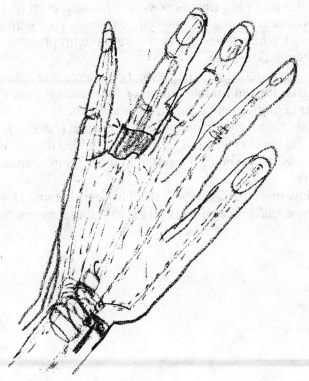

*9. Healing visualization for injury: Hand*    Drawing by Patricia Garfield

*This picture shows a healing visualization that I used for my hand. I pictured energy flowing into my hand from the central part of my body (red dotted lines on the right of each finger) and energy returning out of my hand (blue dotted lines on the left of each finger). I visualized my wedding ring as an additional source of energy, emitting golden light of its own. Although there was residual stiffness in my wrist, as shown by the sensation of a coiled spring and the actual metal plate (drawn in its true shape and size), my fingers and thumb felt strong and capable. In other visualizations, I imagined soothing pink lotion penetrating the numb area and lubricating green oil penetrating the stiff areas, with bone growing solid and firm around the metal plate.*

*Be sure to date any drawings you make of your afflicted body part and save them for comparison. By making a drawing of your healing visualizations you help focus your imagination on what is needed in your particular case.*

## E. GOAL IMAGERY

What is the best-possible recovery you can imagine? Picture this vividly. Dispel any discomforting symptoms. See the body part as normal and pain-free as possible. Make it even better. Visualize yourself moving the injured or ill body part with ease and grace. Let yourself find ways to live life with pleasure and joy. See yourself doing this.

If you practice positive imagery as described here on a regular basis, for ten minutes three or four times a day, especially prior to falling asleep at night, you can actually alter blood flow that may improve your symptoms. Relax and observe your body. Let all the tension flow out. Drift into a guided dream of yourself feeling well and whole. It's possible that you may enhance your recovery.

How does healing reveal itself in your dreams? How can we encourage this process? We will explore these questions next.

# 7

# HEALING DREAMS

> The machine that injured me is going across a mountain road in front of me as I am driving down. I have to swerve the BMW I'm driving to avoid the machine. I almost go over the cliff, if it weren't for the fact that the brakes don't lock up. I stop at the edge with two wheels hanging over.
>
> Injured dreamer
> Three months after surgery

George—the man who was severely injured by a machine that severed his median nerve, nine tendons, and chipped his wrist bones—had several nightmares in which the machine was inflicting even more damage (described in Chapter 6). The above dream was the first one since his operation in which George was not hurt. Although he continued to be in danger in the dream (with two wheels hanging over the edge of a cliff), and he still felt vulnerable (the machine was in his path, causing him to swerve), he felt more in control. It was an important turning point in George's recurrent dreams about his trauma. We'll see its implications below.

## ◇ DREAM IMAGES OF HEALING

During the healing phase, negative dream images about a trauma persist, but alongside them, positive images are born; I call these the healing images. When this stage arises, and how long it lasts, depends largely upon the severity of the initial trauma and the extent of any repair work. My broken arm was limited to fractures of the radius and wrist bones; no muscles, nerves, tendons, or skin were severed during the accident; all cutting consisted of surgical incisions, not jagged tears. I had to recover from the double fracture, the wounds created by the operation that cut skin, flesh, muscles, and ligament, in order to rearrange my wrist bones and the insertion of a metal plate.

People who have incurred greater physical damage than mine, or have crushed, burned, or torn body parts, especially nerves, spend more time in the healing phase before they are fully recovered. Likewise, their dream images of the trauma will linger longer. Those people with acute illnesses may have healing imagery early on; those with chronic illnesses will have healing images during periods of remission. Thus, some dreamers may experience healing imagery almost immediately, or within the first week; others require months. Recognizing the signs of dawning physical and mental health can help dreamers move in this direction more rapidly.

## ◇ Healing as Increased Protection

We saw how injury is accompanied by a sense of heightened vulnerability, a feeling of helplessness, and of being out of control. Not surprisingly, then, the restoration of health is often marked by the opposite feelings. When people who have been badly hurt or have been sick start to recover, they dream of images that give them a sense of greater protection and increased control.

### GEORGE'S MANEUVERABLE CAR

When I asked George, "What makes a BMW different from other cars?" he answered, "It's a good, stable racing car—one you can win with. It handles better than other cars." For George, then, his dream vehicle was one that conferred greater control (its better handling ability), and therefore, ability to cope with his difficult situation. He began to have a chance to "win" over his injury. Other dreamers choose different images of protection.

For George, the car body in his dream provided a protective shell between his body and the self-propelled machine. Previously, George had had no separation between himself and the machine in his dreams; it sliced into him just as it had done in waking life, or it caused even more damage. The fact that

George was now able to imagine himself surrounded by a protective car indicated that the psychological scars were beginning
to mend, as well as the physical ones. Although he was still
"hung up," with his car hanging over the cliff, he had begun to
cope in his dreams. This is a natural healing process that occurs
during dreams.

Watch for any dream image that reflects improved protection and increased control. It may take the form of a knight's
armor or be your own superb grace and skill. When you notice
such an image, encourage it by paying attention to it. Draw it,
as described in the previous chapter. At the very least, turn it
over in your thoughts and feelings, and absorb its power to heal.

### ◇ Healing as Increased Comfort and Acceptance of Limits

#### BRAD'S CADILLAC ON TRACKS

Brad was recovering from an operation that replaced his left hip.
The cartilage between his hip joint and the pelvic area had been
worn out, so that the rubbing of bone on bone caused him considerable pain. About two weeks following his hip replacement,
Brad was feeling better. He was using a hospital bed at home
and was getting around with crutches. During this time he
dreamed:

> My friend Joe has a store where prescriptions are sold. No busi-
> ness. He says he's a year too early for the area. [He actually has
> a different type of store that does very well.]
>
> Then I am in a parking lot. Joe has an old Cadillac with a
> rear window that is crazed and broken. I pull up in an old BMW
> sedan. It's red, rusty, and in need of paint. Joe goes to lunch with
> two old friends. I don't go so they can talk. There is a young man
> with business cards—all with notes on the backs—who sells real
> estate.
>
> I want to see Joe's other car, which is in the parking lot. It's
> an old Cadillac convertible that is surrounded by two vertical
> pipes or railroad-type railings, and it has railroad-type wheels on
> the car so it can roll back and forth. Inside is an army medical
> captain.

Here is a perfect example of the necessity for getting the
dreamer's associations to his or her images in the dream. For
George, a BMW was a highly desirable vehicle—a racing car
that could win with its good maneuverability and control. When

I asked Brad the same question, "What makes this brand of car different from others?" he replied, "It's smaller and more expensive. I don't like it. It's not worth the money. It's underpowered and not well put together."

Obviously, Brad was identifying in this dream with his own sense of being "underpowered and not well put together." Add to this basic negative meaning the idea of the car being "red, rusty, and in need of paint," and we can see that Brad did not yet feel in a good state of repair. In fact, this car may have symbolized Brad's body prior to the hip replacement, when each step was causing pain. The dream phrases of "no business" and being "too early for the area" underscore the same concept of incomplete recovery.

However, the other two cars in the dream begin to offer hope. Brad likes Cadillacs very much, enjoying their spaciousness and comfort. One of the dream Cadillacs was old, with a "crazed and broken" rear window, suggesting the dreamer still felt battered. As we discussed it, the second Cadillac, the one "surrounded by two vertical pipes," turned out to represent Brad's repaired body.

There were at least two sources to the strange arrangement of the second Cadillac described in Brad's dream. At the time of his dream, Brad was sleeping in a hospital bed, with its characteristic vertical railings, that had been installed in his home. These bars could easily be conceived of as the "railroad-type railings" that appeared in his dream. Moreover, the hip prosthesis itself consists of a rolling mechanism with smooth, gliding surfaces but a fairly limited range of motion.[1]

Clearly the person who has had a hip replacement must exercise certain cautions. When I discussed with Brad the odd apparatus surrounding the old Cadillac in his dream, he commented, "It was restrictive, like a good horse in a short corral." Brad suddenly realized that the "army medical captain" in the driver's seat reminded him of his surgeon. Thus, the wheels on the short span of railroad tracks seemed to represent Brad's prosthesis, with its gliding surfaces and limited range of motion. Although Brad felt somewhat "like a good horse in a short corral," and his favorite car appeared in a battered and restricted condition, it was there and functional.

The old Cadillac on tracks was a metaphor for Brad's body with his prosthesis. The limited range of Brad's prosthesis was a reality. Part of his healing involved accepting those limits. The "new" body was still old, it was restricted, but it was roomier than his body before surgery (the old, rusty BMW). Now it was more comfortable (like a Cadillac). In short, the new body was better. The fact that Brad's favorite car was available in the dream, that he might be able to give up the battered one he disliked that he had been driving, suggested the emergence of healing for this dreamer.

In your dreams, the vehicles that you drive or ride in can reveal many of your feelings about your body, especially in men. Women sometimes use car images as metaphors for their bodies, but more often they use clothes or houses. If you dream about a car, ask yourself questions about the brand of car, the model, and its features (using the guide on page 142 in Chapter 5). And don't be surprised if you see your surgeon hitching a ride.

### ◇ Healing as New Plant Growth and Lively Animals

Dream images of flowers, plants, and springtime in general are characteristic in the person who has begun to heal, as already mentioned. These images of fertility, which also often arise during the early months of pregnancy, of falling in love, or of undertaking new projects, are representative of the dreamer's sense of new growth in his or her body.

### MY GROWING PLANTS

Healing imagery began to surface in my own dreams the second night I was home from the hospital—five nights after having surgery. It was reassuring to see positive pictures appear in my dreams again after so many nightmares. In their first appearance, I dreamed:

> I live in a pretty area of a city, a rather historical area. At first I'm sitting in my living room, looking out a picture window onto a small, triangular-shaped "square" that's across from our house. Beyond it is a stone building of a mellow color. This makes a pleasant change. I think how it would be a pity to have some other construction there that would strike a harsh note in the mellow view.

Picture windows in dreams often reveal a change in a point of view, and this view was pleasant. The "mellow" color represented my improved mood. The dream continued:

The idea occurs to me that we could contribute money or raise funds to convert the grassy plot into a beautiful garden. It would complete the historical feeling and make the whole area harmonious. I notice a restaurant called "Dinner Inn" with an old-fashioned lamppost.

My plan to make the green area even more lovely symbolized my hope. A place of nourishment, the restaurant, was part of the picture. The dream continued:

Then I seem to be on the sidewalk in front of the house with a French friend, discussing the differences in tai chi in our respective countries. He demonstrates a move. I show him the parallel movement, *making a complete turnaround.* This stance involves holding up both hands in front of the chest and turning, with the knees bent. I get a good look at my left wrist. The cast is off and my arm is thin. It will need building up, but the shape of the wrist is good.

These dream observations about my wrist, which was still in a cast, proved to be quite accurate when the cast was later removed. The most dramatic metaphor in the dream was the "complete turnaround" I demonstrated to my friend. There is no doubt that my dreaming mind was sensing a change for the better.

The dream concluded with a scene in which I viewed the pretty blue-and-white exterior of my home with a historical marker on it. I spoke with a woman neighbor, who asked me, "How are you doing?" I replied, "Much better, thanks. I was just thinking how pleasant it would be if we were to convert this area into a garden." I pointed out my house, adding, "Wouldn't a garden complete the warm, pleasant feeling?" This dream marked the beginning of a steady improvement for me.

As always, the positive dream images were at first interspersed with negative ones, but as the healing accelerated, the positive pictures occurred more often. These signposts of a shift for the better included more images of growing plant life. A few days later I dreamed I was driving by attractively landscaped grounds, with sweeping green lawns and large spreading trees. The grass was the fresh, new color of early spring, though the trees were still bare. About two weeks after my surgery, a dream included a scene of two girls in a garden gathering blossoms from trees. Then three weeks after my surgery came a dream scene of driving in a pretty, wooded countryside and seeing exquisite blue blossoms on trees, called "delphinium blue." Observe how the flowery growth increased in lushness as I moved toward greater physical health. It seemed to be a literal growth from grass to abundant blossoms.

If you are recovering from an illness or injury, notice when images of green growth appear. Such images usually signal the commencement of your inner and outer healing. Draw them or meditate upon them. Attending to their presence can help bring them to full flower. A chief indicator of healing in dreams is positive "new growth" in various forms.

## MIMI'S FRISKY ANIMALS

Animal life in dreams may also indicate the beginning of a change for the better. This is especially so when the animals are cute and full of life. Cuddly, adorable creatures provide a strong contrast to post-surgical dreams of dead and dying animals. In one of my dreams during the first week home from the hospital, I saw a baby owl with dark feathers. For me, the owl represents the wise bird, particularly because the owl is the symbol of the graduate school I attended. A baby owl, then, suggested a small bit of newborn wisdom.

Mimi was tormented by dreams of being brutally raped following her hysterectomy. About three weeks later, her dreams showed a positive change that included several metaphors typical of the dreamer who is recovering:

> I'm talking on the telephone to a woman friend when I hear noises. I go to the picture window and look out onto our land. There is a beautiful spring scene—a lush field, green grass, trees in bloom. There are animals running around, kicking up their heels. I tell the person on the phone and call my husband to come look. A goose is chasing my favorite cat. They're all playing. I say to my husband, "Like you chase me, honey."

Along with Mimi's sense of new health as depicted in the images of spring, she was also expressing the revival of her "animal spirit." I have said that views through picture windows often describe a newly emerging point of view. Mimi's instincts were returning, her frisky readiness to "play" with her mate, just as the playful animals in her dream were doing. Having been through a period of pain sometimes allows us to enjoy pleasures more intensely. Green growth, fun-loving animals, and sexual interest all suggest the return of health. Be alert for such images whenever you are recovering from ill health or injury. They, too, are milestones on the road to wellness.

### ◇ Healing as Returning Sensuality

#### DINA'S REASSURANCE

When Dina, who was thirty-five, was scheduled for the removal of her uterus because of fibroids, her greatest fear was that she would be "neutered." This was to be her first surgery, aside from the removal of her wisdom teeth. She prepared herself by gathering as much information as she could. She said, "But I still had one compelling fear that research could not dispel— that somehow I would end up neutered, an un-woman, a non-sexual being. I knew I would have to wait many weeks following surgery to have intercourse and I was afraid."

This disturbing thought accompanied Dina into the operating room. Although she went through the operation without incident and was physically out of danger, she still felt terrified. Then, sometime within forty-eight hours of her surgery, Dina had a passionate dream that included a powerful orgasm. When she awoke from this dream, Dina felt great relief. She knew she was going to be all right and, indeed, she made a remarkably swift recovery. She was back at work in two weeks. Reassured by her dreaming mind that her sexual life was not over, Dina was able to embrace living joyfully.

In fact, orgasms are as much a response of the brain as they are of the genitals. Even people who are severely handicapped, such as paraplegics or other paralyzed persons, are sometimes able to enjoy a full sexual response.[2] The crucial factors seem to be prior sexual experience and appropriate mental stimulation. Dina's dreaming mind had given her the reassurance she needed. Notice when sensual images begin to return to your dreams during convalescence; they, too, are welcome dream signs.

### ◇ Healing as a New Body Image

An important aspect of healing is the development of a new body image that incorporates any changes in a person's body caused by injury, illness, or surgery. Women in particular often use clothing in dreams to symbolize the feelings they have about their bodies. Healing imagery may appear as new or beautiful clothes and jewels.

## MY NEW CLOTHES AND JEWELS

About six weeks after my operation, I dreamed of being in a very sunny shop picking out some new clothes to try on. I chose some luscious colors: peach and cream, and a light yellow-green that brings out the green in my eyes. They were all warm colors and attractive styles. A few days later I dreamed of wearing shoes with rosebuds and a wreath made of rose blossoms. I tried on magnificent jewelry of carved rose quartz and green jade. I noticed I was wearing a beautiful pink-and-green opal ring on my left hand, like one I used to own that had been stolen. Such images depict shifts from predominantly painful feelings to good ones. The image of wearing something beautiful on my injured hand was especially important. Dream pictures like these symbolize the reintegrating body image and the treasure of restored health. Dream images of myself with both arms in casts, of fragile things in danger of breakage, and other negative images still appeared, but there was a new, clear note ascending.

## KAREN CHOOSES THE QUEEN OF HEARTS

Karen had an unbroken family line of breast cancer, from her grandmother to her mother to herself. She had her right breast removed because of minimal breast cancer when she was only thirty-seven, and underwent subcutaneous surgery on her left breast six months later.

Karen is a psychologist who has kept a dream diary since the age of seven. Her records show that during her recovery from the first mastectomy, Karen experienced healing elements in her dreams rather rapidly. For instance, ten days after the surgery, Karen had the following dream:

> I am to be in a parade. Have to get a costume ready. Can't remember how, but someone suggests or I decide to go as the queen of hearts. Spent the day making a golden crown with red hearts. Someone else is going to lend me a velvet dress and I am going to put hearts on it.
>
> Then I forget about it until it is almost time for the parade. The dress is there and there are small silver hearts on the bodice. The dress is black velvet. I think I'll be a mix between the queen

of spades and the queen of hearts. Did find some large red hearts to add. There are some disturbances or delays during this time of activity. A woman who doesn't think I should be the queen of hearts. I have a glimpse of a red king and think with surprise that I didn't realize there'd be a king of hearts. I go off just in time for the parade.

This dream showed Karen's ambivalence between her fear of death (queen of spades) and her desire for love and life (queen of hearts). The dress in her dream was black velvet, a somber costume, combined with silver hearts, a more hopeful sign. It was important for Karen to add large red hearts to the dress and to wear the golden crown. Although the balance between life and death felt tenuous at this stage, the dream said, Karen gave greater weight to the symbol of life and even glimpsed the possibility of a loving mate, a "king of hearts." She went off "just in time" to join the parade of life.

In the second dream of the same night, Karen used the metaphor of new construction. In a vast building, she found that "all the rooms had been remade" from the little shops that were previously located there. The appearance of attractive new clothing and newly reconstructed rooms indicated that Karen was already beginning to integrate the changes in her body.

### KAREN ACCEPTS THE PONCHO GIFT

A couple of nights after the dream about the queen of hearts, Karen continued integrating her newly changed body in her dreams. During the first two weeks after her surgery, Karen's images wavered between ominous and inspirational. Dark images alternated with images of light. In one of these:

I was on a mountainside with a young woman who was both a mother and wife figure to a Christ-like figure. He had to go about some dangerous business and wanted to hide her away for her safety. She was upset. Said she wouldn't want to spend her life hiding while he was being persecuted. She said she'd rather go back to heaven. Said she would ascend tomorrow—that it was her choice. She was very indignant that they wanted to decide for her.

So far, Karen's dream emphasized the risk of death, to "go back to heaven." Perhaps her dreaming mind likened the persecution and crucifixion of Christ to her own current suffering. The dream continued:

> Then the Christ-figure brought her a gift—a poncho of white, fine turquoise and blues. He was wearing it, but she knew it was made for her because it had two spaces for her breasts woven in. She reached for it feeling very happy.

The marvelous poncho, which was worn by the spiritual figure before giving it to the woman in the dream, was especially tailored for the dreamer. This garment suggested the emergence of a beautiful and spiritual new body image. The dream concluded:

> Next I was meeting an old boyfriend (always exciting and dangerous). Somehow I have a child. I start to go down a gully to meet him but find it is steep and dangerous. I get trapped there. He's on the other side and can't reach me. A man in a truck rescues me.
> Then switch to a young woman who is going to die tonight. She is with myself and my mother. I get the idea that leukemia is killing her. We're all at a gathering to say good-bye. At the end, my mother and I keep returning to kiss her because I will miss her unbearably.

The dream theme of wavering between the risk of death and the commitment to life was carried on in the scene of being trapped in a dangerous place, yet getting rescued. The final scene again brought up Karen's fear of dying from a fatal disease and the sadness this engendered. Yet, Karen began to thrive following this dream and was soon back to work wholeheartedly. She opted for life.

Unusual images, such as the costume in Karen's dream of the queen of hearts and the unique poncho, are extremely important to notice and understand. Clinician Ernest Rossi believes that unusual images in dreams are essential for the development of identity and consciousness:

> That which is unique, odd, strange, or intensely idiosyncratic in a dream is an essence of individuality. It is an expression of original psychological experience and, as such, it is the raw material out of which new patterns of awareness may develop.[3]

Idiosyncratic dream images, Rossi says, are "growing edges" of change in the dreamer. I believe they are characteristic when the dreamer is recuperating. Idiosyncratic dream images need to be recognized and encouraged, especially in the midst of dismal imagery. Beautiful clothing almost always signifies a change for the better. If you find yourself having an unusual dream image, give it your special attention. If possible, draw or paint it in color and contemplate its significance to you. (See the last section of this chapter, "Benefiting from Your Unique Dream Images," for suggestions.)

### ◇ Healing as New or Rebuilt Structures and Equipment

We saw how dreams of broken or malfunctioning equipment and deteriorated buildings represented the damaged body. As we heal, the opposite imagery makes its appearance in our dreams. Buildings being remodeled, new rooms added, new structures being erected—these images are typical signs of the repair work going on in the body that has been injured or ill. I particularly liked the dream I had about eight weeks after my accident (five weeks after surgery) of "a lot of construction going on to make ramps for a new freeway." The word *freeway* is often a pun in dreams for a smooth movement in life.

Repaired equipment in dreams, like new or rebuilt structures, symbolizes the restored functioning of the dreamer's body. In my dream about a freeway, a large light fixture that had been repaired was being delivered to my house. I had forgotten I had it but was very pleased to see it again. Sources of light in dreams usually represent growing consciousness or flashes of understanding; they are almost always good signs in dream life.

### ◇ Healing as Increased Cooperation

Another good indicator of an improved physical condition is the appearance of cooperative dream figures. While nightmares usually depict the dreamer alone against great odds, dreams of healing typically show the dreamer as part of a loving group. This suggests that, at least at the moment, all the parts of the dreamer are working well together toward a common goal.

## IRENE'S HUMAN CHAIN

Irene, for example, several months after surgery to remove a cancerous tumor in one of her breasts, dreamed:

> My husband and I are with a group of people in the ocean. We're holding onto pieces of a ship from a shipwreck. I say, "I can't swim!" [true]. Some man takes the lead. He asks, "Who else can't swim?" Others raise their hands. He says, "Hold on. We'll make a chain."
>
> We form a chain, like a snake, going up and down over the swells. The water is dark but bright. I feel more comfortable and not so afraid. We go with the swells, riding over the crests of the waves.

Irene found this dream strangely comforting. She was, in fact, deriving much support from a loving husband. In addition, she had joined a support group for cancer victims, as well as experiencing psychotherapy. Although she was still struggling with the repercussions of the shipwreck, which probably was a metaphor for her illness and surgery, there was hope. The water in her dream was "dark" and dangerous, but it was also "bright," and she was not alone. You will not be surprised to hear that Irene had much edema, represented by being immersed in water and "swells" in her dream. Despite other physical problems that were emerging in this plucky woman's life, Irene felt she was able "to go with the flow," as in her dream, with the help of others. This was a good start toward competent swimming on her own in dreams and in waking life, while being supported by others who loved her.

### ◇ Healing Seen in Puns

Be sure not to overlook wordplay in your dreams. It can be like a billboard of improvement written in capital letters. I had to smile when I awoke from a dream of meeting a woman named Faith Hope—a most delightful person.

### ◇ Healing as a Meeting with the Inner Guide

Some of the dreamers I worked with were fortunate to meet a wise guide in their dreams, one who advised them or gave them

gifts. Karen's dream about Christ giving a woman a special poncho that he had worn had some of this quality. It left her feeling
strengthened and encouraged in her efforts to get well. Dawn,
too, had an encounter with a dream guide. In this case, the
guiding image appeared during her operation.

### DAWN SEES GREEN LIGHT

Dawn, a woman in her sixties, had decided to have plastic surgery on her face. Although she elected this operation, she still
had considerable fear about the risks involved and what the
results might be. She decided to prepare herself carefully.

This thoughtful woman arranged with a family member to
make a special cassette tape for use following the operation.
The finished tape contained some of her favorite music, along
with a descriptive journey through an array of colored lights.
Dawn listened to the results and was pleased.

In the hospital Dawn had chosen, each patient could recu-
perate in a small cottage in complete privacy. Dawn arranged
to have twenty-four-hour nursing care, with someone present
when she returned from the operation. The helper was instructed to set up the tape and play it for her while she was
recovering full consciousness. All went according to plans. However, there was an additional bonus Dawn hadn't counted on or
couldn't have anticipated—the imagery of the tape became an
integral part of her operation experience.

In the early morning, Dawn had been given Valium to relax
her for the forthcoming surgery. She was taken into the operating room where an anesthetic, ketamine, was administered intravenously that, though it does not produce deep anesthesia,
put her into a tracelike state. Ketamine is a drug that sometimes
stimulates unpleasant dreams,[4] but not in this case. While the
surgery was underway, Dawn dreamed:

> I'm in an airplane in an aisle seat. Next to me on the left, in the
> window seat, is a "being." There is a kind of curtain with scal-
> loped edges partially separating us, rather like the material of
> tortillas. I can see that he is a large man, almost a giant. He has
> a deep baritone voice that sounds comforting and reassuring. He
> turns to me and says, "We're going on this wonderful journey
> and I'll be with you all the way." I lean down and try to duck
> under the curtain, which is about chest height, saying, "I want to

see your face." He says, "I'm sorry, but these will keep you from seeing my face. These are skin flaps. You can touch them." I see now they have pores. There is a green light pouring down onto him, shining down on his legs.

Then the scene shifts and we seem to be riding on a Grey-hound bus in the same positions and relationship. I say, "I know who you are—you're Hilarian." "That's right," he replies. "We're almost finished now." I hear another voice saying the same thing. I can stay in the dream, but I elect to wake up.

Dawn said that though it was difficult to move her lips when she awoke, she managed to say, "Before you take me back to the room, I must see the doctor." He came around and put his face close to her, wearing a green mask and cap. He said reassur-ingly, "I've been here all along." Dawn had the odd sensation that the energy of her spirit guide, whom she calls Hilarian, was "channeling" through her surgeon. Whatever the case, Dawn felt supported in a loving and healing way by this figure through-out the surgery.

Dawn had already realized within her dream that the image of the curtain was probably the actual flaps of her skin that were being draped and moved—the "tortilla-like" material with pores. Dawn added, "I make such a 'flap' about my skin." She felt that the shift from airplane to bus was a change from a more luxurious mode of travel to a more mundane one. Perhaps it marked the conclusion of the soaring journey—for as she came back to earth, she awoke in reality. Notice how her spiritual guide was almost a giant. Size in dream images frequently por-trays importance.

The green light of Dawn's dream was perhaps partially stimulated by the green operating outfits of the staff, but more so by some of the description in her prepared cassette. It wasn't until she listened to the tape in her cottage that she noticed the phrase, "When you walk into the green light, it's very healing." Dawn's expectations had been largely positive. She had chosen surgery, arranged the circumstances of it, prepared to make the best of it, and had good results. We should all be so fortunate.

Karen felt encouraged by the figure of Christ in her post-surgical dream. Dawn felt supported and sustained by her spir-itual guide during her operation. In rare instances, an afflicted person believes actual healing took place *during* the dream.

◇ Healing as Restored Physical Wellness—Dreaming
Oneself Well

### JUNE RECEIVES THE HEALING TOUCH

Strange as it may seem, healing sometimes occurs *within* a dream state. A woman I will call June, who was described to me by one of my correspondents from Canada, had suffered migraine headaches from the time she was a teenager until she was about fifty-five. These debilitating vascular headaches occurred at a rate of three to five times a year, always immobilizing her for about a week.

During one of these headaches that had been going on for two or three days, June became so dizzy she could no longer stand up. It was afternoon, but she lay down on the couch and went to sleep. After only a few minutes, June dreamed that she was:

> . . . with an old woman and her husband and their son. The old woman was dying. June [who in reality was a nurse] was taking care of the old woman, staying with her for days and nights. She wanted to leave to take care of her own family, but there was no one else to care for the old woman, or be with her in her few conscious moments, so June stayed with the old woman until she died.
>
> The dream continued after the funeral. The husband and son of the old woman who had died came to visit June. In the dream, June was suffering from a migraine [as she actually was]. The two men stood by the bed and the son declared that because she had been so kind to his mother, he would help her. He laid his hand on her forehead and said that she would never again, as long as she lived, have another one of those headaches. When June awoke, the headache had vanished.

Over a year and a half later, June had not experienced a recurrence of a headache, though her past pattern would have amounted to at least five by then. The relief she had obtained from the healing figure in her dream carried over to her waking life, possibly from her powerful reaction to the dream-healing. Perhaps recalling the touch of her inner healer may have helped June relax constricted blood vessels whenever she began to feel tense. Learning takes place in dreams as well as awake.

June, Dawn, and Karen were all helped to a greater or lesser extent by a special figure in a dream. In Chapter 9, *Your*

*Inner Dream Temple*, we will explore ways to deliberately encounter a dream guide in waking visualizations. Some health practitioners call a wise and helpful figure in a visualization the "inner advisor."[5] Others call it the "inner shaman."[6] Regardless of the label and whether or not the figure is actually real, an imaginary wise figure who helps you replenish and use your own inner wisdom and experience is welcome.

If we can help dreamers to draw upon their self-curative powers, as June did, we will be well on the way to maximizing the potential of our dreams. This possibility becomes a greater probability with lucid dreaming. The ability to become conscious in a dream allows the option of deliberately directing healing energies within a dream state. This almost incredible idea may soon become a reality, with the use of Stephen LaBerge's "dream light," as you'll see in Chapter 8, *Convalescence and Wellness Dreams.*

## ◇ THE EMOTIONAL LEVEL OF HEALING

### ◇ Healing as Accepting Death

Eventually we will all die. Some of us will go sooner, some later, but there is no evading the death of our physical bodies. There are times when "healing" is in the acceptance of this inevitability. When we choose to go with dignity, with the chance to say good-bye to our loved ones, moving toward the unknown light, our mode of departure may be a gift to those who are left behind.

### ◇ Charisse Kranes's Dreams

Charisse fought a four-year battle with ovarian cancer before she died this past June at the age of thirty-one. She was a pretty woman with an exquisite singing voice. A rabbi by profession, she also had a devoted relationship with her husband, Winston, who generously gave me access to her drawing journal after she died.

I met Charisse a little over a month prior to her death. At that time, she was ravaged by the disease, weighing only 83 pounds instead of her normal 130. She still clung to life with a zest and was intrigued to explore the possibility that her dreams could be messages to herself. She'd been consulting my husband, Zal, who is a psychotherapist, about coping with her disease and fast-approaching death; he felt that I should meet this extraordinary woman. We met only once in my office shortly before she was hospitalized for the final time.

## THE CONCERT

Charisse brought four dreams to our session, two of which came from the night of May fifth. In the first scene:

> Mom, Dad, and I were together. On campus? I was looking separately for a movie theater. Then at 8:30 P.M., we decided to wait in line for the Grateful Dead concert. This was smart because the concert was scheduled to begin at 8:30 and this way we would not have to wait. We sat down, me in the middle, Dad on the aisle. He said something about how silly this was and then some girl who was distributing Miss America-type ribbons smiled and wrapped one around his shoulder.

The dream metaphor that struck me most profoundly in this first scene was that of waiting for the "Grateful Dead" concert to begin. Although many people are avid fans of this rock group, its name takes on special significance in a severely ill dreamer. I asked Charisse, "Suppose I were a little kid who didn't know what the Grateful Dead was. What would you tell me?"

She replied, "They're a bizarre rock group. They've been around forever. They don't record. They only do live concerts sometimes. They have loyal fans." She added as an afterthought, "It's nice to know someone's grateful to be dead, to be dying. Perhaps I wish I were grateful about it."

Charisse's mother, who in the dream sat on her left, had also died quite young from cancer. So this first dream contained two images of death. We saw how dream images of death, dying, and leave-taking are typical of fatally ill dreamers. Although the same images may also occur in the dreams of those who are recovering, they cease as the dreamer's health improves.

The dream picture of Charisse's father being draped with a Miss America-type ribbon was a personal reference. Charisse did not get along easily with her elderly father. She saw the ribbon in the dream as restricting the man, "keeping him in line and pacifying him." This suggested that Charisse had felt a need to present a Miss America-type persona to her father, to "keep him in line" and make him happy.

The final scene in Charisse's dream related to her difficulty in retaining nourishment:

> Part of the delay [before the Grateful Dead concert began] was that two little girls with paper cups were trying to fill a silo with oatmeal and red farina. There were cows/elephants? waiting to be fed. One of the adults warned that by the time they ate, they would be angry and too dangerous for the little girls, but they chimed in together, "Oh, we always feed them. It's no problem" —something like that. Meanwhile, an older woman (me?) finished filling up the silo without any extra help. She used glass cereal bowls instead of paper cups.

I have said that animals in our dreams often represent our instincts, or basic life force. The animals in Charisse's dreams reflected this general meaning, as well as her specific situation. Since the cancer had spread to her intestines, it was exceedingly difficult for this young woman to stay properly nourished. Charisse felt exceedingly nauseous from the medications and various treatments she was undergoing; eating was a major problem for her. The unfilled silo was another image for Charisse's empty and undernourished body.

The image of cows or elephants waiting to be fed also represented her undernourished body. Charisse liked cows, regarding them as "beautiful, slow animals." Yet the means to nourish the cows or elephants was almost impossible to supply in the dream. Imagine how long it would take two little girls to fill a silo using paper cups! Charisse said the cups were "small, not reusable, and could be thrown away since they were paper." She was actually using paper cups often for drinking the water she carried with her everywhere. She defined the cereal bowl as "bigger, more efficient," but it was still an overwhelming task to fill a silo.

As we discussed the food itself, its symbolism emerged. Both oatmeal and red farina were defined as creamy grains; she hadn't been able to eat either lately. Red farina, she said, was "smoother than oatmeal, more colorful, more stable." She added, "Red lentils are what Esau gave up his birthright for." The giving up of a birthright was an ominous sign.

The good sign in Charisse's dream was that the older woman, perhaps herself, was able to accomplish filling the silo. This suggested that the dreamer was still actively trying to combat her illness. However, though the food in the dream was nourishing, it was not something she could currently tolerate in waking life. The dream said there was a danger that if the animals were not fed, they would become angry and unmanageable. Whatever else the dream may have been saying, it was surely stating that there was a huge need that was difficult to fill.

## THE HOT TUB

In Charisse's second dream, there was a continuation of the struggle to come to a resolution about her father's view of her—and perhaps her own view of herself:

> I was preparing for a play. The director was a woman. Yesterday we practiced at a Kabuki-like tub (but I didn't go in) where there were just women. Today men and women are in the tub.
>
> Meanwhile, I'm discussing a costume. We're deciding I should wear a nightgown and look through mine, forgetting that I had so many. I want to ask whether I should wear a long nightgown or a baby doll.

Charisse defined a "Kabuki-like tub" as "heaven." It was very pleasant to be in the water with naked women; she felt relaxed and safe because it was segregated. At the time, she felt very self-conscious about her figure. "When one is naked, one is more exposed," she said. Charisse's abdominal area was badly swollen by fluid retention, perhaps contributing to the dream image of water. Immersed in the warm tub, as in a warm womb, the dreamer's deteriorating body felt comforted and secure.

When I asked Charisse to describe the differences between long nightgowns and baby dolls, her answers were opposite to what I would have expected—the reason why it is always crucial to ask the dreamer what the images mean. Dreamers typically say that revealing clothes like baby doll nightgowns are more sensual and often more desirable. In contrast, Charisse said that long nightgowns were "for adults." She liked beautiful lingerie and loved buying it when she got married. She thought of the baby doll style as "for little kids," adding that it was generally not comfortable. "My father always wanted me to wear baby doll nightgowns," she added.

Taking her associations to the nightgowns, together with the Miss America-type ribbon in the first dream, these images suggest that Charisse had felt a need to play the childlike woman (the baby doll), and to succeed in a traditional way (the Miss America way), in order to please her father. In her second dream, she seemed to be saying she was ready to be an adult (to wear a long gown). Feeling mature is good whatever the circumstances.

### SCHOOL PAPER DUE

On the night of May eighth, Charisse recorded a short third dream:

> I don't remember where or when. Here's a fragment. I was writing a paper for school. I think in longhand. Then it was a crisis. I had to do it on the word processor. Wow . . . too tired. . .

At this stage, Charisse's energy level was severely compromised. The school crisis represented her physical crisis. She described writing a paper as "a need to organize your thoughts logically and coherently." In the crisis, she recognized a need for speed. Perhaps it was a "term" paper, indicating the end of an allotted time. Longhand, she said, was more personal and what she used for her journal and her diary; word processing was less personal but easier and quicker. There was no longer time for Charisse to go slowly.

### FINAL JOURNEY

On the night of May ninth (the evening before we met), Charisse dreamed:

> Something about animals and movie stars at a country fair. People. I ask Winston—I thought I was awake—if my stomach is more distended. He was packing, perhaps going away on a mission.

Charisse's final dream contained the characteristic image of someone leaving, going on a journey. In her tradition, "missions" are frequently to Israel, which devout Jews view as the "Promised Land," a safe haven. Charisse was literally gone within the month of this last dream.

### SUMMARY OF CHARISSE'S DREAM THEMES

Thus, some of Charisse's dream imagery was characteristic of people on the verge of death; other aspects were unique to her situation and condition. Her four dream themes could be summarized this way:

1. I am waiting to find the way to be grateful about dying. This stage is about to begin. I must still keep Dad in line.
2. I want to feel warm, safe, and comforted. Yet I am ready to be an adult.
3. I am facing a crisis. I must bring my thoughts together coherently and quickly.
4. Life is like a country fair. Is my illness worse? There is going to be a separation, perhaps a mission.

Those aspects of Charisse's dreams that can be found in the dreams of the extremely ill include:

1. *Images of Death or Dying.* Physician Robert Smith, as described earlier, studied the dreams of seriously ill patients in a hospital.[7] He found that the patients' dream content was closely related to their condition two months later. Those men who mentioned death or dying in their dreams were far more likely to have worsened or died themselves within the two-month span than those who had no such references in their dreams. Women patients who mentioned leave-taking or going on a trip in their dreams were more likely to have worsened or died than those who did not.

Charisse's four dreams, taken together, contain both images. In addition to the images of death in the first dream, she mentioned in her last dream the departure of her husband, perhaps symbolizing *her* departure from him.

2. *Images of Hungry, Hurt, or Dying Animal Life.* Animals usually represent the instinctual life of the dreamer, as already mentioned. When this basic animal life is depicted in trouble in dreams, the dreamer's own physical energy is at a low ebb. Charisse's hungry cows or elephants played this role in her dreams. We have seen this imagery appear in post-surgical dreams, and how some dreamers bounce back with imagery of reviving animals or new birth.

3. *Images of Paradise.* Although Charisse's celestial image was not apparent on the surface of these dreams, it readily emerged in her associations to the Kabuki-like tub with its warm womb-immersing water. It is not unusual for dreamers to provide themselves with a divinely safe place prior to death.

At the end, Charisse died in a remarkable way. She entered the hospital for the last time on Wednesday, May twenty-third. That night and the following one, people gathered at her bedside, bringing testimony of how she had inspired them with her vision, her services, and her pure, beautiful singing voice. Her husband assured her that she had done enough work. She could let go of her fears, her pain, and anxiety about not having accomplished enough. Early on Friday morning, while her catheter was being cleaned, Winston had the impression that Charisse was trying to sit up, to reach him on the cot he had set up by her bed. He crawled in beside her on her bed and she fell asleep. Then he returned to his cot and slept himself. Shortly thereafter, others in the room saw Charisse awake and heard her say, "I have faith." She then slipped away.

Charisse kept an incredible drawing journal that documented her last few months; these images are described in "Charisse's Drawing Journal," on pages 211–214. They're a precious memento of a loved woman who found an acceptance of death.

### ◇ Healing as Becoming Self-Supportive after Trauma

When people endure traumatic injuries or illnesses, they sometimes find that their most severe pain comes from the loss of emotional support they had believed was solidly in place. Dee, for instance, whose boyfriend had driven her to the hospital after she had her hand crushed in a machine at work, found him less sympathetic when she came out of the hospital three weeks later. He told her that their relationship was over and that she would have to find another place to live. The agony of the rejection that she felt was worse than the pain in her wounded hand.

### RITA DWYER'S NEW PATH

Rita, too, found herself without the man she had counted on when she was ravaged by injuries and burns from the work-related explosion (described in Chapter 4, *Forewarning and Diagnostic Dreams*). Rita, a scientist, had been in the hospital for five months recuperating from the chemical explosion and fire that nearly killed her. The burns on her face and body were still not healed, and she was getting discouraged over repeated rejection of her skin grafts. Her physician arranged for her to visit home, with the hope that the trip would encourage her.

At home, however, Rita had to confront the knowledge that she had suffered irreversible physical damage. In the hospital, she had been shielded by a covered mirror and her visitors were limited to only family members and a few close friends. In her own home, she was deluged with well-meaning, sympathetic visitors who conveyed to her the sense of being a pitiful victim. It was then that the man whom Rita loved deeply decided to break off their relationship. She said, "His decision devastated me, wounding me more painfully than my physical injuries had done. I knew how terrible I looked—facial burns are never pretty—but others who loved me looked beyond the outer shell and were clearly happy that I was still alive. Yet, if he in whose love I had felt so secure couldn't stand to be with me, to stand by me, to give me hope that our dreams for the future would somehow be realized, how could I go on?"[8]

It was an excruciating experience for Rita. She added, "I went back to the hospital bleeding on the inside, walling up my sadness and feelings of betrayal by love, wanting to get better but wondering if it mightn't have been better for me to have died." Rita was already suffering from recurrent nightmares that replayed the horror of the explosion and fire. Now her trauma was doubled—emotional as well as physical—it was no wonder that her replay nightmares were joined by dreams of rejection, dreams in which she would be trying to reach the man she loved, but never succeeding.

After several years of reconstructive surgery, Rita got on with her life as best she could. She eventually married, had children, and devoted herself to making a good home for her family. Still, she continued to be occasionally haunted by the old dream of rejection. She had long since given up romantic notions about her lost love, yet these dreams stirred up the old sadness, longing, and despair.

### LEAVING BEHIND OLD BAGGAGE

Finally, Rita's dreams helped her to heal from the emotional pain that still rankled. She became intrigued by her dreams and started a dream journal. Having recorded her dreams for about six years, she took a special workshop on the subject and started reading widely about it. Rita decided to ask herself for a dream that would help her work on her life and to cope with her recurrent rejection dream. This is a technique called "incubating a dream" (described more fully in Chapter 8, *Convalescence and*

*Wellness Dreams*). It's a method you may find useful. For Rita, it was a revelation:

> I'm somewhere, such as a campus or resort, and there is a game being played in the field below a sort of residential building. I go up a couple of times to watch some cheerleaders who are not right on the field but up above it, cheering and being filmed. It seems to be hard work to get the cameras up there. I see X [the man who rejected her] maybe twice, and each time I say hello, he either just says hello or answers so briefly as to effectively ignore me.

So far, Rita's dream resembled the usual rejection theme—she was trying to communicate with her lost love and he was unresponsive. The cheerleaders, however, suggested that some part of Rita's dreaming mind was "cheering" her onward. The comment about it being "hard work to get the cameras up there" implied that incubating a dream with a wider view took effort. The dream continued:

> I don't seem to get too bent out of shape, but do go inside where my husband is on a bed watching the same game, but on television. It shows close-up views of the play, compared with what can be seen from outside. I realize that I want to be with him, knowing he is a better partner than X, but as I watch for a while, I also realize that I'd rather watch from outside where I can see all of the action live.

In this second scene, Rita compared her husband with her lost love. She realized she preferred her husband as a life partner, yet she perceived that his view of life was more focused than the broader view she desired for herself.

Rita's dream continued with her returning outside where, with friends and co-workers, she enjoyed seeing the whole field with the players and sidelines. At one point, she communicated with a girlfriend via a walkie-talkie, but put it down when she realized it was possible to talk face-to-face. In the final dream scene:

> I go to leave and wave good-bye to my husband and possibly X, who both are in the building up above, either looking out a large window or standing on a balcony.

I'm carrying a purse and luggage and go to my car, which is a smaller model than I usually drive, maybe a red convertible. I realize that I can't drive the car where I'm going, which is up a hill that I've been to before. Maybe I have to pick something up there. I decide to leave the luggage in the car instead of burdening myself with it on the climb—a path with greenery and tall grass edging it, but steep and somewhat hard to climb.

I put my purse on the floor in front of the front seat, passenger side, and cover it with a teddy bear so that no one will see it. Maybe I only take out my wallet to take with me. I lock the window and set on my way alone. I know the climb will be hard but I can make it.

In this concluding segment of the dream, Rita seemed to be putting aside her past relationship with her lost love to peacefully coexist with her husband. Perhaps she was also saying good-bye to a dependency upon her husband. There was something the dream said, that she needed to find on her own. Rita must make the climb alone, leaving behind all the "baggage," which probably referred to the emotional heaviness she had been carrying. She secured her valuables and took only the essentials. Finding one's own way is always "a hard climb," but her dream told Rita that she was capable of making it.

From the time of this dream, Rita accepted that she must find her way in life, to use her own wide-angle vision and her desire for face-to-face communication, to let go of the past and move forward. She was no longer troubled by dreams of being rejected by the man she once loved. She added, "I often think of this dream when I need to face up to something, to deal with an issue face-to-face, directly, independently." (Another crucial dream from Rita's fascinating journal appears in the following chapter.)

Rita continued to develop her interest in dreams and became actively involved in many spheres outside her home life, including being the 1987–90 chairman of the board of the Association for the Study of Dreams, and the current vice president. Today she is a vital person, full of the joy of living, who gives much to those who know her.

## ◇ ACCELERATING SELF-HEALING WITH ART

### ◇ Expressing Emotions and Sensations with Art

Whenever we are confronting a significant illness or injury, we find ourselves at the beginning of a journey. How rough or smooth the road will be, how strenuous the travel, whether we have companions or not, the nature of directions along the route, and even what our final destination will be are unknown. By recording images of our voyage as we go, making a kind of visual ship's log or travel diary, we do more than create an interesting journal of a trip. We can gain strength and insight; we gather inner nourishment for the trip, and sometimes invaluable guidance to bring our journey to completion.

### ◇ Documenting Your Journey with Art

You will get a sense of what I mean in the powerfully expressive record of Charisse, the young woman who died of ovarian cancer, whose dreams were described in this chapter.

### CHARISSE'S DRAWING JOURNAL

The single time that we met, Charisse had showed me her drawing journal, explaining some of the images. It's a document of a woman's heroic struggle with physical pain. The journal consists of forty-eight pages, mostly with drawings, but several with comments, biblical quotes, or prayers. I'll describe a few of these.

The first picture is a self-portrait. It shows a figure with distorted features: an enlarged abdomen, face, and head, with the mouth open. There are no arms, perhaps reflecting Charisse's sense of helplessness. There is much turmoil drawn in black and brown squiggles inside her intestine, with a small pair of orange eyes "witnessing" what she was feeling. The positive aspect of this illustration is the notes of song still emerging from her mouth.

The next drawing is a powerful rendition of Charisse's immune system. It shows a tree with deep roots in many colors. The heart of the tree trunk almost seems to be the shape of a womb, where her cancer began. On the opposite page is an inscription in yellow-green: "Strongly rooted, drawing up all colors, flaming brightly, hot-white light of God at my innermost, love, wisdom, energy lapping around me."

*10a. Illness: Ovarian cancer*                    Drawing by Charisse Kranes

*Drawing a picture of how one feels during an illness or after an injury helps get emotions out of the body and onto the paper.*

*This self-portrait was a healing activity for Charisse, who was terminally ill with ovarian cancer that had spread into the abdominal cavity. In it, she depicts her physical appearance and her subjective sensations. Although extremely thin at the time, her abdominal area was distended, as shown by the enlarged abdomen. The lack of arms in the picture reflects her sense of helplessness. The act of eating was difficult, depicted by the distortions in the mouth and stomach area. The eyelike marks in the lower abdomen express her sense of "witnessing" what was happening to her body. Yet Charisse shows herself still singing—she had a highly trained voice. Singing was a spiritual activity for her that brought much pleasure to her listeners. It was important for her in her last days to stay in touch with something that brought a special joy.*

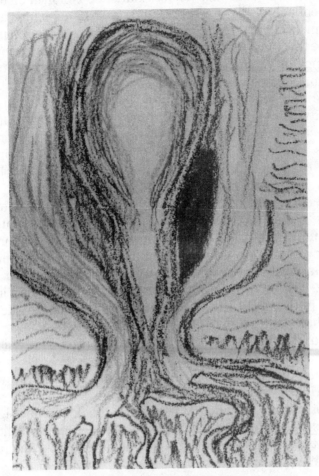

*10b. Healing visualization for illness: The rooted self*

Drawing by Charisse Kranes

In this picture, Charisse intended to visualize her immune system, strongly rooted, gathering strength in many colors from roots in the earth, and from light emanating out of heaven. She imagined "the hot-white light of God at my innermost" with "love, wisdom, and energy" lapping around her. This image suggests the dreamer's need to be rooted, connected, or anchored.

At the same time, Charisse's drawing seems to depict the uterus, where her disorder was centered, with an area of disturbance—the dark spot—mainly on one side.

By focusing on her spiritual side and filling her mind with loving thoughts in her journal and her waking hours, Charisse was able to die peacefully, "rooted" in strong faith, surrounded by her loving husband and caring friends.

Two later drawings depict Charisse's stomach disturbance with leakage in black, brown, and gray. One picture attempts to transform the "shit"; it shows small flowers growing from the earthy brown substance. These pictures are followed by drawings of "calm." Charisse rendered calmness in aqua and medium-deep blue, bluish-pink, and pale gray.

Throughout the forty-eight pages, there is a diminishing of intensity. Early drawings are strong in line and bright in color; these elements grow weaker as the pages progress and time passes. On page thirty-five, the poignant plea "help" appears in letters of green and blue. From page thirty-six, the colors become lighter and the lines unclear, partly from Charisse's dwindling energy, but also from her choice of hue, such as pale, bilious green, pale yellow, and pale pink. Forms continue to grow more simple and vague. On page forty-three is the shape of a cow drawn in gray, perhaps relating to her dream about one. On page forty-seven, the words "heal me" appear in pale purple. The final page used, forty-eight, has inscribed in small letters in the upper left-hand corner in her healing shade of medium blue, the words, "I am, I AM." The remaining twelve pages of the book are blank. Charisse's journal is a visible record of a valiant struggle.

We have much to learn from the dreams and drawings of the seriously ill or dying patient. By discovering the signs of deteriorating health and their opposite, the flourishing signs, we may be better able to guide people through difficult illnesses, supporting their own strength, and helping to ease the passage of those who are ready to depart.

## ALEX'S HEALING ART

"My art saved my life," said Alex Pellegrini, as we discussed his remission from a non-Hodgkins lymphoma. Prior to coming down with cancer, Alex had been a high-school teacher and then a counselor. Lying in bed in the hospital, Alex began to doodle to pass the time. In retrospect, he thinks these early drawings were of his cancer cells—small, abstract, dividing images. He found making them strangely comforting. Alex did not follow any pattern of art therapy; he simply went with his intuition, drawing what pleased him. He found that his artwork was liberating. Having developed from his illness, it came to represent his healing energy. Throughout his nine months of treatment, Alex had plenty of time to further his interest and skills in art, eventually taking professional instruction. Art provided Alex's life with a clear focus and a new direction. He began to re-evaluate his career plans and, some four years later, was fully committed to working as an artist. He has already participated in several gallery exhibitions.

Most people will not develop into professional artists from drawing while they are ill, but everyone is able to benefit from the practice, as Alex did. With a few simple tools (described in the activities section of Chapter 6, *Post-Crisis Dreams*) and the will to face your discomfort, you can begin where you are to picture and eventually transform your pains. Even if you have already drawn a picture of your afflicted body part, now is a good time to draw a picture of whatever residual pain and other sensations you may have. Comparing current drawings to earlier ones often reveals remarkable change. Be sure to date the new drawing.

### ◇ Documenting Pain in Art

Many people find the idea of drawing a picture of their pain repellent. Unfortunately, this attitude leaves the sufferer exactly where he or she always was; the pain remains the same, worsens, or else goes through its usual course before it is resolved. By making a picture of your pain or trauma, you can take a shortcut to recovery.

#### MIGRAINE DRAWINGS
Migraines are vascular headaches that involve rhythmic contraction and expansion of the blood vessels in the scalp and brain, producing a throbbing pain that usually starts and remains on one side of the head.[9] They are characterized by vivid visual effects such as flashing lights, zigzagging lines, and an area of total darkness, called an "aura," which often precedes the onset of the headache pain. There may be impressions of strange odors and confusion as well. The hands and feet become cold. Many sufferers also have severe pain, nausea, vomiting, dizziness, and sensitivity to light and sound. Any of these sensations may appear in the dreams of migraine sufferers.

One of the children I worked with for my book, *Your Child's Dreams*, dreamed of being a baseball that was hit and caught and thrown hundreds of times.[10] He awoke with a pounding headache. A man who was coming down with Lyme disease dreamed of being struck in the head with a hammer, after which he awoke with characteristic head pain.[11]

Art therapy is used as a regular part of the treatment program for migraine sufferers at the Louis A. Weiss Memorial Hospital in Chicago. By drawing their headaches, patients are helped to recognize how they feel, to confront repressed emotions, learn how to cope with them, and ultimately learn how to deal with their pain. Psychotherapists find that migraine sufferers who are able to visualize their hands growing warmer during an attack are able to mitigate their discomfort and even alleviate it.

Last March, the National Headache Foundation and Wyeth-Ayerst Laboratories held a "Migraine Masterpiece" competition.[12] The three top winners were awarded cash prizes totaling $7,000. The work of these three and some of the twenty-two merit-award winners were exhibited in shows in New York and Chicago.[13]

Drawings of migraine headaches by people who are troubled with them reveal similar images to those that appear in the dreams of migraine sufferers. If you recall the dream images reported by people who awoke with headaches described in Chapter 1 on page 36, these dream pictures often involved tight headgear that created pressure, or blows to the head. Likewise, headache illustrations by migraine sufferers often included images of heads with screws boring down into them or ones with heads in a vise. The colors used were fierce and bold; lines were characteristically diagonals, jagged, or fragmented. Some of the drawings depicted piercing, wavelike patterns, violent bolts of lightning, explosions in the head or stomach, and balls of fire.

By giving external form to their pain, regardless of its source, people can gain a sense of control over it. There is something about the directing of energy into drawings that represent one's pain that drains discomfort from the site of injury. When people draw their injury or trauma, they almost always experience relief. The healing process gets underway.

◇ Documenting Traumatic Events in Art

Transferring feelings about pain onto a piece of paper becomes even more valuable when the person has experienced severe trauma.

## TRIAL BY FIRE

Kim, for example, was hospitalized at St. Francis Memorial Hospital's Bothin Burn Center after he had been trapped in a brush fire he and his co-workers were trying to control. When he realized his predicament, Kim had to run through thirty yards of flames to escape the circle of fire. His clothes caught on fire and, although he tucked his body into a ball and rolled to put out the blaze, he was badly burned. With deep burns on the outside of his body, and smoldering anger at his co-workers and supervisor on the inside, the last thing Kim wanted to do was to draw. Art therapist Valerie Appleton persuaded the twenty-five-year-old man to make a picture of the day he got burned, "Just try," she said. "If you don't like it, you can tear it up." [14]

Kim drew. His picture showed a red scribble of a fire truck and rolling smoke. He ripped the drawing into three pieces. "My God, you're right," he said. "It's over." Appleton explains that art can give the artist a sense of mastering his or her feelings. She feels it is important to "make a map of the accident." Even those who have had their hands amputated were able to draw with felt-tipped pens fastened to what was left of their arms. The helpless victim of a trauma gains a feeling of control and is given something to do that more fully expresses his or her pain in pictures. Drawing allows trauma victims to express feelings that are sometimes not possible to put into words. Drawing helps people cope with their pain.

Appleton, in her work with burn patients, finds a progression of themes as people recover. Newly burned people often cover their papers with harsh lines, heavy with red and black. There are often images of heat in hot oranges and reds, such as burning sunsets. As patients recover, the lines in their works soften to curves; the hues tend toward the cooler colors of blues and greens. Appleton notices an uncanny correlation between when patients start using cool colors and the time their fevers abate and healing begins.

I wonder what effect deliberately using blues and greens at an earlier stage would have. Could we hasten the reduction of fever in burn patients by asking them to draw or meditate upon cooling scenes such as a mountain stream or a snow scene?

I recently had an opportunity to observe the effect of a large-scale trauma on the dreams of myself and others, as well as appreciate the relief-producing and healing effects of trauma drawings.

## EARTHQUAKE DREAMS AND DRAWINGS

In Chapter 6, *Post-Crisis Dreams*, I described the traumatic impact the 1989 San Francisco earthquake had upon the population of the Bay Area. Although my family and my home had not sustained any serious damage, I felt badly shaken by the continuous aftershocks.

Since I continued to feel nervous about the possibility of another impending earthquake, I found it helpful to draw the experience I had gone through. It was a literal drawing with my feet in the foreground; rippling walls, tumbling books, and shattering pottery filled the background. Showing the event through my eyes externalized it. No longer trapped inside, it was on the paper where I felt a great deal more comfortable about it.

Dreams that people described to me about the earthquake were realistic at first. Gradually the dream scenarios began to change, providing the seeds of healing. Dreams were no longer the same or worse than the actual traumatic incident. When positive fantasy elements begin to appear in the post-traumatic nightmare content, the dreamer is on the way to recovery.

## PUTTING TOGETHER THE PIECES

Fiona, who had been exceedingly traumatized by the earthquake, wore her clothing for three nights afterward. Keeping a flashlight by the bed was common practice for many people, but she felt unable to disrobe, for fear another earthquake would force her family out to a shelter in the middle of the night. Later, she was willing to undress, but not until the very last moment before she went to sleep, instead of putting on a nightgown to watch television and talk with her husband, as was her usual habit.

I knew that Fiona was finally making a recovery when, two weeks after the big earthquake, she had the following dream:

> I was looking at terra-cotta shards. I thought at first it was my delicate saki cups, but then I saw the pieces had a drawing on them. As I pieced the shards together, I saw it was a beautiful delicate drawing of a fish, rather like a cave wall drawing. Then I seemed to be putting together a wall in Pompei. I could make a wall with the beautiful pattern, which now had all sorts of natural marine life as well as fish. It was esthetically beautiful.

This dreamer associated the color of terra-cotta with herself, a color that is particularly suited to her, as well as being one that often appears in frescoes. The city of Pompei, of course, had been destroyed by a volcano, reminding Fiona of the lesser destruction of San Francisco from the earthquake. Fish, to her, are rather alarming creatures that scared her as a child when she had her toes nibbled at by some fish. She thinks of the city she lives in as a water city.

In her dream language, Fiona was saying, "I fear that something valuable and delicate has been irreparably shattered (the saki cups). But then I discover there is a pattern (the line drawing) that can guide me to restoring the pieces (the shards), to put the pieces of myself back together. This restoration can create something beautiful."

Drawing her special dream image might have helped Fiona further consolidate her learning. The changes occurring in this dream were a spontaneous restoration of health. Perhaps in the future we will be able to guide dreamers to seek and find the images that will help cure them of their emotional and physical pains.

## ◇ Dream Signs of Deteriorating Health

We have already seen that when our health begins to fail, our dreams depict our debilitation in certain images:

- Animal or plant life is neglected, malnourished, or dying
- Sick, dying, or dead animals or people appear
- Clothing is ragged, dirty, or falling apart
- Machines, equipment, or plumbing malfunction
- Buildings or other constructions deteriorate or collapse
- The dreamer is threatened with damage or death

Such themes do not necessarily mean we are seriously ill; they reflect our state at a moment in time, exaggerated and dramatized. They may be symbolic of an emotional state as well as a physical one.

## ◇ Dream Signs of Improving Health

We also saw that when our health begins to improve, our dreams forecast or express these positive changes by different imagery:

- New growth in plants or newborn animals appear
- Protection from images that have endangered us is present
- Flexibility occurs in formerly stiff images
- Permanent loss or limitation is accepted
- New clothing reflecting the new body image is present
- New construction takes place
- Other dream characters provide support
- Healing takes place within the dream

We will explore next how to get the most benefit from these valuable images of healing.

## ◇ DREAM ACTIVITIES: BENEFITING FROM YOUR UNIQUE DREAM IMAGES

### ◇ 1. Select a dream from your journal that contains an idiosyncratic image.

What is the most unusual, fascinating, or idiosyncratic image in this dream? You'll recognize it by the power it has to intrigue or puzzle you. You may wish to choose a personal healing image from your journal (see the preceding list for typical healing images). Select your dream image.

> *Example:* The dream image of a jacket made from turquoise bird feathers in Native American style.

### ◇ 2. Draw, paint, or meditate on your idiosyncratic image.

Render this dream image in color, if possible. Concentrate on expressing what is special or unusual about it. The drawing needn't be "good," "pretty," or "perfect." Instead, capture how the dream image makes you *feel*. Express your emotions on the paper.

### ◇ 3. As you work, observe yourself.

Notice which areas you emphasize. Which colors do you choose? What is important for you to express about the image?

*11. Idiosyncratic dream image: The turquoise jacket*

Drawing by Patricia Garfield

*This drawing illustrates the idiosyncratic dream image of the turquoise jacket described opposite. The box with the seven compartments that was a part of the dream represents seven separated powers, the energy centers in the body. The birds represent these powers activated. There are several birds to indicate the many feathers needed to make the garment. The jacket symbolizes these same powers integrated and used by the dreamer. The caption expresses the message of the dream and the wish of the dreamer: "Oh, spirit birds, will I wear your magic jacket? Will I tame your seven mystic powers?"*

*By drawing any unique and puzzling images from your dreams and by questioning yourself about their elements, you may be able to synthesize meaningful messages to yourself. Odd images usually represent a newly emerging part of the dreamer.*

◇ 4. After you finish your drawing, think about your
dream image.

What do your self-observations suggest? Have you realized or
discovered anything about the image's meaning to you as you
worked or after you finished? In your journal, jot down your
comments.

◇ 5. Ask yourself questions about your
idiosyncratic image.

Consider the whole image and its parts. How would you cate-
gorize this object? What is its shape? Its style? Its color? Its purpose?[15] Contemplate whatever is special about each of these
aspects of the image—whatever distinguishes it from other similar things. Break down a complex image into component parts,
and then ask questions about the part. Remember, each
dreamer will answer questions about a dream image in his or
her unique way.

*Example Questions and Answers About the Bird-Feather
Jacket:*
Q   What is a bird?
A   A bird is a creature capable of flight (usually), unlike
other animals.
Q   How are birds different from other animals?
A   Birds are covered with feathers instead of with hair or
fur.
Q   What are feathers?
A   Feathers are structures designed to support flight.
Q   What is turquoise?
A   Turquoise is a beautiful shade of blue. It combines
warm and cool tones of yellow and greenish-blue.
Q   How does turquoise differ from other colors of gem-
stones?
A   Turquoise is considered sacred by Native Americans,
symbolizing heaven and life energy.
Q   What is special about Native American style?
A   Native American styles are more relevant to the values
of the person who wears them. The designs have spiri-
tual meaning.

Q  What is a jacket?
A  A jacket is an article of clothing used for protection and/
   or warmth.
Q  How does a jacket differ from other clothing?
A  It can be easily put on or taken off; it's convenient to
   use.

◇ 6. Combine your several answers into one answer.

If the above answers were combined, what would it produce?

*Answer:* A garment that would render the wearer capable of
spiritual flight. It would be convenient and easy to use.

◇ 7. What would it be like to be this object
(thing, person)?

Try to imagine how you would feel being this object (thing, person).

*Example:* What would it be like to be a jacket made of turquoise
feathers in Native American style? Or to wear such a jacket?
*Answer:* Warm, protected, beautiful, complete, and surrounded
by spiritual force.

◇ 8. What is the implication of this image
in your dream?

What does this response tell you about yourself at the moment?

*Example:* I'm reaching for a way to contact my spiritual side
easily.

Take any of your newly discovered images and give them
external form. Draw them, write about them, dance them, construct them, or find pictures that capture their essence. Interact
with them in your imagination; let them speak. Listen to their
messages. Make changes in your life.
Jung asserts that by giving the dream content visible form
in the waking state, we are clarifying an aspect of our unconscious. "By shaping it, one goes on dreaming the dream in
greater detail in the waking state." By giving these unusual im-

ages form, he felt, we are beginning the process of widening our consciousness. (The above guide is based in part on some suggestions made by Jung.[16]) By working with our idiosyncratic images, we come to understand things about ourselves that were formerly buried out of sight and mind. By bringing them out and contemplating them, we are able to integrate any opposing aspects of our personality and move forward. These ideas are particularly applicable when we are injured or ill.

This process of working with idiosyncratic images can be repeated for any other key images of the same dream. Then see how the images fit into an overall dream message. You may find it helpful to consult symbol dictionaries *after* you have given your own associations to your dream image. A particularly useful, though expensive, symbol dictionary is Ad DeVries's *Dictionary of Symbols and Imagery*.[17] Good dream dictionaries sometimes stimulate the dreamer's own associations or reveal meanings. But don't be misled. Accept only those suggestions that give you a sense of "rightness" when the connection is made between your dream image and its meaning. If the suggested meaning does not fit, discard it. The dream image was created by your mind; only you will recognize the right meaning. Listen to your heart.

◇ 9. Draw your immune system.

In previous activity sections, you drew your trauma, your afflicted body part, and your physical pain. It is equally important to consider your body's natural defense barrier—your immune system. We don't need to know in detail how this complex, intricate system protects us from invasion in order to mobilize its force. This happens automatically whenever our bodies are injured or ill. But we can help the process along by picturing our responses as active and effective.

Draw a picture of what you imagine your protective white blood cells look like. These are the chief defense elements in your immune system. The drawing can be literal or metaphoric. Show the shape of your white blood cells, their size, color, and what they are doing.[18]

◇ 10. Draw your treatment.

Now draw a picture of your treatment taking place. This may be an operation, using equipment, or undergoing a medical procedure. This drawing, too, can be literal or symbolic. Show how the treatment works inside your body. You may also want to show your white blood cells interacting with your disease or injured site. If you haven't drawn your afflicted body part before, now is a good time to do so. Show what your damaged cells look like. Then show how your treatment combats these.

◇ 11. Strengthen your defense.

How do your defensive elements compare to the attacking or injured ones that you drew earlier? What is their ratio? Which are bigger? Stronger? More active? More colorful? Which are winning? Now make any changes or improvements in your drawing you desire.

"Imaging" the immune system successfully fighting cancer cells is a primary tool in psychotherapy treatment with cancer patients.[19] For instance, the disease cells might be visualized as garbage, and the immune system as troops in white uniforms gathering the garbage and disposing of it. Or, the immune system might be pictured as spacemen in white uniforms who fire laser guns that vaporize the cancer cells. This method of combating the disease organisms with one's immune system is effective in many illnesses. Simply picture your white blood cells winning over any diseased cells.

What do you think would enable you to heal more rapidly? Do certain areas need soothing? Do other areas need stimulating? Should your defenses be more powerful? Imagine ways to supply these needs and draw them. Would any of your unique dream images help here? Add them to the drawing if you like. In whichever way appeals to you, make the healing elements in your drawing satisfy you. If you are injured or ill, repeat these activities daily, if possible, or at least weekly.

Each of us has tremendous healing power within our bodies and minds. We often don't appreciate the strength of our resources. By deliberately looking for the ways we can help ourselves, by imaginatively stirring these inner powers, we invoke them and help them carry forward their natural healing process.

# 8

❖

# CONVALESCENCE AND WELLNESS DREAMS

## ◇ DREAMS OF CONVALESCENCE

As we convalesce, dream images that are positive or neutral in content increase. Although energy and mobility may still be limited at this phase, the healing person begins to dream in ways that are more characteristic of the pre-injury or pre-illness time. Dreams replaying the accident, the sickness, or the operation may still arise, but these images become less frequent. New clothing and buildings, births, thriving plants, and lush blossoms flourish in the dreamscape as we recover. Your dreams during convalescence will differ from the preceding healing stage mainly in the greater proportion of positive dream images, and in the appearance of work themes. The recovering body part continues to appear in dreams until wellness is fully reestablished.

During convalescence, people are often engaged in special exercises or routines that focus the mind on the recuperating body part. For example, the "dynamic splints" I wore several hours each day demanded attention. One splint pulled my wrist forward in a flexed position; another pulled it backward in an extended position. I lifted weights using my wrist and squeezed a rubber toy to strengthen it. I turned a bar to make my wrist flexible. I had residual swelling measured by comparing the volume of water displaced by my repaired arm and hand to the volume displaced by my uninjured arm and hand. Several times a week I dipped my arm and hand into hot paraffin to soften the tissues that were then massaged and manipulated into their full range of motion. The angles of my joints were measured and compared to previous measurements. All night long I wore a flexible "scar mold" with an elastic covering. Small wonder then that my left wrist still appeared in my dreams.

Nightmares during convalescence, when they occur, deal more with the tasks ahead, conflicts over work or disabilities, and only occasionally glance backward to the pain and fright previously experienced.

### ◊ Pets and Plants Assist Healing

Surprisingly, pets and plants speed up convalescent time. Researchers have found that patients recovered from major surgery more swiftly when they owned pets. The responsibility of caring for a loved animal helped mobilize patients sooner, giving them a reason to get up out of bed and stay moving. The affection of a loving pet or the beauty of a healthy plant probably also helped the long hours of recuperation to pass more pleasantly. The mere action of stroking a pet has been found to be soothing to the caretaker. Caring for an animal seems to make people kinder to other people.[1] Possibly tending a plant has a similar gentling effect. It does us good to think about and relate to things other than our own discomfort.

### ◊ Dreams about Work

As convalescents regain enough energy to get restless, but are not yet well enough to return to work, they begin to dream about work. Sometimes these dreams signal readiness to deal with work issues again; at other times, they scream aloud, "Not yet!"

## NINA'S DREAM OF NOT ENOUGH TIME =
## UNREADY FOR WORK

Nina, for instance, was recovering from surgery on arthritic joints in one hand. Being a nurse, she was aware how much her presence was needed, yet three weeks after her operation, she did not feel ready to tackle her job, as indicated by the following dream:

> I am back at work looking for some things and medications. There's a time pressure. There are too many patients, not enough staff. There's too much to do and not enough time.

Although Nina's dream depiction of work did not differ greatly from her actual working conditions, she ordinarily felt able to manage. Her dream suggested the pressure would be overwhelming at the moment. She needed more time to recover.

I have already described my dream of my hand being underneath a grandfather clock. At the time of this dream, I had recently received the edited manuscript for my latest book from my publisher, who wanted it corrected and returned quickly. Despite not being fully well, I felt impelled to get to work on it swiftly because of publication deadlines. I managed to do so, but I, like Nina, would have preferred more time.

## RONA'S DREAM OF THE NEW SHIFT =
## WISH FOR EASIER WORK

Rona, a nurse who had fractured her wrist while on an extended vacation, was kept out of work by her complex injury for three months, long after her return home. As she underwent daily physical therapy to restore lost functions to her hand, she wondered, "How long is this going to go on?" Rona didn't usually recall her dreams, but at this time, she dreamed:

> Someone offered me a nine-to-five job, with a regular eight-hour shift.

Rona's job actually involved working twelve-hour shifts for three days at a time. The thought of an eight-hour shift was so unlikely that it struck Rona as ridiculous. Yet, she added, "If someone did offer me such a shift, I'd take it."

Dreams such as Rona's prepare the mind to cope with upcoming work demands. Dreamers often feel "not quite ready" to function at the same pace as prior to their injury or illness. Their dreams sometimes provide the possibility of an improved work situation as a wish fulfilled. As you recover from an injury or illness, monitor your dreams to assess your readiness to return to work.

## ◇ The God of Convalescence

The ancient Greeks had a special god who ruled over the period of convalescence. He was called Telesphoros, from Greek words meaning "finisher," "accomplisher," or "terminator." [2] According to some myths, Telesphoros was the son of Asklepios. He was depicted as a small boy, or possibly a dwarf, wearing a cap or hood and a long cloak that covered his body. He was sometimes placed beside the statues of the healing god Asklepios and sometimes with Asklepios' daughter Hygieia (the source of the word *hygiene*, the science of health).

In some of the dream sanctuaries, special rooms or temples were set aside for the worship of Telesphoros. He was revered throughout Asia Minor, and especially at Pergamon, where paeans were sung in his honor during festivals. Patients who were recovering at the sanctuaries were known to have made sacrifices to Telesphoros.

This figure of the small boy divinity appeared in some of the celebrated dreams that were incubated at the ancient healing temples. [3] In one dream, he prescribed a healing balsam that was to be applied in the bath; in another, he was reported to have appeared in the vision of a man who was dangerously ill, touched the dreamer's forehead, and cured him.

I find the idea of the image of a small child representing recuperation particularly fitting. We have seen how newborn life and new objects often symbolize returning health for the dreamer. A child wrapped in his cloak of secrecy may indeed be the bringer of new life. Look for him or his modern equivalent as you recover.

## ◇ WELLNESS DREAMS

What are the dreams of fully restored health like and how can we recognize them? After we have regained our well-being, dream content returns to mainly pre-trauma subjects—our relationships with our mates, parents, children, and colleagues. We strive to succeed at our work, to create, to develop, and to enjoy life. We dream about our fears and our hopes for the future.

As our health is becoming reestablished, our dreams often deal with special topics, ones I call "reintegration dreams." These images weave the formerly injured or ill body part into our dream tapestry in a new and attractive way. Here are some examples:

### ◇ Dreams of New Clothing = New Body Image

#### MIMI'S GOLDEN REMARRIAGE DREAM

Mimi, the woman in her early forties who had a total hysterectomy soon after remarrying, had two extraordinary dreams that marked her returning health. You may recall that Mimi had violent dreams of being raped immediately after her surgery. Some four weeks after her surgery, Mimi dreamed she was with her new husband at their church at sunset:

> The light and colors are golden. All the girls look as though they wear halos, with their hair backlit. I am a bride, among many brides, walking on the grounds. We are waiting for a bridal talk. I look down at my stomach and decide that Judd and I will have a baby. I look really young and beautiful. I'm wearing the wedding dress I actually wore, with a floral piece and veil.

This dream might have expressed Mimi's regret over not being able to bear more children after her hysterectomy. Yet she already had delivered two babies, so the dream decision to have another child with her new husband was more indicative of her hope for a positive future together—the birth of a lasting love relationship. Her stomach, which had recently been the site of so much pain, now became the dream site for creating their new life together.

The atmosphere of warm, golden color and light underscored the happy feeling that Mimi expressed in this dream and that lingered on when she awoke. The angeliclike brides strolled in the sunset glow. Mimi saw herself as part of the heavenly group, about to embark on an important life journey. Some of this imagery reflected activities that Mimi was currently participating in at her church. But the dream went further.

Getting remarried is a powerful symbol in dreams. It usually suggests a recommitment to some purpose. In Mimi's dream, it indicated a determination to make her new relationship work, a rededication. The golden color and light, the special dress, and the dreamer's youthful appearance all reflected Mimi's sense of physical well-being and hopeful attitude. You may find similar signs appearing in your own dreams as your well-being returns.

## MIMI'S DESIGNER-DRESS DREAM

A new body image is essential to our complete return to health. We need to accept any losses or changes in our bodies and integrate these into our new view of ourselves. This process is aptly demonstrated in a dream that Mimi had a few days after the one just described. She said it was her favorite of all dreams:

> I go with my family to a dress designer who takes my measurements. Later the same day I return and he has the dress ready. I had asked for minor changes in his pattern, with a kind of V-cut in the front of the skirt, with gathers.
>
> Everybody is happy and cheerful. My mother, my father, my elderly aunt, and my deceased grandmother is there, too. I'm surprised and excited to see her, and introduce her to the dress designer. I sweep up an armful of dusty-rose-colored roses, asking, "How do you like this with the dress? Should I carry them?"

The dream image of having her measurements taken implied that Mimi was making a self-assessment. Notice how Mimi pictured a designer wedding dress that included minor alterations in the pattern. As Mimi described the wedding dress in her dream, she gestured to show me the location of the "V-cut" in the front of the skirt, which was directly above her surgical scar! In four weeks, Mimi had transformed the "big, red, amorphous pain" she had felt in her abdomen after surgery into an intricate "cut" that was part of a beautiful dress—a magnificent integration image. Being a wedding dress, it sealed her commitment to her new mate as wife and spiritual partner.

The presence of happy relatives in the dream, especially her favorite, deceased grandmother, suggest that all parts of the dreamer were approving her renewed commitment.

I asked Mimi, "What makes roses special compared to other flowers?" She replied, "They're the most beautiful and

fragrant of flowers. In the dream their color was extraordinary
—more subtle, more pure—not a color everyone else would
pick." For myriads of dreamers, flowers symbolize pleasure in
romantic love. Mimi's choice, her dream said, was different from
the typical. Her flowers of love offered a sharp contrast to her
nightmares of being raped just a month earlier.

Overall, this dream showed Mimi had accepted and integrated the change in her body image: she had accepted her hysterectomy and was ready to move on with life. Her surgical scar
had become an integral part of her new body image. She was
well.

Stay alert for any indication that your unique dream images
include a former injury in a new way, as Mimi's wedding dress
integrated her surgical scar. Such reintegration images signal a
dramatic renewal of physical and emotional health. You may
have an occasional recurrence of negative imagery about your
health problem, but you will have reached an integrated level
that can be consolidated.

## RITA'S MISSING PIECE DREAM

Rita, as you perhaps remember, was nearly killed in a chemical
explosion. Her condition remained serious for many months.
She underwent repeated operations to restore functions to her
face and hands. I have already described Rita's sense of excruciating loss when the man she loved terminated their relationship a few months after her injury. As her physical condition
stabilized, Rita tried to reestablish her life. In between surgeries,
she attempted to return to work in an administrative post that
had been created for her; it provided a sheltered environment
but "no real sense of purpose or value." Eventually, she married
a man who had loved her before her disfigurement and continued to love her in this difficult time. He became her anchor.

However, Rita did not yet feel whole. She said that during
the daytime, she could pretend to be like everyone else and
repress her true feelings, accepting one surgeon's judgment:
"Like Humpty-Dumpty, there was no way I could be put back
together again as I had been."[4] On the other hand, she suffered
intensely from the rejection and insensitivity of people who reacted negatively to her appearance. These painful experiences
surfaced in repeated nightmares of reliving the explosion, along
with equally unplesant dreams about inadequacy and rejection.

A consultation with a psychiatrist was not helpful to Rita. She did, however, obtain some relief from relaxation and meditation techniques she learned in a special workshop. Later she began exploring dream groups, and it was this work that led her eventually to her own healing and reintegrative dreams. In one of the dream workshops she took, Rita decided to incubate a dream to answer the question, "Where am I going with my life?" (Later in this chapter, I describe a method to incubate your own dreams.)

At this point, Rita knew that her role as a mother and daughter was changing. Her father had recently died; her two sons were in college and her only daughter was almost a teenager. She felt a need for a new direction. Her interest in dreams had spurred her to become a founding life member of the Association for the Study of Dreams. She wanted to attend the first conference to be held in San Francisco in 1984, but was afraid to venture to that city alone from across the country. She was still sensitive about possible rejection.

The question, "Where am I going with my life?" led to a remarkable dream response. In the opening scene:

> I am entering a workroom with a cousin; we are discussing the death of my father and her mother and the illnesses of other aunts. I join three women who are working at the table and I am finishing up a small dress upon which I have been placing bows in a pattern.
>
> I am short one bow and search for the right piece of fabric from a pile on the floor. My cousin and an old school friend say they will help me.

Rita said that the dress in her dream seemed to be a mourning garment, though in a smaller size than she could wear, more the size for a child. Rita, who by now was quite sophisticated in understanding her dream symbols, saw this too-small mourning dress image as an indication that she was ready to leave her grief about herself and her injury behind—the mourning image did not "fit" anymore. Rita's cousin and her old school friend, she thought, symbolized different periods of her own life. She associated her cousin with her first twenty years; her friend, with the second twenty, with some overlap between the two. The dream concluded:

When we find the bow, they want to tape it on the dress but I say it should be glued. The tape is in the dining-room buffet, but the *glue* is in the *study*.

Later we discuss a trip and getting together for dinner with my old school friend and her ex-husband (who both live in San Francisco). They help me carry my suitcase as we leave. I have a definite feeling of traveling on.

Rita entitled this dream, "Finding the Missing Piece." She made a drawing of it that showed her path around the table which looked, she said, "like a yellow brick road." Thinking about the two time periods represented by her cousin and her friend led Rita to draw a "life clock" with time periods. She placed a question mark in the current cycle. Above this clock, Rita drew a hand with a finger moving a "spinner," as in a board game. It was a graphic representation: "What is the next move?" Rita thought that her dream was urging her to go to San Francisco, to "travel on" to this area, where the presence of her old school friend would support her, and to pursue her new interest.

Rita was puzzled at first by the dream reference, "the glue is in the study." What did she need to study? What did she need to glue in place? Pondering this, Rita later realized that the "missing piece" in the dream might be the "missing *peace*" she had been seeking. In her words, "During those nights when I dreamed of searching for the 'missing piece,' I was really looking for the 'missing peace' of my days. In letting go of my struggle to be like everyone else, I found inner peace and myself—in my own unique imperfection."[5]

Perhaps it was the study of dreams that would help her glue things together. Like Dorothy setting out to find the Wizard of Oz, Rita felt ready to go on her own grand adventure. Perhaps for the first time since her near-fatal injury, Rita felt peacefully whole. She undertook her journey and a new life unfolded. Dreamwork helped her to accept the enormous changes in her body and life activities. It helped her acknowledge that she would never again be the person she had been. She would no longer write chemical papers and earn patents. Perhaps now, she thought, her products were love and compassion.

Integration of a new body image and a new self may take a few months or a few decades. It is a process that must be periodically renewed. We will recognize integration by our increasing feeling of wholeness.

## ◇ TRANSFORMATION RITUALS

### ◇ New Behaviors as Health Returns

People who have been injured or ill often mark their return to wellness by specific behaviors (described in Chapter 3, *The Seven Stages of Recovery from Physical Trauma*). These actions are sometimes straightforward "freshening up." Rona, for instance, after being out of work for several months with a mangled wrist, had her hair colored and newly styled and got a manicure the week prior to returning to her job. Hand therapists report that one of the surest signs of increased vigor in a woman with a hand injury is beginning to use nail polish again or getting a manicure. Such women, like Rona, are feeling well enough to want to look attractive. Yet these behaviors imply even more.

We saw how an alienation of the afflicted body part is typical following an injury. Using nail polish indicates that the woman is reconnecting with her formerly disowned body part. We need to "readopt" our body parts to become whole. We can help ourselves do this by deliberately choosing words that repossess our bodies, saying "my scar," and so forth. We are creatures who act upon our environment; we're not simply passive recipients of forces. We can use active verbs to describe what we do or experience and deliberately use integrative imagery.[6]

Getting well is not simply the restoration of functioning. Ideally, our repaired body parts should move and function again with ease and grace. Bridging the gap between walking stiffly and moving with natural ease is crucial. This may not always be possible, of course, as when a body part has been damaged beyond repair or lost, but the closer we can move toward this goal, the better we will feel. Being well means we are able to use our repaired body as naturally and gracefully as possible given our circumstances. Oliver Sacks, whose leg had been so badly injured, found himself walking in a stiff and awkward fashion when he got out of his cast. This condition persisted for some time until he was persuaded by a consultant to do an activity he loved: swimming. By performing actions that felt natural to him in the water, he discovered that his natural grace carried over to moving fluently on land as well. He was once again able to walk with ease. Whether we dance or paint pictures, performing activities we love may help us make the final step to wellness.

Anger is a major problem for people who have been injured, along with depression. We must let go of our anger to get well. Hand therapist Marilyn Armbruster explained, "Many patients get stuck in anger and don't get better. They tell me how long they waited in the emergency room and what the doctor did wrong. They go over this every time I see them. These patients often don't improve."

I saw this fact personified in a young worker who had been injured when the ceiling collapsed while he was applying "mud," a type of plaster, to it. He received only minimal compensation, and so experienced much bitterness and resentment. "Eight years later," he told me, "I still get mad when I'm 'mudding.' " Forgiveness may truly be good for the body as well as the soul.

Another type of completion activity occurs when people arrange meetings with physicians against whom they have held grudges in regard to a misdiagnosis or unnecessary treatment. It even helps to telephone them or write letters, in order to confront them and express what you may have been unable to say while you were ill.

Although my husband and I eventually decided against taking legal action against the orthopedist who had worsened my injury, I had a need to tell him how I felt about his not listening to me. I also thought it was unfair that we should bear the financial burden of his misdiagnosis as well as the physical suffering. I wrote him a letter expressing these concerns and documenting our expenses beyond our insurance coverage. His prompt payment in response was satisfying. I already knew he deeply regretted what happened. I hoped he would be more careful with future patients. Such behaviors by people who are almost well tend to wrap up unfinished business.

If you find yourself harboring resentments toward people involved in an injury or illness you have experienced, try to find a way to resolve your feelings and set them aside for good.

### ◇ Specialized Transformation Rituals

Aside from these straightforward fixing-up and finishing-up behaviors, some people undertake symbolic actions. I was fascinated to observe and hear about the behaviors of some of the men and women who had been patients in the hand clinic I attended. I mentioned in Chapter 3 how one man melted down all his old arm splints and remolded the material into a sculpture; how a woman gave all the old parts of her splints, scar molds (a pink plastic used to compress a scar to keep it flat), stockinette strips, and other equipment to her daughter who modified this treatment apparatus into Christmas ornaments; and how another woman, who had used bags of beans as weights to strengthen her wrist during therapy, planned to cook the beans into a festive dish.

All these actions celebrated wellness by a transformation ritual. By turning the equipment associated with suffering into artful or nourishing objects, these men and women triumphed over their pain. They concretely honored their revival—new bodies for old—the reborn self.

Part of my own restoration to health involved the writing of this book. When I began to think of how other people were suffering over post-traumatic nightmares unnecessarily, as I had, of how they did not know this was a normal part of the healing process, and how many of them did not realize how to change their dreams, I was returning to my role as a psychologist and dream professional. By making my suffering worthwhile, in the sense of sparing others from hurtful misunderstandings, I was transforming my pain into a gift.

Take the time to think about how you could transform any of the equipment or materials you associate with a period of physical suffering into a positive memento. What else could you do? Is there a way others could benefit from what you have experienced? Plan to carry out the most appealing transformation ritual.

## ◊ THE SEQUENCE OF DREAM CHANGE DURING RECOVERY

### ◊ Garfield's Five Steps to Recovery

When I reviewed all the dream images I had during the period from my injury until three months after surgery, I observed a remarkable pattern. I believe this sequence of change in dreams during recovery is characteristic of most illnesses and injuries. During this fifteen weeks—from my injury that took place three weeks prior to surgery until twelve weeks after it—a clear sequence of change was evident in the dream pictures. This time frame divided itself into five periods of three weeks each. The length of these periods will vary for different people with different recovery rates, but the sequence is similar. I named these five phases of dream healing:

1. Replay of trauma
2. Accidental improvement
3. Deliberate improvement
4. Shift in power
5. Reintegration

A variety of images appeared in dreams during these five phases of recovery. Some of these images dealt directly with my injured body parts: my left arm, wrist, and hand, especially the ring and middle fingers, had been badly damaged. I had contusions on my left knee and had struck my left forehead. In the dreams I had during the fifteen-week period, I mentioned my arm, wrist, hand, fingers, and knee forty-six times. (See Appendix K for a documentation of these images.) Other images in my dreams depicted replays of my accident. My dream journal contained twelve scenes replaying my accident of falling and breaking my wrist. None of the twelve replays were exact repetitions of the trauma. (I did not include puns on the words *fall* and *break* that occurred in the dreams during this fifteen-week period.)

Each category of imagery, the injured body parts and replays of the accident, underwent a transformation during the fifteen weeks. I think a parallel pattern takes place in recovery from illnesses and other physical traumas. Perhaps you will recognize your own pattern.

Although I call the five categories "steps," they are more like "waves" because, despite overall differences, they overlap and double back in time. There is a general forward surge, but the steps are more blending than discrete. Every dreamer should be familiar with this natural pattern of metamorphosis. It is crucial information for whenever you may need it. A description of each phase follows.

## 1. REPLAY OF TRAUMA: EQUIVALENT OR WORSENED DREAM IMAGES

During this first phase, the dreamer or some other dream character repeats the waking trauma or illness, or endures a similar, but magnified one. The afflicted body part appears in the dream in the same poor condition, or worse, than in waking life. Nightmares and feelings of terror or horror are typical at this time. There may be a few rare images in which the dreamer receives specific healing treatment. These are consistently positive.

Example: *from injury until surgery (first three weeks).*
Score: *four replay images; eight injured body parts.*

*Injured Body Parts.* For the first three weeks, between my injury and the surgery to repair the damage, most dream references to my injured body parts were negative. Fear or outright terror was common. In these dreams, my injured body parts corresponded to the same conditions I experienced in my waking state, such as seeing a thick, deformed wrist. I had no awareness that I could change the condition. Sometimes the injured body part appeared in the dream in an exacerbated state: for instance, the dream of falling into the sea and getting my hands scraped against rough concrete as I climbed out. This dream image of scraping against concrete corresponded to the sensation of the rough plaster cast that rubbed my hand as I slept. Yet it was worse because both hands seemed affected in the dream.

Sometimes the dream images of my injured body part were emotionally neutral, as when I saw myself wearing long gauntlet gloves (the "glove" was probably stimulated by the sensation of the elbow-length splint I wore). During this phase, only one dream image of an injured body part was positive: an image in which I received a magical treatment—that of a man kissing my injured knee (probably a response to the tingling sensation I felt in it).

*Replays.* The four replay images that were present during this period were all negative: in one, I fell into the sea and climbed out; in the second, a dark pink marble or granite marquee, advertising "The Rocky Horror Show," broke off a movie house and just missed my husband and myself; in the third image, a woman was almost hit by a truck, fell, struck her head, and bled. This injured dream woman most closely corresponded to my actual condition, with a lump on my forehead and my black eye at the time. In the fourth image of this period, I fell into a bog and lost my purse, but I climbed out.

## 2. ACCIDENTAL IMPROVEMENT: CHANGE JUST HAPPENS

In dreams during this phase, there is an improvement in the condition of the afflicted body parts, or the dreamer discovers that he or she can move and function in a way heretofore impossible. Change just happens; it is not caused by the dreamer. These changes may be superior to the actual condition and are uniformly positive.

At this stage, improvement in the outcome of the trauma is present. If the original trauma or an exaggeration of it replays in the dream, the dreamer or some other dream character is able to get out of the situation or esape unscathed. Also, the trauma may take place but misses the dreamer. The danger just happens and escape is fortuitous.

> Example: *from surgery to three weeks post-surgery (second three weeks)*. Score: *five replay images; eight injured body parts*.

*Injured Body Parts.* During the period between surgery and three weeks after it, there were almost the same number of dream images, associated with the accident but their content began to shift. Despite repairs having been made to my wrist, new injuries were created by surgical incisions, insertion of a metal plate with screws, and stitching of the soft tissue and skin. Once again my dream images of the injured body parts were mostly negative images, equivalent to or more aggravated than my waking condition. In one of these, a dog bit a woman on her arm; in others, dream characters had injured hands. A few images were neutral. However, there was one positive image in which my functioning was greatly improved; I dreamed my cast was off and I observed that although my arm was thin, the wrist was well shaped. I was actually still wearing a heavy cast. The dream predicted accurately the good condition of my arm when the cast was removed a few days later, though I still could not move it normally.

*Replays.* In this period, replay images of falling began to change, too. There were five replay images, of which three were negative: one involved a collie falling off a high ledge, breaking its bones, bleeding, biting its owner and dying; the owner then fell and sprained her back; and a thermometer fell and broke into five pieces.

Alongside this negativity, however, healing forces could already be observed in two transformed replay images. In one image, I noticed that a large, fragile vase was tippy and might fall and smash, so I moved it to a safe corner. In the other, I was seated on a vehicle, perhaps a lawn mower, when the seat slowly gave way. As I fell, I became aware that I must not catch myself with my left hand and further injure it, so I turned myself around in midair, and eased my body gently down to the ground onto my bottom, unharmed. These dream images are actually more characteristic of the next phase, "deliberate improvement." This transformation of an ongoing dream marks a major shift in content of the dream replay images. Thenceforth, in the dreams of the remaining nine weeks, there were no further falls that resulted in injury.

### 3. DELIBERATE IMPROVEMENT: CHANGE IS CAUSED

In the dreams of this phase that involve the afflicted body part, dreamers may realize they do not have to accept malfunctions or limitations, at least not in the dream. Dreamers realize they have a choice.

At this stage, replay images are still present in which there is danger of the trauma recurring, or the trauma begins to happen, but it is averted by deliberate action of the dreamer. Behaviors such as moving objects, changing one's position, providing protection, or giving warnings are typical. The outcome of the trauma is improved by an action of the dreamer, not by chance. These replay dream images may begin negatively but become transformed into positive images.

Example: *from three to six weeks post-surgery (third three weeks)*. Score: *two replay images; seven body parts.*

*Injured Body Parts.* During this phase, there were only two negative dream images of my injured body part: in the first, my left hand was held outside a window and I felt frightened; in the second, my left arm was pulled down to the sidewalk and I couldn't move it. I awoke from the latter dream with my arm lying straight on the bed, instead of being elevated as it was supposed to be. There was one marvelous positive image of my injured body part, in which I wore a beautiful pink-and-green opal ring that a man used to bless himself by holding my hand to his forehead.

*Replays.* Only two replay images occurred in dreams of this time period; both included transformation or protection. In the first, my child fell into a tank of deep water during a swimming lesson. I rescued him, and to my surprise, he wanted to go on with the lesson. In the second, I was walking in a dangerous, snowy area with wildcats around. I was afraid I might slip and fall and not be found, but this did not happen. I gathered chunks of earth and ice to protect myself in case the wildcats came. These dream actions—rescuing a person who fell and acting to protect myself from danger—indicate increasing confidence in the inner powers of recovery.

### 4. SHIFT IN POWER: RECOVERY IMAGES TRIUMPH

This is the stage in which the tide turns; images of recovery predominate over images of injury. Dream images of the afflicted body part become largely positive—frequently with treatment or healing taking place within the dream. The dreamer may be able to perform movements heretofore impossible. For some dreamers, replay images stop completely.

Example: *from six to nine weeks post-surgery (fourth three weeks)*. Score: *zero replay images; fourteen body parts*.

*Replays.* Between six and nine weeks post-surgery, the most dramatic shift in my dreams took place. There were no replay dream images at all. Obviously, my dreaming mind was no longer occupied with what had happened in the past and was finding other matters of greater interest.

*Injured Body Parts.* In this period, the largest number of body part images arose. Although a few of these continued to be negative, equivalent to my condition or worse, and some were neutral, nearly half of the body part images were positive. The three negative dream images of my injured body part were: the metal plate in my arm might have to be removed; my finger was too swollen to fit inside a puppet; and I got stung on my left hand by a black bug. Notice how these events are all less serious than the dream images of the injured body part in earlier phases. In the dream in which my finger was too swollen, I realized I was wearing a splint and that I could remove it, thus allowing more hand flexibility. This dream recognition of unnecessary limitations was essential to recovery.

The several positive images of the injured body part were

astonishing and encouraging. These took various forms: in one dream, a door leading to somewhere important was marked with the symbol of a golden hand; in another, an artist wrote a signature with great skill and a fancy flourish. There were two dreams of special treatment: in the first, a woman rubbed and massaged my hands with a healing lotion; in the second, a woman physician made me a hand splint. Most striking of all, I discovered in a dream that I could scratch the middle of my back with my left hand. It felt good and I was very happy to be able to do this, though in the waking state I could not yet accomplish this movement. Such dream images seem to forecast the return of normal functioning.

### 5. REINTEGRATION: NEW BODY IMAGE FORMED

Replays of the original trauma are rare at this stage and may disappear entirely. The dreamer or dream character may witness danger to other characters but is able to rescue them without incurring harm to the self or the other. There is a reversal in the dreamer's role from victim to savior. The sequence is one of increasing control within the dream. The injured or ill person no longer feels helpless and victimized. Formerly traumatized dreamers are able to recognize danger and avert it by changes in their behavior.

In this phase, the dream images of the healing body part become a harmonious part of the symbolism of an ongoing story. The injured or ill body part becomes reintegrated; a new body image forms. The reintegration dream images are always positive. These latter three phases of healing in dreams tend to overlap.

> Example: *from nine to twelve weeks post-surgery (fifth three weeks)*. Score: *one replay; nine body parts*.

*Replays.* During the period of nine to twelve weeks post-surgery, only one replay image occurred. In it, a small boy was in danger of falling or being crushed when a mantelpiece on which he stood began to fall. I shouted a warning in time and he was saved. More than two years after my injury, I can say that replay imagery continues to occur, albeit rarely, probably when I feel anxious about some other situation. My dream characters seldom fall now; if they are in danger of doing so, they are often able to avert it or transform the situation.

*Injured Body Parts.* At this stage, most dream images about my recovering body part were positive. Only one negative image of a hand arose; in it, I pinned a bandage around a man's little finger that had a tiny scratch. Clearly, the size of my problem was shrinking. In an emotionally neutral dream image of my injured body part, I saw three different wrists: one too small and frail; one too large and swollen; one just right. It seemed as though, like Goldilocks, I could pick the one that was just right. Some of the positive dream images about the recovering body part were astounding. In one, women stood in a circle, holding hands while they recited a prayer of blessing or thanksgiving in an ancient tongue. In another, a man put his hand through a screen to shake my hand and thank me. In yet another, I read a wondrous book on dreams with beautiful pictures of *mudras* (hand gestures used in Buddhism to indicate the action of the deity, which is usually beneficent).

SUBJECTIVE SENSATIONS IN HAND DURING POST-SURGERY HEALING

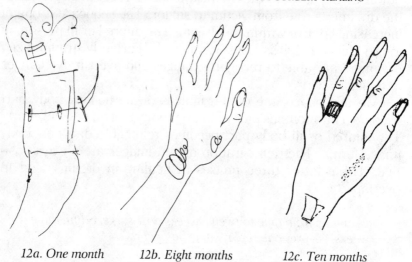

| 12a. One month | 12b. Eight months | 12c. Ten months |

Line drawings by Patricia Garfield

*The process of healing can be observed most clearly in a series of drawings. I drew the first picture, 12a, one month after surgery on my wrist. I had been out of the cast for three weeks, yet had only minimal movement in my wrist. My hand felt like a wooden block attached to a thick arm by a stiff metal hinge. My swollen thumb and fingers felt like weak, almost useless appendages. I sensed additional blockages in my fourth finger and in my thumb.*

*(continued)*

Thus, in the period between nine and twelve weeks post-surgery, the pattern of predominantly positive dream images of my recovering body part was firmly established. This became the stable pattern henceforth, with an occasional negative image of the healed body part, as setbacks or pain occurred. Sometimes a neutral image arose, but most dream images of my recovering body part were positive ones that became increasingly symbolic.

### SUMMARY OF THE SEQUENCE OF INJURED BODY PART IMAGES

Notice how the dream images of the injured body part started out mostly negative, became a mixture of positive and negative imagery, then shifted to mostly positive. Their quantity was moderately high at first (eight body parts in the first three weeks), reached a peak (fourteen body parts in the fourth period of three weeks), then abated (nine body parts in the fifth period of three weeks). The following shows the pattern of body parts in my dreams after injury:

| PHASES OF RECOVERY | NUMBER OF BODY PARTS |
|---|---|
| 1. first three weeks (from injury to surgery) | 8 |
| 2. surgery to three weeks post-surgery | 8 |

---

*The second drawing, 12b, was made over eight months post-surgery. I had weekly physical therapy sessions during this time and practiced daily exercises at home. By then, my hand felt reintegrated. Although movement of my wrist was still restricted, the sensation was that of a strong spring, rather than a stiff hinge. There was still a stiffness at the base of my thumb—depicted by the smaller spring—but the blockage in my fourth finger was gone and my fingers felt useful.*

*The third drawing, 12c, was done ten months post-surgery. It shows normal fingers and a flexible apparatus in my wrist (in fact, I still had a metal plate attached to my radius). The sensation of stiffness at the base of my thumb was reduced to small spots of numbness. For the first time since my injury, I drew my wedding ring on my hand, which I had been unable to wear because of swelling. It was a visible marker of return to near normality.*

3. three to six weeks post-surgery          7
4. six to nine weeks post-surgery         14
5. nine to twelve weeks post-surgery      9

Dream images of the injured body parts peaked at six to nine weeks post-surgery because healing and reintegration images were occurring simultaneously with the images of damage.

### SUMMARY OF THE SEQUENCE OF REPLAY IMAGERY

The overall pattern of replay imagery showed the greatest number of negative images taking place soon after the initial trauma. Positive images, in which the trauma was averted, overlapped with the negative ones and eventually predominated, then disappeared altogether. Dreams of replaying the trauma were moderately high at first (five images in the first three weeks), then increased (six images in the second period of three weeks), then decreased to a low (one image in the fifth period of three weeks). The following shows the pattern of dream images replaying my accident:

| PHASES OF RECOVERY | NUMBER OF REPLAY IMAGES |
|---|---|
| 1. first three weeks (from injury to surgery) | 5 |
| 2. surgery to three weeks post-surgery | 6 |
| 3. three to six weeks post-surgery | 2 |
| 4. six to nine weeks post-surgery | 0 |
| 5. nine to twelve weeks post-surgery | 1 |

This pattern showed that scenes replaying my trauma were most intense closest to the accident. In my replay dreams, characters moved from the role of passive victim to that of active savior.

The natural pattern of healing moves from repetition or exaggeration of a real-life trauma to the ability to recognize the danger of it within the dream, to averting it by changing one's behavior, by protecting oneself, or by rescuing those at risk.

To summarize, there seems to be a natural pattern of healing that appears in dreams consisting of: (1) replay images of the initial trauma in which the afflicted body part appears in an equivalent or worse condition than waking; (2) accidental improvement in the trauma outcome and afflicted body part in which change just happens; (3) deliberate improvement in the outcome of the trauma and the afflicted body part in which change is caused; (4) a shift in power to predominantly positive imagery; (5) reintegration of the recovered body part in which a new body image is formed.

A few other investigators have reported similar dream-healing sequences. Ernest Rossi—a Jungian therapist, hypnotist, and theorist of the mind/body connection—shared with me his observations about the changes in dreaming that take place as a person recovers from smoking and other addictions.[7] Dreamworker Reed Morrison found a pattern of change in the dreams of alcoholics and drug addicts as they recovered from their addictions.[8] Psychologist Stanley Krippner, dealing also with recovery from chemical addiction, described his treatment of a patient named Curtis who kept a dream diary as he was recovering from cocaine addiction.[9] Still other writers speak of stages of recovery that appear in dreams as a person overcomes the effects of sexual abuse.[10] Each of these approaches share principles in common—my "Five phases to Recovery," Rossi's "Four R's to Recovery," Morrison's "Mapping of Recovery," or other similar schemes. In each system, when the dreamer changes his or her behavior in a dream, it becomes easier to accomplish change in the waking state.[11]

Trauma takes many forms. Your recovery may have a beneficent pattern of its own, which you may discover on your road to wellness, using your dreams as a guide. However, being aware of a natural pattern of healing, you have the possibility of deliberately evoking imagery that is characteristic of returning health. Perhaps you can accelerate this process.

## ◇ DREAM ACTIVITIES: HEALING, INCUBATION, AND LUCID DREAMING

◇ 1. Review your dream journal, and count the
number of afflicted body images in your dreams
between any injury or illness and three weeks later.

You can use another convenient time period if you prefer. Also count, if applicable, replay images. Most nightmares abate by six weeks post-crisis. You may want to work on any persisting nightmares with the method described in dream activities four and five below. If you are still troubled by bad dreams about your trauma, consider seeking professional assistance.

◇ 2. Count the number of afflicted body parts and
replay images appearing in dreams from three to six
weeks post-crisis.

If you use a different time period, keep the two periods equal in length. Be sure you are counting the same type of dream images in both time periods. That is, an image of the afflicted body part is the same body part whether the image is pleasant or not. A dream image of a trauma resembling yours is the same image whether the outcome is positive or negative.

◇ 3. Compare the dream themes in the two periods,
and assess your stage of dream healing.

Is there a reduction in the number of afflicted body parts? Is there a shift away from negative content in the dreams to more positive content? Are fewer replays of the trauma taking place? Describe any differences briefly in your dream journal. Which of the five steps to recovery do your dreams match most closely? (You may want to review the definitions of these steps on pages 237–247.) Record your opinion of your current phase of healing. You may wish to repeat this activity at intervals in order to assess changes taking place in your dreams.

◇ 4. Apply the healing sequence to your own dreams.

Select a nightmare or unpleasant dream that replays a trauma you have experienced. Ask yourself:

A. When could I have recognized the danger that was present in my dream?
B. How could I have averted the dream danger?
C. Could I have moved something to prevent the danger from happening?
D. Could I have protected myself with something already present in the dream?
E. What could I have added to the dream to help or rescue myself? (This can be assistance from superhumans, animal helpers, or magical equipment.)

    F.  How could I have changed the dream danger by chang-
ing my own behavior?
    G.  How could I have saved others at risk in my dream?

    ◇ 5. "Replay" the dream now in your imagination.

See the changes that most appeal to you taking place. Repeat
this imagery just before you fall asleep, making it vivid and life-
like.

Changing dream imagery may seem like a small comfort if
you are still suffering from a waking life trauma or illness, but
there is nothing to be gained by continuing to suffer in your
dreams as well. Move in the natural, positive direction of health.
By picturing your dreams differently, you not only have a chance
to change them, you will be providing yourself with a better
mood when you awake. Just visualizing changes taking place
may encourage you to meet the challenges of your day. And it is
possible that you will even be accelerating your physical healing.

People have an inherent urge to move toward health. We
have an inner impulse in the direction of wholeness. By recognizing it in our dream images, by valuing it and encouraging it,
we help ourselves achieve it.

    ◇ 6. Incubate a dream on a specific topic.

You may wish to question your dreaming mind about some aspect of your recovery. This process is a modern version of the
ancient practice of dream incubation. In olden times, as mentioned previously, pilgrims traveled to dream temples to sleep,
hoping to receive a dream in which the healing god would appear to cure them or give them advice about a problem. The first
step is to get ready to dream.

### BEFORE INCUBATING A DREAM
*1. Plan your incubation question or request.*

We saw how Rita incubated a dream to answer the question, "Where am I going with my life?" Some other popular
dream incubation questions or requests that injured or ill dreamers find useful are:

What direction shall I take now?
What's next?
What shall I do about my current problem?
How can I help heal myself?
How can I get well?
Am I ready to return to work?
Help me to move my body naturally.
Teach me what to do.
Bring me relief.
Give me hope.
Give me peace.
Comfort me.
Show me the divine.
Take me where I need to go; show me what I need to know.

Your question or request should be concise and phrased in words that are meaningful to you. It should be a topic you care about. Some people find rhyme or rhythm helps them recall their incubation phrase. The last statement on the list is my personal favorite, because it leaves open the possibility of the dreaming mind to respond with whatever is most needed at the moment. You may prefer to dream about a particular person, place, or activity. It's up to you.

Some dreamworkers object to "setting up" the dream beforehand and to questioning characters during the dream.[12] They would limit the dreamer's interaction strictly to visualizations after the dream is complete. My own point of view is that, so long as the dreamer honors the dream, questioning it before, during, or afterward may be beneficial. Your dreaming mind will not be forced to do something it is unwilling to do. Whatever answers may emerge come from your deepest self; they are not imposed from outside. Incubating a dream takes effort, so the process is not undertaken lightly. Furthermore, I believe dreams are a natural resource. Dreamers should feel free to consult their innermost guide whenever they wish.

*2. Rehearse your incubation question or request.*

After selecting your incubation phrase or sentence, pick a day when you are not overtired and can concentrate on your purpose. Look at pictures or books, or engage in activities that are relevant to your goal. Repeat your incubation request several times during the day. Gently remind yourself of your goal for the night's dream. Write your incubation request in your dream journal, along with your notes about your emotional state and activities during the day. As you drift into the drowsy, hypnagogic period prior to sleep, chant your phrase softly in your mind like a lullaby.

*3. Visualize your incubation question or request being fulfilled.*

Picture your question being answered or your request being fulfilled as you fall asleep, but leave yourself open to whatever response the dream may provide.

### AFTER INCUBATING A DREAM

*4. Record your dream and explore it as an answer to your request.*

Some dreams appear at first to have no connection with the incubation question or request. By patiently working through the chief images in your incubated dream, as explained in the D-R-E-A-M-S method in Chapter 1, and regarding the overall message as a possible answer, you may see a profound connection. If no link is obvious between your incubation request and your responsive dream, you may wish to repeat the attempt. Sometimes three or four nights in a row are necessary to produce a clear dream answer. A few dreamers have found that after trying to incubate a dream, then giving up the attempt, a vivid dream answer appears.

*5. Use your judgment as to whether the advice in the dream is valid.*

As with every piece of advice, we must use our common sense. If following the dream answer makes sense, and the suggestion is not likely to be harmful, you may wish to act on the advice. If you feel uncertain about the dream advice, or are concerned that it might not be good for you, consult your physician or some other health professional who is familiar with your situation. Some dreamers have received remarkably helpful advice in their dreams regarding food that was especially nourishing for their condition, or activities that helped speed their recovery, or simply providing visions of beauty that comforted and replenished their spirit.

### ◇ 7. Incubate a lucid dream.

The main difference between incubating a dream to answer a question or fulfill a request and incubating a lucid dream is what you do *within* the dream itself.

As you work with your dreams, you may find yourself becoming aware that you are dreaming *during* the dream. This remarkable insight, called "lucid dreaming," has been observed since the time of Aristotle.[13] Many dreamers use the awareness they are dreaming to "escape" to the waking world, not realizing that lucid dreaming allows the dreamer a power and freedom that is rarely, if ever, experienced in waking life—the magical ability to fly, to travel instantaneously to distant lands, to converse with the deceased or with distant friends, and to make love with a special person. Lucid dreaming may even provide a unique opportunity to direct the body's natural healing powers.

For centuries, dreamers' descriptions of the amazing state of lucid dreaming were dismissed as mere anecdotes. Sleep researchers thought that lucid dreams were not real dreams, but must be imaginings, the product of the drowsy mind as it drifted toward sleep, or perhaps they were hallucinations or semiawakenings. We know now that lucid dreams are true dreams.

The single most important development in the field of dreams in recent years is the demonstration by Stephen LaBerge, of the Stanford University Sleep Clinic, that lucid dreaming is real dreaming. For the first time, he was able to prove that lucid dreaming occurs during rapid eye movement (REM) sleep.

In 1978, using himself and a few lucid-dreaming participants, LaBerge carried out the definitive experiment. His subjects were able to make eye-movement signals or clench their fists in Morse code when they became aware that they were dreaming; these signals were recorded on a polygraph in the sleep laboratory. Soon LaBerge trained dozens of subjects to become lucid in their dreams, signal when they realized they were dreaming, perform some task—such as singing, counting, or flying—and signal again when they had completed their dream assignment.

When LaBerge's popular book, *Lucid Dreaming*, came out in 1985, lucid-dream groups began forming across the country. The press picked up the subject and wrote about it avidly. Television and radio media probed the implications of this unusual state of consciousness. An event first mentioned by Aristotle became hot copy in the modern world because it had been scientifically measured.

Currently, LaBerge has developed prototypes of infrared goggles that illuminate when a dream period begins. An electrode in the goggles emits a pulsing red light when REM movements start. Using this "DreamLight" while they sleep, thousands of people may soon be able to dream lucidly. However, special equipment is not essential to learn the technique of lucid dreaming. The following are some suggestions for becoming lucid in your dreams:[14]

### BEFORE LUCID DREAMING

*1. Set a goal.*

Plan what you will do when you become lucid in a dream. Will you fly? Make love with the partner of your choice? Rehearse some skills? Travel to some exotic place? Contact another dreamer? Ask your dream characters what they represent? Ask your dream what it is you most need?

Your first goal may simply be to have a lucid dream. It often helps to write your intention down in your journal before falling asleep, as a suggestion to yourself.

*2. Remember your goal.*

Remind yourself of your lucid dream goal during the day by putting it into a short phrase that you repeat like a chant or mantra as you drift to sleep. For instance, "Tonight I fly." If you awaken during the night, repeat your phrase over and over like a lullaby as you fall asleep again.

*3. Visualize your goal.*

Picture yourself remembering your goal during a dream. Imagine what it will look like and feel like.

### DURING PRE-LUCID DREAMING

*1. Be alert to frightening dream images.*

The most common way people become lucid is to become so scared that they realize they are dreaming. Whenever you are chased or attacked in a dream, or something else terrible happens to you or another dream character, you have a chance to recognize that you are dreaming. You might notice yourself having a recurrent nightmare or find yourself dreaming the same old thing again. Use your knowledge that you are dreaming— not to awaken—but to stay asleep. See what happens without being afraid, or change your dream to suit yourself.

*2. Be alert to bizarre, dreamlike elements.*

Notice any incongruities or bizarre elements in the dream story. Recognize those two giant horses in the sky as dream creatures. Test the reality of your dream. Some dreamers find it useful to ask themselves during the day, "Is this a dream?" and test their answer by various behaviors, such as jumping to see if they can fly (if they can, they *know* they're dreaming).

3. *Watch for changes in sensation such as the following:*

*Feeling of Wind*

Wind blowing in your face or a cool draft in a dream may signal the start of lucidity.

*Tingling of Skin*

A tingling sensation on your skin, often associated with the dream image of light rain or drizzle, sometimes marks the start of lucidity.

*Sound/Vibration*

Many lucid dreamers report the presence of a combined buzzing/tingling or a buzzing light when they become lucid.

*Patch of Light*

A crack, patch, or hole of light—sometimes as an open window—often appears in lucid dreams.

*Repeating Dream Story*

When a dream story seems to begin again—a phenomenon I call "doubleness"—this is often a signal that a dream may become lucid.

*Intense Eye Focusing*

An intense staring or focusing of the eyes in a dream may occur at the start of lucidity.

*Shifting Consciousness*

A sense of "going to sleep," "waking up," "going into a trance," "feeling lightheaded," or "feeling tired" in the dream often precedes lucid dreaming.

*Rhythmic Movements*

Lucid dreams are frequently precipitated by dream images of rhythmic dancing, spinning, swimming, or pelvic thrusting.

*Being Suspended in the Air*

Flying, floating, or levitating in a dream are almost certain precursors to becoming lucid.

4. *Analyze the ongoing dream.*

Are you having the same scary dream again? Are you suggesting to yourself what some dream image symbolizes? Recognize it for a dream; become lucid.

5. *Be alert to dream mirrors.*

Pay special attention if you find yourself looking into a reflecting surface in a dream, such as a mirror, window glass, or pond. These images are often a symbol for self-reflection and may provide the opportunity to become lucid.

*6. Maintain emotional balance.*

Once you have become lucid during a dream, stay calm. Keep a balance between becoming so emotional that you awaken, or so unfocused that you forget you are dreaming. Perform your goal, or just let the dream play on while you watch, unafraid and conscious.

### AFTER LUCID DREAMING

*1. Review your pre-lucid moments.*

When you have had a regular, non-lucid dream, reexamine it for the points when you might have realized you were dreaming (see the clues listed in the previous section). When you have a lucid dream, observe which dream images preceded your lucid state. You may wish to head a page in your dream journal "pre-lucid moments" and create a list of these images as you experience them.

*2. Visualize being lucid in your next dream.*

When you awaken from a nonlucid ordinary dream, picture yourself recognizing the next dream as a dream.

*3. Give waking form to your special lucid dream images.*

"Artifacts" from dreams will help you understand their symbolism and remind you of their message. Paint or draw your special lucid-dream images or find pictures that recapture their essence. Place this dream artifact where you can see it until you feel you have absorbed the message of your dream image.

### ◇ 8. Incubate a lucid healing dream.

To incubate a lucid healing dream, amend the directions for incubating a lucid dream as follows:

### BEFORE A LUCID HEALING DREAM:

1. Select your healing goal and put it into words.
   *Examples:* Teach me to reduce or eliminate my pain. Help me heal. Show me contentment.
2. Rehearse your healing goal, repeating it before sleep.
3. Visualize your healing goal being fulfilled.

### DURING A LUCID HEALING DREAM:

1. Become lucid in your dream.
2. Perform your dream healing or allow it to take place.
3. Accept the wisdom of your dream.

AFTER A LUCID HEALING DREAM:

1. Value any dream healing you receive, whether your dream was lucid or not.
2. Find a memento to recall your dream-healing experience and treasure it. Place it where you can see it and recall its message.

The potential for healing in lucid dreams is enormous. Lucid dreams are much more intense than waking visualizations. Our body functions change during dreams just as they would if we were exposed to the things and people being pictured. Yet waking visualizations alone have been found to improve health conditions. Lucid dream visualizations should be even more effective.

As of now, we have no scientific proof that picturing a body disturbance improving in a lucid dream actually changes the physical body. However, many intriguing accounts are accumulating. Psychologist Jayne Gackenbach has collected many of these lucid dream-healing tales.[15] I have encountered several myself. Ed, for example, one of the men I interviewed who is a frequent lucid dreamer, told me that he often uses lucid dreams to heal small wounds. Ed makes drums and occasionally cuts himself while working. Whenever he has been injured, and is able to become lucid in a dream, Ed reminds himself to direct healing energy into his wound. When he succeeds, he says, his wound heals more rapidly than usual.

EXAMPLE OF LUCID DREAM HEALING:
MATTIE CLEANS OUT HER LEG

At the 1988 conference of the Association for the Study of Dreams held at the University of California, Santa Cruz, a young woman I will call Mattie told how she had been helped in a lucid dream. She had suffered a severe ankle fracture that limited her to a wheelchair for many months. She decided to use her ability to have lucid dreams to heal herself.

Whenever she became aware that she was dreaming, Mattie pictured herself "going inside my ankle." There she looked around and saw "all sorts of junk." In these lucid dreams, Mattie busied herself with removing from her injured ankle the debris she found—screwdrivers, bolts, and all sorts of tools. When she was awake, she found her condition improving. For the first time since her injury, Mattie was able to walk.

Such accounts as Mattie's and Ed's are, of course, extremely difficult to verify or study. Stories of healing in lucid dreams do, however, offer hope that injured dreamers may be able to speed their recovery through lucid dreaming. We have little to lose and much to gain. If the idea appeals to you, try directing healing energy into any disturbed body area the next time you have a lucid dream. You will be a pioneer in an exciting new frontier of dream research.

In the last chapter, *Your Inner Dream Temple*, I offer a series of visualizations about an imaginary journey to a dream temple, based on my own visits to ancient ruins as well as on historical records. You may find these visualizations help consolidate your skills in incubating a dream—lucid or not—that will grant you advice or healing. You will be invited to encounter your inner dream guide—an imaginary figure who is powerful beyond your wildest dreams. Your guide awaits you each night.

# 9

# YOUR INNER DREAM
# TEMPLE

The material in this chapter is meant to transport you—
to carry you to another space for a new and nourishing experience. Becoming well is more than a matter of recovering from
physical trauma. Healing may mean an emotional or spiritual
renewal even more than a physical one.

Whenever you are seriously injured or ill, you will set out
on a healing journey. Regardless of what the final outcome may
be, your voyage can become a source of self-understanding and
discovery. As you undertake the outward journey to recover
from an accident or a sickness, you also undertake the inward
journey.

In the next several pages, you are invited to take an imaginative journey by way of a series of visualizations to an ancient
Greek dream temple.[1] In the course of this voyage, you'll have
the opportunity to refine several of the dreaming skills that you
have learned throughout the book. Yet this unique presentation
may help you reach a deeper level, a more mythological and
archetypal level, of your imagination. The highlight of the jour-

ney is an encounter with your inner guide. These visualizations are intended to help evoke the healing power in your dreams.

I preface each stage of your imaginative journey with an introduction that tells the purpose of that visualization and how it might apply to you.

Perhaps you'll want to glance through the entire chapter first, so you'll have some idea of what to expect. Then have someone read the visualizations aloud to you, or record the complete set onto a cassette tape by yourself, or ask a friend with a soothing voice to record it. The groups of dots indicate a pause of about five seconds. The portions to be read aloud are preceded by an asterisk. Hearing the words as you visualize them will give you the full impact of the imagery and your focused imagination working together.

I also describe a set of activities for each phase of the journey that you can perform with basic supplies, if you wish, to heighten the effect of the visualizations. Although some of the activities may seem overly simplistic, they can provoke potent reaction. I suggest you undertake these activities in the spirit of a personal ritual. Some of the activities are best performed before the visualizations; others are better performed during or afterward. Descriptions of the activities are placed before or after the visualizations, according to which is usually most effective. There may be some activities you will want to repeat after the visualization as well as before it.

You can work through the visualizations and/or the activities on separate days, if you prefer. However, the result may be strongest if you can fantasize the journey as a whole.

◇ Adjusting the Visualizations and Activities

You may wish to make changes in the script that fit your personal preference or ability. For example, I describe the voyage as starting out on a ship. People subject to seasickness may prefer to substitute a train or airplane for the means of transport. The necessary element is that you journey outward from where you are now to travel to a different space. How you get there is irrelevant. Tailor the examples to suit yourself. Make it more appropriate for you wherever possible. And, as always, listen to your heart.

If you reroute a portion of the trip, be sure to include all your senses in the picture—how it looks, sounds, feels, or even smells or tastes. All visualizations must contain a few bare essentials:

1. Set a relaxed and receptive mood.
2. Travel to another mental or physical space.
3. Paint the scene using all your senses.
4. Encounter and experience.
5. Discover.
6. Return refreshed.

If you design a personal visualization, make sure it includes these six elements. Be sure to emphasize whatever sensory experiences are most evocative for you.

Let's begin. Settle yourself into a safe, restful place where you will be free from interruption for at least fifteen minutes. Make sure your clothing is comfortable—not too cool or too warm—and loosen any tight belts or restrictive items. You may want to pull on a sweater or blanket and rest against a pillow. Close the door to ensure privacy and open a window or otherwise make sure there is a circulation of fresh air. You'll need a full hour to do an entire visualization in one sitting.

## ◇ PREPARATION

### ◇ Introduction to "Preparation"

To prepare for this journey requires collecting your thoughts and emotions about what you most want or need at the moment. This is equivalent to the activity of incubating a dream. You need to clearly and concisely formulate your purpose. Write down an incubation request or question on a sheet of paper and put it in your journal. This will help you clarify your personal goal.

### ◇ Activities for "Preparation"

Fold the sheet of paper with your incubation request written on it, and place it under your pillow when you go to sleep tonight. The next day put it into your journal when you record your dreams of the previous night. You'll come back to it at the conclusion of your travel.

You may also find it helpful to construct an actual object that represents your problem or question. This "request-object" can be a small reproduction of a body part, such as those votive offerings pilgrims of old carried to the healing shrines, or it may be a representation of a nonphysical problem or a question you have. Actually making this object, or even drawing it in simple form, will help you concentrate your purpose. Set your request-object somewhere in your bedroom where you will see it often to remind you of your wish. Look at your request-object before falling asleep.

## ◇ INVOCATION

*Long ago in ancient Greece, the god of dreams was called Onei-ros (oh-NYE-rus), son of the black-winged Hypnos (HIP-nohss), the god of sleep. Let these grand mythological figures guard your journey and bring you safely home. If you wish, invoke additional favorite figures to accompany you on your imaginative trip.

Wherever you are, make yourself very, very comfortable . . . Lie down or lean back . . . Close your eyes . . . Breathe in and breathe out . . . If you like, allow Hypnos to fan his great feathered black wings in front of you . . . Let yourself drift with the soft currents of air . . . Breathe deeply and evenly, inhale the fresh air and allow any tension to melt away as you exhale . . . Relax your body, but hold your mind alert . . . as though awake in a dream . . .
[Repeat this invocation whenever you begin a visualization.]

### ◇ Visualization for "Preparation"

*As for any journey, you must prepare. Experience yourself now resting in your bedroom at home . . . See it clearly, the colors, the forms. Hear the sounds coming from outside as though far, far away . . . In your mind's eye, get up now and begin to pack a small bag. Take only the absolute essentials, for this voyage is of the spirit. What do you truly need? See yourself putting these few things inside a bag.

When you have packed all that you think you need, ask yourself what it is that you most want in your life at the moment. What troubles you or grieves you or makes you feel anxious? Do you want advice on any subject? Are you feeling out of balance? Focus on one important need. Think about this problem, source of suffering, or question.

When you have clearly defined what it is you want to know or have or feel, find an object that captures the essence of this problem or question. If no such thing exists, create it. Find or make an object that epitomizes your problem or question. See its shape and its characteristics . . . It may be very heavy; it may be light in weight but painful to touch. Create and see this request-object . . . Feel its texture with your fingers . . . Picture yourself placing this object in your bag if it will fit. If this is not possible, arrange a way to transport it with you. This request-object is essential as an offering to your inner guide. Make it and take it with you.

[Note: If you are pausing here in your travel, make the following "reawakening" suggestions given in the Interval that follows. Use this Interval conclusion whenever you wish to stop. When you begin once more, repeat the Invocation, then pick up the journey at the point where you stopped.]

## ◇ INTERVAL

*You have completed an important phase of your inner journey. Let yourself sense this accomplishment . . . Now allow yourself to slowly return to your normal state. See yourself resting comfortably in your own bedroom. Feel refreshed and renewed by your imagination. Stretch and yawn and come back to full awareness. More and more clear and alert. Sit up now and make any brief notes you wish in your journal to recall this part of your experience. Get up and go about your life, keeping a part of your mind in touch with an inner peacefulness.

## ◇ THE VOYAGE

### ◇ Introduction to "The Voyage"

The image of a journey is archetypal. It is a metaphor for the inner journey. As you travel outwardly, you also journey inwardly. The sea voyage, in particular, symbolizes the adventure of self-discovery. You are undertaking an imaginary pilgrimage in quest of your own center. The cyclic movement of a round trip, traveling to and returning from another place, also represents the course of your life, and especially the quest for wisdom. Naturally, there are obstacles and difficulties along the way.

To board a ship, and to set sail, is to make a commitment to this inner journey. Your voyage is intended to help you rise above your ordinary existence in search of transcendent truths.

The ship itself is a symbol of a human body carrying the soul. Traditionally, ships are feminine, as if the people inside them were as children within a womb. In ancient times, when a ship was named, a blood sacrifice was offered to some god. Later on, this practice was replaced with the breaking of a bottle of red wine to symbolize the blood. Nowadays, breaking a bottle of champagne over a ship's prow to christen it is the remnant of this ancient practice. The prows of ancient ships often were carved with a figurehead who served as the tutelary deity to safeguard the voyage.

The sea over which the ship travels is literally the source from which all life proceeded. Symbolically, the sea stands for the unconscious—that vast reservoir of vital energy, dangerous forms hidden in darkness, and sunken treasures. The poet Homer called the sea "wine-dark." In its darkness you may glimpse the sea monsters and sea guides of your own dreaming mind. As you cross the waters, you move through time. When you reach the seaport beyond, a new land and a new experience begin.

◇ Activities for "The Voyage"

On a tray or table near where you plan to sit or lie for the visualization, place the following items:

- Drinking glass
- Bottle or flask of fresh, cool mineral water
- Piece of whole-grain bread or roll
- Piece of fruit

Make any substitutions that are appropriate for your situation. Also, get out your favorite pillow and a soft blanket or shawl. If possible, use a rocker to simulate the movement of a ship.

Get settled in the rocker with your pillow supporting your

neck and head, and cover your body, or part of it, with the blanket. Turn on the tape recorder, or ask a friend to read the visualization aloud. Rock gently as you fantasize about your voyage. When you "awaken" in the morning in the visualization, drink some of the mineral water, eat some bread, and taste a bit of fruit. If you plan to go directly on to the next visualization, pause to refresh yourself with the items on your tray.

### ◇ Visualization for "The Voyage"

[Repeat the Invocation if you are beginning again.]

*Now you see yourself boarding a ship . . . Visualize it in any style that appeals to you—a small schooner, an old-fashioned sailing boat, a great ocean liner. Perhaps there is a figurehead, a unique figure from one of your dreams. Decorate your ship for comfort and convenience in whatever way you like . . .

See yourself aboard your ship. There is a shrill whistle, a lurch, and the vessel begins to move. The ship is underway—your inner journey has begun.

You are moving swiftly through the water. Hear the slapping of the waves against the hull of the ship . . . Feel the whizzing of the wind in your face . . . Smell the salt air . . . Taste the spray on your lips . . . Look down into the water . . . Glimpse the forms moving in its depths—the depths within you . . . Perhaps there is a dolphin alongside . . . Look at the sky above . . . Listen to the call of the gulls.

Visualize your day aboard. Eat and enjoy yourself. Play games, dance, gamble, swim, anything you like. Be yourself. Be comfortable. Have fun.

Night has come . . . The stars are shining brightly. The moon reflects a path across the water . . . You retire to your cabin. You undress and put on your night clothes, if you wear them. You perform your bedtime rituals. You climb into your bunk and turn out the light. Listen to the night sounds—the steps in the corridor, the chatter of distant crew, the purr of the ship, the whoosh of the water as it plows the sea.

Feel the gentle rocking of the ship as you ride . . . You are lulled as in a cradle. On and on the ship rushes, leaving your past far behind, racing toward an unknown shore, with you cradled in its womb . . . Perhaps the water grows turbulent, for your dreams seem dark. On and on the ship speeds. You are going back . . . back . . . back in time.

### DISEMBARKATION

A sound pierces your sleep. You awaken to the scurry of feet in the corridor. Land, land ahead. You arise and wash and dress. You eat from the tray of fruit and bread that has been placed in front of your cabin door. You drink pure, sweet water from a flask. You pull your things together and hasten with your bag to the deck, wondering what is going on.

How fresh the early morning air feels and smells. The sun is just rising over the hills at the port. The crowd around you murmurs in a foreign tongue. How puzzling. You seem to be the only person who speaks your language. Even their garb looks foreign. The ship is docking now at the primitive port. After much clanking of rings and winding of ropes, the ship is secured and you disembark, going down the wooden ramp with the crowd of strangers. Your feet touch new soil. You have reached a new stage of the inner adventure. [Give the Interval conclusion if you are stopping here.]

## ◇ ON THE ROAD

### ◇ Introduction to "On the Road"

To set out on the unknown road is to become a pilgrim. It is a decisive step. You are traveling toward your center in search of truth. A certain amount of trust is necessary as you find yourself in a strange land, confronting the unknown. Your purpose is to extract meaning from your road through life. The baggage you carry contains your essentials, your burdens, and your offering. As a seeker, you must cope with the obstacles of the road, whatever they may prove to be.

You'll be asked to climb an imaginary mountain. Climbing represents an emotional or spiritual ascent. All higher development is achieved with labor. The difficulties of the ascent correspond to your struggle for inner development as well as efforts to cope with external conditions through life. The heat and dust are life's annoyances. But there are compensations, too.

The stream that issues from the rocky crag offers regeneration. Out of the solid rock flows the source of life. By washing in these waters, and drinking of them, you may taste spiritual rebirth. These are waters of wisdom that awaken the dreamer to lucidity. They not only cleanse, but also may restore and refresh your spirit.

The candles set into the rocky niches represent the light of understanding, as yet unlit. The staff you create is your support and protection to help you move forward. As you enter the sacred grove at the crest of the mountain, you come closer to the heart of the matter. From here, you can see the green fertile valley below, with its temples, where the valuables are gathered. As you start the descent, you feel in the breezes, the life force, the living movement of the spirit concentrated below. The olive tree you'll pass is a symbol of fertility because it lives for hundreds of years, flourishing and bearing fruit on sandy soil. Here in the sacred grove you'll have an imaginary encounter with the serpents who are the border guardians to the sacred precincts. These are not the evil serpents of biblical tradition. These are the healing serpents who shed their skins to constantly renew life. On the altar, the table or throne of the gods of this high place, you'll leave a small sacrifice. This will help you begin to restore any balance that's needed in your life.

◇ Visualization for "On the Road"

[Repeat the Invocation if you are beginning again.]

*It is daybreak. You are being jostled along with the throng into the small seaside village. The white buildings of this little seaport gleam pink in the thin morning sun. Everyone seems to be headed the same way, jabbering and gesticulating. You ask someone at the head of the group for directions, but no one understands you. People shrug or smile and turn away. You heft your bag and walk along with the group. They must be going to a place where you can get information, for they seem to have a purpose and direction. As the group passes the local market stands, people pause at one stall or another to make purchases. Some buy fruit; others pick cakes; a few purchase a rooster or a sheep. You find a few coins of odd design in your pocket and buy a bunch of grapes. You are impatient to find out where you are and what is happening.

Crossing through the small village, the crowd reaches a road on the far side marked by a white signpost with old, illegible letters. Here the people change direction and take the road. Although the route is narrow, you can tell it is an important road because it is flanked by columns—tall, white, and slender—leading into the distance.

## THE ROAD ASCENDS

The people grow quiet as they walk, their sandals shooshing across the paving stones. They nod or smile at one another, but speak little as the road rises and requires more effort to climb. Your shoes become dusty and you feel pleasantly warm as the rising sun heats the slabs under your feet. Graceful colonnades cast morning shadows across the rising path. The road widens as the village recedes behind the throng. You climb steadily onward. The day is mild, and the sloping land is rich with green vines. You feel relaxed and serene. You are on the way.

Gradually, the slope steepens. The columns disappear. The green vines give way to monotonous miles of scrub. The climb gets more difficult. Your breathing quickens. But the air is crisp and clean and you climb on vigorously.

You climb on and on . . . Now the sun hangs overhead, hot, bright, and dry . . . Your feet are sore and burning . . . You begin to feel tired and a bit faint with hunger and heat . . . Your spirits droop . . .

## THE SACRED STREAM

Suddenly, the people at the front of the throng slow and stop. The group turns off the path into a shady grove. You slip your shoes off your aching feet. Cool grass lies underfoot. You hear the gurgle of running water and see a crystal-clear stream bubbling from clefts in a wall of rocks and gushing alongside. You sit with the others and dip your feet into its icy-cold water, washing the dust from your face and hands. You feel cleansed. You form a cup with your hands and, holding your fingers together, collect some water from where it issues out of the rocks. You drink it and feel refreshed.

Then you rest on a grassy knoll and watch the soft white clouds shifting shape as they cross the blue sky. You regard the play of sunlight through leafy boughs overhead. You hear the call of birds. People are opening sacks and producing olives and bread and cheese. You wish you had more than grapes, but by sharing what you have, you receive enough to pacify your hunger.

Now you get up and, wading further into the stream, you look with amazement at the saplings that stud the water. In the rocky wall to the right, small niches have been chipped out of the face. Into these niches little candles have been set. Surely this is a sacred stream. How it must glimmer at night when pilgrims light the candles that will flicker onto the rushing water and reflect from the rock face.

Among the cypress trees that line the bank, there are some fallen branches. You select one of these that is long and strong enough to lean upon, stripping the small twigs and leaves from its fragrant bark. This will help you climb. You can use a support. You dry your feet on a piece of clothing, and gather your belongings as others bundle their things. Together you resume the ascent of the mountain.

## THE INITIAL SACRIFICE

You continue to climb, feeling grateful for your staff. Soon your calves and thighs ache from the ascent. The paving stones feel rough and scorching beneath your tired feet. The stiff breeze from the sea at your back dries your sweat. Your small bag grows weighty and burdensome. The road turns higher yet into the mountain. The climb grows arduous. Your breathing quickens.

You are well into the scrubby hillside now. Another few paces and you reach its crest. Everyone stops to gaze at the sight. Down below, on the other side of the mountain, is a green valley . . . How beautiful it is . . . well worth the hard climb. You see clear to the mountains on the other side. The valley forms a bowl surrounded by wooded hills . . . You can perceive buildings, as of a sanctuary, among the great plane trees that rise from the valley floor. This is where you are headed—your goal.

As you start the descent, you feel at once a change in the atmosphere. The breeze blows more gently here, sheltered as you are by the embracing hillsides. You see an ancient olive tree ahead, not far from the road, still putting out fruit even in sandy soil. It looks as if it were twisted by a giant's hand . . .

## THE GUARDIAN SNAKES

The road bends suddenly and you find yourself in a magnificent hollow. Here you catch the scent of laurel leaves and the spicy resin of pine. As you approach the grove of trees, you notice a twisted loop of rope hanging from one of them. Is it? No—it couldn't be! It is! A tree snake!

As long as a man, the serpent coils its yellowish body around a low branch. Incredible—it must be dangerous! You pick up a rock to throw at the snake's glistening head as you draw near. You nudge your neighbor to warn him. He grasps your arm, knocking the stone from it. He points excitedly to the others and they nod and mumble in their strange tongue. By their happy expressions, you understand they are glad to see this creature—a holy serpent, then.

Now you notice more of them—many more. The snakes drop from the trees and slither across the grassy earth, as though to welcome the pilgrims. Each person pauses as a snake glides near. The creatures hiss and rear, darting their brassy heads up and down, flickering their forked tongues. You sincerely hope they are not poisonous. It must be so, for no one else seems afraid.

Some of them even touch your fellows. Horrors! One coils around the base of your staff and you freeze. Then the snake unwinds its slender body and slithers onward.

## THE ALTAR IN THE HOLLOW

The crowd presses forward carefully through the snakes into the grove. You are carried with them—your mind awhirl with emotion. There in the hollow you see a small altar.

Now the pilgrims pull small offerings from their sacks— pieces of fruit and cup-shaped cakes, shiny with honey. You take your few remaining grapes, and reaching into your bag, you find something you no longer seem to need. You set these items with the other offerings.

Women in white gowns come forward—they must be attendants of this altar. One of them whistles in a high pitch and, quite unbelievably, the snakes respond to her signal, looping and winding their way toward the altar where they are fed honey cakes by the attendants. Tame snakes!

The men, the women, the elderly, and the children bow their heads in worship. You offer a silent prayer to your own deity for safekeeping in whatever is to come. You renew your purpose.

Down to the valley you head with the pilgrims. You feel

less weary now,—cooled by the green grove and excited by the encounter with the guardian snakes.

[Give the Interval conclusion if you plan to stop here.]

◇ Activities for "On the Road"

For this activity, you'll need:

- Comfortable walking shoes
- Stick that you find en route
- Mineral water
- Bunch of grapes or a small box of raisins

Adjust the supplies as necessary for your condition. Then take a walk of at least ten minutes, perhaps around a block. Try to follow a route with an up-and-down slope. As you walk, concentrate on the feeling of your feet upon the ground. Think about your journey through life, where you have been, and where you are going. Watch for a small branch with a nice shape or foliage you like. Pick it up and bring it home with you. Place it with your request-object.

If walking outside is impractical, climb a flight of stairs a couple of times. Take each step deliberately, thinking about ascending as a symbol for increments of inner development.

When you have finished, wash your hands slowly and thoughtfully. Consider how any dirt that is being removed is a cleansing of your past. Let the clear, running water renew you. Then, if possible, form a cup with one of your hands and drink from it. You may need someone to pour the mineral water for you. As you swallow, imagine the water refreshing you internally. Eat some of your grapes or raisins. Chew them carefully, picturing their life cycle—how they grew, how they came to reach you. Feel them nourishing your body in a way that is important for you. Then find some object that you can do without and give it away or discard it.

These activities may be best performed after you have listened to the visualization for "On the Road."

## ◇ ENTERING THE SACRED SPACE

### ◇ Introduction to "Entering the Sacred Space"

In a sense, a temple is the throne of the deity it honors. Its beauty, balance, and symmetry represent the order in the universe and the order within the human body. Some traditions think of the altar inside the temple as the "heart" of the divinity. The entry steps symbolize the pilgrim's journey to the center of the self. Contemplation is the appropriate behavior for a temple. Your purpose is to understand the meaning this space has for you personally.

The flowers and trees surrounding the temple all have symbolic significance. I was particularly intrigued to see the poppies growing on the grounds around the temple at Epidaurus. These soporific blooms anticipated the divine sleep that was to be granted the pilgrim. They offered consolation.

Likewise, the carvings and other building decorations all relate to the divinity who is worshiped within and to the goals of the pilgrim. Asklepios, as the son of Apollo, was partly a solar deity; as son of his mother, Coronis, he was also a deity of the depths of the earth. Emblems of the powers of heaven and earth decorate the shrines to him. Pilgrims of every religion and age seek the inner light and the ability to understand the inner darkness.

By passing through the gate, you are making a transition from one realm into another. The materials used inside the temple, like the decor on the outside, signify the various qualities of the deity that are sought by the pilgrim. Smooth ivory, for instance, symbolizes purity; gold represents nobility, incorruptibility, insight, and love. The open door of the temple offers you the opportunity to pass through and learn the secrets within.

Immersing yourself in water is a kind of baptism. Here one's body and spirit are refreshed. Being anointed with oil is an ancient symbol for absorbing special powers and divine blessing. The flames of torches and the fire on the altar correspond to the enlightenment you seek.

Remember that although the ancient way may not be your way, you can learn from it. It can enrich your present.

◇ Visualization for "Entering the Sacred Space"

[Repeat the Invocation if you are beginning again.]

*As you leave the sacred grove, you can see in the distance another road of the same size as the one you are treading. Approaching from the plain, as you have come from the sea, the other road is also populated with pilgrims. Some wave and shout to their fellows. You glance at your watch; it is midafternoon.

Soon the roads merge into a single wide path. You, too, smile and nod at the newcomers. In a little while, the road again narrows, then twists and winds to the very base of the valley. Here the tall columns begin again, leading you forward. You round a corner and see a magnificent building ahead. Beyond it, there are other buildings, with the whole enclosure marked by a boundary wall only a few feet high. One could enter by simply stepping over the boundary, but the building ahead is obviously the proper way.

It must be important to take off your shoes, because people stop and remove their sandals. Someone gestures sharply at you, indicating that you should do the same. Small children, older people, and even those who seem ill do likewise. You hasten to remove your shoes, too, and tuck them into your satchel.

You stare at the majestic, classic columns of the gateway as you approach. Encircling most of the buildings are pedestals topped with marble statues, the shapes of which set your mind fluttering with vague memories of an ancient past.

The people fall silent. There is a stir of suppressed excitement, murmuring, and hushed whispers as you approach the door. Now, as your group passes under the arch, you see strange writing overhead, carved in ancient script. Although its letters are unknown, you can somehow sense their meaning. You are entering a holy place. You must be worthy of it.

## THE GATEWAY

You reach a grand vestibule by means of a ramp. You see how those people who are handicapped can more easily manage this entrance than stairs. The polished marble Ionian and Corinthian columns are dazzling in the afternoon sun. On the frieze, rosettes alternate with wreathed ox heads. Above them on the cornice, palmettes spread between lion heads and spirals of growing plants. The rose, flower of the sun; the lion, with his radiating, sunlike mane; the ox; the palm—some being of light must be honored here.

How cool and soothing the smooth black-and-white marble feels underneath your aching feet.

### THE FURTHER SACRIFICE

A tall man in a white garment comes forward to greet your group —obviously some priest or official. Each person speaks to him in turn and then is directed to one of the many other white garbed men and women who wait behind him. These attendants take their assigned person to a side bench where they speak in the person's native tongue. You hear the babble of many languages spoken at once.

At last you are able to make yourself understood. You tell your attendant who you are, where you have come from, and what you seek. The kindly face responds with comprehension. "And what have you brought to sacrifice?" you are asked. You describe the object you carry. "Not yet," you are told. "Have you nothing else to give? We must learn first whether you will be called."

Sacrifice—but what? All you carry is essential. Your eyes fall upon your watch. Perhaps this golden timepiece will do. You are in another time anyhow. You remove your watch. The attendant nods, and you both get up. Following as directed, you pass through the far door where the whole sacred space lies revealed. Now you see the marvelous structures within, each more sumptuous than the other.

You are taken to an outdoor altar adjoining the entrance hall. There, among the gifts of rich and poor, you place your watch, the material link to your past. Some people carry animals, cakes, fruit, and other objects.

### THE HOT SPRINGS

You follow your attendant, with your bare feet now treading the sacred way. It's time to refresh yourself from your journey, you are told. Up ahead you see a steaming pool carved into solid rock. Fresh water spouts from the rocky outcropping—an effervescent thermal spring. Nearby, a cubicle is pointed out for your belongings and you set your bag inside. You receive a clean white robe to wear after your bath. You slip off your dusty clothing and, unabashed by the presence of others, dip into the comfortably warm water. The area is protected from the sun by a lavishly decorated roof, with the sides open to the light breeze.

Other people—some shy, some confident—are pouring the warm fluid over themselves with reverence, as if it were holy water. You select a pitcher from the poolside and fill it with the clear, warm fluid. You can smell the minerals it contains: a bit of sulpher, perhaps some iron, more fresh than strong. How heavenly it feels to wash off the dust of the road . . . Then you slowly immerse your body . . . Your head floats effortlessly in the buoyant liquid as the sacred water penetrates every pore . . . Soon all the aches in your body melt away with the heat . . . Your worries seem to evaporate with the tiny bubbles fizzing and popping on the surface of the water . . . Peace, a deep peace, begins to soak into your body.

Now your attendant gestures for you to come out. Rather reluctantly, you leave the pool, dry yourself with the thick, absorbent cloth, and pull on the clean robe of soft, white linen. You pass as others do into a low room where masseuses and masseurs are oiling the prone pilgrims.

You climb onto the marble slab indicated for you and lie down. Your muscles are still warm from the sacred hot spring. Now you are massaged and rubbed with fragrant oils . . . Feel the comfort of the pungent, spiced oil penetrate . . . Sense the soothing movements, the stroking, kneading, pulling, and rubbing that delight you . . . Each movement seems to be exactly right, as though your masseuse/masseur is reading the needs of your muscles . . . Somewhere in the background floats the sound of double flutes . . . Every last fragment of pain from your long walk dissolves; your body opens, rested and calm . . . You sink into a deep and drowsy stupor . . .

When you arise, you feel clean and pure and revived. You towel off the excess oils and put on your robe. Someone indicates a door for you to pass through where you enter a kind of commissary. Here fresh fruit, bread, olives, and cheese are set in bowls before you. A flask filled with icy mountain water is given to you to drink.

Comforted within and without, you wander into the splendid courtyard, and beyond it onto the open grounds. At first you stroll, content to marvel at your surroundings. Then you find a sheltered stone bench under a broad tree where you sit and contentedly watch all that passes. Small groups of pilgrims at distant benches listen to readers and musicians, but you stay where you are. A profound peace seems to have entered your body. Somewhere, in the back of your mind, you remember there was a problem or question you had, but you don't quite recall what it was. Never mind. You will deal with it eventually. For now, you rest and watch the changing colors in the sky as the sun sets.

## THE CEREMONY AT THE TEMPLE

The darkness deepens. Then a light flares up. Another . . . and another. Torches spot the sanctuary. And now . . . the sound of singing voices and rich music reach you from afar . . .

You rise and move toward the lights and rhythmic harmonies. Returning past the galleries, their marble colonnades glittering in the torchlight, you see ahead a procession of torchbearers in front of a great building. As you approach, you surmise this must be a temple. From it, you can see the great gate where you entered the sanctuary. The imposing building is surrounded on all four sides by columns. Hundreds of people mill in the open space before this temple, with their voices blending in some ancient paean. The rhythm of this piece stirs some memory of long ago.

You squeeze through the crowd toward the steps of the temple where its great doors are flung wide. The singing flows out from here into the crowd who follow the words. Underneath the voices, pure, harmonic tones are struck. Something inside you reverberates, as though your body were an instrument. You feel like weeping with joy at the sounds. Something new awakens in you.

Standing on tiptoe, you can glimpse the interior of the temple. In the flickering light, you can see at the farthest end of the temple sits a huge statue. It gleams of polished ivory and its golden fittings shimmer in the moving light.

On the richly colored side walls, you can barely discern curved niches set with smaller statues, resembling images you once knew. But where?

Standing near the altar, a priest and priestess are chanting. Then one pours a libation from a golden vial. The chant stops. Five pure tones ring out. All is done. The crowd silently moves away, mindful of all that took place.

Someone touches your arm and there is your attendant again, gesturing to you to follow. You are led into a hostel across the grounds to a simple bed in a large niche where your things have been set. There are walls on three sides, but the fourth side is open with columns beyond to let in the soft, fragrant air.

You crawl onto the pallet with relief. You did not realize how tired you were. You sleep heavily, without dreams . . . [Give the Interval conclusion if you are going to stop here.]

### ACTIVITIES FOR "ENTERING THE SACRED SPACE"

Take off your shoes. Walk around your room three times while thinking what it would be like to walk on sacred ground. If weather permits, you may prefer to walk barefoot on grass in a yard. I once walked barefoot in the grass that grew above my father's grave. Although on one level I knew perfectly well that nothing physical was happening; on another level I felt that I was actually absorbing some of my father's fine qualities. While you move, imagine going through a passageway to a sacred place.

Now run a hot bath. Bathe with attention. Feel the cleansing of the water. Take a washcloth or cup and pour the water over your head and shoulders. After you get out and dry off, rub your body with a soothing moisturizer or fragrant oil.

You may wish to have a massage while you listen to the cassette tape. If you do so, "follow" with your mind the movements of the masseuse or masseur. Allow the hands to penetrate your muscles and flesh as if they were light entering dark places. Imagine that you are absorbing the qualities you desire through the hands and the oil. This activity is best performed during or after the visualization.

Find something else you no longer need and give it away.


## ◇ THE SECOND DAY


### ◇ Introduction to "The Second Day"

Among the many symbols for spiritual awakening is the crowing of a rooster. The rising of the sun, like the light emanating from lamps and torches, relates to the light of understanding. Their illumination symbolizes the pilgrim's inner enlightenment.

In your imagination, you'll continue to experience your body in a new way while you also stimulate your emotions and thoughts. The library you'll enter in your mind's eye represents the storehouse of hidden knowledge, with its unique personal lessons. Knowledge, too, is an inner light.

These symbols of light are a sharp contrast to the black mud you'll be asked to immerse yourself in. Mud is an integration of two powers of the earth: the soil itself, softened and pliable, and the water springing from deep, hidden sources. Mud is a union of receptive earth and transforming water. By absorbing these powers, you absorb their power of transformation. Your purpose is to permit the transformation to begin its work.

During this phase of the visualizations, you draw nearer to the central secret, and begin to participate in invoking its power.

### ◇ Visualization for "The Second Day"

[Repeat the Invocation if you are beginning here.]

*At sunrise, you hear the crowing of many cocks. Then silence. Now singing again—a morning hymn. You dress in your robe and move with the others to a fountain where you splash yourself with cold spring water and eat at the table set outside with simple foods, honey cakes, and water from the well. How nourishing it all tastes. When your attendant appears, you rise quickly and follow. The morning air is a delicious blend of warmth and coolness. A mild breeze lifts your hair.

### THE GYMNASIUM

You perceive a large building ahead; you hear the buzz of low voices of many people. Entering through another astoundingly lavish doorway, you reach the spacious inner room. Here, people are performing various exercises under direction. Your attendant presents your instructor.

This tutor also seems to know exactly what your body requires. By touching here and there, probing and pulling, a diagnosis is made. You are given a light garment to wear. You slip this on under your robe. Next you are shown a sequence of movements and exercises to perform.

See yourself with your instructor doing the movements that your body most needs. Feel yourself reaching outward and gathering inward. Sense the easy play of your muscles, the gliding of your tendons over your bones. It's almost as though you can perceive all parts of your body simultaneously. You are present everywhere at once inside your body. When your flesh takes on a warm glow, you slip off your outer robe.

Your instructor demonstrates each new movement, then watches you perform it. With infinite patience, the instructor corrects you by moving your body for you with a few pertinent comments, rather than explanations of what to do. You discover an inner rhythm. These exercises are so adapted to your needs that each repetition seems smoother, more flowing, more graceful. Your instructor notices at once when you have the correct "feeling" of the movement, and progresses to teach you more and more.

Now there is a sort of dance step demonstrated. You follow and are astounded at how easy it seems . . . Again and again the steps build upon preceding ones until there is a flowing line, a rhythmic pattern that seems to unroll from inner depths . . . You feel vibrantly alive . . . light . . . easy . . . free . . .

How long you have been lost in these intricate patterns, you could not say. Your teacher stops. You see the other people moving toward the far door. You replace your robe and pull off your damp exercise clothing to place in the big baskets provided. You feel profoundly appreciative to your teacher and try to communicate this before you join the others.

Outside on a table, under a large shade tree is spread another light meal. As you sit and eat, flute players wander around the group. The people eat silently, letting the harmonious strains penetrate them, along with the nourishing foods. Your body tingles with life.

## THE LIBRARY

Once again, your attendant appears and leads you across the grounds. Whenever you raise questions as to why things are being done a certain way, or what is the purpose of this teaching, you are told only, "This you must learn for yourself."

Soon you enter the cool interior of a marble library. The floor is decorated with multi-colored marble. The light is golden here. Looking up, you see that the windows are covered with thin slabs of translucent alabaster. The coffered roof is made of wood. The niches are lined with shelves full of scrolls. Your attendant selects one of these. You are taken to one corner away from the few other quiet students and are given the scroll written in your language. Your attendant leaves you to read.

Unrolling the parchment, you find a long poem decorated with a curious design. You begin to read. As your eyes examine the first few lines, your heart quickens. These words speak directly to you. They express an emotion you have been unable to put into the right words. But it is all here—your very thoughts. In charming form, in lovely phrases, the words leap from the pages into your heart.

The poem touches you so profoundly that your eyes brim with tears of pleasure. What is this place that dazzles the mind and body? You look up and gaze around at the splendid statues on pedestals between the niches, and the harmonious proportions of the room. Everything seems calculated to evoke a sense of beauty. Your finger traces the perfect design. You continue to read and absorb and wonder until once more your attendant returns. The scroll is set back in place and you leave.

## THE MUD BATH

Walking across the grounds as directed, you notice here and there some of the large yellow serpents you saw before slithering through the grass, or sunning themselves on the rocky outcroppings. You still feel apprehensive, but not fearful.

You reach a spring quite different from the one you visited yesterday. This water is not clear, but dark, glossy, black, and muddy. Surely you are not expected to get into this? Yes, it is certain that you must for your attendant so indicates, and you see others already sunk deep into the mucky pit.

Discarding your robe, you sit down on the rock ledge and ease yourself into the glistening muck. Water and earth together form the thick mud. It squishes beneath your feet and between your toes. It clings to your body. With a heavy, sucking splash, you sink into the sticky mass. Now another attendant comes with a trowel-like instrument and layers the mud up to your neck. Again you inhale the metallic odors of minerals.

Heat begins to penetrate your flesh to the very bones. Sweat breaks out on your brow. It is almost painful, but not quite. And somehow, good. Just at the point when you think the experience is unendurable, the attendant returns to help you out of the mud. Gooey and limp, you totter after the attendant to a large fountain where, under the carved heads of spouting lions, you rinse all traces of the mucky substance from your skin and hair. The lukewarm water cools your burning body. But something has entered your flesh that will not be rinsed off, for you still sense the penetrating minerals. You feel different yourself—transformed.

Again you are led to the massage room. Again you crawl

upon the marble slab. Feel the amazing contrast between the hot, squishy mud and the cool, smooth marble . . . Again yield yourself to the soothing essences of sweet oils and herbs . . .

Asleep but not asleep . . . Your body listens as it is lost, suspended in the pleasure of abandoning all effort . . . Your mind hovers in a semi-world, dim but awake, feeling the perfect touches your body needs . . .

When you arise and put on a clean, white robe, you once more partake of the pure foods set before you in the courtyard and drain your cup of the sparkling, cool water. Once more you stroll the grounds in a sunset glow, finding even more attractive glades and walks as you cross the grassy carpet dotted with red poppies, yellow buttercups, and minute bluebells.

## INSIDE THE TEMPLE

As the sky darkens, you hasten your step toward the temple where you visited the previous night. This time you want to see more clearly what is happening.

The sunset sky reflects gold and rose against the flanks of white marble columns, as the sun goes down behind the temple. You can still see well enough to discern the decorations on the outside of the building. Above the chiseled tops of the Doric columns, the frieze is adorned with a meander, over which the shapes of large roses open petals wide to the setting sun. Spaced on the cornices at the long sides of the temple are lion heads with flaring manes. In between these solar beasts swirl spirals, suggesting energy and growth. At intervals above these ornaments appear palmlike shapes, their clustered branches spread upward and outward to the sides. Surely each, as on the entry gate, has some special significance—something to do with radiance.

On the shorter sides of the temple, the triangular space of the pediments is filled with sculptures of agitated figures, depicting a battle. At the four corners of the roof, shapely women in flowing gowns sit sideways upon prancing horses. Highest of all, atop the peak of the pediment, like a bird alighting to rest, perches the statue of a woman with widespread wings. What did they call her? Nike [NYE-key], you remember, the winged Victory. Victory over what? Your mind is full of questions.

In the center of the columns, like a cottage set amid a grove of trees, is the glowing inner chamber. The outer walls of these are of stone tinted pale red and blue, and around the base is a design comprised of large, looping serpents. A great portal, its tall doors made of wood set with ivory sunbursts, swings open. As you draw nearer, you perceive its glimmer comes from the studs of nail heads made from pure gold.

A warm light and a delicious fragrance issue from this inner room. Outdoors, torches are lit. The crowd that has been shifting about with controlled excitement silently forms a line. Music resounds from the strings of lyres and harps inside, and the people begin to move slowly as they commence a chant.

Something strangely familiar strikes you about their movements. Yes—part of the slow pacing involves steps your body already knows because, almost without willing it, you start to sway and your feet join the pattern. You step into line with the others and allow your body to move itself, remembering its lesson of the morning.

Rhythmically and steadily, the line moves forward toward the ramp to the interior. Swaying, pausing, swaying. You seem able to follow effortlessly even parts of the dance you have not seen before. Someone on either side grasps a hand and, as one body—curving, stretching, curving—you are part of a long, sinuous line that moves through the portal to the interior of the temple, lit by torches without and wavering oil lamps within.

You know not the words of the chant you utter, but sounds flow from you, too. Each utterance seems perfectly fitted to each movement. The music here is clear, sweet, and pure; the harmonious voices of the singers in the front blend with the dancers' voices as you slide smoothly across the black-and-white stone floor. You move with a pulse, a heartbeat, as a single living being, into the very heart of the temple. Swaying, swinging, singing, you pass in front of the large figure.

## THE STATUE

Only now can you see it unobstructed. The flames of many oil lamps flicker across the smooth polish of a monumental hero or god. His flesh is formed from carved ivory; the decorations are in pure gold. He is seated on a throne the base of which is decorated with tortured images, one depicting the head of a woman with snakes for hair. This heroic man-god is bearded, with a serene and compassionate expression. He wears a wrap similar to those of the attendants. In one hand he holds a long staff. The other hand rests atop a sculpted golden serpent. At his feet lies the statue of a dog. The gilded decorations glimmer in the wavering light. This enshrined figure must be the healing god of these people, and the ritual some kind of appeal for help. Internally, you invoke your own inspirational or spiritual figure.

As the dancers pass the figure of the healing god, each in turn releases the right hand, touches the statue reverently, and then touches a part of his or her own body. They join hands once more and proceed. You follow their lead, touching the figure and then some part of your own body.

The dancers move slowly back out of the temple in a serpentine line, then down the ramp until they reach the high altar outside that faces the temple doors. Here the line forms a spiral around the stone altar ablaze with fragrant woods under the dark skies. The great, dancing spiral, still chanting to the musical strains, doubles back until a continuous living spiral encircles the altar . . . The moving light, the moving voices, the moving bodies all merge . . . You sense as you sing and sway, the undulations of a giant serpent composed of living people . . . Time vanishes . . .

At last the links are broken and the group steps slowly and silently away into the starlit night. You are not surprised to see your attendant waiting to take you to the hostel where your bed is ready. You slip under the covers, with your body still reverberating from the temple music and dance. Sleep comes gently. In your dreams, you see a vague figure on a mountain top wave to you, gesturing as though to ascend. You smile in your sleep and all is quiet.

[Repeat the Interval conclusion if you are stopping now.]

### ◊ Activities for "The Second Day"

Put on a piece of favorite music. Perform some set of exercises, dance, or movements you know. Or simply let the music dictate your steps. Let the movement flow upward from your feet, through your body, rippling effortlessly up and out of your head. If you are unable to move to the music, simply listen to it. But hear the music in a new way.

Let the music pass through your body. See the high notes as though they were emanating from your head. See the low notes as though they came from the depth of your abdomen and your legs. See the inbetween notes coming from your torso. Allow the sounds to wash over you and through you. Let the pulse of the music move from side to side within your body. Left, right, left, right, while the musical notes resonate in different areas of yourself. You may feel a pulse coming from your central core to the outer surface of your body. If so, go with that rhythm. When the music finishes, remain still and sense its reverberations still echoing inside your body.

Next reread a favorite poem and contemplate how it might apply to your life.

For the following activity, you'll need clean hands and these supplies:

- Jar or tube of thick hand cream
- Towel
- Candle or oil lamp
- Matches

If possible, massage the hand cream thoroughly into every area of your hands. Let it serve as a substitute for the thick mud in the visualization. Perhaps you'll want to listen to the tape as you perform this action with total awareness. Then blot your hands on the towel, but do not rub away the residual cream. If an injury or illness prevents you from doing this activity, you may want to arrange with someone else to massage your hands or feet gently.

Now light the candle or oil lamp with a match. Focus on the light for a few seconds. Then close your eyes and see the light in your mind's eye. Contemplate how the cream is absorbing into your body. Imagine it penetrating not only the pores of your skin but entering deeply. See it penetrating your very bone marrow with healing energy. Touch your body wherever it is most needed.

Then picture the light, like the cream, being absorbed into your body. Open your eyes to glimpse the light again, if you wish, to remind you of its appearance. Close your eyes again and watch the flickering light on the inside of your lids. Imagine the energy of the light entering deep within and healing you.

Recite quietly, in a low voice or to yourself, any prayer, psalm, chant, or mantra you know by heart. Select one you like. Let its words enter you, too. Feel their healing balm. Now open your eyes, blot your hands, and blow out the light. For each activity henceforth, relight your light.

These activities are most beneficial following the visualization for "The Second Day."

## ◇ THE THIRD DAY

### ◇ Introduction to "The Third Day"

Having a propitious dream was the "entrance fee" to the sacred sleeping space in the dream temples. The attendants required a dream from the pilgrims that suggested they were being invited by the deity before being taken to the final step. You may wish to continue to incubate a dream as you proceed to this phase.

In fantasy, you'll be asked to explore an ambivalent place. On the grounds of the sanctuary was a round building called the "tholos," which means a rotunda. The base of this building contained a concentric labyrinth covered by a stone. The domed ceiling was pierced with a circular opening. This repetition of the circular form suggested not only an association with the deity of the sun, but also of heaven and perfection. Holes, whether they be in floor or ceiling, imply an opening to the unknown, an entrance to another world.

Other contrasts existed in this building. The floor made of alternating black-and-white marble slabs recalled the parentage of Asklepios—the light of his sun-father and the dark of his earth-mother. They further symbolized the initial and final stages of life, the beginning and the end of all things. The blue and red of the building stones underscored the idea of contrast—the blue of heaven and spirit, the red of the underworld and the human body. Your purpose at this stage is to understand these contrasts.

The theater you'll attend in your imagination, with its classical drama, allows you the chance to participate by identifying with the actors. Drama is a special form of teaching. While acting a part, one also remains oneself, thus forcing a heightened and sustained awareness. While watching the play, the viewer can see one's own troubles in a different perspective. Either way, your emotions are aroused. What can they teach you about your life?

### ◇ Activities for "The Third Day"

If possible, attend a play or film. This activity may be done before or after the visualization for "The Third Day." Select something with value, preferably a classic work. If this is impossible, find a dramatization with worthwhile content on television. Watch this dramatization while remaining "conscious" throughout the program. Stay aware of how your emotions shift and how certain contrasts portrayed on the stage and screen exist within yourself.

Continue your activities to incubate a dream. You may wish to ask for a lucid dream to teach you what you need to know.

Light your candle or oil lamp before this visualization and keep it burning throughout.

## ◇ Visualization for "The Third Day"

[Give the Invocation if you are beginning here.]

*At sunup, you wake with the crowing of roosters, then quiet, followed by the faraway sound of voices in a morning hymn. As before, you go with the others outside to the sacred fountain to wash and to eat the simple foods set on the tables. This morning your attendant asks what you have dreamed and you describe the shadowy figure atop the mountain. Smiling, the attendant walks along with you to the center of the sanctuary, saying that you are on your own this morning.

Meandering about the grounds, you breathe deeply. This tranquil valley has become a haven of serenity. Occasional pilgrims you pass exchange cordial greetings with you in their tongue. As you stroll, your eyes scan the harmonious proportions of the columns and walls of the various buildings you have entered. Your attention is caught by a totally round structure you had not paid attention to before. You decide to investigate.

### THE THOLOS

Of all the buildings in the sanctuary, only this one is circular. Its exterior, like the others, is surrounded by white marble columns. Behind the columns, the outer walls of the inner chamber are made of stone with pale blue and red tints. On the ceiling between the columns and these walls, there are sumptuous decorations of coffered wood. Each coffer contains a giant flower spreading its petals. Around the base of the walls of the inner chamber is another sculpted design of great snakes rising in loops. You have seen similar ones on the other buildings, yet something strikes you as different about this sanctuary.

Curious, you step up the three stone levels and approach the large double door. Pushing open one of the leaves cautiously, you perceive a magnificent interior. A few white-robed attendants move about in the hushed atmosphere, but they do not appear to object to your presence.

Beneath your feet spreads cool, polished marble in a pattern of large, alternating black-and-white diamonds. Around you rise walls of multi-colored marble topped with a design of graceful dancing women or goddesses. Overhead, you see with surprise that the center of the domed ceiling is pierced with a circular hole through which you can see the sky. The effect is startling, almost as though you were looking directly into heaven. The sunlight pours in a stream through this aperture onto the floor, where it illuminates a large round white stone set in the middle of the diamond-shaped slabs encircling it.

Before you, and dominating the space, is another statue of the healing god. Is this his temple, too? If so, how odd to have two temples of the same god so close together. Set in front of this statue is a brazier held aloft by bronze figures of upright snakes; in it, a flame is perpetually burning. You move closer to inspect the figure. Its gesture and attributes are much the same. Again the throne is decorated with a classical scene with a Greek warrior conquering the snake-headed Medusa. What can all this mean?

Now several more attendants appear. Fragrant herbs and spices are thrown upon the fire, which cause it to sizzle and leap up. Another chant begins, one that is darker and more solemn. The singers form a circle excluding you as they move around the central white stone. Their steps are unfamiliar and you are content to step back into a niche and simply watch.

### THE PIT

The fragrance from the brazier wafts sweet and pungent. The dancers' slow steps accelerate to a frenzied pitch that suddenly ceases. The group kneels in a circle. Leaning forward together, many hands shove the white stone aside.

A dark pit is revealed. Is it a tomb? Inside the inky blackness you discern movement. A mass of something is seething inside. Creeping forward a little, you can see that the interior of the pit is divided into three concentric rings of stone. Between these inner walls lie hundreds, perhaps thousands, of the yellow snakes. Writhing almost like a single, breathing body, the entangled mass swells, rises, and falls.

You turn and grope toward the outer door, then stagger

down the steps and slump onto a curved stone bench to catch your breath and quiet your inner turmoil. From the round building, you can hear more singing and movements. What are they doing now? Feeding the creatures? Do they breed them there? Why keep that gruesome pit in a place of such beauty? Why is this place so filled with wonders and horrors?

After a while, the sounds cease and your mind stops reeling. You walk swiftly away from that awesome spot, heading toward the hostel and more familiar sights.

Reaching the usual dining table, you find there is not much to eat today. Only crusty bread and the cold spring water is set at your place. In any case, you're not very hungry at the moment.

When your attendant appears, you ask many questions. His only answer is, "You must ponder these things." But this afternoon, you are to have a treat, you are told. A performance is being held at the theater, and as soon as you are ready, you will be taken there.

## THE THEATER

As you walk with your attendant under the huge shade trees, you realize you are going in a direction that you have not taken before. Down a path, beyond the buildings, out of the sacred grounds, you walk quite far.

At last you can see a structure through the trees and you hear the rumble of many voices and scuffle of many feet. You reach a wide path with hundreds of people moving toward the entrances to what you now perceive is an outdoor amphitheater.

Along with the crowd, you enter under high arches to the huge stone amphitheater carved into the side of a mountain. Your attendant points out your place along one of the stone benches about halfway back, with a good view of the stage. You are left to enjoy the performance.

The stage must be set to the north, for the afternoon sun does not trouble you. Some sort of ceremony precedes the show. Although you do not know the words, it is obviously a dedication, something to honor one of their gods, as though acting itself were an offering. The acoustics are startling. The tiniest whisper easily reaches your ears. The surrounding ring of mountains must form a natural funnel.

With music, dancing, and a chorus of voices, the play begins. The actors are masked, with each painted expression revealing the quality of the character portrayed. You forget any sense of hunger as you watch in fascination. After a short while, impossible as it is, the play appears to transform into your language, and you comprehend everything.

Moreover, the content is exactly what you need to hear and see, what you need to feel. Is it a comedy? A tragedy? What do these figures say and do? They seem to be depicting a portion of your life. See the actors moving, interacting, and speaking. The show continues. Then you seem to be inside the play, acting your part, as in a dream. Do you laugh? Do you weep? Do you rage with anger? Do you feel inspired? Whatever it is you most need to feel—that emotion swells within you. It builds with the climax of the play. It washes through you and over you.

The thunderous applause that marks the end of the performance is like the shock of awakening. And yet the play stays with you and within you. You feel serene and uplifted.

As the sun begins to set, you get up and move out with the throng. When your attendant rejoins you, you return together the way you came, separating from the others who leave by the main road, while you take the narrow path back to the sanctuary. You have no questions for your attendant, feeling content for the moment to be within yourself.

### THE COLD SPRINGS

Now you are led to a third bubbling spring that gushes in abundance from a cleft in the rock through the mouth of a large lion spout. This stream must come straight from the mountains, since it is icy cold. Your guide says you are to wash here this evening, so you shed your robe and step gingerly into the frigid waters. Quickly washing any dust and sweat from your body, you cleanse yourself with this sacred water.

As you step out of the cold water into the cool air, an attendant wraps you in a big, heavy, warm robe, and briskly rubs your skin until it glows with warmth. Then you put on a dry, white robe and you once again follow your guide . . . [Give the Interval conclusion if you are stopping here.]

## ◇ THE ABATON

### ◇ Introduction to "The Abaton"

The tunnel you'll be asked to go through in your imagination is a passageway to the encounter with your inner guide. Traveling through the secret passage underground is sometimes the way to the brightest light. In the dream temples, this encounter took place in the "abaton," the innermost chamber of the sanctuary where the pilgrims withdrew for their sacred sleep. Here is where they incubated dreams and hoped to receive an answer from the god.

People of all times and traditions have sought to reach a higher power within themselves. Some call such a figure the "Inner Advisor"[2] or the "Inner Shaman"; others think of it as the "Guardian Angel" or the "Voice of the Soul." Whether you conceive of this figure as an actual entity or an imaginary embodiment of a creative power, it is possible to visualize an encounter and exchange with the figure and to receive its advice and help.

### ◇ Activities for "The Abaton"

Light your candle or oil lamp before you begin the visualization. Place on your tray some sweet cake or piece of candy, preferably made with honey. At the conclusion of the visualization, eat this with awareness, contemplating the sweetness of life.

Place your request-object and your stick (or a piece of it) into an attractive box or basket with a lid. If these items are too large to fit, cover them with a sheet. Add to the items something you often wear or use—for instance, a ring, watch, or a favorite pen. Keep the items covered during the visualization. At the end of the fantasy, open the box or remove the sheet and allow three drops of candle wax to fall within. If you are using an oil lamp, take out each object separately and pass it slowly over the flame. Then put back the object you usually wear or carry.

You may wish to further prepare for this last phase of the visualization with rituals that include bathing, singing, praying or meditating, and sleeping in a different place or way. Choose the supplies and methods that have been the most evocative for you.

◇ Visualization for "The Abaton"

[Repeat the Invocation if you are beginning here.]

### THE TUNNEL

*Your attendant now leads you to an odd structure near the cold spring—a kind of tunnel into the earth. You can still hear the sound of rushing water from the sacred spring. You are led down a short flight of steps, feeling a bit lightheaded with hunger.

Before you is a long tunnel that is wide enough to lie across. You see that beds are set at intervals along the walls. Above these are rectangular openings through which you can glimpse snippets of the sunset.

The water from the sacred stream must flow beneath the tunnel, since the muffled sound of rushing water reverberates throughout. You can hear water splashing down steps in a small waterfall and streaming below you. In the dim light and mysterious atmosphere, you make your way to the bed specified by your guide, as other pilgrims do the same. Here you see your satchel has been set. An attendant brings a tray with a warm drink and two honey cakes that you accept eagerly.

Grateful for food and drink at last, you drain the warm fluid; its honey flavor is sweet and satisfying. You have eaten only one of the sesame honey cakes when you feel extremely drowsy. Putting the other cake into your satchel for later, you place it under the bed, lie down, and pull up the cover.

Water splashing down steps and flowing underneath you fills your ears as you drift . . . and . . . drift . . . a voice—or is it the water? Is someone speaking through the hole above your head? Are you dreaming?

How long you have been entranced you do not know, but you are touched, roused, and led half-awake, deeper into the tunnel, wrapped in your blanket and toting your satchel.

### THE SACRED SLEEP

Climbing a short flight of steps, you enter an inner chamber. This room is above ground, since you can glimpse stars through the windows. You are guided to a niche where you again lie down on a fluffy, warm sheepskin. Your mind hovers in a half-sleep. The darkish room is in a semi-gloom, lit by the flames of dozens of flickering oil lamps.

Around a small altar, white-robed attendants scatter spices

over the fire in a brazier. Other attendants in white gowns intone a low chant.

### THE GIFT

Your attendant tells you to get out your offering, then disappears. You see other pilgrims placing objects into the large baskets carried by attendants. Models of ears and breasts, legs and thumbs—all sorts of forms—some of terra-cotta, some of gold or silver are being set into the baskets. You open your small satchel and get out the request-object you have carried so long.

As the collectors reach you, you set your offering into the basket and they pass on. The music ceases. A chief attendant calls for quiet and all the oil lamps are extinguished.

You lie in the fragrant-smelling darkness. Your body still resonates with the vibrations of music and moving water. Your eyes close, letting the waves flow over you. Your body folds and falls asleep. Your mind hovers, resting but alert. Asleep but awake, you lie in the dark, waiting.

### THE HEALING

Blackness . . . silence. Then there is a small light. Somewhere in your mind, a light glows and grows. Soon the whole inner space of your head is illuminated, and turning, you discover that light streams out from your eyes. Wherever you look is bright with luminous color. Light out of darkness.

There is a swishing sound. You look toward the noise and see one of the sacred snakes slithering across the floor. Somehow it seems natural and right. You reach into your bag and pull out your remaining honey cake. As the snake approaches you, rising up and flicking its tongue, you hold out the cake and the creature eats it peacefully.

You hear footsteps approaching. Looking up, you see beyond the snake a figure that you recognize with a shudder of joy. This is the one you have been awaiting—your inner guide. Let this figure appear before you now. Regard it clearly with your new sight. Examine its form, its shape, and its color. It may be a spiritual figure or a person you once knew or one you imagine. It may be any living or mythical creature. It may have the kindly face of your attendant. Whatever or whoever it is, it is totally good. Light within darkness.

Watch your guide move around the group of sleeping pilgrims . . . Let your guide reach you . . . Greet your guide . . .

Let your guide touch you . . . Ask your guide for its name . . . And hear the response . . . Ask the guide again for its *real* name . . . And hear the answer . . . Now is the time to ask your question, to get advice for your problem. Whatever it is that you need or want, tell it to your figure. Let it respond to you now. Hear its response. In your imagination, hear the words of your inner guide. Let it give you what you need to have, and tell you what you need to know. Let your inner guide provide the perfect treatment for you.

Now ask your guide, "What can I do for you? What can I do for you?" Hear the reply . . . Do or be or understand whatever it is that your guide has said . . . Let yourself feel healed in the way that is best for you . . . Understand how you can continue this feeling and doing in the future . . . Arrange to contact your guide again, whenever you need.

When these exchanges are complete—greeting your guide, asking your guide for its name, its *real* name, and hearing its response, making your request, and hearing the answer, asking what you can do for your guide, and listening to its reply—just continue to luxuriate in the presence of your guide in any way you desire . . . Let your guide be with you in any way you wish . . . Let your guide's loving care fill and satisfy you . . . Continue to be with your inner guide for as long as you wish . . . Plan how to meet again whenever you wish . . . Say good-bye for now, knowing you can meet again . . .

*THE LEARNING*
Now you seem to lift up from your couch and fly—fly out of the building of sleepers into the night sky. See yourself soaring over the sacred grounds, above the white buildings in the moonlight. Feel the wind in your face, the vibrations in your body as you fly freely . . . *Experience* flying . . .

Below you lies the rectangular temple. Dip and glide between its columns, around and into the great portal. See the dancers below you, sinuously moving like a snake. Feel the undulations moving through your spine—the snake within your body—as you swerve and lift through the air. Fly up and circle the ceiling.

Below you see the enthroned figure is no longer their healing god, but your inner guide, full of life. Even the statues in the niches seem to live and breathe. The paintings on the walls and the carvings on the throne blend and merge. No longer scenes of

classic Greek myths, but images from your dreams. Watch them
metamorphose into your nightmare demons and your own glo-
rious heroes and heroines of nights long gone. But, of course—
this is the victory that stands atop the roof of the temple. Those
bloody scenes of battle and struggle—they are within you.
Those nightmare figures on the throne of the healing god are
yours. The victory is the triumph over them. The victory on the
temple is your victory. You conquer your inner demons by transforming them. The light within you reshapes the dark.

You soar onward, out the door and beyond, above the tops
of the trees. Now you see the round temple below. You dip and
circle it. Skim through its columns and wide doors. There, too,
your guide is enthroned. Look at the walls. Written in carved
letters across their surface is a word or a phrase—a message to
you. It is something you need to know. Read it and remember.

See the black-and-white diamond marble slabs below you
as you fly. Watch how they blend—the dark and the light merg-
ing. The pit below; the splendor above. The tomb in the earth;
the rebirth in the air. You fly out of the circular opening in the
dome and onward, over the hot springs and the cold springs, the
sparkling waters and the black mud.

Your eyes radiate outward; turn them inward. Your dark
parts below; your light parts above. You need them both. Each
is part of your wholeness. You were stuck in the blackness or
dazzled by the light. Change is all . . .

See the sacred well within your lower parts . . . Now let its
shining waters rise, radiating like a fountain, spreading up and
over your head and down your whole body, washing it with
healing energy . . . Feel the fountain rising from a deep well
within your body. Watch its sacred waters rise up your spine
and over your head, cascading energy down over your face and
front . . . Feel its healing power . . . Let the radiant waters en-
circle your whole self.

Like the snake shedding its skin, you are continuously reborn. *You* are the creator, molding light from dark, transforming
your inner being, over and over, making a new self. You climb
high into the night sky, wind rushing without, sacred water circulating within. Higher and higher . . . Awake in your sleep.
Light in the dark.

## THE DEPARTURE

The cry of roosters rouses you from your temple sleep. The attendants return to the sleeping quarters with song and prayer. Around you, some of the pilgrims are weeping with joy and hugging one another. You smile, too, as you accompany them through a hidden door to the courtyard. You join the morning hymn. You wash in the sacred spring, knowing it is the last time for now. You eat the fresh fruit and bread waiting on the table. Your clothes are returned to you, clean and fresh. You dress and return your robe. You are given a bundle of food for the road.

## THE FINAL SACRIFICE

When your attendant appears, you embrace with genuine gratitude. One thing remains, you are told. You retrace the sacred way, barefoot to the great gate. Here at the altar near the exit, you are asked to leave one last gift. You open your satchel, although you know you have given all you brought to give. There you see, among the things you thought absolutely essential, is one you no longer need. It's so obvious, so right. You lift this last object out of the bag and place it with others upon the altar.

You embrace your attendant once more, promising to come again, and exit through the gate, heading homeward.

## THE RETURN

The road is familiar now. You have put on your shoes and stride along with the few other pilgrims. You wave to those who separate at the divided path. The climb up the hillside seems easy. You stop at the sacred grove to give some portion of food from your bundle to the guardian snakes. You turn and gaze back at the sanctuary below, then proceed forward with renewed spirit.

Down, down the dusty paved road, pausing at the sacred stream to wash and eat, and share your food, you soon reach the small seaport. There, as you knew it would be, is your ship.

You board. The ship departs. You dine, socialize, then undress and retire to your bunk. The ship rocks you as before, and you fall asleep eagerly, ready to meet the light within your dreams as your ship speeds home . . .

## ◇ CONCLUSION

You awaken in your own bed. . . . You feel refreshed . . . renewed. Open your eyes. Stretch. Sit up and write in your dream journal whatever you wish. Look at your initial incubation request. Look at your request-object. What have you learned from your visualization? What have you learned from any incubated dream? What did you discover? Perhaps your request was answered directly. More likely, it was answered in a way you didn't expect. Perhaps the answer you received was more than you anticipated. How can this response help guide your life? Put out your candle or oil lamp, yet keep the light alive in your heart.

As you come to the end of this book, you are well on your way to completing your healing journey. You have seen how your dreaming mind warns you of danger ahead, alerts you to present disturbances in the body, expresses your reactions to crises, portrays sensations in your ailing body parts, depicts their malfunctioning, even sometimes heals your pain, and offers you inspiring images of integration.

By recording your dreams in a journal, you have begun to create a valuable document for self-discovery. By working with the images in your dreams, you can read messages relevant for your days. You saw how healing from a physical trauma begins by telling your story, expressing your emotional responses to what has happened in words and pictures. You sought to find a meaning in an illness or injury, and created a proverb to express that meaning. You looked for an image to represent your loss and an image to symbolize your wholeness. Perhaps by now you realized the importance of fortifying yourself with a daily pleasure break.

You saw how to identify the afflicted body part in your dreams. You found the value in understanding the dream image on a psychological as well as literal level. You reviewed the characteristic forms that various types of diseases and disabilities take in dreams.[3] You explored how the dreaming mind operates in metaphors. You learned to watch your dreams for signs of speeded-up or slowed-down metabolism, how to recognize dream images of excessive cold or heat, and moisture or dryness that indicate changes in body functioning. You learned the implications of broken or damaged structures and wounded or dying people and animals. You worked with dream cars in trouble and dream houses in danger.

You practiced "redreaming" unsatisfying dreams. You drew a picture of a crisis and of the afflicted body part. You saw how drawings of the wounded or ill body part changed over time. You held "conversations" with the ailing body part. You supplied it with missing needs. You drew your nightmares. You found refocusing images and used them in visualizations. You transformed the image of injury or illness using imagery to oppose it, to dilute it, to redirect it, to color it, and to imagine it healed. You worked with idiosyncratic dream images and found a way to appreciate their vital messages. You used art to visualize strengthening your immune system.

You saw how there was a sequence of dream changes during recovery from illness or injury. First came the dream pictures replaying the trauma. Then accidental improvement in the trauma arose in dreams, followed by deliberate improvement caused by the dreamer. Next there was a shift in power to predominately positive dream images. Finally, the images in dreams revealed that reintegration has occurred. You became familiar with the images characteristic of each of these steps of healing, and learned how to recognize the dream images of returning wellness. You saw how to incubate a dream on a specific topic, and how to incubate a lucid dream, using this altered state of consciousness to improve your condition.

Finally, you saw how to use your imagination to create a journey to your "inner dream temple." You may set out on this inner healing journey again and again because the temple of dreams lies within you. There your inner guide sits enthroned. The wisdom, the great truths, and the knowledge of this guide is yours for the asking. Visit your inner dream temple whenever you wish. Contact the healing power of your dreams. Seek guidance there. Dream well and prosper. May your journey be a blessing.

# APPENDICES

## ◇ CONTENT

Dream images associated with injured body parts in:

NOTE:
The dreams listed in these appendices are not the only ones reported by subjects with these physical problems. They are chosen to illustrate the typical close connection between an injury to, disease of, or surgery on a particular body part and the imagery of the same person while dreaming. The injured dreamer dreams about other topics as well. Also, please note that it was only possible to give a representative sample of the disorders and their associated imagery, not an exhaustive survey.

# ◇ KEY TO ABBREVIATIONS IN APPENDICES

Name indicates source of the dream cited (details in bibliography):

| | |
|---|---|
| B. | Robert Bosnak. |
| E. | Havelock Ellis. "Ellis/E." indicates Ellis himself. |
| G. | Indicates the example is from the author's collection of interviews with dreamers. When identified as "Garfield/G." the subject is the author herself. |
| Gt. | Emil Gutheil. |
| H. | Robert Haskell. |
| K. | Vasillii Kasatkin. "Kasatkin/K." indicates Kasatkin himself. |
| L. | Harold Levitan. |
| Lk. | Russell A. Lockhart. |
| M. | Patricia Maybruck. |
| Pt. | Dennis Potter. "Potter/Pt." indicates Potter himself. |
| R&C | Ernest Rossi and David Cheek. |
| S. | Alan Seigel. |
| Sk. | Oliver Sacks. "Sacks/Sk." indicates Sacks himself. |
| VdC | Robert Van de Castle. |
| W&F | H. Warnes and A. Finkelstein. |
| Z | Alfred Ziegler. |
| unk. | Unknown. The dreamer is referred to by the name supplied in cited text; if no name or number is given, he or she is identified by the abbreviation for unknown. |

## ◇ APPENDIX A

### ◇ Dream Images of Injured Body Part in Cardiovascular Disorders
### *(heart and blood vessel disorders)*

| DREAMER IDENTITY/ SOURCE* | DISORDER† | DREAM IMAGE |
|---|---|---|
| 1. "P"/K. female age 51 | Myocardial infarct one month before; woke up with rapid heartbeat, pain in heart, spasm in throat. | Dreamer in cemetery, sat on husband's grave; two hands came out of grave; one hand grabbed throat, other put bony fingers into heart; hard to breathe, couldn't scream. |
| 2. "L"/K. male age unk. | Heart attack eleven days before dream; felt fine before sleep; woke in pain with heart spasm. | Dreamer was lying in his country house; not enough fresh air; bandits broke into the house, fought with his brothers and sisters; one bandit tried to crush roof with beam; it fell onto the dreamer's chest; he tried to lift it or to scream but could not. |
| 3. "P"/K. male mid. age | Heart disease for three years; mild pain during day; awoke in fear and pain. | Dreamer was fighting in war; enemies surrounded him; one hurt him in the heart. |
| 4. unk/W&F female age 62 | Coronary | Dreamer's 64-year-old brother was killed in a car accident; his head was severed from his body; when she approached, his head turned into a chicken's head with milk around it. (One brother had died of a coronary.) |
| 5. unk/W&F female age 65 | Coronary | Somebody was killed in a car accident and dreamer saw blood; she wondered if the victim was a person close to her; she felt upset. (Her parents and two sisters died of myocardial infarction.) |

* See *Key to Abbreviations* used in appendix for the source of examples cited here.

† The terms used to describe the disorder are those given by the original source.

| | | |
|---|---|---|
| 6. unk/W&F<br>male<br>age 63 | Coronary; woke up in fear and pain. | A man was chasing dreamer; he tried to run away; he felt a pressure in his chest; he couldn't breathe. |
| 7. unk/W&F<br>male<br>age 50 | Myocardial infarction; awoke with pain spreading to chest. | Dreamer was in a war; enemies were chasing him; he was fighting for his life when he felt pain in his left arm; thought he was injured. |
| 8. unk/Z.<br>male<br>age 50 | Arterial infarct† that occurred during the dream; awoke with pain in heart and neck, cold sweat. | Dreamer was at a reception at a palace; knew he or the ruler would die; he warned the ruler of a plot; he was chased by a man with a white blank instead of a face; four of the guests shot at the dreamer; he felt the bullets pierce his heart; he saw blood flow out; he fainted from pain and died. Dead, but visible, he was talking with the king; he tore the skin off a courtier's face; he pulled off other masks; he fought a soldier and also a skinny man. The hall emptied, the wind gusted but the air was sultry; an evil giant came and strangled him; he felt as if a bomb exploded. |
| 9. unk./H.<br>male<br>age unk. | Myocardial infarction; patient complained only of a "fluttery feeling in stomach." | Dreamer fell from the wharf into water between the wharf piles; a yacht moored alongside squeezed him into the pier structures. |
| 10. unk./E.<br>female<br>age unk. | Heart "weakness"† | Dreamer was driving sweating horses up a steep hill, urging them with a whip in order to avoid an express train behind them. |
| 11. unk./W&F<br>male<br>age 41 | Angina pectoris | A helicopter was destroying a "bombed out" house with its blades. Dreamer ran to save the pilot who was sitting on a tractor with blades; dreamer felt afraid and helpless. (His father died of a coronary.) |

† The terms used to describe the disorder are those given by the original source.

| 12. "P"/K. male age unk. | Hypertension | Dreamer saw himself on top of a tall building that was made by his design (he was an engineer); it was built with negligence; there were cracks in the walls and the structure was showing; he was afraid he could be tried for such poor work; then the whole building collapsed, trapping him inside with a heavy weight on his chest and head; it was hard to breathe; felt afraid. |
|---|---|---|
| 13. unk./W&F female age 58 | Hypertension | Dreamer saw a boy killed in a car accident; he lay on the ground full of blood; felt very upset. (Her mother died of hypertension.) |
| 14. unk./Z. female age 20 | Tachycardia episodes (rapid heartbeat); woke with pulse of 130 beats per minute | Dreamer was half-human, half-monster, lying in bed; here and there, especially on her arms and legs she was covered with scales; in place of her normal feet she had prehensile ones (capable of clutching, like birds' feet) with which she could hold fast to the foot of the bed; she was appalled. |

*Typical dream images with heart disorder:*
Dreamer or other character is hurt in accident, war, or fight.
Wounds typically appear in left arm, heart area or neck.
Pain in heart, left arm, or neck often accompany the wound.
Squeezing or clutching pressure on heart, chest and/or neck.
Sense of heavy weight falling on chest.
Sense of strangulation, of suffocation, of difficulty breathing or of stagnant air.
An impression of an explosion, as with shots or bombs.
References to death, blood, pain.
Effortful behavior with sense of urgency and/or fear.
Objects capable of clutching or squeezing.

*Antidote images for visualizations:*
Wounds are being treated with soothing balm.
Lightness, spaciousness, openness.
Gentle breezes bringing fresh, clean air.
Letting go, floating freely and pleasantly on air or water.

On a swing or seesaw, swaying in ordered, easy rhythm.
Harmonic music washing over the body.

## ◇ APPENDIX B

### ◇ Dream Images of Injured Body Part in Gastrointestinal Disorders
#### *(stomach, intestinal disorders)*

| DREAMER IDENTITY/ SOURCE* | DISORDER† | DREAM IMAGE |
|---|---|---|
| 1. Garfield/G. female age 56 | Overeating | Dreamer in tight cubicle could barely move as she tried to change clothes. |
| 2. Ellis/E. male age unk. | Indigestion | Dreamer was eating bread mingled with cinders and mouse's excrement; tried to avoid impurities; found his mouth full of cinders. |
| 3. "P"/K. female mid. age | Anacidic gastritis† | Dreamer was eating raw or spoiled fish. |
| 4. "Z"/K. male age unk. | Ate suspect sausage in evening; awoke with stomach pain after second dream. | Dreamer was fishing in muddy, brown water; spoiled fish on river banks with feces; unsafe to eat. |
| | | Dreamer was attacked by hoodlums in public toilet covered with feces and vomit; they caught him and kicked him in stomach. |
| 5. "N"/K. male elderly | Chronic gastritis | Dreamer was eating earthworms or raw, bloody meat; or long strings and globs of mucus came from mouth and stomach. |
| 6. "N2"/K. sex unk. age unk. | Chronic colic | Dreamer saw furuncle (boil) in stomach opening; blood, pus to left of navel, more furuncles with feces, pus. |

* See *Key to Abbreviations* used in appendix for the source of examples cited here.

† The terms used to describe the disorder are those given by the original source.

| | | |
|---|---|---|
| 7. "N3"/K. male age unk. | Chronic acidic gastritis; awoke nauseous, feeling full. | Dreamer in room with feces; wanted to vomit but no place to do so because of people. |
| | Awoke feeling full and queasy. | Dreamer was eating strange, light-yellow fish, half raw, with unpleasant yellow dressing; felt disgusted but ate it. |
| | Acute episode; awoke with unpleasant sensation in stomach; throat irritated, mild nausea. | Dreamer had mucus in throat; had difficulty breathing; tried to cough out; with hands pulled out a mushroomlike object with a rough base, with pale spiders and worms; thought he might have cancer. |
| | Awoke with slight nausea and felt bad in stomach. | Dreamer saw river with murky, dirty water, a dirty bank with dead fish and snotlike material. |
| 8. unk./K. male elderly | Hyperacidic gastritis with heartburn. | Twice dreamed he drank vinegar and felt it dripping into his stomach. |
| 9. unk./K. sex unk. age unk. | Dysentery; awoke after second dream with headache and pain in lower abdomen; had to defecate. | Dreamer was in apartment dirtied with feces and water that was yellowish-grey. Dreamer was fighting in war; he hid in a rest room dirty with feces; he was caught by one enemy who hit him on head with rifle-butt and another who struck him in stomach with bayonet. |
| 10. unk./Lk. female age unk. | Stomach cancer; awoke screaming. Nightmares began a few months before diagnosis and lasted for two weeks. She died three months after diagnosis. | Recurrent nightmares of dogs tearing at her stomach; fires burning her flesh. |
| 11. unk./W&F male age 85 | Peptic ulcer; awoke terrified. | Dreamer's house was burning; he shouted for help but nobody came to rescue. |

| 12. unk./W&F male age 57 | Duodenal ulcer | Dreamer was in a closed building trying to get out but unable to find an exit; a woman showed him the door, but when he got there he was attacked, clawed, and scratched by cats; he felt hopeless, angry, and helpless. |
| 13. unk./W&F male age 35 | Duodenal ulcer; dream followed an argument with his boss; he felt rage, helplessness. | Dreamer saw himself tearing out his teeth one by one, breaking them between his fingers, which were full of blood. |
| 14. unk./W&F male age 29 | Perforated ulcer; dream was on the night prior to the perforation. | Dreamer was eating pizza when his stomach "broke open"; he felt afraid and helpless. |
| 15. Ward/M. male age 51 | Incipient ulcer; awoke with bad stomach pains. | Dreamer saw what looked like an X-ray of his stomach . . . full of grapes with little Italian peasant women stamping on them; one huge grape burst. |

*Typical dream images with stomach disorders:*
Dreamer is confined by small space or tight clothing.
Dreamer consumes unpleasant or spoiled food or liquid, inedible material or feces.
Dreamer is in the presence of spoiled food, dirty water, or feces.
Dreamer is attacked and injured in the stomach.
Dreamer has large amounts of mucus or pus in digestive tract.
Dreamer sees unhealthy fish [elongated shape of fish in dream may correlate with shape of stomach or intestine].
Dreamer is wounded or hurt in stomach area.

*Additional typical dream images with ulcers:*
Dreamer's house is on fire [images of heat are associated with inflammation in a body part].
Something breaks or bursts in the dreamer's abdomen.

*Antidote images for stomach visualizations:*
A bland potion soothes the digestive tract.
Fresh, clear waters wash away all debris and flow freely.
Healthy fish are swimming rhythmically in calm waters.
Stomach is wrapped gently in soft, comforting cloth.
Smooth hands stroke and soothe the body surface.

*Additional antidote images for ulcer visualizations:*
Cool, soothing fluids inundate the abdominal area.
River waters or firehoses douse all flames.
A building is repaired or reconstructed.
Feelings of peacefulness and love flow through the person.

## ◇ APPENDIX C

### ◇ Dream Images of Disturbed Body Part in Pulmonary Disorders
### *(lungs, bronchial tubes, etc.)*

| DREAMER IDENTITY/ SOURCE* | DISORDER† | DREAM IMAGE |
|---|---|---|
| 1. Jake/G. male age 8 | Pneumonia; dream recurred three times during illness. | A man holding all the people in the world in his arms was standing on the dreamer's chest; the people were dead. |
| 2. Rosie/G. female age 6 | Pneumonia; dream a few nights after return from hospitalization. | Dreamer was playing with the brakes in her mother's car; the car ran away; her mother couldn't help; she didn't know how to stop car; then she got lost and a witch captured her; she got away and the witch came back with a shiny red convertible. |
| 3. Christopher/ B. male age unk. | Pneumocystis (from AIDS). | Dreamer was in speedboat with a friend, going fast; lake water was mucky (vile green slick); dam prevented water from running out; he turned boat around and went back. |
| 4. "A"/K. female age unk. | Tuberculosis in lungs for 3 years; awoke in fear. | Dreamer was lying naked on the ground, the earth sunk, opened, the edges closed in and squeezed her chest, it was hard to breathe. |

* *See Key to Abbreviations* used in appendix for the source of examples cited here.

† The terms used to describe the disorder are those given by the original source.

| 5. "S"/K.<br>female<br>age unk. | Tuberculosis in lungs for 2 years; pleurisy in left lung. | Mountain slide, earth, fell onto dreamer's chest; she tried to crawl through a small hole but her chest, especially the left side, did not fit. |
|---|---|---|
| 6. unk./K.<br>male<br>age unk. | Acute bronchitis; awoke with clogged passages, headache, lying on his chest, with chest squashed. | Dreamer was climbing up a mountain with friends, fell behind; he wore some obstructive headgear; fell from high bank into the dirty, yellow river, was drowning. |
| 7. "R"/K.<br>male<br>age unk. | Acute catarrh of breathing passages; awoke afraid, had trouble breathing, a stuffed nose, headache. | Dreamer was fighting in a war, was attacked, thrown to the ground, an enemy was strangling him. |
| 8. Emerson/G.<br>male<br>age 40 | Asthma from 4 to 10 years old; recurrent dream with attacks. | Dreamer saw a brainlike material, all wrinkled; he tried to smooth it out carefully with his hands or a machine; it wrinkled up behind him again (spasms in bronchial tubes?). |
| 9. unk./W&F<br>female<br>age 22 | Bronchial asthma; woke up wheezing. | A man tried to kill dreamer. He had invented a machine to kill people by holding them under water for three minutes; it was dangerous, had to be stopped; eight women were in the room; dreamer was mad at her physician in the dream. |
| 10. unk./W&F<br>female<br>age 62 | Bronchial asthma; woke up crying; soon had attack. | Dreamer's mother brought her two glasses of water, told her not to worry because she would get well; dreamer felt helpless, unhappy. |
| 11. unk./E. | Asthma, during attack. | Dreamer saw sweating horses trying to draw a heavy wagon uphill. |
| 12. unk./Z.<br>male<br>age 41 | Asthma; woke with attack. | Dreamer was suspected of committing murder; police followed him in car to see he had nothing to do with the deaths; the earth began to tremble as in a landslide or an earthquake; dust and dirt |

swirled in the air; he sank deeper and deeper; earth began to cover him; he screamed for grandparents; he hurried naked from square to square while chunks of earth fell on him.

| | | | |
|---|---|---|---|
| 13. | Frank/M.<br>male<br>age 39 | Chest cold started the next day after the dream. | Walls in a store collapsed; refrigerator fell onto the dreamer; he couldn't get his breath, but got out okay. |
| 14. | Sarah/M.<br>female<br>age 30 | Head cold started the next day after the dream. | Dreamer was in a meadow full of beautiful wild flowers; she started sneezing uncontrollably. |
| 15. | Susan/G.<br>female<br>age 35 | Head cold; awoke with stuffy nose. | Dreamer was breathing through two long straws. |

*Typical dream images with lung disorder:*

Chest area is being weighted or squeezed or struck by earth or other heavy objects or is generally constricted.

Dreamer's chest is squeezed by tight clothing.

Dreamer's chest is stuck in narrow space.

Dreamer is sinking into earth (characteristic of more serious lung disorders).

Instabilities of earth or buildings—quakes, landslides, opening of crevices.

Climbing is effortful, causing labored breathing.

Feelings of fear, unhappiness, and/or suffocation.

Seeing objects or animals that worsen condition—dust, horses, flowers, etc.

Sensations of drowning or moving through polluted water (dirty water indicates presence of mucus).

Dreamer is in speeding or in an out-of-control vehicle (general symbol for rampant illness).

Dreamer has difficulty breathing.

*Antidote images for visualizations:*

Clear, sparkling, freely moving water flows through and cleanses body.

Breathing passages widen while inhaling steam from a kettle.

Firm foundation of solid land and buildings.

Balance, harmony, peacefulness.

Strolling at ease in clear, pure mountain air.

Openness, vast skies, space above.

Flying above clear waters.

## ◇ APPENDIX D

### ◇ Dream Images of Injured Body Part in Dental Disorders
*(toothache, infection, abscess, surgery)*

| DREAMER IDENTITY/ SOURCE * | DISORDER † | DREAM IMAGE |
|---|---|---|
| 1. "F"/K. male age unk. | Slight pain in tooth after dream; severe toothache developed during day. | Dreamer lost lower right tooth, saw roots of a yellowish-black color, almost all destroyed. |
| 2. Fiona/G. female age 49 | Two days after apicoectomy (oral surgery to remove infection from around root of tooth and in jaw bone). | Dreamer was in dirty water, swimming through seaweed [strings from stitches] that tangled and caught her legs. |
| 3. Garfield/G. ‡ female age 55 | Abscess in gum above infection in root of tooth erupted day before dream (1/7/90). | Dreamer entered a filthy bathroom that needed a lot of work; saw a dried-out white African violet in the toothbrush holder; she thought she would try to revive the root [root of tooth] stock because it probably produced beautiful flowers. |
| | 1/13/90: one week post-apicoectomy (surgery in jaw around root of tooth, on 1/8/90). | Dreamer saw termites swarming on mirror in bedroom, and table; people gather small bugs. |

* See *Key to Abbreviations* used in appendix for the source of examples cited here.

† The terms used to describe the disorder are those given by the original source.

‡ In order to demonstrate how dream images depict on-going conditions in the body, I have excerpted a set of images relating to an infection in the root of my tooth and jaw during the first month the disorder was apparent. Following oral surgery the conditions worsened and surgery had to be repeated about six months later. Dream images continued to reflect this condition during the intervening months, but were too numerous to cite.

| | |
|---|---|
| 1/14/90: one week post-apicoectomy. | Dreamer drove a beat-up car to get gas; saw that a nearby car had a rusty bullet hole in the body [hole in jawbone]. |
| 1/23/90: two weeks post-apicoectomy. | Dreamer's speech was thick, as if had a gauze pad at front of mouth. |
| 1/25/90: abscess suspicious again; two weeks after having had apicoectomy. | Living room drapes, inner and outer, caught on fire and were ruined; would have to be replaced.<br><br>Dreamer passed a mirror and observed her jaw oddly swollen; thought she must return to dentist. |
| 1/27/90 | Woman had problem of some kind with rug; small bugs like boll weevils; carpet must be specially cleaned. |
| 1/31/90 | Some blood of dreamer was tested, poured from a tube onto tray where it sizzled and turned from red to brown; afraid it would prove infected.<br><br>Jade earring—shaped like a tooth and its root—was broken. |
| Infection recurred; surgery repeated 8/21/90. | |

*Typical dream images with tooth disorder:*
Dreamer experiences pain in or loss of tooth.
Dreamer has unusual objects in mouth.
Objects representing dental apparatus hamper dreamer.
Fire or heat indicates presence of inflammation.
Bugs such as termites or boll weevils indicate presence of infection.

*Antidote images for visualizations:*
Infected material drains out of mouth and washes away.
Swimming freely in clear water.
Opening the mouth wide and singing joyfully.

## ◇ APPENDIX E

### ◇ Dream Images of Injured Body Part in Arthritic Disorders
### *(rheumatoid arthritis, etc.)*

| DREAMER IDENTITY/ SOURCE* | DISORDER† | DREAM IMAGE |
|---|---|---|
| 1. unk./Gt. female age 26 | Arthritis; awoke with stiff shoulders and arms. | Dreamer was being held captive in a large apartment; her arms were bound to her sides like in a strait jacket; she was permitted to roam the house, but captors would not let her out; all they gave her was hard candy; it seemed her mother was holding her captive. |
|  | Condition improved morning after this dream. | Dreamer was leaving her house to go to another house; the streets were very icy. A model T Ford turned the corner and turned over, fell to pieces. Her mother said to be careful; dreamer fell but was able to get up easily. She crossed over and entered her aunt's house; dreamer realized she was partly dressed. |
| 2. unk./Gt. female age unk. | Rheumatic pains (champagne brings on her pains, but she had not drunk any recently). | Dreamer was drinking glass after glass of champagne, saying to herself she would have to pay for it afterward. |
| 3. "No. 9"/L. female age 56 | Rheumatoid arthritis for nine years. | Dreamer was visiting a house in middle of the night; she heard terrible noises, opened a door, and saw two men making love, the older man tearing the flesh of the younger man with his teeth. |

* See *Key to Abbreviations* used in appendix for the source of examples cited here.

† The terms used to describe the disorder are those given by the original source.

Dreamer was biting someone's hand, drawing blood; she desired to hurt them but was revolted by the flesh and bones under her teeth.

Dreamer was bitten by a snake on the toe; felt his little teeth penetrating her flesh.

| | | |
|---|---|---|
| 4. "No. 4"/L. female age 40 | Arthritis for five years. | Dreamer was killing her loved cat by putting it into an electric warming tray going full blast. |

Dreamer had wolves for pets; she was deathly afraid of them; saw chunks of meat, bone in the living room; she felt afraid, whom did they eat?

A man was killing the dreamer's squirrels, taking them in his hands and crushing their bones, making a horrible sound; dreamer was afraid he was going to do the same to her.

| | | |
|---|---|---|
| 5. "No. 10"/L. female age 59 | Arthritis for fifteen years. | Two boys were keeping a man hostage by holding him down and cutting out his liver with a long carving knife, preparing to eat the liver. |

| | | |
|---|---|---|
| 6. "No. 5"/L. female age 30 | Arthritis for eight years (recurrent dream after being angry at cat for soiling furniture). | Dreamer was biting her cat. |

| | | |
|---|---|---|
| 7. "No. 1"/L. female age 38 | Arthritis for thirteen years. | Dreamer in rage at her mother; she took a bite out of her mother's arm, a whole piece of flesh was in her mouth. |

Dreamer's loved dog was leaping at her throat with teeth bared; dog didn't want to kill her but was being forced to do it.

Dreamer was cuddling on her sister's lap, getting very close to her; suddenly sister jabbed a lit cigarette into the dreamer's eye.

| 8. unk./Z. | Arthritis; | Dreamer was filling glasses from |
| female | hospitalized with | heavy pitchers for a large |
| age 35 | attack in right wrist. | number of people seated at |
| | | tables, probably waiting for |
| | | something to eat; she was the |
| | | only one to whom task was |
| | | entrusted; was being forced to |
| | | do it by a man with benevolent |
| | | grin; was some kind of |
| | | blackmail. |
| 9. Potter/Pt. | Arthritis with | Dreamer's fingers were gnawed |
| male | psoriasis. | by rats. |
| age unk. | | |

*Typical dream images with rheumatoid arthritis:*
Dreamer's free movement is restricted—captive, held down.
Dreamer performs behavior that brings on rheumatic pain.
Dreamer performs behavior that strains the afflicted part.
Dreamer or some other dream character is enraged.
Dreamer or some other character bites or otherwise injures a helpless
   dream animal or person;
Animals chew or bite dreamer's painful parts (oral aggression is com-
   mon).
Bones are being crushed.

*Antidote images for visualizations:*
Free, easily fluid movement; gliding over ice, water, or air.
Dancing or swimming with joy.
Letting anger and resentment flow out of the body.
Flooding the body with radiant light or healing waters.
Washing the body with love and peace.
Handsome jeweled rings and bracelets with smooth, articulated parts.
Wearing beautiful, light-colored clothing that gives body a feeling of
   easy, free-flowing grace.

## ◇ APPENDIX F

## ◇ Dream Images of Injured Body Part in
## Neurologic Disorders: Migraine

| DREAMER IDENTITY/ SOURCE * | DISORDER † | DREAM IMAGE |
|---|---|---|
| 1. unk./W&F female age 17 | Migraine; awoke with left hemicranea. | A man broke into dreamer's bedroom through windows; she tried to escape to bathroom, but man shot her on left side of head; she felt scared. |
| 2. unk./W&F female age 38 | Migraine; awoke with headache. | Dreamer's husband invited his mother to stay with them for three months because dreamer was having such a time with their child; dreamer shot her husband in the face by accident and yelled, "Oh my God." |
| 3. unk./Gt. female age unk. | Migraine; awoke with headache. | Dreamer was alone with father who was a widower; she was not married; she was sitting quietly when the door opened and her mother came in, dead, with a bloody band around her forehead, showing she had been slain. |
| | Migraine; awoke with headache. | Dreamer was taking a walk; a storm broke out; a bolt of lightning struck her head; she turned around her longitudinal axis several times and then fell down. |
| 4. Case 75/Sk. male age unk. | Migraine. | Nightmare, suddenly changing to cinematographic vision of flickering stills persisting for ten minutes in the waking state. |

* See *Key to Abbreviations* used in appendix for the source of examples cited here.

† The terms used to describe the disorder are those given by the original source.

| | | |
|---|---|---|
| 5. Sacks/Sk.<br>male<br>age unk. | Migraine; awoke with left visual field missing. Patient was in the hospital for treatment of an injured leg. | We were at war and the enemy had an ultimate weapon, a "Derealization Bomb." It could blow a hole in reality. Dreamer was outside in garden; he saw his pear tree was missing, part of the garden wall was gone; the road gone; his mother had no left half . . . [dreamer was awakened by nurse who saw how pale he was]. |
| 6. unk./L.<br>sex unk.<br>age unk. | Migraine; awoke with throbbing headache. | Dreamer was in a shipwreck . . . many people were drowning . . . he managed to save his favorite niece . . . as he swam away he looked back and saw the other people being eaten up by seamonsters . . . the heads of the people were in the mouths of the monsters . . . it was very scary. . . . |
| 7. Ellis/E.<br>male<br>age unk. | Fell asleep with a headache. | Dreamer was waiting for an express train to London; one comes up to platform, but he cannot ascertain if it is the train he wants. [Rail travel provoked headaches for the dreamer.] |
| 8. Ellis/E.<br>male<br>age unk. | Awoke with slight headache. | Dreamer was in vast, gloomy English cathedral and on the wall he observed a notice that on a certain day, evensong would take place without illuminating the cathedral to avoid attracting moths. [Coolness, such as in the cathedral and lack of glare were soothing when dreamer had a headache.] |
| 9. Ellis/E.<br>male<br>age unk. | Fell asleep with headache. | Nails were being hammered into the floor. [The pounding corresponded to the thump of the dreamer's throbbing arteries.] |

*Typical dream images with migraine:*
Dreamer or some other character is wounded in the head—by acci-

dent, by an assailant, by lightning—usually on the side experiencing the headache pain.

Dreamer observes distorted or detached heads of people or animals.

Dreamer or some other character has bandaged head or wears head-gear that is tight or obstructs vision.

Dreamer is dizzy and falls.

Dreamer sees odd visual patterns in stills, flickers, moving abstracts, or objects that expand rapidly or expand and contract. [Changing visual patterns probably represent the aura present during migraine.]

Part of the dreamer's visual field is missing.

Dreamer is in the presence of objects that ordinarily induce a headache for him or her.

An unpleasant jarring or pounding rhythm is present.

*Antidote images for visualizations:*

Hands are being warmed by holding a cup of hot chocolate, steaming coffee, or other hot beverage attractive to the person. [Warming hands draws blood away from cerebral centers, lessening congestion.]

Hands are being warmed by holding them to a fire in fireplace or a campfire.

Relaxing in a safe and comfortable place, allowing the visual effects to pass through and subside.

Being in a place that is comfortably cool and dim.

Any pounding rhythm is transformed into light-footed, joyful dancing.

Letting any pain melt and drip out of the body.

Letting soft breezes pass over and carry away all discomfort.

◇ APPENDIX G

## ◇ Dream Images of Injured Body Part in
## Throat Disorders

| DREAMER IDENTITY/ SOURCE* | DISORDER† | DREAM IMAGE |
|---|---|---|
| 1. "K"/K. female age unk. | Throat infection began day after dream; awoke with pain in throat. | Dreamer had diphtheria, saw white spots on her tonsils; her son became infected too. |
| 2. "W"/K. female age unk. | Throat infection two days after dream; awoke with pain in throat, had difficulty breathing. | Dreamer was followed by hooligans; some caught her by the throat, choked her; she couldn't breathe. |
| 3. unk./K. male age unk. | Influenza present; awoke with pain in throat, especially on the left side; body ached, his face was hot, his head heavy and with a noise in both ears. | Dreamer was fighting in the war; shouting horsemen with red faces approached; his small group was overpowered; the soldiers wore large helmets; an enemy tried to stab him in the left side of the throat; dreamer tried to cry out. |
| 4. Garfield/G. female age 49 | Influenza present; awoke with pain, inflammation in throat. | Dreamer struck in throat by devil with a pitchfork. |

*Typical dreamer images with throat disorder:*
Dreamer's throat is squeezed or wounded.
Dreamer observes indications of disease in throat.
Heat in dream indicates presence of inflammation in throat.

*Antidote images for visualizations:*
Drinking cool, soothing liquids, or eating soft, melting ice cream.
Snowflakes falling gently on sore areas.
Cool waterfall or stream rippling down throat.
Green, blue, aqua sea lapping in waves over throat area.

---

* See *Key to Abbreviations* used in appendix for the source of examples cited here.

† The terms used to describe the disorder are those given by the original source.

## ◇ APPENDIX H

### ◇ Dream Images of Injured Body Part in
### Dermatologic Disorders
### *(damaged skin)*

| DREAMER IDENTITY/ SOURCE* | DISORDER† | DREAM IMAGE |
| --- | --- | --- |
| 1. Garfield/G. female age 15 | A large acne pustule arose during the day after the dream. | Dreamer saw a soldier wounded in the cheek by a bullet. |
| 2. Lila/G. female age 39 | Pox from chicken pox erupted day after dream. | Dreamer had poison ivy all over her body. |
| 3. "K"/K. female age unk. | Inflammation appeared on the back of the right hand during next day. | A neighbor touched the back of dreamer's right hand with a burning cigarette. |
| 4. Kasatkin/K. male age unk. | A small furuncle (abscess) appeared on the right temple the evening following the dream. | The dreamer had a black swelling with pus on his right temple; he feared blindness. |
| 5. "N"/K male age unk. | Pain present in nail of right thumb when awoke; inflammation arose during the day. | A large splinter pierced dreamer's right thumb from nail to wrist; pus, pain were present. |
| 6. "S"/K. male age unk. | Intense pain from skin disease was present in first joint of the left index finger prior to dream; pain worse and headache on awakening. | Dreamer was fighting in the war; he wore a huge helmet that obstructed his vision; one of the enemies cut him with a knife on the left index finger. |

* See *Key to Abbreviations* used in appendix for the source of examples cited here.

† The terms used to describe the disorder are those given by the original source.

*Typical dream images with skin eruptions:*
Dreamer has pain from a wound in the area of a present skin eruption or one that emerges the day after dream.
Heat or swelling in the dream indicates the presence of inflammation at the site of the disorder.
Dreamer suffers from skin disorder similar to impending one.

*Antidote images for visualizations involving skin eruptions:*
Soothing ointments or cool creams are applied to the area of disturbance.
Healing light or flowing water floods the disturbed area, dissolving and carrying away all discomfort.

## ◇ APPENDIX I

### ◇ Dream Images of Injured Body Part in Obstetric Disorders
### *(damaged fetus)*

| DREAMER IDENTITY/ SOURCE * | DISORDER † | DREAM IMAGE |
|---|---|---|
| 1. Brenda/G. age 30 | Induced abortion; dream was few days after the abortion. | Dreamer's garage doors were torn off and her car was stolen; angry women tore up the land around her house with bulldozers. |
| 2. unk./M. age unk. | Miscarriage two or three days after dream. | Dreamer saw her deceased grandfather who smiled and said, "I'm going to take your baby now." |
| 3. unk./VdeC. age unk. | Miscarriage. | Dreamer was in a bathtub when the water turned red. |
| 4. unk./VdeC. age unk. | Miscarriage. | A strange lady told the dreamer three times, "You can't take care of it!" |

* See *Key to Abbreviations* used in appendix for the source of examples cited here.

† The terms used to describe the disorder are those given by the original source.

| 5. | Sonia/R&C age 34 | Spontaneous abortion; began bleeding during this dream. | Dreamer's baby was taken from her by the Nazis [her first pregnancy was aborted by surgery in prison camp]. |
|---|---|---|---|
| 6. | Mrs. M./ R&C age 26 | Spontaneous abortion; began bleeding after this dream. | Dreamer's husband was dying. |
| | | Second spontaneous abortion. | Dreamer had to abort baby or husband would be killed. |
| 7. | unk./M. age unk. | Fetus in distress; premature birth; C-section performed; infant survived. | Dreamer was drowning at the beach where she was washed up on the shore; her mother started cutting dreamer's abdomen with a knife. |
| 8. | unk./VdeC. age unk. | Later found fetus had died in womb. | Dreamer saw her infant on examining table; her obstetrician discontinued the exam because the baby was too cold. |
| 9. | unk/VdeC. age unk. | Fetus later was born dead. | Dreamer's mother was baby-sitting her child and put it into the refrigerator where dreamer found it icy cold. |

*Typical dream images with damage to fetus:*
Destruction to entrance of a house and/or to land.
Abnormal coldness of a child.
Someone threatens or harms the dreamer's fetus or a relative.

*Antidote images for visualizations:*
Reconstruction of house; reclamation of land.
Warming and nurturing of infant.
Saving and healing the threatened person.
Cherishing the internal child; rocking, soothing, comforting it.

# ◇ APPENDIX J

## ◇ Dream Images of Injured Body Part in Gynecologic Disorders
### (hysterectomy)

| DREAMER IDENTITY/ SOURCE* | SURGERY | DREAM IMAGE |
|---|---|---|
| 1. Mimi/G. early 40s. | Uterus and ovaries removed. | Dreamer forced to have sex in 50 ways by ex-boyfriend. |
| | Both dreams during hospitalization. | Dreamer was raped by two young strangers. |
| 2. Bejay/G. age 47 | Uterus removed; dream during hospitalization. | Dreamer gave birth to jagged, metal, half-fender of a car. |
| 3. Julia/G. mid 30s | Uterus removed; dream during hospitalization. | Dreamer had orgasm. |
| 4. Maggie/G. age 40 | Left ovary removed during cesarean; dream about six weeks post-surgery. | In mirror, dreamer saw left breast boarded up; her right breast was long and droopy; she feared cancer. |
| 5. Eileen/G. age 60 | Uterus and ovaries removed, extensive pelvic surgery. | Dreamer saw dead and dying animals on a hillside field, retreated. |
| | Dream during stay in intensive care unit. | |
| | Dream first night out of I.C.U.; still had tube in stomach, no solid food. | 2 men and 2 women were waiting at a table for food to be served; white tablecloth, pink flowers. |

*Typical dream images following hysterectomy:*
Pain in area of genitals depicted as attack or difficult birth.
Fear of death, fear of aging, fear of loss of femininity
Deceased people, dead or dying animals (general for surgery)

* These five subjects are from the author's collection of dream interviews.

*Antidote images for visualizations:*
Making passionate but pleasant love.
Giving birth to new self.
Reborn, rejuvenated animal and human life.
Radiant light or sparkling waters flooding site of operation, washing
  away all trace of pain, leaving body glowing, renewed.

## ◇ APPENDIX K

### ◇ Dream Images of Injured Body Part in
### Fractured Limbs
### *(broken wrist)*

| DATE OF DREAM | LITERAL IMAGES* | SYMBOLIC IMAGES |
|---|---|---|
| | [Left arm, wrist, hand, head, knee, associated injuries, sensations, treatment or equipment are pictured directly in dream.] | [Left arm, wrist, hand, head, knee, associated injuries, sensations, treatment or equipment appear symbolically in dream pictures.] |
| | **DREAMER IDENTITY:** Author† Female age 54 | |
| 3/1/88 | *Date of Injury:* radius bone broken, wrist bones crushed, fingers hurt, knee hurt, neck wrenched. Misdiagnosis of sprain in wrist. | |
| 3/3/88 | 1. My *hands* rub on rough concrete as I climb out of sea [plaster splint on arm]. | |

* The numbers refer to individual dream images. Literal dream images scored included: left hand, wrist, arm, finger, knee, head, operation or surgery, surgeon, plate in arm, cast, splint, baton, and spirometer. In the symbolic dream images, only a sample of those that appeared during this time frame are given.

† In order to give a comprehensive picture of the changing dream imagery during the healing process, I have excerpted this set of images from my own dream diary. Examples from other dreamers with fractured limbs appear throughout the text.

3/4/88

2. Balloons are attached to my *arms* and one *knee* [swelling in these areas].

1. Eagle has shutters for wings [could not fly].

2. Woman dreams about her pet octopus [eight arms].

3. I wear a cream-colored fur jacket with attached gloves of long gauntlet style in tooled leather [splint on arm].

3/6/88

3. Puff to the *forearm* [swelling].

4. M.D. means mud; also means movement in Rorschach test, where it's good; here movement is not good [can barely move].

3/7/88

5. Bare branches are covered with ice [reduced circulation in fingers].

3/9/88

6. Hot day but can't cool off because water in the swimming pool is hot [inflammation in wrist].

3/11/88

4. Man kisses my sore *knee* [sensation in knee].

5. Man gives lecture with diagram of a break—I recognize it's my broken *arm* [growing suspicion it's broken, not a sprain].

3/14/88

6. Injured woman bleeds a glassful of blood from her *head* [sensation in head].

3/16/88

*Date Multiple Fracture was Diagnosed*

3/17/88

7. Huge fire may trap us [inflammation in wrist].

3/18/88

8. House is being restored after fire [hope to repair cause of inflammation and other damage].

3/19/88

7. My *operation* may be postponed because numbness in ring *finger* is "cardiac" [concern about numb ring finger. Predictive? After

operation had brief cardiac change].

3/20/88     8. Woman has deformed, thick *wrist* [like mine looks now].

3/21/88     *Date of Surgery*
(three weeks post-injury)

3/24/88                                        9. A place with a broken pipe or pipe connection [breaks in arm].

9. Dog bites woman on *arm* [surgical wound].       10. Dog falls, breaks bones, dies [replay of break plus fear of death].

3/25/88     10. *Cast* is off; my *left arm* looks thin but shape of *wrist* good [arm in cast now, feel hopeful].

3/28/88     One Week Post-Surgery
(four weeks post-injury)

11. Man and I have broken *arms* in *cast* [as mine is].

4/2/88     12. An older girl has many problems with her *hand* [as I've had].

13. Her younger brother hurts his middle or ring *finger*, tip of little finger bent, not so bad, but serious; he is cuddled by his mother [continued discomfort in fingers].

4/3/88     14. Airplane seat has no support for my *head* on left side [still have neck pain].

4/4/88     Two Weeks Post-Surgery
(five weeks post-injury)

4/5/88     15. I'm in a vehicle that mows lawns, when the seat starts to give way; I start a slow fall and have time to think I should not land on the *left hand*, which would injure it further; I decide to turn and fall on my butt, easing myself gently down.

| | | |
|---|---|---|
| 4/9/88 | 16. A man has *large hands* from being *operated* on while young; the operation probably stimulated the growth of his hands [my hand still swollen]. | |
| 4/11/88 | **Three Weeks Post-Surgery (six weeks post-injury)** | |
| | 17. My *left hand* is held outside a window; I feel excited and frightened [I wear compression bandage at night and arm is elevated]. | 11. Someone has a right hand underneath a grandfather clock [time "pressure" about getting back to work]. |
| 4/13/88 | 18. I set down a *black baton* [apparatus used to increase flexibility in wrist]. | |
| 4/18/88 | **Four Weeks Post-Surgery (seven weeks post-injury)** | |
| 4/20/88 | 19. Man uses a *spirometer* [apparatus used to clear lungs after operation]. | |
| 4/21/88 | 20, 21. I wear a beautiful pink-and-green opal ring; a man blesses himself by holding my *hand* and ring to his *forehead* [sensation in fingers, hand, and possibly head]. | |
| 4/24/88 | 22. My left *arm* is pulled down to sidewalk; I can't move it; I picture it going deep into a bag of nuts [wake with my arm stretched straight, unsupported, and in discomfort, instead of elevated as should be]. | |
| 4/25/88 | **Five Weeks Post-Surgery (eight weeks post-injury)** | |
| | 23. A new *splint* is made for me [this is a continuous process in treatment]. | 12. A landmark that is a cut-down tree stump [my arm still has limited functioning]. |
| 5/2/88 | **Six Weeks Post-Surgery (nine weeks post-injury)** | |

5/4/88

24. If the *metal plate* in my *arm* rotates it will have to be removed says a *surgeon* [my concern about this possibility].

5/5/88

25. I shake *hands* with a woman who greets people at a reception [sensation in hand].

26. A man who is being held by detectives presses coins with a message into my *hand* [pun on "change" in my hand].

27. I make a print of a plant by running my *fingers* along the leaves and trace the stems; this conveys its shape onto a paper; part of plant is sick [this may refer to a local infection unrelated to hand].

5/6/88

28, 29. My *finger* is too fat to fit inside small finger puppets; my *hands* are to be photographed with full-sized puppets and won't look good; I realize that's because I'm wearing a *splint* and I can take it off [fingers still have edema but are much better].

5/7/88

30. A special door that is marked by a *gold hand* and a stick [the hand may lead somewhere special].

5/9/88

Seven Weeks Post-Surgery (ten weeks post-injury)

31. I discover I can scratch the middle of my back with my *left hand;* I'm very happy because it feels good [I cannot yet do this].

5/11/88

32. An artist writes a signature with right hand and makes a fancy flourish with *left hand;* it's very skilled [greater flexibility in repaired hand].

| 5/16/88 | **Eight Weeks Post-Surgery**<br>**(eleven weeks post-injury)** |
|---|---|

33. I wear a white wrist band on my *left wrist* [instead of the complex apparatus I'm using].

| 5/17/88 | |
|---|---|

34. Woman rubs and massages my *hands* with a special lotion [pleasant sensation in hands].

| 5/18/88 | |
|---|---|

35. A woman doctor makes me a *hand splint* [my swelling is reduced, but splint fitting in day was painful; I tried to find better brace for driving; I want a better splint].

36. I get stung by a tiny black bug on my *left hand* [painful splint fitting during day].

37. Woman in church performance beats her chest and *arms* to make an aural pattern.

| 5/23/88 | **Nine Weeks Post-Surgery**<br>**(twelve weeks post-injury)** |
|---|---|

38. Women *hold hands* in a circle and recite a prayer of blessing or thanksgiving in an ancient tongue [feeling grateful with improvement in hand].

| 5/29/88 | |
|---|---|

39. I see three different wrists; one too small and frail; one too fat; one in-between [possibility of restored normality].

| 5/30/88 | **Ten Weeks Post-Surgery**<br>**(thirteen weeks post-injury)** |
|---|---|

| 5/31/88 | |
|---|---|

40. I pin a bandage around a man's little *finger* and make a tiny scratch [may be sensation, but probably is a mild psychological "injury"].

| | |
|---|---|
| 6/6/88 | <u>Eleven Weeks Post-Surgery</u> <u>(fourteen weeks post-injury)</u> |
| 6/7/88 | 41. Male teacher puts his *hand* on my bottom [sexuality returning]. |
| 6/8/88 | 42. A kindly older man tells a young one who's usually messy but is now well dressed, "We hold our *hands* by our jackets" [change in hand]. |
| 6/11/88 | 43, 44. I read a book on dreams that has *pictures of hand mudras;* people are to assume various *hand postures* with one or both hands in order to influence the dreams in sleep that follows; it's a surprising technique [hands may be important for writing about dreams]. |
| 6/13/88 | <u>Twelve Weeks Post-Surgery</u> <u>(fifteen weeks post-injury)</u> |

45. I part streamers with my hands and can see clearly.

46. A man puts his *hand* through a hole in a screen to shake my *hand* to thank me [continued sensation in hand plus feeling of gratitude for improvement.]

## ◇ SUMMARY OF GARFIELD'S DREAM IMAGES OF INJURED BODY PARTS FROM INJURY TO TWELVE WEEKS POST-SURGERY
### (fifteen-week period)

| 1. First three-week period (from injury up to night before surgery), 3/1/88–3/20/88 | Value of image * | | |
|---|---|---|---|
| | Neg. | Nt. | Positive |
| 1. my hands are scraped | x | | |
| 2. balloons lift my arms and knee | | x | |
| 3. my forearm is puffed | x | | |
| 4. my sore knee is kissed | | | x |
| 5. my broken arm is diagrammed | | x | |
| 6. a woman's head bleeds | x | | |
| 7. operation postponed because of my numb ring finger | x | | |
| 8. woman has a deformed wrist | x | | |
| Summary of images first period | 5 ng. | 2 nt. | 1 p. = 8 |

2. Second three-week period
(from day of surgery to three weeks after surgery),
3/21/88–4/10/88

| | Neg. | Nt. | Positive |
|---|---|---|---|
| 9. dog bites woman's arm | x | | |
| 10. my cast off, arm thin but my wrist shape is good | | | x |
| 11. man and I have arms in casts | x | | |
| 12. girl has problems with hand | x | | |
| 13. boy has hurt finger | x | | |
| 14. no support for my head | x | | |
| 15. I avoid falling on my left hand | | | x |
| 16. man with large hands from growth-stimulating surgery | | x | |
| Summary of images second period | 5 ng. | 1 nt. | 2 p. = 8 |

* A value of negative, neutral, or positive was assigned to each image.

## 3. Third three-week period
(from three weeks post-surgery to six weeks post-surgery),
4/11/88–5/1/88

| | | Neg. | Nt. | Positive |
|---|---|---|---|---|
| 17. | my left hand outside window, feel frightened | x | | |
| 18. | I set down a black baton | | x | |
| 19. | man uses a spirometer | | x | |
| 20. | I wear opal ring on hand | | | x |
| 21. | man blesses himself by touching my ring to forehead | | | x |
| 22. | my left arm is pulled down | x | | |
| 23. | I get new splint made | | x | |
| Summary of images third period | | 2 ng. | 3 nt. | 2 p. = 7 |

## 4. Fourth three-week period
(from six weeks post-surgery to nine weeks post-surgery),
5/2/88–5/22/88

| | | Neg. | Nt. | Positive |
|---|---|---|---|---|
| 24. | if my metal plate in arm rotates, surgeon will remove it | x | | |
| 25. | I shake hands with woman | | x | |
| 26. | man presses coins in my hand | | x | |
| 27. | I run fingers along leaves | | x | |
| 28. | my finger too fat to fit puppet | x | | |
| 29. | my hands won't look good for photo so I take off splint | | x | |
| 30. | gold hand marks special door | | | x |
| 31. | I scratch my back with my left hand | | | x |
| 32. | artist makes flourish with left hand | | | x |
| 33. | I wear white wrist band on left wrist | | x | |
| 34. | woman massages my hands | | | x |
| 35. | woman doctor makes me a hand split | | x | |
| 36. | tiny black bug stings my left hand | x | | |
| 37. | woman beats arms in pattern in performance in church. | | x | |
| Summary of images fourth period | | 3 ng. | 7 nt. | 4 p. = 14 |

5. Fifth three-week period
(from nine weeks post-surgery to twelve weeks post-surgery),
5/23/88–6/13/88

| Neg. | | Nt. | Positive |
|---|---|---|---|
| 38. | women hold hands in circle | | x |
| 39. | three different-sized wrists | x | |
| 40. | I bandage and scratch a man's little finger | x | |
| 41. | male teacher puts hand on my bottom | x | |
| 42. | older man says "We hold hands by our jackets" | x | |
| 43. | I look at fascinating book on hand mudras | | x |
| 44. | hand postures influence dreams | | x |
| 45. | I part streamers with hands and can see clearly | | x |
| 46. | man shakes my hand in thanks | | x |

Summary of images fifth period          1 ng.   3 nt.   5 p. = 9

Total                                    16 negative images
                                         16 neutral images
                                         14 positive images
Grand total                              46 dream images

Summary of Distribution of Dream Images of Injured Body Parts:

| | | | | |
|---|---|---|---|---|
| First three-week period | 5 negative | 2 neutral | 1 positive | = 8 |
| Second three-week period | 5 | 1 | 2 | = 8 |
| Third three-week period | 2 | 3 | 2 | = 7 |
| Fourth three-week period | 3 | 7 | 4 | = 14 |
| Fifth three-week period | 1 | 3 | 5 | = 9 |
| Total | | | | = 46 |

*Typical dream images with broken limb:*
Dreamer or other character injures limb in equivalent or worsened way.
A person or animal deliberately wounds dreamer's limb.
Dreamer or some other character has part of limb larger than normal (usually represents swelling).
Dreamer or some other character has limb that looks deformed or is nonfunctional.
Dreamer's limb is partially or completely disconnected from body.
Dreamer or other character undergoes normal treatment or uses equipment or apparatus.
Dreamer has fear of further injury.

*Antidote images for visualizations:*
Receiving special treatment for injury—loving touch, special medicine or food, special equipment.
Seeing injured limb in healthy and whole condition.
Being able to avoid any further injury.
Engaging in acts of blessing or thanksgiving.
Wearing beautiful jewelry on injured limb.
Seeing limb made of precious metal or jewels.
Seeing limb used in new and positive ways.

# REFERENCE NOTES

## Chapter 1
### Your Body in Dreams

1. Patricia Garfield, *Creative Dreaming*, New York: Simon & Schuster, 1974; New York: Ballantine, 1976; *Pathway to Ecstasy: The Way of the Dream Mandala*, New York: Holt Rinehart & Winston, 1979; Prentice Hall, 1989; *Your Child's Dreams*, New York: Ballantine, 1984; *Women's Bodies, Women's Dreams*, New York: Ballantine, 1988.

2. Joseph Campbell, *The Hero with a Thousand Faces*, Princeton, NJ: Princeton University Press, 1949.

3. Roger Dafter, "Individuation in Illness: Moving Beyond Blame in Mind-Body Healing," Ernest Rossi, ed., *Psychological Perspectives*, vol. 22, 1990, pp. 24–37. Robert Bosnak, *Dreaming with an AIDS Patient*, Boston: Shambala, 1989, p. 97. According to Jungian analyst Robert Bosnak, "The word *individuation* alludes to an ancient concept stating that every creature in its unfolding will manifest according to its innate form. A chicken's egg will not produce a dog." Jung extended this concept to mean the process of unfolding one's interior blueprint, the emergence of the integral

wholeness of the human being. This wholeness, "the Self," is usually symbolized by the number four and by a circle.

4. Stage I is identified on the electroencephalograph (EEG) when the brain waves slow slightly from a fast, irregular pattern called *beta* (12–18 cycles per second) and a restful but awake pattern of *alpha* (8-12 cycles per second). These slower waves are called *theta* (4–8 cycles per second). When less than 50 percent of the brain waves are *alpha*, stage I begins. Slow, rolling eye movements are often present during stage I, also called descending stage I, and the person feels extremely drowsy.

Stage II is characterized by the appearance of mostly *theta* waves (4–8 cycles per second) and sleep spindles (brief bursts of 12–14 cycles per second). When a person dozes off while reading or watching television, sleep spindles occur. K-complexes (high-amplitude negative waves followed by positive activity) also arise in stage II.

Stage III is identified by the presence of *delta* (high-amplitude waves of 1–3 cycles per second) in 20–50 percent of the EEG record.

Stage IV is identified by more than 50 percent *delta* waves. It is difficult to arouse sleepers from this stage. The longest period of stage IV usually occurs early in the night, during the first cycle. There are often only two or three periods of stage IV each night.

REM, or ascending Stage I, follows Stage IV. In the normal adult the sleep stages are distributed as follows:

| | |
|---|---|
| REM | 25 percent |
| Stage I (descending) | 5 percent |
| Stage II | 50 percent |
| Stage III | 10 percent |
| Stage IV | 10 percent |

For more information on sleep stages, see: J. Allan Hobson, *The Dreaming Brain*, New York: Basic Books Inc., 1988, Chapters 6 and 7; Also see Carl F. Wiedemann, "REM and Non-REM Sleep and Its Relation to Nightmares and Night Terrors," Henry Kellerman, ed., *The Nightmare*, New York: Columbia University Press, 1987, pp. 75–97.

5. Richard M. Coleman, *Wide Awake at 3:00 A.M.: By Choice or by Chance?*, New York: W.H. Freeman & Co., 1986.

6. See Carl F. Wiedemann, "REM and Non-REM Sleep and Its Relation to Nightmares and Night Terrors."

7. See Jerome L. Singer, *Imagery and Daydream Methods in Psychotherapy and Behavior Modification*, New York: Academic Press, 1974, p. 173.

8. Aad van Ouwerkerk, "The Elements of Dreaming" worksheet and his paper "The Seven Step Process—A Practical Dreamwork Method," presented at the Association for the Study of Dreams annual conference, Chicago, 1990.

9. This method is based on the Jungian technique of "amplification" with the additional step of feeding back to the dreamer his or her dream with the personal associations substituted in the dream text, using the dreamer's own words. This step often leads to profound insights for the dreamer.

10. Again, this is a technique suggested by Jung. See Carl G. Jung, *Modern Man in Search of a Soul*, New York: Harcourt Brace Jovanovich, 1933. For the reader's convenience, here is an excerpt of one of the key passages (pp. 13–14): "We shall best succeed in reading dreams by establishing their context . . . To do this, we must keep as close as possible to the dream-images themselves. When a person has dreamed of a deal table, little is accomplished by his associating it with his writing-desk, whch is not made of deal. [Author's note: deal is an old-fashioned term for pine or fir wood of a standard size.] The dream refers expressly to a deal table. If at this point nothing occurs to the dreamer, his hesitation signifies that a particular darkness surrounds the dream-image, and this is suspicious. We would expect him to have dozens of associations to a deal table, and when he cannot find a single one, this must have a meaning. In such cases we should return again and again to the image. I say to my patients: 'Suppose I had no idea what the words "deal table" mean. Describe this object and give me its history in such a way that I cannot fail to understand what sort of thing it is.' We succeed in this way in establishing a good part of the context of that particular dream-image. When we have done this for all the images in the dream, we are ready for the venture of interpretation."

11. Aad van Ouwerkerk, "The Elements of Dreaming" worksheet and his paper "The Seven Step Process—A Practical Dreamwork Method," presented at the Association for the Study of Dreams annual meeting in Chicago, 1990.

12. This discussion of metaphors is based on the theories of George Lakoff and Mark Johnson, *Metaphors We Live By*, Chicago: The University of Chicago Press, 1980. We say that "time is money" (we can waste it, save it, or spend it); "argument is war" (we defend ourselves, or attack a position, win or lose); and "love is a game" (we gain points, quit, or score). We are continuously defining our experiences by a metaphor—usually without being aware we are doing so. A metaphor is useful when it helps us understand

an experience or a complex concept; but it can also limit our self-concept and, consequently, our behavior. One businessman thinks, "I'm a young Turk"; another may decide, "I'm a mouse." A metaphor always highlights some features while hiding others. A man may be "a bull" at work yet "hen-pecked" at home. Each metaphor focuses on a different aspect of the same man.

13. Aristotle, *De Divinatione Per Somnum (On Prophesying by Dreams)*, Richard McKeon, ed., *The Basic Works of Aristotle*, New York: Random House, 1941, p. 630. Aristotle, a pupil of Plato's, lived between 384–322 B.C. He added, "But, speaking of 'resemblances,' I mean that dream presentations are analogous to the forms reflected in water . . . if the motion in the water be great, the reflection has no resemblance to its original, nor do the forms resemble real objects . . ." By this, Aristotle meant that if our sensory organs are agitated during sleep, dream images will be distorted, but if the sense organs are more tranquil, dream images will be clear.

14. George Lakoff and Mark Johnson, *Metaphors We Live By*, Chicago: The University of Chicago Press, 1980, p. 233. A large part of self-understanding is finding appropriate metaphors that make sense of our lives. Psychotherapy involves locating and recognizing the metaphors we have been using to guide our lives, such as, "I'm a poor little match girl," or "I'm a lazy bum." We need to become aware of the metaphors we dream by and live by. Then we need to construct new metaphors that give wider meaning to past experiences. "I'm a wounded victim" may be recast as "I'm a sensitive measuring instrument." New metaphors create new understandings and therefore new realities. "The process of self-understanding is the continual development of new life stories for yourself." In our dreams, the metaphors "bodies are containers" and "bodies are buildings" are basic. We project our own physical shape onto other objects with surfaces.

15. U. Jovanovic. Cited in Charles Fisher, H. D. Cohen, R. C. Schiavi, D. Davis, Barbara Furman, K. Ward, A. Edwards, and J. Cunningham, "Patterns of Female Sexual Arousal During Sleep and Waking: Vaginal Thermo-Conductance Studies," *Archives of Sexual Behavior*, vol. 12, 2, 1983; Charles Fisher, J. Gross, and J. Zuch, "Cycle of Penile Erection Synchronous with Dreaming (REM) Sleep," *Archives of General Psychiatry*, vol. 12, 1965, pp. 29–45; Lorna Tener and Carlyle Smith, "Vaginal Blood Volume Changes During Sleep," *Sleep Research*, vol. 6, 1977; I. Karacan, A. Rosenbloom, and R. Williams, "The Clitoral Erection Cycle During Sleep," paper presented at the meeting of the Association

for the Psychophysiological Study of Sleep, Santa Fe, New Mexico, 1970.

16. Charles Fisher, H. D. Cohen, R. C. Schiavi, D. Davis, Barbara Furman, K. Ward, A. Edwards, and J. Cunningham, "Patterns of Female Sexual Arousal During Sleep and Waking: Vaginal Thermo-Conductance Studies."

17. Ismet Karacan, et al., "Uterine Activity During Sleep," *Sleep*, vol. 9, 3, 1986, pp. 393–97.

18. Vasilii N. Kasatkin, *Theory of Dreams*, Leningrad: Meditsina, 1967. The material from Vasilii Kasatkin's research was especially rich in case studies of this type of dream.

## Chapter 2
## Dreamer, Heal Thyself

1. For further reading on exploring one's personal story, see: David Feinstein and Stanley Krippner, *Personal Mythology: The Psychology of Your Evolving Self*, Los Angeles: Jeremy P. Tarcher, 1988; Lucia Capacchione, *The Well-Being Journal: Drawing on Your Inner Power to Heal Yourself*, North Hollywood, CA: Newcastle, 1979; *The Creative Journal: The Art of Finding Yourself*, North Hollywood, CA: Newcastle, 1989; Tristine Rainer, *The New Diary*, Los Angeles: Jeremy P. Tarcher, 1978.

2. This "preventive medicine" behavior I first saw suggested by Irving and Susan Oyle in an article in *New Dimensions* newsletter, September–October, 1989. Simple pleasures are beginning to be recognized as making active contributions to long-term health.

## Chapter 3
## The Seven Stages of Recovery from Physical Trauma

1. Thomas Holmes and Richard Rahe, "The Social Readjustment Rating Scale," *Journal of Psychosomatic Medicine*, 1967, vol. 11, pp. 213–18.

2. This case was described by Medard Boss, *Analysis of Dreams*, New York: Philosophical Library, 1958. See also Robert E. Haskell, "Dreaming, Cognition, and Physical Illness: Part II," *Journal of Medical Humanities and Bioethics*, 1985, vol. 6, pp. 115–16.

3. H. A. Savitz, "The Dream as a Diagnostic Aid in Physical Diagnosis," *Conn. Medicine*, vol. 33, 1969, pp. 309–10. Quoted in Robert E. Haskell, "Dreaming, Cognition, and Physical Illness: Part II," p. 111.

4. Hippocrates, *Regimen IV, or Dreams*, W. H. S. Jones, trans., Cambridge, MA: Harvard University Press, Loeb ed., vol. IV, 1931, p. 423.

5. R. Wadeson, "Anxiety in the Dreams of Neurological Patients," *Archives of General Psychiatry*, 1966, 14, 249–52. Quoted in R. Haskell, p. 113.

6. Robert E. Haskell, "Dreaming, Cognition, and Physical Illness: Part II," p. 119.

7. Hippocrates, *Regimen IV, or Dreams*, p. 443.

8. Described in Robert E. Haskell, "Dreaming, Cognition, and Physical Illness: Part II," p. 110.

9. T. French and L. B. Shapiro, "The Use of Dream Analysis in Psychosomatic Research," *Psychosomatic Research*, vol. 11, 1949, pp. 110–12. Described in Robert E. Haskell, "Dreaming, Cognition, and Physical Illness: Part II," p. 110.

10. Leon Saul, E. Sheppard, D. Selby, W. Lhamon, and D. Sacks, "The Quantification of Hostility in Dreams with Reference to Essential Hypertension," *Science*, March, 1954, pp. 119, 382–83. Quoted in Robert E. Haskell, "Dreaming, Cognition, and Physical Illness: Part II," p. 109.

11. H. L. Levitan, "Dreams Which Precede Asthmatic Attacks." In A. Krakowski and C. Kimball, eds., *Psychosomatic Medicine: Theoretical, Clinical and Transcultural Aspects*, New York: Plenum Books, 1983. Described in Robert E. Haskell, "Dreaming, Cognition, and Physical Illness: Part II," p. 110. See also Thomas French and Franz Alexander, "Psychogenic Factors in Bronchial Asthma, Part I and II," *Psychosomatic Medicine Monographs*, *II*, vol. 1 and 2, 1941. Described in H. Warnes and A. Finkelstein, "Dreams that Precede a Psychosomatic Illness," p. 318.

12. Emil Gutheil, "Dreams as an Aid to Evaluating Ego-Strength," *American Journal of Psychiatry*, vol. 12, 1958, pp. 338–57. Described in H. Warnes and A. Finkelstein, p. 318. See also H. L. Levitan, "Dreams Which Culminate in Migraine Headaches," *Psychotherapy and Psychosomatics*, vol. 41, 1984, pp. 161–66. Described in Robert E. Haskell, "Dreaming, Cognition, and Physical Illness: Part II," p. 110.

13. Hippocrates, *Regimen IV, or Dreams*, p. 427.

14. Hippocrates, *Regimen IV, or Dreams*, p. 437.

15. Hippocrates, *Regimen IV, or Dreams*, p. 443.

16. Hippocrates, *Regimen IV, or Dreams*, p. 435.

17. Albert S. Lyons and R. Joseph Petrucelli, II, *Medicine: An Illustrated History*, New York: Harry N. Abrams, Inc., 1978, pps. 193, 207. See also Walter A. Jayne, *The Healing Gods of Ancient Civilizations*, New Haven: Yale University Press, 1925, pp. 298–99.

18. Douglas J. Guthrie and Phillip Rhodes, "Medicine and Surgery before 1800," *The New Encyclopaedia Britannica*, 15th ed., Chicago: Encyclopaedia Britannica, Inc., vol. 23, 1988, p. 889. Guthrie and Rhodes render Hippocrates' first aphorism as, "Life is short, Art long, Occasion sudden and dangerous, Experience deceitful, and Judgment difficult."

19. Hippocrates, *Aphorisms*, W. H. S. Jones, trans. Loeb Classical Library, vol. IV, Cambridge, MA: Harvard University Press, 1931, p. 99. In Jones's translation, the aphorisms begin, "Life is short, the Art long, opportunity fleeting, experiment treacherous, judgment difficult."

20. Hippocrates, *Regimen IV, or Dreams*, p. 425.

21. Carl G. Jung, *Modern Man in Search of a Soul*, New York: Harcourt Brace Jovanovich, 1933, pp. 13–14.

22. Aristotle, *De Somniis (On Dreams)*, Richard McKeon, ed., *The Basic Works of Aristotle*, New York: Random House, 1941, p. 623.

23. Aristotle, *De Somniis*, p. 624. Aristotle thought that the activities in the sensory organs create dream images that possess true resemblance to actual objects ". . . after the manner of cloud-shapes, which in their rapid metamorphoses one compares now to human beings and a moment afterward to centaurs."

24. J. Allan Hobson, *The Dreaming Brain*, New York: Basic Books, Inc., 1988.

25. J. Allan Hobson, p. 15. Of course, Aristotle was not aware of the periodic bursts of rapid eye movements (REM) that occur in sleep during brain activation; this discovery was made by Eugene Aserinsky and Nathaniel Kleitman in 1953. Recent research has even pinpointed the precise cells in the brain stem that turn dreaming on, and the body chemical, acetylcholine, which acts as a trigger.

26. Vasilii N. Kasatkin, *Theory of Dreams*, Leningrad: Meditsina, 1967, p. 179. Kasatkin quotes the dreams of pickled cucumber, coleslaw, and herring in patients with heartburn. The dream of the patient with the perforated ulcer is quoted in H. Warnes and A.

Finkelstein, "Dreams that Precede a Psychosomatic Illness," *Canadian Psychiatric Association Journal*, vol. 16, 1971, p. 320.

27. H. Warnes and A. Finkelstein, p. 319.

28. Vasilii N. Kasatkin, p. 181.

29. H. Warnes and A. Finkelstein, p. 319.

30. A. Ziegler, "A Cardiac Infarction and a Dream as Synchronous Events," *The Journal of Analytical Psychology*, vol. 7, 2, July, 1962, pp. 142–43.

31. Vasilii N. Kasatkin, *Theory of Dreams*, p. 182.

## Chapter 4:
### Forewarning and Diagnostic Dreams

1. Rita Dwyer, "Dream Story," *The Dream Network Bulletin*, vol. 4, 3, May/June, 1985, pp. 1–3. Also, personal communication, 1989.

2. Montague Ullman and Stanley Krippner with Alan Vaughan, *Dream Telepathy: Experiments in Nocturnal ESP*, London: McFarland, 1989.

3. Jule Eisenbud points out that telephoning, as well as other images of indirect or exotic communication, often symbolize telepathic communication in dreams. Ullman, Krippner, and Vaughan, p. 32.

4. J. Kales, C. Allen, T. Preston, T–L Tan, and A. Kales, "Changes in REM Sleep and Dreaming with Cigarette Smoking and Following Withdrawal," *Psychophysiology*, vol. 7, pp. 347–48. 1970. Cited in Carolyn Winget and Milton Kramer, *Dimensions of Dreams*. Gainesville: University Presses of Florida, 1979, p. 361.

5. Ilza Veith, *The Yellow Emperor's Classic of Internal Medicine*, Berkeley: University of California Press, 1949. This book's Chinese title is *Huang Ti Nei Ching Su Wên*.

6. Ilza Veith, p. 163.

7. For references on Asklepios, see: C. Kerényi, *Asklepios: Archetypal Image of the Physician's Existence*, Princeton: Princeton University Press, 1959; Ralph Jackson, *Doctors and Diseases in the Roman Empire*, Norman, OK: University of Oklahoma Press, 1988; Walter A. Jayne, *The Healing Gods of Ancient Civilizations*, New Haven: Yale University Press. 1925; Emma and Ludwig Edelstein, *Asclepius: A Collection and Interpretation of the Testimonies*, Baltimore: The Johns Hopkins University Press, 1945; Richard

Caton, *The Temples and Ritual of Asklepios at Epidauros and Athens*, London: C. J. Clay and Sons, 1900.

8. For references on Hippocrates, see: Hippocrates, vols. 1–4, W. H. S. Jones, trans., Cambridge, MA: Harvard University Press, 1984 (Volume 4 contains the section on dreams.); Francis Adams, *The Genuine Works of Hippocrates*, New York: William Wood & Co., 1886.

9. For references on Aristotle's thoughts about dreams, see: Aristotle, vol. 7, *On the Soul; Parva naturalia; On Breath*, W. S. Hett, trans., Cambridge, MA: Harvard University Press, 1986; Richard McKeon, *The Basic Works of Aristotle*, New York: Random House, 1941.

10. For references on Galen's thoughts about dreams, see: George Sarton, *Galen of Pergamon*, Lawrence, Kansas: University of Kansas Press, 1954; Rudolph E. Siegel, *Galen on Psychology, Psychopathology, and Function and Diseases of the Nervous System*, London: S. Rarger, 1973; Joseph Walsh, "Galen's Writings and Influences Inspiring Them," *Annals of Medical History*, vol. VI, no. 1, January, 1934, pp. 1–30; Margaret T. May, *Galen On the Usefulness of the Parts of the Body*; Ithaca: Cornell University Press, 1968.

11. Lawrence W. Way, *Current Surgical Diagnosis and Treatment*, San Mateo, CA: Appleton & Lange, 1988, pp. 408–411.

12. Lawrence W. Way, p. 411

13. Marcus Aurelius (121–180 A.D.) was emperor of Rome from 161–180 A.D.

14. Rudolph E. Siegel, *Galen*, p. 170.

15. For references on Artemidorus, see: Artemidorus, *The Interpretation of Dreams: The Oneirocritica of Artemidorus*, trans. and commentary by Robert White, Park Ridge, NJ: Noyes Press, 1975. Rudolph E. Siegel, *Galen*, p. 172.

16. Vasilii N. Kasatkin, *Theory of Dreams*, Leningrad: Meditsina, 1967.

17. Robert Smith, "Dreams Reflect a Biological State," "Evaluating Dream Function: Emphasizing the Study of Patients with Organic Disease," papers presented at the Association for the Study of Dreams, Ottawa, 1988.

18. Although this connection was not so strong as it was for the men; women showed no relationship between dream references to death and outcome. Robert Smith, 1988.

19. Abraham Kardiner, "The Bioanalysis of the Epileptic Reaction," *Psychoanalytic Quarterly*, vol. I, 1932.

20. Jill Caire, "A Holographic Model of a Psychosomatic Pattern: Freud's Specimen Dream Reinterpreted," *Psychotherapy and Psychosomatics*, vol. 36, 1981, pp. 132–42.

21. Sigmund Freud, *The Interpretation of Dreams*, New York: Avon, 1965, pp. 138–39.

22. Irma's dream appears in Freud's *The Interpretation of Dreams* on pages 139–40:

> A large hall—numerous guests, whom we were receiving. —Among them was Irma. I at once took her on one side, as though to answer her letter and to reproach her for not having accepted my "solution" yet. I said to her: "If you still get pains, it's really only your fault." She replied: "If you only knew what pains I've got now in my throat and stomach and abdomen—it's choking me"—I was alarmed and looked at her. She looked pale and puffy. I thought to myself that after all I must be missing some organic trouble. I took her to the window and looked down her throat, and she showed signs of recalcitrance, like women with artificial dentures. I thought to myself that there was really no need for her to do that.—She then opened her mouth properly and on the right I found a big white patch; at another place I saw extensive whitish grey scabs upon some remarkable curly structures which were evidently modelled on the turbinal bones of the nose.—I at once called in Dr. M., and he repeated the examination and confirmed it . . . Dr. M. looked quite different from usual; he was very pale, he walked with a limp and his chin was clean-shaven . . . My friend Otto was now standing beside her as well, and my friend Leopold was percussing her through her bodice and saying: "She has a dull area low down on the left." He also indicated that a portion of the skin on the left shoulder was infiltrated. (I noticed this, just as he did, in spite of her dress.) . . . M. said: "There's no doubt it's an infection, but no matter; dysentery will supervene and the toxin will be eliminated." . . . We were directly aware, too, of the origin of her infection. Not long before, when she was feeling unwell, my friend Otto had given her an injection of a preparation of propyl, propyls . . . propionic acid . . . trimethylamin (and I saw before me the formula for this printed in heavy type) . . . Injections of that sort ought not to be made so thoughtlessly . . . And probably the syringe had not been clean.

23. Jill Caire, "A Holographic Model of a Psychosomatic Pattern: Freud's Specimen Dream Reinterpreted," *Psychotherapy and Psychosomatics*, vol. 36, 1981, pp. 132–142. Freud's surgeon's comments are quoted in this paper.

24. Sigmund Freud, *The Interpretation of Dreams*, p. 141.

25. Bernie Siegel, *Peace, Love and Healing*, New York: Harper & Row, 1989, pp. 64–65.

26. Bernie Siegel, *Love, Medicine and Miracles*, New York: Harper & Row, 1986, pp. 113–14.

27. Described by Ernest Rossi and David Cheek, *Mind-Body Therapy*, New York: Norton, 1988, pp. 375–76. Jung knew Latin and must have recognized the word for slime is *pituita*. "From this word comes pituitary. The slimy colloidal secretions of the pituitary gland are essential to certain bodily processes. These secretions flow into the third ventricle, one of those hollow subterranean womb-like caverns through which the cerebrospinal fluid also flows." This fluid has the function of lubricating these cavities and it provides a mechanical barrier against shock to the brain, allowing the brain to float in it. The fluid flows through aqueducts in its course. If these are cut off or blocked, the effect is a drainage of the cerebrospinal pool downstream. The two extinct animals in the dream may have represented the hypothalamus and the pituitary that lie beneath the cerebrospinal pond. Jung accurately diagnosed this dreamer as having a neurological disturbance in the third ventricle.

28. From the author's personal collection. This woman's imbalance had been gradually building since the partial removal of her thyroid and parathyroid glands when she was in her forties.

29. Oliver Sacks, *Awakenings*, New York: Dutton, 1983, pp. 67–79. Rose was one of the last victims before the epidemic of 1916–1926 vanished.

30. Oliver Sacks, *Awakenings*. At that time, Rose sat motionless and unblinking in her wheelchair for endless hours. She gazed into space with a blank expression; her soft speech and her unsteady movements were severely limited, although she underwent periods of agitation. When L-dopa, a "miracle" drug that sometimes relieves such conditions, became available, Sacks tried it on Rose and she "awakened." At first she improved in every way. Her voice and ability to walk were fully restored; she became cheerful and smiling. Unfortunately, Rose went from elation to manic excitement to extreme irritability. It proved impossible to find the

right dosage of medication to keep her mood even, and she became "spellbound" again. Later attempts to reawaken her proved futile. In retrospect, Sacks saw Rose as "a Sleeping Beauty whose awakening was unbearable."

31. Oliver Sacks, *Awakenings*, pp. 188–201.

## Chapter 5
### Crisis Dreams

1. Oliver Sacks, *A Leg to Stand On*, New York, Harper & Row, 1984, p. 46.

2. Louis Breger, Ian Hunter, and Ron Lane, *The Effect of Stress on Dreams*, New York: International Universities Press, 1971. See the case of Al, pp. 106–123. Al's other pre-operative dream images were: a pocketknife with three blades fallen out; a roof with missing shingles; a set of false teeth needing repair; a building damaged by a nasty boy.

3. Louis Breger, Ian Hunter, and Ron Lane, *The Effect of Stress on Dreams*. See the case of Penny, pp. 141–159. Another of Penny's pre-operative dream images was a rickety hot-dog stand with makeshift stools.

4. Louis Breger, Ian Hunter, and Ron Lane, *The Effect of Stress on Dreams*. See the case of Al, age 64, pp. 106–123.

5. Louis Breger, Ian Hunter, and Ron Lane, *The Effect of Stress on Dreams*. See the case of Melvin, pp. 124–140. Another of Melvin's pre-operative dream images was a model airplane blown apart by a fan before he could glue it together.

6. The author observed slides of the drawings done by migraine sufferers that were submitted to a national contest held in 1989 by the National Headache Foundation and Wyeth-Ayerst Laboratories.

7. Vasilii N. Kasatkin, *Theory of Dreams*, Leningrad: Meditsina, 1967. Kasatkin cited the dreams of sauerkraut, herring, and pickles, on page 16 of the translation of Chapter 6. The case of the man who dreamed of eating pizza when his stomach "broke open" the night before his ulcer perforated was described by: H. Warnes and A. Finkelstein, "Dreams That Precede a Psychosomatic Illness," *Canadian Psychiatric Association Journal*, vol. 16, 1971, p. 318.

8. Dianne Hales, *The Complete Book of Sleep: How Your Nights Affect Your Days*, Menlo Park, CA: Addison-Wesley, 1981, pp. 35–36. More than half of all heart attacks and all strokes occur

during the night. Many ailments are worsened at night: epileptics have more seizures; ulcer patients secrete more acid (three to twenty times more than the normal person); asthmatics wheeze more; chronic lung disease patients gasp for oxygen; persons with gastrointestinal reflux or kidney disease are worse; eczema and psoriasis patients itch more. REM sleep triggers more cases of retinal hemorrhage (bleeding in the eye) in diabetics than in the daytime.

9. Described in Carl G. Jung, ed., *Man and His Symbols*, New York: Doubleday, 1964, p. 78.

10. Carl G. Jung, *Man and His Symbols*, p. 78. Jung described a case in which a physician friend of his fell ill with a deadly gangrenous fever and had just been hospitalized. A former patient of this friend's, who had no awareness of his doctor's disease, dreamed that his doctor died in a great fire. Three weeks later, the doctor died. Jung believed that the dream was predictive, representing his colleague's diseased body as a house, and the fever as the fire that destroyed it.

11. Hippocrates, *Regimen IV, or Dreams*, p. 441.

12. Vasilii N. Kasatkin, *Theory of Dreams*, p. 4 of translation of Chapter 6.

13. Charles Witt, "Portraits of Pain," *San Francisco Chronicle*, July 21, 1986, p. 15. This article quotes the observations of art therapist Valerie Appleton.

14. Louis Breger, Ian Hunter, and Ron Lane, *The Effect of Stress on Dreams*. See the case of Al, age 64, pp. 106–123. Four days before surgery to remove a damaged portion of a blood vessel in one of his legs, he dreamed. . . .

> . . . it was somethin' about driving a car . . . there was some people in the car and I was driving the darn thing . . . When we come out of this place where I had it parked, it was icy, you know, icy. And as I came out of this place, there was quite a little hill and there was ice . . . And I realized I wasn't gonna make it, so I didn't even try to . . . It was in some city or some small town . . . it was Christmastime and we was shopping. It was cold, awful cold, and it was just solid ice all across and at the bottom of this hill where you turned up, so many people had come down with their cars that there was a big slush hole there was all water [laughs]. This damn place was kind of like a toboggan place . . .

The "slush hole" Al mentioned may have symbolized a pool of blood from one of his leaking vessels. The "hill" in his dream suggested his difficulty walking.

15. Robert Van de Castle, "Pregnancy Dreams," paper presented at the Association for the Study of Dreams annual conference, Ottawa, 1986.

16. Robert Van de Castle. See note 15.

17. If the dreamer happens to be familiar with the term "ice" for the street drug that is an odorless, colorless form of crystal methamphetamine, and possibly using it, the dream image could refer instead to the drug and its dangers.

18. Vasilii N. Kasatkin, *Theory of Dreams*, p. 181 of translation of Chapter 6.

19. Robert Bosnak, *Dreaming with an AIDS Patient*, Boston: Shambala, 1989, pp. 139–41. Christopher's dream no. 39 is:

> I'm on a boat, a speedboat. I'm with my friend. We're going very fast. The water of the lake is mucky. We are close to the dam. It is concrete and manmade, and it prevents the water of the lake from running out. At that point the water is most dirty. That's when we turn around and go back.

His dream no. 40 is:

> Conversing with a beautiful woman from my house boat to hers. She has attendants like royalty and they are dressed romanishly. The water between us is icky.

He described this water as "brown, filthy, rotten, and putrid."

20. H. Warnes and A. Finkelstein, "Dreams that Precede a Psychosomatic Illness," *Canadian Psychiatric Association Journal*, vol. 16, 1971, pp. 317–25. Her dream was:

> A man was trying to kill me. He invented a machine to kill people by suffocating them by holding them under water for three minutes. It was very dangerous and he had to be stopped. There were eight women in the room. I felt very mad at you [her physician] because you left me there. I woke up wheezing.

21. Hippocrates, *Regimen IV, or Dreams*, pp. 441, 427.

22. Hippocrates, *Regimen IV, or Dreams*, p. 441. In such cases, he recommended treatment with food and exercise that was "drying."

23. See Chapter 4 of this book, p. 106.

24. Louis Breger, Ian Hunter, and Ron Lane, *The Effect of Stress on Dreams*. See the case of Al, pp. 106–123. His dream, p. 114, was:

> . . . we were trying to travel up a river bed or coming down-stream every so often in the rocks. You know how the water is down and the rocks . . . they was up, out, dry . . . there was boulders about the size of your feet or something like that, round rocks . . . we was staggerin' along trying to look up into the clouds and stumblin' over these damn rocks . . .

25. Sigmund Freud, *The Interpretation of Dreams*, New York: Avon, 1965, p. 157.

26. Hippocrates, p. 439

27. Hippocrates, p. 439

28. Hippocrates, p. 439

29. Louis Breger, Ian Hunter, and Ron Lane, *The Effect of Stress on Dreams*. See the case of Melvin's dream, p. 130: In his dream, he was standing on a ladder held by his wife, extended over the roof in heavy rain and wind. He was hanging onto the house while trying to brush off the wood moths. Perhaps Melvin's dreaming mind was likening his body "trunk" to a tree trunk.

30. Louis Breger, Ian Hunter, and Ron Lane, *The Effect of Stress on Dreams*, p. 138.

31. Louis Breger, Ian Hunter, and Ron Lane, *The Effect of Stress on Dreams*. See the dream of Paul, p. 161–162.

32. Robert Bosnak, *Dreaming with an AIDS Patient*, pp. 76–77.

33. Louis Breger, Ian Hunter, and Ron Lane, *The Effect of Stress on Dreams*. See the case of Melvin, p. 130–131.

34. Vasilii N. Kasatkin, *Theory of Dreams*, p. 178 of translation of Chapter 6.

35. Oliver Sacks, *A Leg to Stand On*, p. 21. Sacks, who injured his left leg when hiking on a mountain, had suddenly come face to face with a bull and ran to escape him. He misstepped on loose rock and fell over a precipice. "It is as if there is a moment missing from my memory—there is 'before' and 'after' but no 'inbetween,' " he said. Sacks remembered thinking at first that "someone" was hurt, without realizing it was himself.

36. Once, when I was having Sunday brunch with my family in an outdoor restaurant, I was happily eating and engaging in conversation. Suddenly I heard someone scream. It took a second or so

for me to realize that I had screamed. From the heavy branches of trees overhead, a black walnut, the shell covered with characteristic thorns, had fallen full force onto the top of my head. I wasn't badly hurt, though there was a cut and some minor swelling. The shock of the sudden injury, however trivial, had set off an automatic alarm response.

37. Ernest Rossi, *The Psychobiology of Mind-Body Healing*, New York: Norton, 1986. Some of these neurotransmitters contain norepinephrine that activates the sympathetic nervous system; others secrete acetylcholine, which affects the parasympathetic nervous system. There are similar routes by which the endocrine system, immune system, and the neuropeptide system can also transduce information from the mind to the body cells.

38. This study by industrial sociologist Robert Karasek at the University of Southern California is described by Valerie Adler, "Little Control = Lots of Stress," *Psychology Today*, April, 1989, pp. 18–19.

39. The first scene of this dream was:

> Zal and I are staying at some sort of fancy castle-resort. It's set on the water with beautiful lawns and wooded areas (rather like an Irish castle we once stayed in). The first scene involves a picnic on the grounds. There is a special disposal chute for trash. I'm amazed how much trash I have. A woman offers me some odd food she calls a half-pancake that looks like a half chicken with dark flesh, telling me, "You'll have to cut it yourself. I have a bad wrist." I notice that her wrist has a thick, deformed look (as mine did at the time).

Here we see the typical portrayal of the afflicted body part. My injured wrist, however, was attributed to another woman in my dream rather than myself. The references to meat or poultry flesh and cutting are characteristic of dreamers about to undergo surgery. In the dreamer's mind, the surgeon's knife is transformed into various instruments that cut; the body flesh is likened to meat. There may have been a pun on the word *chicken*. I was certainly fearful of the operation. In my dream, I provided an apt container to get rid of my "trash"—probably the debris that was accumulating in my wrist from crushed bones and the healing that had begun in the misshapen fashion. The dream continued in the second and third scenes described in the text.

40. Louis Breger, Ian Hunter, and Ron Lane, *The Effect of Stress on Dreams*, New York: International Universities Press, 1971.

41. Louis Breger, Ian Hunter, and Ron Lane, p. 170. See the case of Al, pp. 106–123. In one dream, Al was trying to saw a 45-degree angle on a board; in the same dream, he was cutting a circle with a scissors on a picture. In the second dream, he was discussing how a quarter of beef should be cut up to preserve it; this dream included an operation and a pocketknife with blades that fell out.

42. For instance, the man scheduled for surgery to repair a vascular blockage in his legs referred to cutting three times in two of the four dreams of the first night he was measured. Prior to his hip replacement, Brad, one of the men I interviewed, recorded two references to cut meat in his four pre-operative dreams. In one, he saw himself slicing two pieces of beef; in the other, his son was cooking hamburgers, which he does not like. As in my dream with the half-chicken, when the body is going to be cut by a surgeon's knife, the dreaming mind often likens human flesh to edible animal flesh.

43. Louis Breger, Ian Hunter, and Ron Lane. See Melvin's dream, p. 137.

    Dreaming about buying a new car I think . . . we went to a car dealer and we started looking for a car that I had . . . we had been given an invitation to drive a new Ford for two days without obligation . . . nothing to sign or anything . . . with the exception of a card for insurance purposes . . .

44. See Associated Press article, "Fat Women at Risk for Gallstones," *San Francisco Chronicle*, August 31, 1989.

45. Louis Breger, Ian Hunter, and Ron Lane. See the case of Penny, pp. 141–156. She had been forced to lose 30 pounds when hospitalized for 13 days for stomach pains a month earlier. In waking life, Penny sewed new dresses before she went to the hospital, anticipating a newer, slimmer figure. Several of her dreams contained new clothing. In one, four nights before her scheduled surgery, she dreamed of cutting material for a new wedding dress out of old material, and of wearing "different clothes" with three-inch heels on her shoes (she was short).

46. An exhibition that I viewed of the drawings of burn patients at St. Francis Hospital in San Francisco revealed their incredible differences as the patients healed. Drawings of the accident and other pictures made early in the process were filled with fiery colors, and scenes with heat, such as a burning sun on a beach. As the patients began to heal, cool blues and greens appeared in the drawings.

    Some of the patients I interviewed or worked with came to believe that "art saved my life" or "art saved my sanity."

47. Based on an exercise suggested by Betty Edwards, *Drawing on the Artist Within*, New York: Simon and Schuster, 1986, p. 103.

## Chapter 6
### Post-Crisis Dreams

1. Nina's surgery was performed under a nerve block, so she was conscious most of the time. As the nerve block wore off, she was given a general anesthetic.

2. Oliver Sacks, *A Leg to Stand On*. Three nights after an operation under general anesthetic, during which a torn tendon in his left leg had been reconnected, Oliver Sacks dreamed that he was back on the mountain where he had been injured. In his dream, he was impotently struggling to move his leg without any result. He could see the stitches from the surgery but, though his leg had been repaired, it would not budge. No matter how he tried to move it, it remained inert, as though dead. He awoke in dread from this dream.

   Sacks persuaded himself to return to sleep, and had another nightmare in which he was confronted by a kind of fish-bull-monster emerging from the depths of river water [p. 57]:

   > As he turned—his vast face towards me, his vast eyes upon me—a wild and terrible panic overcame me, and frantically I tried to leap backwards up towards safety, *up* the riverbank behind me. But I couldn't spring. The movement came out wrong and instead of throwing me backwards threw me violently forwards, beneath what I now saw were the *hooves* of the fish . . .

   Sacks woke himself up with the violence of his sudden movement in the dream to find that he'd contracted his hamstrings so vigorously that his right heel had actually kicked his buttock, while his left heel was digging into the edge of his cast.

   Sacks' nightmare contained several typical responses to surgery. It depicted an attack by an animal shortly after having had surgery on his leg. The dream involved some elements of his actual accident (being hurt when he was chased by a bull), exaggerated and worsened. His nightmare also depicted the lack of sensation in his injured body part. The dream said he could not escape and he fell forward into even greater danger.

   Instead of being cured by surgery, Sacks feared that an additional problem had been created. Now he could not only not move his leg, he could no longer feel it. Images that arise from deep water often emerge from a deep part of the dreaming mind. The vast bull-creature may have been this newly emerging anxiety looming up out of the depths. Before the operation, his leg had sensation; now it had none. Was it the "hooves" of the surgeon's knife that created his further problem?

3. This dream was cited by Raymond Friedman, M.D., Ph.D., in a workshop sponsored by the California State Psychological Association, held at the Marriott Airport Hotel in San Mateo, California, a few days after the 1989 San Francisco earthquake, on October 22, 1989. The man's dream was:

> I am standing by a body of water. Suddenly an alligator rises up from the water. I back away onto dry land, thinking, "It's O.K., alligators can't run too fast." But this one runs swiftly after me. I decide to fly. I rise into the air. But then I see with horror that the alligator can fly, too, and is coming after me.

4. This earthquake is generally referred to as the Loma Prieta earthquake, as it centered on the fault of that name. The 7.1 earthquake struck San Francisco at 5:04 P.M. on October 17, 1989. Within two weeks, there had been over 2,000 small aftershocks, with about half a dozen ones larger than 4.0. In addition to loss of life and serious injuries, the earthquake caused problems with housing, added commute time, and general post-traumatic stress for the Bay Area population.

5. Peter's nightmare was:

> I see the blade stopped in a clean open cut. As I watch, the severed tubelike artery curls, shrinking back into my hand—it looks like white meat. Suddenly the artery begins to squirt like a hose out of control. The blood sprays all over the plywood and the other guy. I can still hear the slush sound as the blood lands, and I hear the sound of the blade ripping. I feel a screaming pain as I roll onto the floor . . .

6. Dee's nightmare was:

> I'm at work. There are these machines all around. The roll-former (the machine that injured her) had me. And another machine that I run, which is actually across the building, was coming and it was moving toward me . . . like it was going to push me into the first machine. And at the same time, in the background, this third machine came chugging along cutting sheet metal, like it was going to push me into the other two machines. It felt like everything was closing in. There's a sound like, "I'm gonna eat you." I can't get my hand out.

7. Brad K. Grunert, Decilia A. Devine, Hani S. Matloub, James R. Sanger, and N. John Yousif, "Flashbacks after Traumatic Hand

Injuries: Prognostic Indicators," *The Journal of Hand Surgery*, 1988, 13A:125-7.

These researchers interviewed 61 workers whose hands had been traumatically injured on the job. They found that nightmares decreased markedly during the first two months after injury occurred. They grouped the flashbacks into three types: *replay/flashbacks*, dreams or waking images repeating the events that occurred just before the accident and continuing until the injury; *appraisal/flashbacks*, dreams or imagery which showed the injury just after the accident; and *projected/flashbacks*, dreams or imagery which portrayed an injury more severe than the one that actually occurred. Some dreamers combined these categories. After a period of recovery, all of the patients were judged by the surgeon as being able to return to their former work.

8. The exact frequency of types of flashbacks was: appraisal/projected (47.5 percent), replay (34.4 percent) and replay/projected (13.1 percent).

9. Regardless of the type of injury the patient in this study had—amputation, functional disability, scarring, or deformity—those people who experienced only replay flashbacks were able to return to jobs at their former workplace sooner (95.2 percent), and with less counseling, than those people who suffered appraisal/projected flashbacks (10.3 percent). Patients with replay/projected flashbacks had a return-to-work rate in between these extremes, about 50 percent.

10. Hilary, for example, had gone through several surgeries for breast cancer, including the removal of both breasts and reconstructive surgery. Her chest felt like one vast, raw wound. She added, "My illness felt like a wall of tears inside." Hilary told me that she felt so fearful someone would bump into her chest while she was outside that she virtually stopped going out. For a period of months, she became almost a recluse, only taking short walks at her husband's side.

Hilary described her series of surgeries as "invasions." Everything seemed treacherous. Even her home began to feel unsafe. She related how the raccoons began coming into her garden, digging up things, destroying plants, eventually reaching her back door and upsetting pots of flowers on her porch. She felt persecuted, as though no place was a safe refuge.

It was then that one of Hilary's friends took action that probably saved the woman's life. She brought Hilary a bouquet of beautiful ice poppies, with a message, "They remind me of you, fragile but sturdy. You can bend them and they bound back." Her friend expressed her fear that Hilary was killing herself, that she must get out of the house to live again. Hilary was so touched by this gesture, that she began to do things to help herself. In particular, Hilary started taking art classes. It was something she had always wanted to do but had always been too busy. She enrolled and found herself blossoming with the color and line that flowed through her hand onto the paper. She also started some religious classes at her church. Hilary began meeting new friends and finding new interests; as she did so, the old fears dropped out. She had begun to truly heal.

11. Gilda Radner, *It's Always Something*, New York: Simon & Schuster, 1989. The survival rate that is usually given for ovarian cancer is about 20 percent.

12. Gilda Radner, *It's Always Something*, p. 109.
Radner's surgery included a hysterectomy, the removal of a grapefruit-sized tumor, a scraping of her internal organs, a second operation to insert a portable catheter, and her first round of chemotherapy. Her weight was down to 95 pounds. She said her head felt like "the inside of a radio," a clear plastic one with pink neon light inside, the electrical wiring all hot and exposed from the toxicity of the chemicals. Nighttime was especially difficult:

> I should have known then that Gene thought I was going to die because he would never have said, "Wake me up in the middle of the night." His performance convinced me. And it happened that I did wake Gene almost every night. I would wake up sweating and out of breath, running from a nightmare that didn't end when I woke up. I would cry in deep moans, wailing like a wounded animal—getting louder and louder to try to drown out what had happened, what I looked like, what could be. Gene held me, rocked me, but he couldn't protect me from the cancer. The night was the scariest time.

Although she did not say what she was running from in the dream, Radner's imagery undoubtedly represented her fear of the disease, the unknown future, and death itself.

13. Gilda Radner, *It's Always Something*, p. 218.

14. Barbara Tedlock, "Dreaming Among the Anthropologists," paper presented at the Association for the Study of Dreams annual conference, Chicago, 1990.

15. Stephen LaBerge, *Control Your Dreams*, Los Angeles: Audio Renaissance Tapes, 1987.

16. Carl G. Jung, *Psychological Types: or the Psychology of Individuation*, New York: Harcourt, Brace and Co., 1924, pp. 574–575. For an excellent discussion of active imagination, see: Gerhard Adler, *Studies in Analytical Psychology*, New York: Norton, 1948, pp. 56–73.

17. Oliver Sacks, *A Leg to Stand On*, New York: Harper & Row, 1984.

18. Sigmund Freud, *The Interpretation of Dreams*, New York: Avon, 1965, p. 263.

19. Evelyn Simon, personal communication and workshop at the Association for the Study of Dreams annual conference, Chicago, 1990.

20. Ann Sayre Wiseman, *Nightmare Help: A Guide for Parents and Teachers*, Berkeley, CA: Ten Speed Press, 1989, p. 26.

## Chapter 7
## Healing Dreams

1. *Total Hip Replacement: Walking Again* (no author cited), Daly City, CA: Krames Communications, 1985.

2. J. Money, "Phantom Orgasm in Dreams of Paraplegic Men and Women," *Archives of General Psychiatry*, vol. 3, 1960, pp. 373–83.

3. Ernest Rossi, *The Psychobiology of Mind-Body Healing*, New York: Norton, 1986, p. 180.

4. Joseph Freidin and Vernon Marshall, *Illustrated Guide to Surgical Practice*, New York: Churchill Livingstone, 1984, p. 110.

5. Martin Rossman, *Healing Yourself: A Step-by-Step Program for Better Health Through Imagery*, New York: Walker, 1987.

6. David Feinstein and Stanley Krippner, *Personal Mythology: The Psychology of Your Evolving Self*, Los Angeles: Tarcher, 1988.

7. Robert Smith. "Dreams Reflect a Biological State," "Evaluating Dream Function: Emphasizing the Study of Patients with Organic Disease," papers presented at the Association for the Study of Dreams, Ottawa, 1988.

8. Rita Dwyer, "Dream Story," *The Dream Network Bulletin*, Vol. 4, no. 3, May/June, pp. 1–3, 1985. Also, personal communication, 1989.

9. This material was supplied by the National Headache Foundation.

10. Patricia Garfield, *Your Child's Dreams*, New York: Ballantine, 1984.

11. Anthony Schmitz, "After the Bite," *Hippocrates*, vol. 3, no. 3, May/June, 1989, pp. 78–84.

12. My thanks to the National Headache Foundation and Wyeth-Ayerst Laboratories for sharing their findings with me.

13. The winning entry is titled, "Violent Passages," by Louise Woodard from Mattydale, New York. It is a time-lapse painting of her migraine sequence. The work focuses on the pain surrounding her eye, the piercing wavelike patterns, flashes of intense reds, blues, and yellows, and the confusion she feels, especially with the numbers two and five, as a result of the migraine. The spiderlike shape reflects the irregularity of blood vessels and flow during the violent attack. The pills represent the end of this ordeal because they can at least subdue the pain.

    The second-place winner, Rebecca Whitcanack, a stenographer from Miline, Illinois, called her work "Nemesis." The recurring phantom masks and chains illustrate her fear of attacks; the violent bolt of lightning depicts the severe piercing pain. She found that by combining art with exercise and piano playing, it provides relaxation and an outlet for stress.

    The third-place winner, Constance Mariels from Davis, California, entitled her picture, "Migraine Figure." This drawing portrays the overall experience of her body, with a meteor like ball of fire illustrating the one-sided pain she feels. She shows her sensitivity to light in the turning of her head. The explosion in her stomach depicts the nausea she experiences along with the pain.

14. Charles Petit, "Portraits of Pain," *San Francisco Chronicle*, July 21, 1986.

15. This concept of questioning the dreamer about the dream image in this fashion is suggested and described by Carl G. Jung, *Modern Man in Search of a Soul*. New York: Harcourt Brace Jovanovich, 1933, pp. 13–14.

16. Carl G. Jung, "The Transcendent Function," Joseph Campbell, ed., *The Portable Jung*. Penguin USA, 1971.

17. Ad DeVries, *Dictionary of Symbols and Imagery*, Amsterdam: Elsevier, 1984. Although less complete, another helpful dictionary is: Herder Freiburg, Boris Matthews, trans., *The Herder Symbol Dictionary*, Wilmette, Illinois: Chiron, 1988.

18. Jeanne Achterberg, *Imagery in Healing*, Boston: Shambhala, New Science Library, 1985. Also see Jeanne Achterberg and G. Frank

Lawlis, *Imagery and Disease*, Champaign, IL: Institute for Personality and Ability Testing, 1984.

19. Jeanne Achterberg, *Imagery in Healing*.

## Chapter 8
## Convalescence and Wellness Dreams

1. "Loving a Pet is Good Kid Therapy," *San Francisco Chronicle*, January 11, 1990, p. B1. Researchers examining the bonds between humans and animals observed several psychological benefits for children. Boys and girls who cared for a puppy, in one study, were found to be more cooperative, more sharing, and better able to understand the feelings of other children. In a study with neglected children, the pets became confidantes who were buffers against loneliness and who were comforting when the child was upset. I suspect these benefits apply to adults as well.

2. Walter Jayne, *The Healing Gods of Ancient Civilizations*, New Haven: Yale University Press, 1925, pp. 348–50.

3. Walter Jayne, *The Healing Gods of Ancient Civilizations*.

4. Rita Dwyer, "Dream Story," *The Dream Network Bulletin*, vol. 4, no. 3, May/June, 1985, pp. 1–3.

5. Rita Dwyer, personal communication with author, 1989.

6. Emily Martin, *The Woman in the Body: A Cultural Analysis of Reproduction*, Boston: Beacon Press, 1987.

7. Ernest Rossi, personal communication with author and lecture as part of program on "Dreams: Creativity, Consciousness, and Healing" at the University of California, Los Angeles, November 11, 1989.
   Rossi's steps seem to be similar to the steps I observed in dreams when recovering from an injury or illness. It may seem odd to liken recovery from an illness or injury to recovery from an addiction. Yet, similar steps likewise lead to the door to health.
   In his work as a clinician, Rossi has treated a number of patients who were struggling to overcome addictions. Consider, for example, giving up smoking (although Rossi says that the same pattern applies to all addictions). The changes that occur in the smokers' dreams as they conquer their addiction are fourfold:

   1. *Repetition.* At first the patient smokes as usual in dreams. There is no change in behavior and no awareness.
   2. *Recognition.* Then the patient smokes in the dream but recognizes that she or he should not be doing so. The

dreamer may say, "What am I doing smoking? I don't smoke anymore!" There is no change in the behavior, but there is awareness of its inappropriateness.

3. *Resistance.* At this stage, the patient is not smoking in the dream but feels tempted to do so and is upset about it. Another dream figure may offer him or her a cigarette and the dreamer may respond, "What are you doing? You know I don't smoke now!" Or the dreamer may be smoking, but realizes she or he does not want to do so and puts out the cigarette, feeling distressed. "How could I blow it?!" In this case, there is a change in behavior but it is accompanied by an emotional struggle.

4. *Resolution.* Finally, the dreamer accepts himself or herself as a nonsmoker in the dream. Another dream character may offer a cigarette and the dreamer replies calmly, "No thanks, I don't smoke." Not only is there a behavior change, but it is accompanied by comfort. Dreams move on to other current concerns.

In the same way that I found a progression toward reintegration of the injured body part in dreams, and a movement in replay imagery from passive victim to active savior, Rossi found a sequence in which the dreamer gradually accepted himself or herself as a nonaddict. The former addicts were integrating the image of themselves as nonaddicts in the same way that injured persons integrated the change in their body image; they were moving from helpless replays of their addiction to becoming actively in control of their behaviors—essentials for the new behavior to become permanent. Change in dream behavior is a vital cue to change in waking life.

8. Reed Morrison, "Dreams Mapping Recovery from Chemical Dependency," *Association for the Study of Dreams Newsletter,* vol. 6, no. 5, Sept./Oct., 1989, pp. 1–3. Morrison's map of recovery:

Morrison bases his labels for the stages on Joseph Campbell's concept of the "hero's journey." He says that "the dark night of the soul" describes the experience of the active alcoholic or drug addict whose night contains dreams of death, destruction, guilt, and persecution. Of course, alcohol and some drugs temporarily suppress dreams; when they return, the dreamer suffers extreme nightmares. As an alcoholic or drug addict makes an effort to recover from the addiction, Morrison finds that dreams change as follows:

1. *Pandora's Box.* This stage, which begins when abstinence begins, usually involves the return of violent dreaming.

During the first 45 days or so of abstinence, dream themes commonly contain alienation, violence, mutilation, bizarre sexuality, and persecution.

2. *The Dragon Fight.* Confrontation and battle characterize this stage, as denial of the problem is relinquished and the addiction accepted. This stage may begin as early as day 20 from abstinence or as late as day 90. Typical dream themes are battles against the victim role. The dreamer is fighting inner fears.

3. *Rebirth.* At this stage, the dreamer may feel relief and calm. Often a relationship with a "higher power" occurs. This stage starts somewhere between days 30 and 120 into recovery.

4. *The Descent.* This stage is marked by descent into the darkness of trauma and conflict. It starts sometime between days 60 and 150. The dreamer confronts unfinished business in life, but now with greater hope, based on the earlier stages.

5. *The Return.* This stage contains dreams of forward movement, ownership, new discoveries, and behaviors. Spiritual or archetypal images predominate, with a sense of renewal and well-being. It may arise between days 90 and 180. However, its appearance does not signal the end. There is a continuous recycling between stages four and five, as the dream experiences are confronted and integrated. Eventually, intervals of the stage of descent lessen and the dreamer consolidates inner strength.

9. Stanley Krippner, "Storytelling and Sobriety: Dreams vs. Drugs," *Association for the Study of Dreams Newsletter,* vol. 6, no. 5, Sept./Oct., 1989, pp. 5, 16. Krippner observed three stages of dream change: early on, Curtis dreamed of blatantly using the drug; then he dreamed of being concerned about the consequences of using it; finally he maintained sobriety in the dream. Describing a dream of the third stage, Curtis said, "I put some crack in my pipe and put it in my mouth. But I realize that I would lose my sobriety so I decide not to smoke. This is the *first time I can remember that I ever took responsibility for myself in a dream* and am not passive and powerless." Curtis had only three minor relapses during the twelve months since he completed the program.

10. Karen Surman Paley, "The Dream as a Higher Power," *Association for the Study of Dreams Newsletter,* vol. 6, no. 5, Sept./Oct., 1989, pp. 3–4.

11. Summary of the healing sequences in dream images:

   1. *Replay of Current or Former Condition in Dream.*
      At this stage, the person who has been injured or ill continues to be the same or worse in the dream. The victim of trauma continues to be victimized, as the addicted victim smokes, drinks, or continues to use drugs according to the waking habit, without awareness or change in the dream.

   2. *Recognition of Inappropriateness of Condition in Dream.*
      At this stage, the dreamer notices that the current (or former) behavior or condition is not desirable or appropriate. There is awareness that the behavior is occurring or that the condition exists, without any change in it. This stage may involve struggle and negative emotions.

   3. *Accidental Change of Condition in Dream.*
      During this stage, the outcome of the dream is different. There is change in the condition or behavior without ability to create it; change just happens. Dreamers may feel great relief.

   4. *Deliberate Change of Condition in Dream.*
      In this phase, the dreamer recognizes the condition or behavior and deliberately acts differently within the dream. There is awareness and change. Emotions may run high. Control of change by the dreamer begins to occur.

   5. *Reintegration of New Condition in Dream.*
      Eventually the new behaviors or conditions become part of the accepted dream scenario. The formerly injured or ill person appears in dreams with a newly integrated body image. The former victim of trauma accepts a new role. The former addict defines the self as a nonaddict in dreams, without emotional turmoil. Awareness and change have become natural.

12. Listen to the tape of the panel discussion: "Should You Control Your Dreams?", annual conference of the Association for the Study of Dreams, Chicago, 1990.

13. Aristotle, in the fourth century B.C., referred to "something in consciousness which declares that what then presents itself is but a dream." Aristotle. *On Dreams.* From *Great Books of the Western World*, Vol. 8, ed. R. M. Hutchings. Chicago: Encyclopedia Britannica, 1952.

14. Patricia Garfield, introduction to second edition of *Pathway to Ecstasy: The Way of the Dream Mandala*, Prentice-Hall, 1989.

15. Jayne Gackenbach and Jane Bosveld, *Control Your Dreams*, New York: Harper and Row, 1989.

## Chapter 9
## Your Inner Dream Temple

1. To read more about ancient dream temples, see the books and articles on Asklepios listed in reference note seven, in Chapter Four.

2. To read more about "Inner Advisor," see Martin Rossman's book *Healing Yourself;* to read more about an "Inner Shaman," see David Feinstein and Stanley Krippner's book *Personal Mythology.*

3. Ernest Rossi and David Cheek state, (p. 377), "The phenomenological experience of dreams in the languages of imagery, metaphor, symbol and analogy is isomorphic with organic brain-body processes down to the cellular-genetic-molecular level." Thus, these symbols can mediate mind-body communication in illness and healing.

# BIBLIOGRAPHY

Achterberg, Jeanne. *Imagery in Healing*. Boston: Shambhala, New Science Library, 1985.

Achterberg, Jeanne, and G. Frank Lawlis. *Imagery and Disease*. Champaign, IL: Institute for Personality and Ability Testing, 1984.

Adams, Francis. *The Genuine Works of Hippocrates*. New York: William Wood & Co., 1886.

Adler, Gerhard. *Studies in Analytical Psychology*. New York: Norton, 1948.

Adler, Valerie. "Little Control = Lots of Stress," *Psychology Today*, April, 1989, pp. 18–19. (Describes work of Robert Karasek.)

Aristotle. *De Divinatione Per Somnum (On Prophesying by Dreams); De Somniis (On Dreams)*. In Richard McKeon, ed. *The Basic Works of Aristotle*. New York: Random House, 1941.

————. "On Dreams"; "On Prophesy in Sleep." In *Parva Naturalia*. Translated by W. S. Hett. Cambridge, Mass.: Harvard University Press, The Loeb Classical Library, Vol. VIII, 1986.

Artemidorus. *The Interpretation of Dreams: The Oneirocritica of Artemidorus*. Translation and commentary by Robert White. Park Ridge, New Jersey: Noyes Press, 1975.

Associated Press article. (Unsigned). "Fat Women at Risk for Gallstones." *San Francisco Chronicle*, Thursday, August 31, 1989.

Bosnak, Robert. *Dreaming with an AIDS Patient*. Boston: Shambhala, 1989.

Boss, Medard. *The Analysis of Dreams*. New York: Philosophical Library, 1958.

Breger, Louis, Ian Hunter, and Ron Lane. *The Effect of Stress on Dreams*. New York: International Universities Press, 1971.

Caire, Jill Bond. "A Holographic Model of a Psychosomatic Pattern: Freud's Specimen Dream Re-Interpreted." *Psychotherapy and Psychosomatics*. Vol. 36, 1981, pp. 132–142.

Campbell, Joseph. *The Hero with a Thousand Faces*. Princeton, N.J.: Princeton University Press, 1949.

Camporesi, E. M., W. J. Greely, P. D. Lamb, and W. D. Watkins. "Anesthesia," in David Sabiston, ed., *Textbook of Surgery*. Philadelphia, PA: W. B. Saunders Co., 1986.

Capacchione, Lucia. *The Creative Journal: The Art of Finding Yourself*. North Hollywood: Newcastle, 1979.

———. *The Well-Being Journal: Drawing on Your Inner Power to Heal Yourself*. North Hollywood: Newcastle, 1989.

Caton, Richard. *The Temples and Ritual of Asklepios at Epidauros and Athens*. London: C. J. Clay and Sons, 1900.

Coleman, Richard M. *Wide Awake at 3:00 A.M.: By Choice or by Chance?* New York: W. H. Freeman & Co., 1986.

Cowels, Ellyn H. "The Healing Dream." Master's thesis, Goddard College, 1980.

Dafter, Roger. "Individuation in Illness: Moving Beyond Blame in Mind-Body Healing." In Ernest Rossi, ed., *Psychological Perspectives*, 22, 1990, pp. 24–37.

Demling, Robert H. "Preoperative Care." In Lawrence W. Way, ed., *Current Surgical Diagnosis and Treatment*, pp. 6–13.

DeVries, Ad. *Dictionary of Symbols and Imagery*. Amsterdam: Elsevier, 1984.

Dwyer, Rita. "Dream Story." *The Dream Network Bulletin*. Vol. 4, no. 3, May/June, 1985, pp. 1–3, and personal communication, 1989.

Edelstein, Emma and Ludwig. *Asclepius: A Collection and Interpretation of the Testimonies*. Baltimore: The Johns Hopkins Press, 1945.

Edwards, Betty. *Drawing on the Artist Within*. New York: Simon & Schuster, 1986.

Feinstein, David and Stanley Krippner. *Personal Mythology: The Psychology of Your Evolving Self*. Los Angeles: Tarcher, 1988.

Fisher, Charles, H. D. Cohen, R. C. Schiavi, D. Davis, Barbara Furman, K. Ward, A. Edwards, and Jerry Cunningham. "Patterns of Female Sexual Arousal During Sleep and Waking: Vaginal Thermo-Conductance Studies," *Archives of Sexual Behavior*, 12, no. 2, 1983.

Fisher, Charles, J. Gross, and J. Zuch. "Cycle of Penile Erection Synchronous with Dreaming (REM) Sleep." *Archives of General Psychiatry*, 12, 1965, pp. 29–45.

Freiburg, Herder. Translated by Boris Matthews. *The Herder Symbol Dictionary*. Wilmette, Illinois: Chiron, 1988.

Freidin, Joseph and Vernon Marshall. *Illustrated Guide to Surgical Practice*. New York: Churchill Livingstone, 1984.

French, Thomas, and L. B. Shapiro. "The Use of Dream Analysis in Psychosomatic Research." *Psychosomatic Research*, Vol. 11, 1949, pp. 110–112.

French, Thomas, and Franz Alexander. "Psychogenic Factors in Bronchial Asthma." Part I and II. *Psychosomatic Medicine Monographs*, II, no. 1 and 2, 1941.

Freud, Sigmund. *The Interpretation of Dreams*. New York: Avon, 1965.

Furth, Gregg M. *The Secret World of Drawings: Healing Through Art*. Boston: Sigo Press, 1988.

Gackenbach, Jayne, and Jane Bosveld. *Control Your Dreams*. New York: Harper & Row Publishers, Inc., 1989.

Gackenbach, Jayne, chair, Walter Bonime, Patricia Garfield, Johanna King, Eugene Gendlin, and Jane White Lewis. "Should You Control Your Dreams?" Panel discussion, annual conference of the Association for the Study of Dreams, Chicago, 1990. ASD Audiotape.

Garfield, Patricia. *Creative Dreaming*. New York: Simon & Schuster, 1974; New York: Ballantine, 1976. *Creative Dreaming* audiotape. Los Angeles: Audio Renaissance Tapes, 1988.

————. *Pathway to Ecstasy: The Way of the Dream Mandala*. New York: Holt, Rinehart & Winston, 1979; Prentice Hall, 1989.

————. *Women's Bodies, Women's Dreams*. New York: Ballantine, 1988.

————. *Your Child's Dreams*. New York: Ballantine, 1984.

Grunert, Brad K., Cecilia A. Devine, Hani S. Matloub, James R. Sanger, and N. John Yousif. "Flashbacks after Traumatic Hand Injuries: Prognostic Incidators." *The Journal of Hand Surgery*, 13A, 1988, pp. 125–27.

Gutheil, Emil. "Dreams as an Aid to Evaluating Ego-Strength." *American Journal of Psychiatry*, Vol. 12, 1958, pp. 338–357.

Guthrie, Douglas J., and Phillip Rhodes. "Medicine and Surgery before 1800." *The New Encyclopaedia Britannica*, 15th Edition. Chicago: Encyclopaedia Britannica, Inc., Vol. 23, 1988, p. 889.

Hales, Dianne. *The Complete Book of Sleep: How Your Nights Affect Your Days*. Menlo Park, Ca.: Addison-Wesley, 1981.

Hall, Calvin. *The Meaning of Dreams*. New York: Harper and Brothers, 1953.

Hall, Calvin, and Robert Van de Castle. *The Content Analysis of Dreams*. New York: Appleton-Century-Crofts, 1966.

Hall, Calvin, and Vernon Nordby. *The Individual and His Dreams*. New York: Signet, 1972.

Hamel, Peter Michael. *Through Music to the Self*. Boulder, Colorado: Shambhala, 1979.

Hartmann, Ernest. *The Biology of Dreaming*. Springfield, Illinois: Charles C. Thomas, 1967.

Haskell, Robert E. "Dreaming, Cognition, and Physical Illness: Parts I and II." *Journal of Medical Humanities and Bioethics*, Vol. 6, 1985, pp. 46–56 and pp. 109–122.

Hay, Louise L. *You Can Heal Your Life*. Santa Monica, Ca.: Hay House, 1984.

Hippocrates. *The Oath.* Translated by W. H. S. Jones. Cambridge: Harvard University Press, The Loeb Classical Library, Vol. I, 1923.

———. *Aphorisms; Regimen IV or Dreams.* Translated by W. H. S. Jones. Cambridge: Harvard University Press, The Loeb Classical Library, Vol. IV, 1931.

Hobson, J. Allan. *The Dreaming Brain.* New York: Basic Books, 1988.

Holmes, Thomas, and Richard Rahe. "The Social Readjustment Rating Scale." *Journal of Psychosomatic Medicine*, Vol. 11, 1967, pp. 213–218.

Hunt, Thomas K., and William H. Goodson, III. "Wound Healing." In Lawrence W. Way, ed., *Current Surgical Diagnosis and Treatment*, pp. 86–93.

Jackson, Ralph. *Doctors and Diseases in the Roman Empire.* Norman, OK: University of Oklahoma Press, 1988.

Jayne, Walter A. *The Healing Gods of Ancient Civilizations.* New Haven: Yale University Press, 1925.

Jung, Carl G. *Modern Man in Search of a Soul.* New York: Harcourt Brace Jovanovich, 1933.

———. *Psychological Types: Or the Psychology of Individuation.* New York: Harcourt, Brace & Co., 1924.

———. "The Transcendent Function." In Joseph Campbell, ed., *The Portable Jung.* New York: Penguin, 1971.

Jung, Carl G., ed. *Man and His Symbols.* New York: Doubleday, 1964.

Kales, J., C. Allen, T. Preston, T. L. Tan, and A. Kales. "Changes in REM Sleep and Dreaming with Cigarette Smoking and Following Withdrawal." *Psychophysiology*, Vol. 7, pp. 347–48, 1970. [Cited in Carolyn Winget and Milton Kramer. *Dimensions of Dreams.* Gainesville: University Presses of Florida, p. 361, 1979.]

Karacan, Ismet, A. Rosenbloom, and Robert Williams. "The Clitoral Erection Cycle During Sleep." Paper presented at the meeting of the Association for the Psychophysiological Study of Sleep. Santa Fe, New Mexico, 1970.

Karacan, Ismet, Constance A. Moore, Max Hirshkowitz, Sezai Sahmay, Erdem M. Narter, Yaman Tokat, and Lale Tuncel. "Uterine Activity During Sleep," *Sleep*, Vol. 9, no. 3, 1986, pp. 393–97.

Kardiner, Abraham. "The Bioanalysis of the Epileptic Reaction. *Psychoanalytic Quarterly*, Vol. 1, 1932.

Kasatkin, Vasilii N. *Theory of Dreams.* Leningrad: Meditsina, 1967.

Kaufman, Tamar. "Writer Dreams Her Way to Health, Returns to Jewish Roots." *The Northern California Jewish Bulletin.* June 15, 1990.

Kellogg, E. W., III. "A Personal Experience in Lucid Dream Healing." (Unpublished account), 1989.

Kerényi, C. *Asklepios: Archetypal Image of the Physician's Existence*. Princeton: Princeton University Press, 1959.

Krippner, Stanley. "Storytelling and Sobriety: Dreams vs. Drugs." *Association for the Study of Dreams Newsletter*, Vol. 6, No. 5, Sept./Oct., 1989, pp. 5, 16.

LaBerge, Stephen. *Lucid Dreaming: The Power of Being Awake and Aware in Your Dreams*. Los Angeles: Jeremy P. Tarcher, 1985.

———. *Controlling Your Dreams*. Audiotape. Los Angeles: Audio Renaissance Tapes, 1987.

LaBerge, Stephen, and Howard Rheingold. *Exploring the World of Lucid Dreaming*. New York: Ballantine, 1990.

Lakoff, George, and Mark Johnson. *Metaphors We Live By*. Chicago: The University of Chicago Press, 1980.

Levitan, Harold L. "Patterns of Hostility Revealed in the Fantasies and Dreams of Women with Rheumatoid Arthritis." *Psychotherapy and Psychosomatics*, 35, pp. 34–43, 1981.

———. "Dreams which Precede Asthmatic Attacks." In A. Krakowski and C. Kimball. *Psychosomatic Medicine: Theoretical Clinical and Transcultural Aspects*. New York: Plenum Books, 1983.

———. "Dreams which Culminate in Migraine Headaches." *Psychotherapy and Psychosomatics*. Vol. 41, 1984, pp. 161–166.

Lippman, Caro W. "Recurrent Dreams in Migraine: An Aid to Diagnosis." *Journal of Mental and Nervous Disorders*, pp. 273–276.

Lockhart, Russell A. "Cancer in Myth and Dream." *Spring*, pp. 1–26, 1977.

Lyons, Albert S., and R. Joseph Petrucelli, II. *Medicine: An Illustrated History*. New York: Harry N. Abrams, Inc., 1978.

Martin, Emily. *The Woman in the Body: A Cultural Analysis of Reproduction*. Boston: Beacon Press, 1987.

May, Margaret T. *Galen On the Usefulness of the Parts of the Body*. Ithaca: Cornell University Press, 1968.

McFadden, E. H., and E. C. Giblin. "Sleep Deprivation in Patients Having Open-Heart Surgery." *Nursing Research*, 20, 1971, 249–254. Described in Robert L. Williams, Ismet Karacan, and Constance A. Moore, *Sleep Disorders: Diagnosis & Treatment*, p. 276. New York: John Wiley, 1988

Money, J. "Phantom Orgasm in Dreams of Paraplegic Men and Women." *Archives of General Psychiatry*, Vol. 3, 1960, pp. 373–83.

Morrison, Reed. "Dreams Mapping Recovery from Chemical Dependency." *Association for the Study of Dreams Newsletter*, Vol. 6, No. 5, Sept./Oct., 1989, pp. 1–3.

Naunton, Doré. "Occupational Therapy and the Treatment of the Colles' Fracture." In Florence S. Cromwell and Jane Bear-Lehman, eds., *Hand Rehabilitation in Occupational Therapy*, pp. 111–113, New York: The Haworth Press, 1988.

*The New York Times* article. (Unsigned). "Loving a Pet is Good Kid Therapy." *San Francisco Chronicle*. Thursday, January 11, 1990, p. B1.

Olson, Fred. Paper presented at the annual conference of the Association for the Study of Dreams, Chicago, 1990.

Oyle, Irving and Susan. *New Dimensions* newsletter, September-October, 1989.

Paley, Karen Surman. "The Dream as a Higher Power." *Association for the Study of Dreams Newsletter*, Vol. 6, No. 5, Sept./Oct., 1989, pp. 3–4.

Radner, Gilda. *It's Always Something*. New York: Simon & Schuster, 1989.

Rainer, Tristine. *The New Diary*. Los Angeles: Jeremy P. Tarcher, 1978.

Rossi, Ernest. *The Psychobiology of Mind-Body Healing*. New York: Norton, 1986.

Rossi, Ernest, and David Cheek. *Mind-Body Therapy*. New York: Norton, 1988.

Rossi, Ernest. Lecture in program "Dreams: Creativity, Consciousness, and Healing." University of California, Los Angeles, November 11, 1989, and personal communication, 1989.

Rossi, Ernest. "The Eternal Quest: Hidden Rhythms of Stress and Healing in Everyday Life." *Psychological Perspectives*, 22, pp. 6–23, 1990.

Rossman, Martin. *Healing Yourself: A Step-by-Step Program for Better Health Through Imagery*. New York: Walker and Co., 1987.

Sabini, Meredith, and Valerie Hone Maffly. "An Inner View of Illness: The Dreams of Two Cancer Patients." *Journal of Analytical Psychology*, 26, 1981, 123–150.

Sacks, Oliver. *A Leg to Stand On*. New York: Harper and Row, 1984.
———. *Awakenings*. New York: Dutton, 1983.
———. *Migraine*. Berkeley, CA: University of California Press, 1985.

Sarton, George. *Galen of Pergamon*. Lawrence, Kansas: University of Kansas Press, 1954.

Saul, Leon, E. Sheppard, D. Selby, W. Lhamon, and D. Sacks. "The Quantification of Hostility in Dreams with Reference to Essential Hypertension." *Sciences*. March, 1954, pp. 119, 382–383.

Savitz, H. A. "The Dream as a Diagnostic Aid in Physical Diagnosis." *Conn. Medicine*, Vol. 33, 1969, pp. 309–310. Quoted in R. Haskell, p. 111.

Schmitz, Anthony. "After the Bite." *Hippocrates*. Vol. 3, no. 3, May/June, 1989, pp. 78–84.

Shakespeare, William. *Pericles, Prince of Tyre*, Act III, Scene II, *The Complete Illustrated Shakespeare*, Howard Staunton, ed., New York: Park Lane, 1979.

Siegel, Alan. *Dreams That Can Change Your Life*. Los Angeles: Jeremy P. Tarcher, 1990.

Siegel, Bernie S. *Peace, Love and Healing: Bodymind Communication and the Path to Self-Healing: An Exploration*. New York: Harper & Row, 1989.

————. *Love, Medicine and Miracles*. New York: Harper & Row, 1986.

Siegel, Rudolph E. *Galen on Psychology, Psychopathology, and Function and Diseases of the Nervous System*. London: S. Rarger, 1973.

Simon, Evelyn. "Artfully Exploring the Dreamworld." Workshop at the Association for the Study of Dreams annual conference, Chicago, 1990, and personal communication, 1990.

Singer, Jerome L. *Imagery and Daydream Methods in Psychotherapy and Behavior Modification*. New York: Academic Press, 1974.

Smith, Robert. "A Possible Biologic Role of Dreaming." *Psychotherapy and Psychosomatics*, 41, pp. 167–176, 1984.

Smith, Robert. "Dreams Reflect a Biological State." "Evaluating Dream Function: Emphasizing the Study of Patients with Organic Disease." Papers presented at the Association for the Study of Dreams, Ottawa, 1988.

Steinberg, Jerry. "An Investigation into the Healing Properties of Dreams." Unpublished paper, September, 1980.

Tedlock, Barbara. "Dreaming among the Anthropologists." Paper presented at the Association for the Study of Dreams annual conference, Chicago, 1990.

Tener, Lorna, and Carlyle Smith. "Vaginal Blood Volume Changes During Sleep," *Sleep Research*, 6, 1977.

*Total Hip Replacement: Walking Again*. (Unsigned). Daly City, CA: Krames Communications, 1985.

Ullman, Montague, and Stanley Krippner with Alan Vaughan. *Dream Telepathy: Experiments in Nocturnal ESP*. London: McFarland, 1989.

Van de Castle, Robert. "Pregnancy Dreams." Paper presented at the Association for the Study of Dreams annual conference, Ottawa, 1986.

Van Ouwerkerk, Aad. "The Elements of Dreaming" worksheet. "The Seven Step Process—a Practical Dreamwork Method." Paper presented at the Association for the Study of Dreams annual meeting in Chicago, 1990.

Veith, Ilza. *The Yellow Emperor's Classic of Internal Medicine. (Huang Ti Nei Ching Su Wen)*. Berkeley: University of California Press, 1949.

Wadeson, Harriet. *The Dynamics of Art Psychotherapy*. New York: John Wiley and Sons, 1987.

Wadeson, R. "Anxiety in the Dreams of Neurological Patients." *Archives of General Psychiatry*, 14, 1966, 249–252. Quoted in R. Haskell, p. 113.

Walsh, Joseph. "Galen's Writings and Influences Inspiring Them." *Annals of Medical History*, Vol. VI, No. 1, January, 1934, pp. 1–30.

Ware, J. Catesby. "Sleep and Anxiety," in R. L. Williams, ed., *Sleep Disorders: Diagnosis and Treatment*, pp. 205–207.

Warnes, H., and A. Finkelstein. "Dreams That Precede a Psychosomatic Illness." *Canadian Psychiatric Association Journal*, Vol. 16, 1971.

Way, Lawrence. *Current Surgical Diagnosis and Treatment*. San Mateo, California: Appleton-Lange, 1988.

Wiedemann, Carl F. "REM and Non-REM Sleep and Its Relation to Nightmares and Night Terrors." In Henry Kellerman, ed., *The Nightmare*, pp. 75–97. New York: Columbia University Press, 1987.

Williams, Robert L. "Sleep Disturbances in Various Medical and Surgical Conditions." In Robert L. Williams, Ismet Karacan, and Constance A. Moore, eds. *Sleep Disorders: Diagnosis and Treatment*, pp. 265–292. New York: John Wiley and Sons, 1988.

Wiseman, Ann Sayre. *Nightmare Help: A Guide for Parents and Teachers*. Berkeley, California: Ten Speed Press, 1989.

Witt, Charles. "Portraits of Pain." *San Francisco Chronicle*, Monday, July 21, 1986, p. 15.

Ziegler, Alfred J. "A Cardiac Infarction and a Dream as Synchronous Events." *The Journal of Analytical Psychology*, Vol. 7, No. 2, July, 1962, pp. 142–43.

———. *Archetypal Medicine*. Gary V. Hartman, translator. Dallas, Texas: Spring Publications, 1983.

# Index

# About the Author

Patricia Garfield, Ph.D., is a world wide authority on dreams. A clinical psychologist who graduated *summa cum laude* from Temple University in Philadelphia, she has been studying dreams professionally for over twenty years.

Dr. Garfield's *Creative Dreaming* is considered a classic in the field. First published in 1974 (hardcover, Simon & Schuster), it is in its nineteenth paperback printing (Ballantine, 1976), was a best-seller on the *Los Angeles Times* list, and has appeared in nine foreign languages.

The author and illustrator of *Pathway to Ecstasy: The Way of the Dream Mandala* (Holt, Rinehart and Winston, 1979; Prentice Hall, 1989), Dr. Garfield also wrote *Your Child's Dreams* (Ballantine, 1984) and *Women's Bodies, Women's Dreams* (Ballantine, 1988). She is a frequent contributor to magazines and professional journals and has recorded a cassette on *Creative Dreaming* (Audio Renaissance Tapes, 1988).

Dr. Garfield travels widely, collecting material for her work. She lectures and teaches special seminars on dreaming for universities and other organizations around the world. She has taught at Temple University, worked as an assistant professor at the Philadelphia College of Textiles and Science, and lectured for the University of California Extension system. Frequently appearing on radio and national television—including three features on ABC's "20/20" news magazine show—her work has also been described in many magazines, including *People*, *Harper's*, *Woman's Day*, *Reader's Digest*, *Omni*, *Psychology Today*, *Bride's*, *Family Circle*, *Parents*, *Parenting*, and *American Baby*, as well as several foreign magazines.

She has served as a dream consultant for the *National Geographic* magazine, the American Broadcasting Corporation, the Canadian Broadcasting Corporation, and Globe Communications. She was one of the six original co-founders of the international organization, the Association for the Study of Dreams.

Dr. Garfield somehow finds time to record her dreams, in a diary of over forty-one years, which contains more than 20,000 dreams—perhaps the most extensive dream journal in the world. Author, speaker, and dream consultant, she lives with her husband, a psychotherapist, in San Francisco.